REFORMIST MUSLIMS IN A YOGYAKARTA VILLAGE

THE ISLAMIC TRANSFORMATION OF CONTEMPORARY SOCIO-RELIGIOUS LIFE

REFORMIST MUSLIMS IN A YOGYAKARTA VILLAGE

THE ISLAMIC TRANSFORMATION OF CONTEMPORARY SOCIO-RELIGIOUS LIFE

Hyung-Jun Kim

Department of Anthropology
Division of Society and Environment
Research School of Pacific and Asian Studies

February 1996

ANU
THE AUSTRALIAN NATIONAL UNIVERSITY

E PRESS

ANU
E PRESS

Published by ANU E Press
The Australian National University
Canberra ACT 0200, Australia
Email: anuepress@anu.edu.au
This title available online at: http://epress.anu.edu.au/reformist_citation.html

---

National Library of Australia
Cataloguing-in-Publication entry

Kim, Hyung-Jun.
Reformist muslims in Yagyakarta Village : the islamic
transformation of contemporary socio-religious life.

Bibliography
ISBN 1 920942 34 3 (pbk)
ISBN 1 920942 35 1 (online)

1. Religious life - Islam. 2. Muslims - Java. 3. Religion
and culture - Indonesia - Java. 4. Java (Indonesia) -
Religion. I. Title.

299.9222

Cover design by ANU E Press

Islam in Southeast Asia Series

Theses at The Australian National University are assessed by external examiners and students are expected to take into account the advice of their examiners before they submit to the University Library the final versions of their theses. For this series, this final version of the thesis has been used as the basis for publication, taking into account other changes that the author may have decided to undertake. In some cases, a few minor editorial revisions have made to the work. The acknowledgements in each of these publications provides information on the supervisors of the thesis and those who contributed to its development. For many of the authors in this series, English is a second language and their texts reflect an appropriate fluency.

Table of Contents

List of Tables

List of Figures

List of Plates

Foreword

This study by Hyung-Jun Kim of a village in Yogyakarta presents a remarkable case-study of the processes of reform and renewal that are occurring widely throughout Indonesia today. Rarely have these profoundly important processes been examined at the local level in such detail. As a case study, this work offers significant insights that carry well beyond a single village. Such insights provide the basis for a critical understanding of contemporary socio-religious change.

Hyung-Jun Kim's stated objective in this work is to consider how Islam is "understood, interpreted and practiced". In many villages, perhaps most villages in Java today, this is no longer a simple matter. Taken for granted practices can be questioned and abandoned, reaffirmed or reinterpreted. To a certain extent, this has become part of the quiet dynamic of daily life. In the case that Kim Hyung-Jun studies here, however, this whole process has come much more to the fore in an effort to Islamize daily life.

When as a graduate student, Hyung-Jun Kim set out to find an "ordinary Javanese village" in which to do his fieldwork, he had no idea that the village he had selected was the site of concerted efforts by a small group of committed young men to remake their village and its traditions in the light of their understanding of a reformist Islam. In his study, Hyung-Jun Kim provides an understanding of this village setting and then proceeds systematically to examine local efforts at reform and their consequences for the social life of the community.

The particular value of this work as a whole is in the way that Hyung-Jun Kim concertedly probes the way villagers now think about rituals such as the communal meal — *kendhuri* — that they share with one another to celebrate life-cycle events and the way that the reformers are have endeavoured to alter accepted practices to better define these practices as Muslim. If tradition is the accumulation of practice, such simple, intimate changes at the local level eventually become of defining importance.

It is perhaps no accident that this Yogya village has, among its population, Christians, both Catholics and Protestants. Their presence in the village adds a further dimension to this study prompting among villagers a heightened sense of what it means to be Muslim or Christian. The value of this study is in the range of its considerations and the quality of its attention to the living reality of contemporary village life.

Hyung-Jun Kim is a graduate of Seoul University. He completed his BA in anthropology in 1988 and his MA in 1990. He then transferred to the Research School of Pacific and Asian Studies at the Australian National University for his PhD. He did 22 months of fieldwork in Java over a period from 1992 to 1994 and submitted his doctoral dissertation in 1996. He is currently an Associate Professor in the Department of Cultural Anthropology at Kwangwon National

University in Chunchon, Korea where he has continued his research on Islam in Indonesia. Most recently, in 2003 and 2004, he carried out nine months research focusing on Muhammidiyah. Parts of his ANU PhD thesis were used in a number of published papers: parts of Chapter 2 in "Agrarian and Social Change in a Javanese Village" in the *Journal of Contemporary Asia*, 32(4): 435-455. 2002; parts of Chapter 3 in "From Bamboo Langgar to Brick Masjid: Islamic Development in a Javanese Village", in Oh, M-S and Kim H-J (eds) *Religion, Ethnicity and Modernity in Southeast Asia*, 131-165. Seoul: Seoul National University Press. 1988; parts of Chapter 4 in "The Islamization of Others' Everyday Life: A Case from Yogyakarta", in *Antropologi Indonesia* 57: 61-69.1988; parts of Chapter 7 in "Unto You Your Religion and Unto Me My Religion: Muslim-Christian Relations in a Javanese Village", in *Sojourn*, 13(1):62-85. 1988 and parts of Chapter 8 in "Changing Concept of Religious Freedom in Indonesia", in the *Journal of Southeast Asian Studies*, 29(2): 357-373. 1988.

James J. Fox

Abstract

This study examines the religious life of reformist Muslims in a Yogyakarta village. The foci of this discussion are on Muslim villagers' construction, with the help of the reformist paradigm, of the image of the 'good Muslim' and 'Muslim-ness', on their efforts to incorporate an (reformist) Islamic framework to question taken-for-granted practices and ideas, on the position of traditional practices and ideas and their relation to reformist Islam, and on the interplay of villagers who show a strong commitment to reformist Islam with those who do not. Another topic which is investigated in this study is the interactions between Muslim and Christian villagers and the impacts of Christian presence on the process by which Muslims define themselves, their neighbours, their religion and their religious community.

After examining the recent socio-economic developments in a Yogyakarta village in Chapter two, this study deals with the development of reformist Islam, the process whereby a group of reformist villagers has been formed and its impact on the religious life of Muslim villagers in Chapter three. The formation of this group precipitated a differentiation of Muslim villagers in terms of their religious outlook and of their participation in religious activities, and has accelerated the diversification of the meaning of 'Muslim-ness'.

Chapter four looks at the notion of 'Muslim-ness', or of 'being a Muslim' supported by the reformist villagers and the interactions between villagers who show a strong commitment to reformist Islam and those who do not. The analysis shows that the profession of faith (*sahadat*) or circumcision, which was once considered to be a sufficient condition to make someone a Muslim, is no longer regarded so by the reformist villagers. Instead, they put absolute emphasis on the fulfilment of faith, such as carrying out daily prayer and the fast, as the central part of the notion of 'Muslim-ness'. The different religious understandings and practices among Muslim villagers have not become a basis of social conflict. No villagers try to involve themselves in the religious life of others, are willing to instruct other people and to make explicit the controversial aspect of others' religious behaviour in public. These attitudes help to create a social environment where the norm of harmony is maintained.

From Chapter five to Chapter eight, the focus is placed on several changes which have taken place as Islamic development has accelerated. Chapter five examines the way traditional rituals are interpreted by Muslim villagers and the emergence of a new Islamic tradition. It shows that the process by which an Islamic tradition emerges from a syncretic background is not simply one of imposing a certain criterion on traditional practices and ending them, but of questioning their relevance, abandoning what cannot be accommodated, reinterpreting what can be made harmonious with reformist Islam and recontextualising them in Islamic terms.

In Chapter six, traditional belief in supernatural beings, supernatural power, and related practices are examined. The reformist villagers try to challenge and reformulate the nature of supernatural beings by equating them with the Islamic concept of the malevolent *jinn* and by condemning villagers' contact with them as *syirik*, or the negation of the Oneness of Allah.

Chapters seven and eight deal with the impact of the presence of Christians on the religious life of Muslims. The study shows that their presence has prompted the formation of a clear boundary based on religious identity and of the idea of 'in-group' and 'out-group', and that the importance of religious identity has begun to extend into non-religious domains. The alleged threat of Christians have also prompted the reformist villagers to defend the *umat* Islam, and their specific mode of attacking Christianity has instated the concept of *akal* (reason) not only as a way to expose the absurdity of Christian theology but as a way to evaluate their own religious practices and ideas.

Acknowledgements

This thesis was made possible by a Korean Government Overseas Scholarship. I am grateful to the Korean Government for the scholarship which enabled me to undertake a PhD program at the Australian National University and field research in Indonesia. I am also thankful to Bu-wung Lee in the Korean Consulate in Sydney for his assistance.

The debt that I owe to my main supervisor, Dr. J.J. Fox may not be easily described. It was he who transformed me from one who did not know exactly where Java is located to one who can say at least something about people in Java. Without his continuous support, encouragement and constructive criticism, it may have been impossible for me to complete this thesis. I would like to express my thanks to him.

I am also indebted to my supervisors, Dr. S. Supomo and Dr. P. Guinness, who willingly sacrificed their valuable time to read my drafts and gave me invaluable and stimulating advice. Dr. Supomo provided me with an insight into looking at and interpreting things Javanese correctly. Dr. Guinness critically appraised my earlier writings, which brought me countless headaches, but, nonetheless, was vital to the completion of this work. I also thank my former supervisor, Dr. P. Graham, for her support and advice during my pre-fieldwork period.

I am truly thankful to Dr. B. Holloway who willingly carried out the most tedious work of correcting the language of this thesis and of proof-reading. Without her careful reading of earlier drafts, this thesis might have been still unreadable to English readers.

A large number of scholars and members of the Department of Anthropology and of the Australian National University have helped me to complete this work. Among them, I would like especially to mention Dr. W. Keeler, Dr. S. Ryang, G. Craswell and D. Porter who read parts of my thesis and gave me their brilliant ideas and suggestions. I am also grateful to P. Taylor, Yunita Winarto, Bambang Hudayana, Jamhari Makruf and Endang Turmudi for their support, inspiration and friendship. My thanks also go to my fellow Korean students who contributed in many ways to clarifying my ideas and to making me feel at home in Canberra. Among them are Charles Shin, Duksan Lee and Hyunhee Moon.

I also thank the administrative staff in the Department of Anthropology for their support and hospitality. Susan Toscan has never forgotten to show her deep concern about my progress and my life, Ria van de Zandt provided me with invaluable technical support and Margaret Tyrie drew a wonderful map for me.

Research in Indonesia was sponsored by Gadjah Mada University in Yogyakarta and carried out under the auspices of Lembaga Ilmu Pengetahuan Indonesia (LIPI). I would like to express my gratitude to both institutions for their support.

I also want to thank Dr. Syafri Sairin, Dr. P. M. Laksono and Dr. Budi Susanto in Yogyakarta, who provided me with priceless suggestions and hospitality throughout the whole period of my fieldwork. Many thanks go to Romo Budi who helped me to find a research site, and to my research assistant and friend, Surono, who willingly sacrificed his time to share the most critical moment of my research with me.

There are far too many people in the village of Sumber to whom I am indebted. I would like especially to mention Bapak Susilarto who introduced Sumber to me, and Bapak Suramto and Bu Suramto who were generous enough to share their life with me and accepted me as a member of their family. I thank other people in Sumber, all of whom were my teachers and were willing to share their life with me. I apologise for not listing individual names due to space limitation. I also would like to apologise and ask forgiveness to people in Sumber for my intentional and unintentional wrong doings during my stay, hoping that the portrayal of their life in this work does not distort what their life really was.

Finally, I would like to express my gratitude to my parents. Although they did not and still do not understand completely why their son was attracted to anthropology and selected Java as a research site, and won't understand what is written in this thesis, their love and support were essential for the completion of my work in Australia and in Indonesia. It is to them I would like to dedicate this thesis.

Chapter 1: Introduction

One of the surprises that Kolojonggo (a pseudonym for the hamlet in which I did my field research) gave me came a few days after I had settled there. Walking aimlessly along a hamlet path, I found a house, or more precisely a building, that looked different from other houses in the hamlet. It was taller than the other houses and had a loud-speaker on top of the roof. Getting closer, I recognised that it was a *masjid* (mosque). I could see the place for ablution, decorations taking the shape of the dome and a large hall inside the building. The reason I was surprised at the presence of a *masjid* in Kolojonggo, a scene which might not surprise anyone from Yogyakarta, was simple: I had not expected hamlets (*dusun*) in rural Yogyakarta to have their own *masjid*. I assumed that I might see a *masjid* at the village (*kelurahan*) level. My surprise, however, did not end there. The next day, I obtained more surprising information from village officials: Sumber (a pseudonym for the village to which Kolojonggo belongs) which consisted of 19 hamlets had 23 *masjid*, signifying that a few hamlets had more than one *masjid*. After this encounter, I could not help reconsidering my decision to do research in Kolojonggo. To me, Sumber did not seem to be 'the ordinary village' in Yogyakarta that I had looked for as my research site.

It is not certain what the notion of 'the ordinary village' meant to me at that time. This concept probably consisted of several elements that I had selected as the characteristics of 'the ordinary village' in Yogyakarta while reading the literature: the significant role of agriculture in villagers' economic activities; a dominant socio-economic position of large landholders and village officials; increasing influences from the city; and, in terms of religion, the dominance of syncretism characterised by an integration of the Javanese folk tradition, Hindu-Buddhist, and Islamic elements. Whatever the exact meaning of 'the ordinary village' might be and irrespective of whether this notion was relevant or not, the first few months of my stay in Yogyakarta were marked by my search for 'the ordinary village'. The strategy that I used to select a fieldwork site also reflected my obsession with this concept. I did not employ any specific criterion in selecting the site. Instead, what I relied on was something like luck or fate. Behind this attitude lay my belief that, if I chose a hamlet according to certain criteria, the hamlet thus selected might not represent 'the ordinary village'.

After making several short trips to rural Yogyakarta, I at last discovered a more specific way to select my research site. As I could hardly communicate with villagers either in Indonesian or in Javanese, I decided to use English teachers living in rural areas as guides. I met five English teachers, visited five hamlets and met five village and hamlet heads. In these meetings, my obsession with 'the ordinary village' hindered me from asking any specific questions about the hamlet or village. I just observed their degree of hospitality and the scenery of each village. My decision to settle in Kolojonggo was based on these considerations. The English teacher who introduced Kolojonggo to me and the village head in Sumber reacted more enthusiastically to my plan to do research in their village than others, while, unlike the other villages, all paddy fields in Sumber were located on flat land and this gave me a good impression.

It took almost three months after the discovery of the *masjid* for me to reach the final decision to continue my fieldwork in Kolojonggo. This decision was based on two considerations. First, for these three months, I visited other villages once or twice a week in order to ask how many *masjid* were in these villages. The finding was rather surprising: most villages in the western part of Yogyakarta had as many as, or more *masjid* than, the hamlets. This implied that, contrary to my previous assumption, Kolojonggo was not such an unusual hamlet. The second factor which made me stay in Kolojonggo was inconsistent with my search for 'the ordinary village'. A few days after I had found the *masjid*, I also discovered a Protestant chapel (*kapel*) in Kolojonggo. Although no clergyman lived there and it was used only for Sunday services, a chapel was what I had least expected to see in a rural village. At first, this extraordinariness gave me an additional incentive to search for another fieldwork site. Later, especially after I knew that the presence of the *masjid* in Kolojonggo was not extraordinary, however, the co-existence of the *masjid* and *kapel* prompted me to continue my research in Kolojonggo and, consequently, I stayed there until the end of my fieldwork. I lived in Kolojonggo from October 1992 till June 1994 except for one month's absence. The major focus of my research throughout this period was placed on Islam while I also dealt intensively with agricultural development.

Looking back on the first stage of my fieldwork, I am perplexed at my groundless obsession with the notion of 'the ordinary village'. What surprises me even more is that I expected to see the *masjid* only at the village level. This might have been based on another assumption that I had at that time, namely that villagers' commitment to Islam may not have been strong enough for them to build their own *masjid* in their hamlet.

The whole period of my field research was a process of realisation that, to put it simply, there was a group of villagers for whom Islam was more than a veneer on their life, and that the influence of this group over others was on the increase, although the process was gradual. Therefore, one of the main themes in this thesis follows my changing perception of Islam. This, however, does not mean that I now have another image of 'the ordinary village', although I probably would not be able to stop myself from saying, on seeing a hamlet without its own *masjid*, 'what has made this hamlet so extraordinary?' One of the insights that my stay in Yogyakarta gave me was that the people of Yogyakarta and the villages where they live are extremely diverse. Each village has its own dynamics and, in some cases, each hamlet in one village shows more distinguishing features than sameness. This diversity makes it futile for me to claim that the portrait of Islam in Kolojonggo can be generalised to include other Yogyanese or Javanese villages. Rather, this thesis describes one possible mode in which Islam in Yogyakarta may be developed and manifested.

Before I go further, it seems necessary to examine previous studies of Islam in Java. Such an examination will help to put my study into a certain perspective and will provide a chance to understand better the notion of, and my search for, 'the ordinary village'. As I had never been to any Javanese village before I started my fieldwork, all my preconceptions about Javanese villages had been constructed from the literature on Java.

1.1. Review of Studies about Islam in Java [1]

It may not be an exaggeration to say that the ideas C. Geertz presented in his books, *The Religion of Java and Agricultural Involution*, have dominated the scholarly discussions about the socio-political, cultural, economic and religious behaviour of the Javanese. Although there are abundant discussions of these books, there are reasons for me to carry out another review of Geertz's work and of scholarly debates on it. My orientation in doing field research was influenced by these debates and, although the main purpose of this thesis is not to support nor to refute Geertz, his paradigm has influenced the course of my writing. The 'spectre' of Geertz has been with me throughout the whole period of doing fieldwork and of writing this thesis. [2]

In *The Religion of Java*, Geertz proposes three main cultural types which reflect the moral organisation of Javanese culture, the general ideas of order in terms of which the Javanese shape their behaviour in all areas of life: *abangan, santri, and priyayi* (1976:4-5). The *abangan* sub-tradition is characterised by a balanced integration of animistic, Hinduistic, and Islamic elements, a basic Javanese syncretism which is the island's true folk tradition, the *santri* sub-tradition by a stress on the Islamic aspects of the syncretism, and the *priyayi* sub-tradition by a stress on the Hinduist aspects. These three religious sub-traditions are associated in a broad and general way with three major social-structural nuclei in Java, namely, the village, the market and the government bureaucracy (ibid.:5-6).

One of the debates concerning Geertz's trichotomy has centred on the relevance of the *priyayi* variant. Some scholars argue that *santri* and *abangan* are the terms designating differences in the religious outlook cutting across social classes, while *priyayi* is a term referring to a social class, namely, the aristocrats (Bachtiar,1985; Boland,1982:4; Koentjaraningrat,1963:188-189; Noer,1973:19).

---

[1] This review includes only the major works written in English.
[2] In this review, I will focus only on *The Religion of Java*. For the review of Geertz's *Agricultural Involution*, see Alexander & Alexander (1978 &1979), Collier (1979 &1981) and White (1983).

People belonging to the *priyayi* may show strong *santri* or *abangan* orientation, implying that *priyayi* on the one hand and *santri* and *abangan* on the other are not mutually exclusive. Those dissatisfied with Geertz's trichotomy on this basis support one of the two alternative positions. The first is to drop the *priyayi* variant in favour of the dichotomy of *abangan* and *santri*: the Javanese should be grouped into two, those who look on their Islamic duties seriously and those who do not. [3] The second position tries to incorporate a concept or concepts comparable to *priyayi*. One of the concepts thus selected is *wong cilik* (literally, small person), a term referring to the lower class living mainly in rural areas. With the introduction of this concept, the Geertz's trichotomy expands to quadri-partite system: *wong cilik-abangan*, *wong cilik-santri*, *priyayi-abangan* and *priyayi-santri*. The incorporation of new concepts, however, also has an analytic problem: the concepts which can be included seem to be almost inexhaustible. For example, Ricklefs, in addition to his use of *wong cilik* as opposed to *priyayi*, incorporates a lateral axis of *kolot-moderen* (old fashioned-modern) (1979:118), while Koentjaraningrat contrasts *priyayi* to *wong cilik* and *wong sudagar* (traders) and includes another axis of urban and rural (1967:245-46).

These two alternative positions seem to be based on different understandings of Geertz's paradigm and its applicability. Those who confine the relevance of Geertz's paradigm to the study of Javanese religion take the first position, while those who apply his paradigm to the general study of the Javanese worldview take the second. To the latter, religion is not a sufficient condition to understand the world outlook of the Javanese, so that social class, *kolot-moderen* and city-urban should be included as relevant variables to understand the different world outlooks. Whatever positions are taken, however, all scholars supporting either of the two positions agree on one point, namely, that in terms of the religious orientation, the Javanese are divided into two groups, those who take their Islamic duties seriously and those who do not. Some of them prefer the term 'kejawen', 'agami Jawi' (literally, Javanese religion) and 'Javanism' to the term *abangan*. 'Javanism' in this context may be defined as the indigenous elements of Javanese religion which have remained constant in the face of the tremendous impact of foreign ideas (Zoetmulder,1967:16) or, more broadly, the religion of those who do not take their Muslim religious duties seriously (Jay,1969; Koentjaraningrat,1985a; Mulder,1978).

---

[3] The dichotomy of *abangan* and *santri* was used as a framework to understand the religious orientation of the Javanese by the scholars in the Dutch colonial period. As early as the 19th century, the terms *abangan* (literally, the red people) and *putihan* (equivalent to *santri* used by Geertz, literally, the white people), were used by a Dutch writer to show the contrast between orthodox and syncretist Javanese (Poensen, C. 1886, *Brieven over den Islam uit de Binnenlanden van Java*, cited in Ellen (1983:58)), while Snouck Hurgronje is said to have used the term *santri* to designate the purist Muslims and *abangan*, the syncretists (Peacock,1986:344). Berg and Djajadiningrat also adopt these terms. To Berg, *abangan* refers to slackers and *putihan*, pious Muslims (1932:303), and to Djajadiningrat, *abangan* designates those who do not live religiously but nevertheless are Muslims and *putihan*, those who live religiously (1958:384).

By contrast with the critics of Geertz who generally agree to the dichotomy of *abangan-santri* but try to modify the *priyayi* variant, another group of critics evaluates Geertz's paradigm from a different angle. Their basic premise is that the *abangan-santri* dichotomy is not relevant to an understanding of the religious orientation of the Javanese. In this respect, their criticism is directed not only at Geertz but at the majority of scholars who have argued for the presence of division among Javanese Muslims in terms of their attitude toward and commitment to Islam. Interestingly enough, the precursor of this group of critics was not a scholar of religion in Java *per se*, but an Islamologist who probably came to know Islam in Java by way of Geertz. According to Hodgson, many of the ethnographic data interpreted by Geertz as proofs of syncretic tradition are actually Islamic. He attributes this shortcoming to Geertz's prejudicial view in identifying 'Islam' with what the school of modernists (reformists) happens to approve of and in ascribing everything else to an aboriginal or Hindu-Buddhist background. Hodgson suggests that the data presented by Geertz show how little has survived from the Hindu past even in inner Java and raises the question as to why the triumph of Islam has been so complete (1974 vol.2:551). Although his argument is persuasive, Hodgson is not generous enough to share his understanding with others. He proposes that his conclusion can be appreciated by 'one who knows Islam' (ibid.), and does not clarify, for example, how the invocation of such beings as *dhanyang* (a local guardian spirit), the spirits living in the rafters of the house, the animals that crawl along like snails, 'mother earth', guardian of the land and the water, and the as yet unborn child alongside Allah, the Prophet Adam, Eve and Muhammad (Geertz,1976:40-41) in order to ask all of them not to bother people, not to make people feel ill, unhappy, or confused (ibid.:14) can be an evidence of the triumph of Islam over the local religious tradition rather than that of syncretism.

Recently, Woodward claims that he is the 'one who knows Islam'. He argues that Islam is the dominant force in the religious beliefs and rites of the Javanese, shaping the character of social interaction and daily life in all segments of Javanese society (1989:3). Although his effort to incorporate the Sufi tradition of Islam as a framework with which to examine religious practices and ideas may be considered as a contribution to the study of Islam in Java, Woodward's argument suffers from several shortcomings. [4] The first of these is his method of interpreting historical and ethnographic data. In order to show that certain religious practices or ideas in Java are Islamic or fully Islamised, Woodward does not present any direct evidence that these have textual references in the Quran and Hadith or have an Islamic origin. What he uses instead is corresponding examples, namely, the presence of similar ideas and practices in the Quran and Hadith, and sometimes in the lives of people in other parts of the

---

[4] For more about criticism of Woodward's argument, see Ricklefs (1991) and Stange (1990).

Islamic world. For example, in order to argue that *slametan* (communal feast), which has been considered by many as a typical example of Javanese syncretism, is based on the textual tradition of Islam, he does not show that the Prophet Muhammad actually celebrated *slametan* nor that Allah commanded human beings to celebrate *slametan*. Instead, he selects a few features arbitrarily from *slametan* such as inviting neighbours for a communal feast and giving the left-over food, and then shows these features are in the Islamic scriptures. Seen within this framework, the fact that the Prophet Muhammad accepted the invitation to a meal from his follower, ate together with his companions and asked the latter to give the left-overs to people is already enough evidence to prove that *slametan* is based on the textual tradition of Islam (1988:62-3). As Geertz notes (1976:11), the communal feast is the world's most common religious ritual. This implies that, if I apply Woodward's method and argument, all parts of the world where the communal feast is practised and the left-over food is distributed are areas whose religious practices may be Islamic. Woodward, who is bold enough to say that 'Roman legal principles or Neoplatonism becomes Islamic if interpreted in terms of a system of symbolic knowledge derived from Quranic or other Islamic principles' (1979:63), may not object to my application of his idea, if I add a phrase, 'as long as the actors who participate in the communal feast consider it Islamic'.

At this point, we encounter a second weakness in Woodward's argument. He relies heavily on the interpretation of actors to examine religious practices in Java. This method itself does not seem to be wrong. What is problematic, however, is his acceptance of actors' interpretation as an absolute criterion on which to judge whether certain practices or ideas are Islamic or not. In the paradigm of Woodward, therefore, interpretation and judgement merge. It may be beyond the capacity of an outside researcher to argue that informants' interpretation of certain practices is factually or historically wrong on the basis of written materials to which he or she has access but informants do not. However, it may be a mistake to use actors' interpretation as an absolute basis to judge the 'Islamic' or 'non-Islamic' nature of certain practices and ideas. An outside researcher may say that 'such and such practices are interpreted as being Islamic' but cannot argue, from this interpretation, that 'such and such practices are Islamic'. On the other hand, this method of Woodward can easily be proved to be wrong, if one uses his method in attacking his argument: if there are Javanese who have a different interpretation of certain practices from that of Woodward's informants - for example, if some interpret *slametan* to be Hindu-Buddhist - this, according to Woodward's method, shows that *slametan* is Hindu-Buddhist, not Islamic. Woodward tries to avoid this issue by using the phrase, 'many people'. For example, he writes 'many people believe that if he chose to, the sultan [in Yogyakarta] could rule the world, and that Yogyakarta is the center of the universe' (ibid.:21) and 'the prince's personal opinion, which is shared by many modern Javanese, is that because books are written by men ... they are less reliable sources of historical knowledge than meditation' (ibid:35). In one sense, this form of argument cannot be falsified, since no one will be able to seek after the opinions of people in Java whose number reaches more than a hundred million and to say confidently that many people do not share the same opinion with those called 'many people' by Woodward. However, it is legitimate to ask from which segment of the Javanese society do Woodward's 'many people' come. Do 'many people' refer to many of the informants whom Woodward questioned during his fieldwork, many people in Yogyakarta or many people in Java? This question is essential since many people in Kolojonggo and Sumber may not agree with the interpretation of the 'many people' in Woodward's book.[5]

Whatever the pros and cons concerning Geertz's ideas, it cannot be denied that his conceptual framework in *The Religion of Java*, namely, that the Javanese can be divided into two groups in terms of their religious orientation and of their attitude toward and commitment to Islam, has been an axis with which the scholarly discussions of religion in Java have been developed. Throughout this process, two contrasting views have emerged: the first argues that Islam has been gaining influence over a much wider circle of the Javanese, while the second puts much more emphasis on the maintenance of the syncretic tradition or 'Javanism' and its continuing popularity with the Javanese. The studies of Mulder, Stange and Nakamura give us good examples of both positions in the study of Islam in Java. The comparison of these studies is all the more interesting since these scholars carried out their research in the early 1970s and in places sharing a similar historical background, Mulder in Yogyakarta city, Stange in Yogyakarta and Surakarta regions, and Nakamura in a town not far from Yogyakarta city.

The starting point of Mulder and Stange is quite similar. They note the popularity of *kebatinan* mysticism and try to understand its contents and implications. According to Mulder, the *kebatinan* or mystical world view in Java is characterised by its emphasis on the oneness of the order of existence, on the superiority of the inner (*batin*) over the outer (*lahir*), on the superiority of the intuitive feeling (*rasa*) over the rational, and on the harmonious order of society. These characteristics have persisted to guide and interpret action in spite of structural change and modern developments (1978:xv), constituting the generic type of Javaneseness (ibid.:100) and providing tools to understand significant social change (ibid.:103). Mulder admits that Islamic doctrines have influenced Javanese mystical thinking and terminology. However, these influences have

---

[5] The criticism that I make here does not mean that Woodward's work does not have any significance for the study of religion in Java. As noted earlier, one of his contributions is to show that the influences of Sufism are visible in traditional Javanese culture. In this respect, he helps us to have a more balanced view of traditional religious ideas and practices in Java which have been considered to be related closely to Hindu-Buddhist tradition (e.g. Hadiwijono,1967).

not been strong enough to replace the Javanese world view, are felt to be foreign to Java (ibid.:10-11) and have reached only a small segment of the Javanese who are isolated from the mainstream (ibid.:105). Accordingly, for virtually all the Javanese, mysticism and magical-mystical practices have always been a most powerful undercurrent of their culture (ibid.:1).

Stange shares much of Mulder's understanding of *kebatinan* mysticism, but he takes a slightly different position to locate mysticism in the present life of the Javanese. He argues that the syncretic and traditional factors within each religious community have lost ground to modern scripturalism (1980:48) and that Javanese mysticism is no longer a fundamental element within the polity of ethnic Javanese (ibid.:43). This does not mean that Stange argues for the dominance of Islam in the religious life of the Javanese. He suggests Islam is integral to, but not at the heart of, local culture, noting that mosques are often little more than gateways to the graveyard in the rural religious pattern of contemporary Java (ibid.:33). In evaluating the position of Islam and Javanese mysticism, what Stange has in mind seems to be a religious polarity (ibid.:47). The syncretic and mystical religious tradition has gradually lost ground to the surge of (scriptural) Islam but the latter has not been successful in replacing the former.

Nakamura gives a contrasting picture of religious life in Yogyakarta to that of Mulder. He finds that an increasingly large number of individuals in the *abangan* category have moved and are still moving towards the category of *santri*, becoming more orthodox in their thought and deed as Muslims (1993:13). To Nakamura, this development is not a recent phenomenon but a part of the ongoing process of Islamisation. One of the interesting findings of Nakamura is that, in contrast to the conventional view of reformist Islam in Java, Javanese reformism is not severed from Javanese traditions nor is it anti-Javanese, but it actually embodies Javanese traditions (ibid.:183). He shows how such basic concepts as '*lahir*' (outer self) and '*batin*' (inner self), and '*kasar*' (literally, coarse) and '*halus*' (literally, refined), which have been employed to analyse 'Javanism' or 'Javanese religion' (Geertz,1976:232-234; Moulder,1978), are used by reformist Muslims to interpret Islamic doctrines and to introduce Islamic virtues to the mass (1993:159-167). [6] In this respect, Nakamura's study gives us a chance to

---

[6] In an article published in 1984, Nakamura extends this idea to criticise Geertz's treatment of the *abangan* variant. He notes that such concepts as *slamet*, *sabar* and *ikhlas* which constitute the central values in the *abangan* outlook have their origin in Islam, so that, he argues, the traditional Javanese outlook cannot be considered to be Hindu-Buddhist or animistic but Islamic. Nakamura's criticism seems to be based on his misinterpretation of the *abangan* variant. In *The religion of Java*, Geertz does not argue that the *abangan* variant is immune to the Islamic influences, but he proposes that the *abangan* variant is characterised by a balanced integration of animistic, Hinduistic, and Islamic elements (1976:5). It is obvious from this that Islamic elements should be included in the *abangan* variant as one of its main constituents. If syncretism is the central feature of the *abangan* variant, Nakamura's criticism of Geertz ironically shows that Geertz's understanding of the *abangan* variant is exactly to the point. This is because not all key concepts which constitute the central values in the *abangan* outlook originate from Islam. For example, such notions as *rasa, nerima, rukun* and *cocok* which have been considered by many

appraise the dichotomy supported by Geertz and others from a different angle. The division between *santri* and *abangan* variants may not be as neat as Geertz unconsciously portrays [7] and the elements constituting each variant may be understood and interpreted by the Javanese in a different fashion from the ways these are interpreted by Geertz and others (see also Dhofier,1978:71-2).

From the 1970s on, observers of Islam at the national level have shown that a remarkable change has been going on in Java. Increasing numbers of Javanese show their strong commitment to Islam; the participants in Friday prayers and in the fast have increased and more Indonesians have made the pilgrimage to Mecca (Johns,1987:224); Islamic activities such as prayers and studies take place everywhere and nominal Muslims participate in these activities (Adnan,1990:444); publication and public discussion about Islam have flourished (Tamara,1986:5-8); the number of students in Islamic boarding schools (*pesantren*) has increased dramatically (Dhofier,1978:68); and the appeal of Islam among modern people has increased (Tamney,1987:62). In spite of these forms of change, the argument for Islam's increasing influence in Java has not been shared by everyone. Many consider that Islam has not been successful in taking a strong grip over the population even after the 1970s (Koentjaraningrat,1985a; McVey,1983; Ricklefs,1979; Slamet,1977:35), while Johns, who reports the increasing popularity of Islam, suggests that, in observing Islam in the rural areas, their (Javanese peasantry) cultural traditions through which they perceive Islam are strongly animist with an Indic religious overlay (1987:226). Some of these scholars use the key symbols of traditional Javanese culture to explain the position of Islam in Java: 'given the depth and comprehensive character of traditional Javanese culture, in any struggle for allegiance which may develop ... between the *wayang* (shadow play) and the Quran, the *wayang* is likely to win' (Ricklefs,1979:126); and 'Javanese society still cannot dispense with the *dhukun* (traditional medical and magical practitioners) (Koentjaraningrat,1985a:426).

The continuing importance of traditional religious ideas in the life of Muslim Javanese is also noted by Keeler who did field research in Central Javanese villages. Keeler argues that people's actions, their speech, their fortunes and their interaction within the family, in village life and among those of different status are thought to be affected by the spiritual potency they wield and by the potency others wield (1987:19). Accordingly, Javanese are preoccupied with asceticism which is considered to be an ideal way to accumulate spiritual potency

---

as the key Javanese value terms (see Anderson,1965; Koentjaraningrat,1985a; Mulder,1978; Stange,1984) are not Arabic but Javanese. These diverse origins of the key notions in the *abangan* outlook imply that the central feature of the *abangan* variant is syncretism.

[7] In *The Religion of Java*, Geertz proposes clearly that the division of *abangan*, *santri* and *priyayi* is not absolute and these variants should be understood as 'cultural types', or probably as 'ideal types' in the Weberian sense. This statement of Geertz, however, seems to be easily overshadowed by the way he presents his book. In *The Religion of Java*, he divides the three categories and explains them one by one, a presentation which gives an impression that this division is clear-cut.

(ibid.:112), and traditional belief in spiritual beings maintains its popularity as a way to accumulate spiritual strength (ibid.:44). Keeler mentions the existence of villagers who disregard spiritual potency and asceticism, but he suggests these villagers, who are identified as some of the most highly educated reformist Muslims (ibid.:114), are exceptions and most villagers are more syncretic than orthodox in their attitude toward Islam (ibid.:23). Keeler's view is also echoed in Bråton's study of a Central Javanese village. Differing from Keeler, Bråton gives us a more balanced view by incorporating Islamic development in rural Java into his discussion: he notes the mushrooming of mosques and villagers' incorporation of Islam as one of the frameworks to interpret traditional rituals (1989). In spite of this, however, he interprets the villagers' commitment to Islam and their acceptance of an Islamic paradigm more as a strategy to present their actual identity actively in a distorted or even opposite way rather than as a genuine sign of the growing importance of Islam in their life (ibid.:72). Accordingly, Islamisation leads primarily to changes in ritual forms while the traditional interpretations, meanings and beliefs still pertain (ibid.:93). Bråton's view can be summarised in the comment of his informant concerning the use of Arabic verses from the Quran in casting spells: '[when you verbally recite Arabic prayers], you can utter a Javanese phrase in your thoughts' (ibid.:76).

Recently, the argument emphasising the continuing importance of 'Javanism' has been challenged by several scholars who argue that Islamic development in rural Java has been accelerated since the 1970s and that Islam has become a much more important factor in determining the religious life of rural villagers. Noting the institutional advantage of the orthodox community, the unprecedented scale of Islamic missionary activities and the continuing and increasing effectiveness of Muslim organisation in the countryside (1978a & 1978b), Hefner maintains that the social forces unleashed under the New Order contribute to the partial realisation of one of the Muslim community's primary religious goals: the Islamisation of Java (1987a:551). The children of many 'abangan' are becoming good Muslims and Javanese culture is giving way to Islam (ibid.:547). Hefner's view is paralleled in the works of two Indonesian scholars. Pranowo, who studied Islamic development in a Central Javanese village, finds that a genuine resurgence of Islam has taken place in the New Order period and that the villagers show strong affiliation and commitment to Islam (1991:152-179), while Mansurnoor shows that the influence of the *kiyai* (religious leaders) over the rural Madurese populace has not been weakened with the advent of modernisation, indirectly implying that Islam's strong grip over the villagers in rural areas has been maintained in the face of rapid changes (1990).

1.2. Organisation and Objectives of the Study

The review of previous studies shows that there have been two streams of thought regarding the position of Islam in Javanese religious life: one emphasises the continuing importance of traditional values and religious ideas, while the other highlights the increasing importance of Islam. This review then shows how prejudiced was the notion of 'the ordinary village' that I had at the initial stage of my fieldwork. I did not consider the view of such scholars as Hefner and Pranowo, assuming that villagers' commitment to Islam would not be strong enough to lead them to build a *masjid* in their hamlet. [8] In spite of this shortcoming, however, the notion of 'the ordinary village' provides one of the keys to understand my orientation in doing field research, in that it reflects my dissatisfaction with some of the studies dealing with religion in Java. In reading the literature, I had an impression that some scholars avoid 'the burden of complexity' (Roff, 1985:26) in the interest of 'a patterned understanding' (ibid.:8). They select and focus on a specific place or group where a certain religious orientation of the Javanese is manifested more clearly and, in doing so, neglect how people with different religious orientations interact and how they interpret and evaluate their own and others' religious ideas and practices. [9] These latter aspects of religious life should be taken into more serious account since those who are committed strongly to Islam and those who show less commitment to it do not live separate lives, but share the same living space and interact with one another.

My dissatisfaction with the approach which focuses on either the *abangan* or *santri* variants and which puts less emphasis on the complexity of religious life became stronger while I stayed in Yogyakarta city. During this time, I could easily observe two contrasting trends in the religious life of the Yogyanese. Each Friday, I could see the *masjid* full of people carrying out their religious duty. In a hotel where I stayed, the female receptionist wore a *jilbab* (female headgear that exposes face but not ears, neck, or hair), went from time to time to the inner part of the hotel to carry out daily prayers, did not sell alcohol and forbade the guests from bringing a local woman to their room. If there were complaints from the guests, she was kind enough to point out the hotels where the guests could do what they wanted freely. On the other hand, when I visited the *alun-alun* (city square) where a night market was open in commemoration of the birth of the Prophet Muhammad (*Sekaten*), the sound I could hear from loud speakers

---

[8] There were several reasons I paid less attention to the view that Islam has increased its grip over the Javanese villagers. First, my research site, Yogyakarta, has been considered to be a place where tradition is much stronger than in other parts of Java. Second, Pranowo's and Mansurnoor's researches were carried out in places where *pesantren* (Islamic boarding school) was located and the *kiyai* (the head of the *pesantren)* had a strong influence over the villagers. In this respect, it was plausible to assume that the villagers living in the research areas of Pranowo and Mansurnoor might show much stronger attachment to Islam than those in other parts of Java where there are no *pesantren* and *kiyai.* Although I expected that there would be some villagers trying to carry out their Islamic duties seriously in rural Yogyakarta, I assumed that they would be few and their influence over the religious life of others might not be strong.
[9] Notable exceptions are Bråton (1989), Hefner (1985, 1987a & 1987b) and Pranowo (1991). See also Siegel (1986:59-80).

was not the recitation of Arabic prayers but popular music called *dangdut*. One of the most crowded places in the *alun-alun* was where several troupes opened stages for *dangdut* performance. There, female singers, wearing mini-skirts or short pants, swayed their body to the rhythm of music, mimicking the dancers in Western pop videos. It might not be a surprise if I had seen the *dangdut* performance in any other place. However, this was done in front of the Sultan's palace and to commemorate the birth of the Prophet Muhammad. My visit to one *kebatinan* group also impressed me a lot. There, I could see people exercising to strengthen their spiritual power. What interested me the most at that time was the diverse composition of its members. There were teenagers and men in their forties, while there were teachers, civil servants, and manual labourers, the composition implying that the popularity of the *kebatinan* group was not confined to a certain segment of the Javanese society.

These contrasting experiences in Yogyakarta gave me an impression that, if I wanted to find a place where villagers might show their strong attachment to Islam or 'Javanism', I could easily do so. This then prompted me to give up employing any criterion in selecting a research site. By doing so, I believed, however naively, I might be able to find 'the ordinary village' where I could see the diversity and complexity of religious life among people who had different degrees of commitment to Islam.

My emphasis on the study of the diversity and complexity of religious life was also influenced by a recent shift in studying Islam from a search for an ahistorical Islamic 'essence' to an examination of the multiplicity of Islamic expression, and historical, socio-political and cultural contexts in which a certain understanding of Islam is adopted, maintained and reproduced (Eickelman,1982; see also el-Zein,1977). [10] This approach opposes the assumption that Muslims' life is dominated by one interpretation of Islam and Islamic practices. Instead, it focuses on the pluralistic character of Muslim life where more than one competing frameworks coexist, ready to be appropriated by human actors. There are always ambiguities and contradictions which allow for various interpretations and which allow some of these to be accepted as more 'orthodox' than others or to be rejected as 'non-Islamic' at particular times and in particular contexts.

One of the main objectives of this study is to look at *the* Islam understood, interpreted and practiced by villagers In Kolojonggo which has been influenced by the surge of reformist Islam for the last two decades. The foci of my discussion are on Muslim villagers' construction, with the help of the reformist paradigm, of the image of the 'good Muslim' and 'Muslim-ness', on their efforts to incorporate a (reformist) Islamic framework to question taken-for-granted practices and ideas, on the position of traditional practices and ideas and their

---

[10] For more about the trend and recent shift in the studies of Islam in Western scholarship, see Bowen (1993:3-8).

relation to reformist Islam, and on the interplay of villagers who show a strong commitment to reformist Islam with those who do not. Another topic which will be dealt with at length is the interaction between Muslim and non-Muslim villagers. Although the co-existence of Muslims and a substantial number of Christians in Kolojonggo is a peculiar phenomenon, it provides an opportunity to understand the dynamics of Islam. The presence of Christians has had an impact on the process by which Muslims define themselves, their neighbours, their religion and their religious community.

The organisation of this thesis parallels the ways I designed and carried out my research. For the first half year of my research, I focused on the socio-economic developments in Kolojonggo. This was essential, although not directly related to my main research topic, since the last three decades have witnessed the introduction of the so-called green revolution and the transformation of the national economy from an agriculture-based to a non-agriculture-based one, both of which have had enormous impacts on the socio-economic structure of rural Java. By looking at these developments, it is expected that the socio-economic circumstances of villagers in Kolojonggo will be clarified.

The aim of Chapter three is to examine the development of reformist Islam in Kolojonggo. We will see the process whereby a group of reformist villagers has been formed and its impact on the religious life of Muslim villagers. The formation of this group precipitated a differentiation of Muslim villagers in terms of their religious outlook and of their participation in religious activities, and has accelerated the diversification of the meaning of 'Muslim-ness'. In Chapter four, the notion of 'Muslim-ness', or of 'being a Muslim' held by the reformist villagers will be examined. In this discussion, the religious activities of Muslim villagers, their understandings of the most important normative duties in Islam, namely, the daily prayer and the fast, and their efforts to adopt an Islamic perspective with which to re-interpret their everyday life will be highlighted. In the last section of this chapter, the attitude of Muslim villagers who show a strong commitment to reformist Islam toward those who do not will be discussed in order to see the basis of interactions between these two groups of villagers.

After examining the development of reformist Islam and its characteristics as understood and practised by Muslim villagers, my discussion proceeds to look at several changes which have taken place as Islamic development has accelerated. In Chapter five, the focus will be placed on traditional rituals. By looking at how traditional rituals are interpreted by Muslim villagers, we will see the complicated process by which an Islamic tradition emerges from a syncretic background. This process is not simply one of imposing a certain criterion on traditional practices and ending them, but of questioning their relevance, abandoning what cannot be accommodated, reinterpreting what can be made harmonious with reformist Islam and recontextualising them in Islamic terms. In Chapter six, traditional belief in supernatural beings, supernatural power, and related practices will be examined. We will see the efforts of the reformist villagers to impose their own paradigm on interpretation of traditional belief in supernatural beings and the achievement and limitation of these efforts. In the last section of this chapter, emerging new paradigms through which to look at the supernatural world and their impact on the process of 'religious rationalisation' will be discussed.

Chapters seven and eight deal with a peculiar situation in which the Muslim community in Kolojonggo is located. In Chapter seven, the development of Christianity in Java, Yogyakarta and Kolojonggo, and the impact of the Christian presence on Muslims' conceptualisation of their own community, will be discussed. In Chapter eight, the focus will be placed on the interactions between Muslims and Christians in Kolojonggo and the ways Muslims conceive Christians, Christianity and Christianisation.

As I emphasised earlier, this portrait of reformist Islam and reformist Muslims in Kolojonggo cannot be generalised to show the dynamics of Islam in Yogyakarta and in Java. Rather, this portrait may be just one possible manifestation of Islam and of Muslim religious life that may be deployed in Java. In this respect, I would like to consider this thesis as a response to the appeal of Hefner who, after examining Islamic development at the eastern edge of Java, wrote 'the Pasuruan example awaits ethnographic comparison with other areas of rural Java' (1987:551).

Chapter 2: Recent Socio-Economic Developments in Kolojonggo

The Special Region of Yogyakarta (*Daerah Istimewa Yogyakarta*) lies in the southern central part of Java, one of the most densely populated islands in the world. Its special treatment, as the term '*istimewa*' (special) implies, stems from the Indonesian government's recognition of its historical importance as the heir of the Javanese kingdom, Mataram, and as the centre of the war of independence against the Dutch.

The Islamic kingdom, Mataram, which had replaced Hindu Majapahit in the 16th century, was partitioned into two self-governing Principalities in the mid-18th century when the Dutch established themselves as the dominant foreign power and involved themselves in power struggles amongst rival princes in Mataram. After the partition, Yogyakarta and Surakarta, located northeast of Yogyakarta, became the respective capitals of the two Principalities. From that time till 1942, both regions remained enclaves governed by indigenous rulers under the supervision of the Dutch residents whereas other parts of Java were subsumed under direct Dutch rule. The competition between the two Principalities for the status of legitimate heir of Mataram favoured Yogyakarta. Unlike the ruler in Surakarta who did not show his strong support to the provisional Indonesian government in the war against the Dutch, the Sultan in Yogyakarta was an enthusiastic supporter of it. The triumph of the provisional Indonesian government then signalled the defeat of Surakarta in its competition with Yogyakarta. The Yogyakarta Sultanate was given the privilege of becoming a special region, whereas Surakarta was amalgamated as part of the Province of Central Java.

Yogyakarta consists largely of two physiographically different areas; barren mountainous regions and fertile lowlands. The mountainous regions, constituting more than half of the total territory of Yogyakarta, incorporate the areas of Mt. Merapi in the north, the mountain range of Seribu in the east and the hilly areas in the west, creating a natural boundary for Yogyakarta surrounded by Central Java. The remaining regions are the lowlands, which are situated largely in the centre of Yogyakarta. Young volcanic soil (regosol) covering most of the lowlands and two rivers of the Progo and the Opak running across it from north to south make these regions one of the most fertile and densely populated areas in Java.

Figure II-1: The Special Region of Yogyakarta

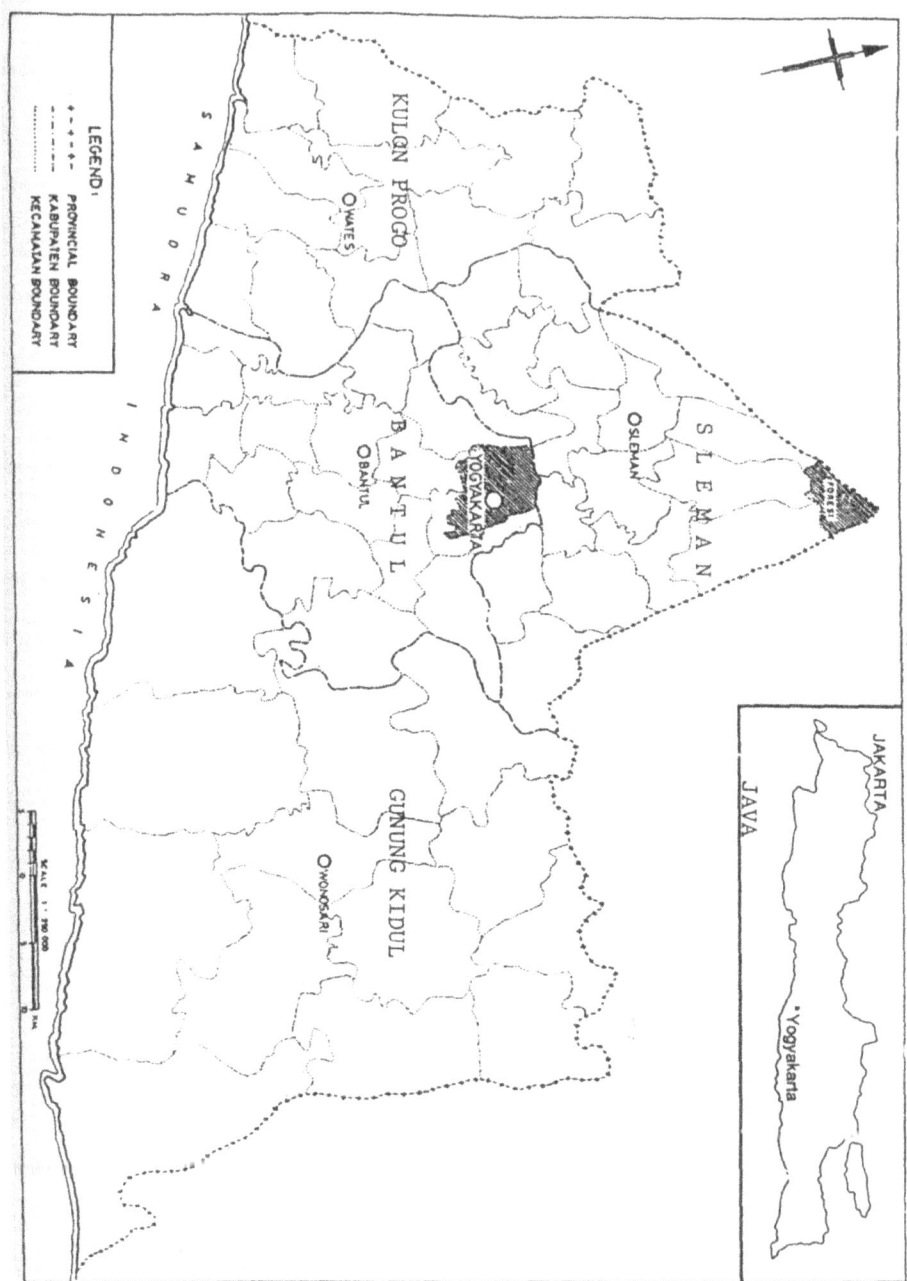

There are four districts (*kabupaten*) and one municipality (*kotamadya*) in Yogyakarta. Each district consists of sub-districts (*kecamatan*), each *kecamatan* of villages (*kelurahan*), and each *kelurahan* of hamlets (*dusun*). The present district and sub-district boundaries were established in 1945 after slight modifications were made to the pre-existing ones (Soedarisman:1984:85-90). The boundaries of the *kelurahan* were also drawn in 1945 but only after massive amalgamations. A few of the lowest administrative units in the colonial period (*desa*) were combined and restructured into a new *kelurahan* while *dusun* were instated as the new lowest administrative unit(ibid.:201-2). This amalgamation makes the size of *kelurahan* in Yogyakarta much larger than their counterparts in other parts of Java. It is not unusual to find *kelurahan* in Yogyakarta which have more than 10,000 residents.

The right to appoint officials in the *kabupaten* and *kecamatan* offices has been left in the hands of the central and regional governments, while the way to appoint *kelurahan* officials and the head of the *dusun* (*kepala dusun* or *kadus*) has oscillated between election by the residents and selection by a committee formed at the district level. Today, *kelurahan* officials except for its head (*lurah*), and the *kadus* are chosen by a committee formed at the district level from a few applicants who are pre-selected by a committee at the *kelurahan* level. The *lurah* is elected by direct votes from the residents.

Of the four districts in Yogyakarta, Sleman and Bantul share a few common geographical and population characteristics which differentiate them from Kulon Progo and Gunung Kidul. Both of them surround the city, providing areas which have accommodated the expansion of the city, and have a higher ratio of irrigated land (*sawah*) and higher population density than the other two districts.

Table II.1: Area and Population in Yogyakarta in 1990

	Area (km²)	*Sawah* (km²)	Population	Population density (per km²)
Municipality	32.50	3.43	412,059	12679
Sleman	574.82	259.98	780,334	1358
Bantul	506.85	174.03	696,905	1375
Kulon Progo	586.24	108.13	372,309	635
Gunung Kidul	1,485.36	79.96	651,004	438
Yogyakarta	3,185.80	625.53	2,912,611	914

Source: Area and *Sawah*: *Daerah Istimewa Yogyakarta Dalam Angka* 1990; Population: 1990 National Census.

The most important economic activity in Yogyakarta has been agriculture. It has employed the majority of the population, especially in rural areas, and has provided the largest part of the regional income. During the colonial time, the most intensively cultivated crop was sugarcane. In many parts of its lowland regions, the percentage of land in sugar cultivation was more than 33 percent in 1920, one of the highest ratio in Java (Geertz,1963:73). Since foreign plantations were expelled after independence, sugarcane has never recovered its dominant position. Instead, rice, the staple food of the Javanese, has been the most popular crop planted in the lowland regions while other crops such as maize, cassava, peanuts and soybeans are cultivated either as the secondary crops in the irrigated areas or as the major crops in the mountainous ones.

For the last two decades, the primary position of agriculture in the Yogyanese economy has been gradually threatened. The Gross Regional Domestic Product, one of the indicators of the economic trend in Yogyakarta, shows that the share of agriculture in GRDP has been in decline. In 1969, it was 38.9 percent (Hill and Mubyarto,1978:30) while it dropped to 30.5 percent in 1988 (KSY,various issues). The number of people working in the agricultural sector has also decreased from 56.3 percent in 1971 to 45.5 percent in 1990 (BPS,various issues). These changes show increasing importance of non-agricultural sectors as ways of obtaining livelihood for the people in Yogyakarta.

2.1. Kolojonggo: A Hamlet in Yogyakarta

The main road connecting the city of Yogyakarta to other major cities in the western part of Java is always crowded with speeding buses, petrol tanks, trucks, cars, motorbikes and other non-motorised vehicles such as animal-drawn carts, *becak* pedalled by manpower and bicycles. Every morning, this two-lane road is filled with rows of motorbikes and bicycles which carry villagers from rural areas to the city. The same panorama is unfolded in the late afternoon, but in the opposite lane. The expansion of the city has greatly changed the scenery alongside the road. The first *sawah* is visible only after riding about 4 kilometres further westwards from the edge of the city. Up to this point, the road is walled by one or two storey buildings accommodating shops and small restaurants. Further westwards from this point, first a large block of *sawah* halved by a narrow path and then a residential area surrounded by tall palm trees appear in turn. This scenery reminds one of the impact of the Dutch colonial policy, which divided *sawah* into two, one for sugar plantation and the other for paddy cultivation, on Yogyanese rural landscape.

Kolojonggo, the hamlet (*dusun*) considered in this thesis, is situated around 300 metres north from this road. It is located about 9 kilometres westwards from the city center and around 7 kilometres from the western edge of the city. It takes around fifteen to twenty minutes to arrive at the city from Kolojonggo by motorised vehicles, around thirty to forty minutes by bicycle, and less than two hours on foot. As this geographical proximity implies, the lives of villagers in Kolojonggo have been closely related to the city. All the policies to control the rural population, designed by court functionaries when the Yogyanese Sultanate had its independent power, by the Dutch colonial government when it overruled the Sultanate, by the Japanese from 1942 to 1945, by the Old Order government before 1965 and by the New Order Government since then, have had an immediate impact on villagers in Kolojonggo, shaping their modes of life.

Administratively, Kolojonggo belongs to *kelurahan* Sumber, *kecamatan* Gamol, and district Sleman. [1] Kolojonggo lies about 150 metres above sea level and its soil is composed mainly of young volcanic soil. The water supply is stable throughout the year and no shortage of water has been experienced since the construction of Mataram channel during the Japanese occupation period. This gives favourable conditions for the development of wet-rice cultivation. In the 1950s and 1960s, double cropping was a common practice, which has become triple cropping per year or five crops in two years after the introduction of new rice varieties in the 1970s. The fertile land in Kolojonggo has been a factor in supporting a large population. In 1993, the population density in Kolojonggo reached approximately 1800 persons per km^2, well above the average population density in Yogyakarta.

For the last two decades, population growth in Kolojonggo has been almost stagnant. In 1971, its population was 522 while in 1993, 544. The low population growth can be attributed to, among others, migration and the success of the family planning program. The impact of the family planning program can be appreciated by comparing the age group below 10 with that between 10 to 19 in 1993. As table II-2 shows, there were 73 children below 10, while the number of teenagers was 115. The comparison of the age group below 10 in 1971 with that in 1993 also shows a sign of declining birth rate. The number of children belonging to this group has dropped from 159 in 1971 to 73 in 1993. [2]

Table II.2: Population in Kolojonggo in 1971 and 1993 [a]

	1971				1993		
Age	Male	Female	Total		Male	Female	Total
0- 9	75	84	159		37	36	73
10-19	58	52	110		48	67	115
20-29	27	37	64		45	47	92
30-39	31	36	67		36	32	68
40-49	22	28	50		36	33	69
50-59	16	23	39		33	34	67
60 +	14	19	33		23	37	60
Total	243	279	522		258	286	544

[a] According to the official statistics made by the kelurahan office, the population of kelurahan Sumber in 1990 was 11590, of which 5749 were male and 5841 were female.

Source: 1971: Census data; 1993: Records kept in the *kadus'* (hamlet head's) house and interview data

The second factor contributing to a stagnant growth in population is out-migration, which has taken place in two ways. First, ten households recorded in the 1971 census emigrated from Kolojonggo as a group. Four of them moved

---

[1] The names of the hamlet, *kelurahan* and *kecamatan* used in the text are pseudonyms.
[2] A similar trend is also visible in the population of Yogyakarta. The number of children aged between 0 and 9 in Yogyakarta declined from 693,135 in 1971 to 490,755 in 1990, while people belonging to the age group of 0-9 and that of 10-19 were respectively 490,755 and 626,915 in 1990 (1971 and 1990 Census data).

to Sumatra following the government transmigration program, while six of them went to other parts of Yogyakarta. Migrations have also occurred individually, caused mainly by marriages and job-seeking. Table II-3 shows the places where the villagers who were registered in the 1971 census lived in 1993:

Table II.3: Places Where the Villagers Registered in the 1971 Census Lived in 1993

	Age in 1971								
	0-9	10-19	20-29	30-39	40-49	50-59	60 +	Total	(%)
In Kolojonggo	73	37	37	50	33	18	4	252	48.3
In the same *kelurahan*	8	13	8	4				33	6.3
In the same region	29	22	11	5	1	1		69	13.2
In Java	29	27	2	1				59	11.3
Outside Java	12	7	2	1				22	4.2
Deceased	3	1		5	16	18	29	72	13.8
Unknown	5	3	4	1		2		15	2.9
Total	159	110	64	67	50	39	33	522	

Source: As for Table II-2.

Of the seven age groups in table II-3, that between 10 and 19 reflects the trends in villagers' mobility most clearly, since people belonging to this group were on the verge of changing their residence by marriage, job-seeking or transmigration in 1971. Of the 110 teenagers belonging to this group, 50 still lived in *kelurahan* Sumber, 22 in other parts of Yogyakarta, and 34 outside Yogyakarta in 1993. Lack of data on the population mobility before 1971 makes it difficult to judge whether the mobility of this group since 1971 has been higher than that of their parents' generation before the 1970s or not. However, considering that most siblings of the villagers older than 50 lived in the vicinity of Kolojonggo in 1993, work opportunities in big cities in Java have increased rapidly over the last two decades, and the transportation revolution in the 1970s, called '*revolusi colt*', shortened the distance between different parts of Java (Hugo,1985:62-65), it is probable that the mobility of this group since 1971 has been much higher than before. The high mobility since the 1970s is also visible in the age group below 10 in 1971, whose search for permanent settlements is not yet complete. Slightly less than a half of them had already left *kelurahan* Sumber and lived in other parts of Yogyakarta or outside of it in 1993.

Having considered a few characteristics in population development, I will focus on the socio economic developments in Kolojonggo since the 1970s. Developments in the agricultural sector after the introduction of the green revolution, diversification of the occupational structure and changes in the structure of land tenure will be the focus of this discussion. [3]

---

[3] For the economic history in Kolojonggo before 1965, see Appendix A.

2.2. Introduction of the Green Revolution

In the process of securing political power after 1965, the New Order government had to face the same issue that had troubled its predecessor: an escalating rice price and a shortage of rice. From the end of May 1967 to mid-January 1968, the rice price rose four times while the import of rice was interrupted by limited supply in the world market (Timmer,1981:37). This economic situation precipitated the government's intervention in the agricultural sector, without which political stability would have been threatened. The most important strategy adopted by the government was to initiate the rice intensification program on a large scale. From the late 1960s, the rice intensification program has continued until now, changing its names and major focuses from time to time. [4] With unprecedented investments in agriculture, the program has succeeded in achieving rapid increase in rice production, allowing Indonesia to secure self-sufficiency in rice in 1985 (Pearson et al.,1991:16). The rice intensification program has impacted on every domain of rural life. Cropping intensification and higher yields have freed villagers from periodic hunger and made rice cultivation more profitable while new technologies have transformed the traditional ways of cultivating rice and of mobilising labour. These changes in agriculture have triggered chain reactions in non-agricultural domains.

The motto of *panca usaha* (five efforts) popularised by the government summarises the goal of the initial phase of the rice intensification program: to use high yielding rice varieties (*bibit unggul*); to apply chemical fertilisers; to use insecticides; to improve irrigation systems; and to improve methods of ploughing and planting. Although more than two decades have passed from that time, *panca usaha* is still a golden rule for peasants, but with slight modifications. Insecticides are now recommended to be used only in limited circumstances while previous emphasis on using fertilisers has been replaced by that on the right combinations and timings of application.

High yielding rice varieties, called PB-5 and PB-8 [5] , were released in 1967 with the initiation of the *Bimas Baru* program. These new varieties had several characteristics which distinguished them from local varieties and which promised higher yields than the latter. They overcame a 'nitrogen to yield threshold', could be grown in many latitudes regardless of season, could support numerous heavy panicles of grain without lodging and could be harvested in a relatively short period of time (Fox,1991a:65). The acceptance of high yielding varieties by peasants was rapid. 31 percent of the rice planted for the 1971/1972 wet

---

[4] For *Bimas Gotong-royong* in 1968/69, see Franke (1973:29-47) and Utrecht (1973:157-160); for *Bimas Gaja Baru* in the 1970s, see Palmer (1977:36-47) and Timmer (1981:38-40); and for *Insus* starting from 1979, see Mubyarto (1982:49-50).
[5] For the breeding history of these new seeds, see Fox (1991a:65-66).

season in Indonesia consisted of new seeds and the figure reached 67 percent for the 1979/1980 wet season (ibid.:66-67).

To the peasants in Kolojonggo, where water supply is constant all year round, the most advantageous feature of high yielding varieties was their shorter growth duration. Compared with the traditional varieties, which required 150 days or more to be harvested, PB-5 or PB-8 could be harvested in 130-140 days. The growth duration was shortened further in the later released varieties which mature in 105-110 days (Khush, 1985:456). The shorter growth duration opened an era of triple cropping in one year or of five crops in two years, which made rice cultivation even more profitable.

The use of chemical fertilisers for rice cultivation was already reported in the Old Order. However, the high price and inconvenience in purchasing fertilisers hindered their extensive use (Soemarjo, 1959:32-33; Utrecht, 1973:159). Therefore, one of the aims of the rice intensification program was to secure peasants' easy access to chemical fertilisers at an affordable price. The government extended distribution networks of fertilisers, subsidised their prices, and extended credit for purchase (Mears, 1981:123-132). With these efforts, chemical fertilisers were introduced into farming with the rapidity that new seeds were. Only a few years after the implementation of the government program, around 70 percent of the peasants in a Yogyanese village were using chemical fertilisers, ranging from 67 to 245 kg. per hectare (Penny and Singarimbun, 1973:32-33). The amount of fertiliser application increased quickly, so that the average amount rocketed from 163 kg. per hectare in 1972 to 300 kg. in 1981 (Fox, 1991a:77-78). The same trend has continued with the average amount of fertiliser application reaching 426 kg. per hectare in Yogyakarta in 1990 (KSY, 1990).

The outcome of the adoption of high yielding varieties and chemical fertilisers has been a remarkable increase in yields per hectare. In Yogyakarta, the average rice production, which had been below 35 quintals (1 quintal = 100 kg.) of unhusked rice per hectare before 1962 (KSY, 1957 & 1963), increased to 45 quintals per hectare in 1975 and to 58 quintals in 1989 (KSY, various issues). As the cropping ratio has changed from double to triple in some parts of rural Yogyakarta, the yields that Yogyanese peasants can obtain from the same size of *sawah* have been more than doubled since the implementation of the rice intensification program. This increase in yields has subsequently decreased the size of *sawah* required to secure a staple rice supply for a household. If it is assumed that a household consisting of five members consumes about 1.5 kg. of rice per day[6], less than 1000m² of *sawah* is now required to satisfy its annual rice consumption in an area where triple cropping is possible. Table II-4 calculates

[6] This is a figure obtained from 25 sampled households in Kolojonggo. Penny and Singarimbun report a figure which is slightly higher than that presented in the text, namely, one-third of a kilo per day or 120 kilos per year per person (1973:20).

the returns that a peasant could obtain from 1000m² of *sawah* in 1993 with the premise that yields per hectare were 60 quintals of *gabah basah* (unhusked paddy containing approximately 25 percent of moisture). [7]

Table II.4: Inputs and Outputs for Rice Cultivation Per Cropping (per 1000m2)

Cost	Unit	Amount (kg.)	Note
Inputs			
Seeds	GB	15.6	4.9 kg. of seeds purchased in the market; 1 kg. of seeds = Rp 800; 1 kg. of *gabah basah* = Rp 250
Ploughing	GB	35.9	Rp 8990.5 per 1000 m²
Planting	GB	21.7	Rp 5428 per 1000 m²
Fertilisers	GB	59.5	45.14 kg. per 1000 m²; Rp 330 per 1 kg. of fertiliser; family labour for fertilising
Weeding	-	-	Family labour
Harvesting	GB	75.0	1/7 of the total production
Total Costs	GB	207.7	
Yields	GB	600.0	
Returns	GB	392.3	
Loss in Drying	-	58.8	Loss in drying = 15 percent[a]
Returns after Drying	GK	333.5	
Loss in Milling	GK	116.7	Conversion Ratio of 0.65 from GK to B[b]
Cost of Milling	B	13.9	Rp 25 for 1 kg. of GK; 1 kg. of *Beras* = Rp 600
Net Returns in Rice	B	202.9	

Source: 101 households in three hamlets in *kelurahan* Sumber
Note: GB = *Gabah Basah*; GK = *Gabah Kering* (unhusked dry rice); B = *Beras* (Milled Rice).
[a] The loss in the process of drying is dependent on the season and geographical characteristics of *sawah*. Although these make it impossible to calculate the exact amount of loss during drying, it is estimated to be 15 percent in the text for convenience' sake. This is based on the consideration that new rice varieties contain 25 percent of moisture when harvested and many farmers dry paddy for their own storage to less than 14 percent of moisture (Mears,1981:48 & 146).
[b] 0.65 is a conversion ratio used by the Indonesian Central Bureau of Statistics (BPS) for calculating the amount of *beras* derived from *gabah kering* (Fox,1991a:80).

Table II-4 shows that 1000m² of *sawah* can yield 202.9 kg. of milled rice per cropping. If a household owning 1000m² of *sawah* cultivates rice three times a year, it can acquire about 50 kg. of rice per month or more than 1.5 kg. per day. This implies that the size of *sawah* required to secure annual food consumption is just half of what villagers in double cropping areas needed for the same purpose in the 1950s. [8] One effect of the increase in yields has been eradication of rice

[7] According to the government statistics, yields per hectare in Yogyakarta have been about 50-60 quintals of unhusked dry rice *(gabah kering)* since the 1980s. In this respect, the yields of 60 quintals of *gabah basah* used in the text are 10-15 percent less than the official statistics. As most villagers commented that the average yields per 1000 m² reached 6 quintals of *gabah basah* and the average yields per 1000 m² in the 52 cases of the harvest measured by a rice trader were 5.9 quintals of *gabah basah*, 6 quintals of *gabah basah* is used in the text for convenience' sake.

[8] In the 1950s, the average yields (unhusked dry rice) per hectare in Yogyakarta were 25.05 quintals (KSY,1957 & 1963). From this, it can be assumed that 0.2 hectare of *sawah* could produce about 500 kg. of unhusked dry rice per cropping. When a household cultivated 0.2 hectare of *sawah* with its own family labour, the production cost could be dropped to 60-70 kg. of unhusked rice, leaving 430-440 kg as net yields. If unhusked rice was converted to husked one at the rate of 1:0.65 and pounding was carried out by family labour, the household could secure about 280 kg. of rice. As double cropping was

scarcity in rural areas. Villagers in Kolojonggo who were born after the mid-1960s unanimously commented that they have not experienced any shortage of rice from their childhood on.

2.3. Development of the Rural Labour Market in Kolojonggo

It has been suggested that the introduction of labour saving mechanisms and rationalisation of labour use after the 1970s reduced work opportunities in the agricultural sector. The examples chosen to show this trend are the replacement of the *ani-ani* (finger knife) by the sickle, of hand threshing and pounding by the diesel-powered threshers and hullers, of hand weeding by rotary or toothed weeders, the introduction of tractors, and adoption of the *tebasan* system for the harvest (Collier, 1981:161-5; Hüsken and White, 1989:254; White, 1989:76). Of these practices, the most substantial impact on the rural labour market in Yogyakarta has been from the introduction of the rice hullers and sickles. The diesel-powered threshers have not been adopted widely, rotary or toothed weeders had already been used in the 1950s (Soemarjo, 1959), tractors have operated side by side with animals instead of replacing them, and *tebasan*, which existed even before the 1970s (Syafri, 1978:7), has not limited the number of harvesters.[9] This implies that labour saving mechanisms adopted after the 1970s affected largely the labour market of women whose major agricultural work involved harvesting and hulling.

In dealing with the rural labour market of men, what should be considered is cropping intensification. As no substantial difference exists in the pre-harvest labour input before and after the use of high yielding rice varieties (Montgomery, 1974:204; Collier, 1979:10-11), it is obvious that change in cropping intensification from double to triple has increased the annual labour input into a certain size of *sawah*. This means that more work opportunities have been created for men in the rural agricultural market since the green revolution.

Papanek suggests that the effect of cropping intensification in creating more work opportunities may have been offset by an increase in the rural population (1985:28-29). Although persuasive, this explanation does not consider one

---

possible, this amount of rice could be harvested once every six months. This indicates that when there was no severe crop failure, 2000 m² of *sawah* could give its holders about 1.5 kg. of rice per day. This amount of rice was large enough to meet daily rice consumption of a family of five members, which ranged, according to Pandam, 100 to 200 grams per person (1958:42). For more about the production cost and rice consumption in the 1950s, see Appendix A.

[9] *Tebasan* refers to a system where peasants sell their rice before the harvest to a middleman (*penebas*) who will do the harvest by himself or herself. As Hayami and Hafid point out, the introduction of *tebasan* does not change directly labour requirements for the harvest. The more important factor to determine labour requirements for the harvest is whether the introduction of *tebasan* is accompanied by a change in payment from output shares to cash wages or not. When cash wages are not applied, the *penebas* has no strong incentive to decrease the number of workers since a share that he or she can secure will not change much irrespective of the number of harvesters (Hayami and Hafid, 1979, 104-5), although the problem of controlling harvesters may prompt him or her to keep their number lower.

important factor, namely, the changing orientation of teenagers who constitute the major providers of new labour. Traditionally villagers began to be involved in agricultural work in their early teens. According to White, in the early 1970s, Yogyanese teenagers between the ages of 10 to 13 started agricultural work such as ploughing, planting and harvesting both in their parents' *sawah* and as wage labourers. By their late teens, the proportion of time allocated to productive labour was almost similar to that of adult villagers (1977:275-282). Beginning sometime in the late 1970s or in the 1980s, teenagers' early involvement in the rural labour market gradually slowed to the extent that in 1993-94, it seldom happened that teenagers worked either in their parents' *sawah* or as daily agricultural labourers. [10] One of the factors accelerating this trend is the expansion of secondary education as table II-5 indicates:

Table II.5: Last School Attended by Villagers Aged between 15 and 34

	Year of Birth			
	1960-64	1965-69	1970-74	1975-79
	I	II	III	IV
None	0	0	0	0
Primary School	24	18	3	0
Junior High School	4	7	12	5(15)
Senior High School	5	17	25	7(22)
Tertiary education	3	5	6	3

Source: Records kept in the *kadus*' house and interview data.
Note: Numbers in parenthesis are the teenagers who were enrolled in junior or senior high school in 1993.

One of the notable features in table II-5 is the contrast in the length of the schooling period between Group I and the other Groups. While two thirds in Group I stopped their study at the primary school level, more than half of those in Group II proceeded to secondary school. The period of schooling becomes longer for the younger cohort, so that all in group IV continued their study at least to junior high school and the majority of them proceeded to senior high school.

Although education and withdrawal from agricultural work does not have any evident causal relation [11] , no teenagers in Kolojonggo work as wage labourers

---

[10] During three months afternoon observation of around 10 hectares of *sawah*, I witnessed only a few cases where teenagers worked in the *sawah* of their parents. Of these, there was one case where teenagers worked as daily labourers. However, this case was an exceptional one triggered by an extraordinary situation. A man who cultivated about 2500 m^2 of *sawah* lost his chance to weed at the right time and the whole *sawah* was covered with weeds. For a couple of weeks, he tried to find labourers to help him weed, but in vain. At last, he asked his grandson to bring his friends, promising to pay almost twice what was usually paid to daily labourers. His grandson succeeded in bringing five friends. After working three afternoons, however, all of them disappeared from the *sawah* without finishing weeding the whole plot.
[11] Asked why they did not work in *sawah*, most teenagers answered that they were lazy or that they felt shame if they worked in the agricultural sector. This attitude was different from that of a few villagers in their late thirties and forties who were quite proud to say they had earned the money to continue their study to secondary and tertiary schools by working in their parents' *sawah* or in some cases, by share-cropping others' *sawah*. Their attitude points out that before the mid-1970s, teenagers

in the agricultural sector while they attend school, and their status as students is accepted, both by teenagers and their parents, as an uncontested excuse for not working in *sawah*. This implies that, unlike what Papanek suggests, rural population growth, especially after the 1960s, has not played a significant role in offsetting the favourable impact of cropping intensification on the rural labour market for men, at least in Kolojonggo. On the contrary, teenagers' late involvement in productive labour has worked to widen work opportunities in the agricultural sector.

In sum, cropping intensification after the green revolution and the gradual withdrawal of teenagers from the agricultural labour market have been two of the factors helping to ease the pressure on the existing labour market of men in Kolojonggo. [12] In addition to these factors, expanding work opportunities in non-agricultural sectors from the mid-1970s have also played a role in hindering the shrinkage of the agricultural labour market. In order to understand this development, a summary of the primary occupations of all male villagers above the age of 15 in Kolojonggo is presented in table II-6.

were not reluctant to work in *sawah* and saw no incompatibility between one's status as a student and as an agricultural labourer. It is not certain why this change has happened.
[12] The positive impact of crop intensification on the rise of employment in rice cultivation is also noticed by Hinkson (1975:333) and Schweizer (1987:66).

Table II.6: Primary Occupations of All Male Villagers Aged above 15 in Kolojonggo

	Year of Birth					
	- 1939	1940-49	1950-59	1960-69	1970-79	Total
A Agriculture						
Owner Cultivation	10	5	5	1		
Owner Cultivation + Tenant	2					2
Sawah Owner	5					5
Tenant	3	4				7
Labourer	4	2	1	1		8
Tenant + Labourer	3	2	2			7
Owner Cultivation + Labourer	1	1				2
Sub Total	**28**	**14**	**8**	**2**		**52**
B Non-Agricultural works mainly in village						
Rice Trader			1			1
Livestock and Fish		2	3			5
Non-agricultural Labourer		2	2	2		6
Self-employed/Entrepreneur	2	3	2	2		9
Sub Total	**2**	**7**	**8**	**4**		**21**
C Non-Agricultural works mainly outside village						
Trader		2	2	4	1	9
Self-employed/Entrepreneur		2		1		3
Construction Labourer	3	2	9	14	1	29
Factory Labourer			2	9	3	14
Driver/Conductor	1		4	2	1	8
White Collar Worker		5	7	3		15
Blue Collar Office Worker	1	2		2		5
Sub Total	**5**	**13**	**24**	**35**	**6**	**83**
D Students and Unemployed						
Student				3	32	35
Unemployed	2	2	1	1	6	12
Sub Total	**2**	**2**	**1**	**4**	**38**	**47**
Total	**37**	**44**	**40**	**45**	**44**	**203**

Source: As for Table II-5.
Note:
A. Tenant: those who sharecrop or rent others' *sawah*; *Sawah* owner: those who own *sawah* but give it to others on a sharecrop basis, receiving one-half of the yields.
B. Livestock and Fish: duck and pig breeders and an owner of a freshwater fish nursery; Non-agricultural Labourer: workers making bricks and *emping* (chips made of *Gnetum gnemon*); Self-employed/Entrepreneur: bicycle repairers, a bamboo furniture maker, a metal worker, a masseur, owners of places making bricks and *emping,* and a vendor of iced drinks.
C. Trader: shop owners (fruit) and middlemen dealing with *emping,* freshwater fish and chicken; Self-employed/Entrepreneur: a gatherer of red ants' houses in mountainous areas, a street vendor and a barber; Factory Labourer: one technician employed in a motorbike repair shop was included in this category; White Collar Worker: civil servants, teachers, a nurse and policemen; Blue Collar Worker: a night watchman, security guards and clerks.

Table II-6 shows that non-agricultural work provides the primary source of livelihood for two-thirds of male villagers in Kolojonggo. Of 203 male villagers aged over 15, those who work primarily in the agricultural sector number 52 while those who work in non-agricultural sectors number 104 excluding students and unemployed villagers. When considering age, table II-6 indicates the changing pattern of employment: the younger villagers are, the less they are employed in the agricultural sector. The majority of villagers born before 1940 are employed in the agricultural sector while the ratio of those working outside this sector gets higher as villagers are younger. In the case of those born after 1960, only two chose agriculture as their primary occupation. The second notable feature in table II-6 is that villagers' occupations are distributed in diverse sub-sectors of the economy. This occupational diversity is not a new phenomenon. Even before the 1970s, villagers' efforts to maximise their income led them to take employment opportunities wherever possible. White gives us a finding that slightly less than 50 percent of villagers in the early 1970s had their primary occupation in non-agricultural sectors (White,1976:139). What makes the period after the 1970s distinctive is that the majority of those working in non-agricultural sectors work outside the village, mostly in the city. Of the 104 villagers who are employed primarily in non-agricultural sectors, 83 work outside the village. [13] The third interesting point is the importance of the construction sector as a source of employment. Twenty-nine villagers work in the construction sector as masons, carpenters or assistants. [14]

The expansion of the labour market for construction labour, especially after the second half of the 1970s, was triggered by increasing government subsidies for rural development and the expansion of the city. [15] Development funds were allocated to build infrastructure such as roads, schools and government buildings (Mubyarto,1982:46-7), while the expansion of Yogyakarta city involved constructing new buildings and houses. These two developments brought favourable conditions for the expansion of the construction sector. The booming construction sector then accelerated demands for construction labour to the extent that from the late 1970s on, villagers from rural areas have been readily employed as assistants of artisans irrespective of their previous work experiences. Apart from this easy access, relatively higher wages in construction labour than

[13] In the case of construction labour, work opportunities are also available within the village. However, as all construction labourers are not reluctant to work outside the village and the majority of construction sites are placed outside it, all of them are classified as working outside.

[14] Widening job opportunities in the construction sector after the 1970s do not seem to have been a peculiar phenomenon in Kolojonggo but to have been widespread in other parts of rural Java. According to statistics, the most rapid annual growth in non-agricultural employment in the 1970s occurred in the construction sector, followed by the transport and service sector. The construction sector accounted for 21 percent of all non-agricultural employment growth in rural areas. This pace was not halted in the later period, so that employment in the construction sector grew at 3.7 percent per annum and accounted for 27 percent of all non-agricultural employment growth in the first half of the 1980s (Manning,1988: 52-54).

[15] In 1963-73, Yogyakarta was the only province to record a decline in the area of *sawah* under cultivation by a yearly average of 1.4 per cent, or over 6,500 hectares (Hill and Mubyarto,1978,42-43). In 1980-1990, the *sawah* area in Yogyakarta decreased by 3881 hectares (BPS,various issues).

in agriculture have been an incentive for rural villagers to work as construction labourers. [16]

Sometime in the 1980s an interesting development took place which helped to expand work opportunities in the construction sector. Traditionally the labour needed to build a private house in the hamlet was provided by close neighbours (*gotong-royong*). The mobilisation of *gotong-royong* was based on reciprocity, so that the duty of the host was to reciprocate his neighbours' labour in the future and no cash payment was involved. [17] In 1993-94, *gotong-royong* was still used but only for the purpose of improving a house and on the condition that it lasted for one or two days. According to villagers, the increasing number of those working outside the village made it impossible to initiate a *gotong-royong* during weekdays and this forced the replacement of *gotong-royong* with wage labour to construct a house. The result of the use of wage labour for constructing a house is that the chances for working as construction labourers have increased even in rural areas.

The withdrawal of people working in non-agricultural sectors from agricultural wage labour has also been a factor in hindering the shrinkage of the agricultural labour market since the 1970s. Their withdrawal may be explained by the negative cultural value attached to agricultural wage labour. When work chances in non-agricultural sectors were not as many as in the period after the 1970s, one's access to agricultural wage labour was dependent on the favour of the landowners and this allowed the extension of unequal economic relations into non-economic domains. Wage labourers did unpaid work for their employer on a regular basis and when the employer hosted certain celebrations, not only the labourers but their family members had to assist in the preparation process. In this respect, employers and labourers were not bound by pure economic relations but by patron-client relations where the former could exert authoritative power over the latter. It seems that this previously embedded inequality has been a factor hindering the involvement of labourers in the agricultural labour market, although the basis of the relations has become increasingly economic. Villagers' easy access to construction work can also explain the withdrawal of non-agricultural labourers from agricultural wage labour. When one is laid off work, he can be easily employed in the construction sector until he finds a new job. As a result, the construction sector now plays the role of provider of

---

[16] In 1993, the daily wage in the construction sector reached Rp 2500 for the novices, Rp 4000 for masons, and Rp 5000 for carpenters, whereas remuneration in agricultural work (hoeing) was Rp 1500-2000. The higher wage in the construction sector seems to have continued from the early 1970s on. In the early 1970s, the daily wage of agricultural labour (hoeing) reached Rp 60-90 in the Bantul district and Rp 60-80 in the Kulon Progo district while that of construction work, Rp 100-125 and Rp 80-100 respectively (Maurer,1991:108-109; White,1977:184 &188). In 1981, the daily wage of unskilled work in public construction projects was as high as Rp 1,000 (Mubyarto,1982:55), equivalent to about 4 kg. of rice, which must certainly have been higher than that in the agricultural sector.

[17] Carpenters were exceptional, so that they were given cash payment even before the 1970s.

temporary job opportunities for the unemployed, a role previously played by the agricultural sector.

In sum, no rapid decrease in agricultural wage labour, expanding work opportunities in non-agricultural sectors, the longer periods of education and the formation of a boundary between agricultural and non-agricultural wage labour have helped to lessen pressure on the rural labour market. Many of those employed previously in the agricultural sector have sought new employment in non-agricultural sectors while most villagers who are newly incorporated in the labour market now start their career in non-agricultural sectors. One impact of this change is that a shortage of agricultural labour has started to be felt by the peasants in Kolojonggo, although they can see many unemployed youngsters or temporary unemployed villagers. [18] As a result, if someone has the intention to work as an agricultural wage labourer, he is instantly given a job by those who are desperately in need of labour. The decreasing pressure on the rural labour market is reflected in the amount of daily wage that agricultural labourers can secure. While agricultural labourers in Yogyakarta had received about 1 kg. of rice for a day's ploughing in the early 1970s (Penny and Singarimbun,1973:26; White,1991:109; Maurer,1991:109), they received about 3 kg. of rice in 1993 for the same amount of labour. [19]

Compared with the rural labour market of men, that of women has followed a somewhat different developmental course. The introduction of labour saving mechanisms, namely, the sickle and diesel powered huller, replaced, although not totally, the *ani-ani* and hand pounding, and brought about a significant decrease in work opportunities. While 200 or more man-days were needed to harvest 1 hectare of *sawah* with the *ani-ani*, 75 man-days were enough to carry out the same work after the introduction of the sickle (Collier,1981:162). In some parts of Java where the *tebasan* system limited the number of harvesters and the *penebas* (rice trader) employed the same person over time (Collier et al.,1974:20-3), or where the *penebas* employed men rather than women (Hüsken,1979:146), the majority of those who had once been permitted to participate in the harvest were deprived of any chance to do so. The diesel powered huller was another novelty having a similar effect on the women's rural labour market. All work opportunities in pounding disappeared and women villagers who usually received 10 percent of the amount they pounded lost this important source of income (Stoler,1985:59). These changes make it possible for Collier to comment that 'the imperatives of efficiency and profitability are

---

[18] Labour shortage in the rural area is also reported by several scholars. See Collier et al. (1982,97), Manning (1987:72), and Naylor (1991:74-77).

[19] Lack of reliable statistical data concerning trends in agricultural wages makes it difficult to know at which point in the last two decades this increase in daily wages began, but the trend was clearly evident in the mid-1980s. According to Maurer, a day's ploughing in Bantul district was worth 4 to 5 kg. of rice in 1984 (1984:118) and was equivalent to slightly more than 4 kg. in 1987 (1991:109).

beginning to exact their toll in the erosion of traditions where elasticities in the production function allowed for high rates of labour absorption within the rice producing sector' (Collier,1981:171).

In Kolojonggo, the position of female labourers has not been as bad as that of their counterparts in other parts of Java, although much worse than before the 1970s. The primary reason for this is that the *ani-ani* has not been replaced by the sickle. It is not certain why the sickle has not been accepted by villagers [20] but the effect of the continuing use of the *ani-ani* isquite clear. A sudden shrinkage of the agricultural labour market was hindered and the benefit of cropping intensification, that is, absolute increase in opportunities to participate in the harvest, could be shared by a much wider circle of female labourers.

The shift in the mode of mobilising harvest labour has also helped to ease pressure on the rural labour market for women. Before the 1970s, the mobilisation of labour for the harvest in Kolojonggo was based on a semi-open system. All of those who wanted to participate in the harvest could do so, if they received permission from the owner. This system allowed participation of women living outside Kolojonggo in harvesting *sawah* in Kolojonggo. In the 1950s, it was reported in a hamlet located around 5 kilometres northeast of Kolojonggo that one third of harvesters came from the hamlet to which the *sawah* owner belonged, one third from neighbouring hamlets and other *kecamatan,* and the rest from different districts (Soedjito,1957:132). This composition shows that there was room for manipulation in the harvest, should a change occur in the existing structure of labour market. When the rice huller replaced hand pounding and more female villagers wanted to participate in the harvest, the pattern of mobilising harvest labour was modified. The semi-open system was gradually replaced by a semi-closed system, namely, one in which the owner did not prohibit villagers living in the same or neighbouring hamlets from participating in the harvest but did not allow those from a different *kelurahan* to do so. With this shift, the work opportunities in harvesting once taken by outsiders were

---

[20] When asked about the use of the *ani-ani*, most villagers commented on the duty to neighbours at first. As the use of the sickle reduces harvest labour greatly and decreases the chances of poor village women earning income, it is better, according to them, not to replace the *ani-ani* with the sickle. They also mentioned the production loss entailed by the use of the sickle. As more grains drop off when harvested by the sickle than by the *ani-ani*, the *ani-ani* can secure more rice for *sawah* owners. The same opinion is retained by the *penebas*, who are more sensitive to the introduction of new technology. Four *penebas* who were interviewed answered that they have never tried to use the sickle due to potential production losses. What is interesting in this explanation is that most villagers including *penebas* have had no experience of using the sickle and, accordingly, no chance to compare these two harvest tools. In this respect, what has a more serious impact on the use of the *ani-ani* is not that the *ani-ani* actually guarantees more paddy than the sickle but that villagers believe the sickle brings lesser yields than the *ani-ani*. This belief is based on villagers' assumption that the bodily movements of harvesters are much larger and rougher when they use the sickle than when they use the *ani-ani*, so that harvesting with the sickle will cause higher ratio of grain loss. Irrespective of whether this assumption is right or wrong, this belief seems to have been one of the most important factors in the continuing use of the *ani-ani* in Kolojonggo and its vicinity.

given to those living in the same or neighbouring hamlets. The change in the mode of mobilising harvest labour entailed a change in the method of fixing harvest wages. When harvesters from distant places were allowed, the dividend allocated to them (*bawon* or *maro*) was up to 1:17, that for harvesters from the same village was between 1:6 to 1:8 and that for harvesters who had close relations with the owner, less than 1:6. After the prohibition on outside harvesters, the share allocated to ordinary harvesters from the same and neighbouring hamlets dropped up to 1:13. With this modification in *bawon*, the share that the owners could secure did not decrease much; they probably could get more than before.

It is not certain whether the increase in harvest work caused by cropping intensification and the change in the mode of recruiting harvest labourers could compensate the loss that the diesel-powered huller brought in or not. However, it is clear that these helped to hinder an abrupt shrinkage of the labour market of women at the first stage of the green revolution and gave female villagers a better chance to adjust to the new economic environment. In this process of adaptation, female villagers were less fortunate than their male counterparts since they did not have access to the construction sector. The only sector which they could easily move into was trade, which brought about a striking influx of ex-female agricultural labourers into local small-scale trade (Stoler,1975:59).

The development of the agricultural labour market of women in the 1980s has also been influenced by factors which have affected that for men. As Javanese parents do not discriminate between male and female children in the matter of education, the schooling period of female teenagers has also become longer, impeding the flow of new agricultural labourers into the labour market. Widening work opportunities in the manufacturing and service sectors after the 1980s have also helped to ease the pressure on the labour market. The primary occupations of female villagers who are older than 15 are summarised in table II-7.

Table II.7: Primary Occupations of All Female Villagers Aged above 15 in Kolojonggo

		Year of Birth				
		- 1939	1940-49	1950-59	1960-69	1970-79	Total
A	**Agriculture**						
	Self Cultivation			1			1
	Planter and Harvester	1	2	3	2		8
	Casual Harvester	11	4	1	1		17
	Professional Harvester		2	2	1		5
	Sub Total	**12**	**8**	**7**	**4**		**31**
B	**Trade**						
	Trader - *warung* and shop	2	2	6	2		14
	Trader - *jamu*	1	4	2	3		10
	Trader - *mlinjo* and *emping*	8	6	4	2		20
	Trader - *pasar* (local market)	3	2	2	2		9
	Trader - others (brokers)		2	2	2		6
	Sub Total	**14**	**16**	**16**	**11**		**57**
C	**Non-Agricultural Work**						
	Tempe Producer	4					4
	Entrepreneur/Self-employed	1	1	2	3		7
	Animal Husbandry		2	1	2		5
	Non-agricultural Labourer	1	4	1	3		9
	Factory Worker			1	2	2	5
	Shopkeeper				3	4	7
	White Collar Worker		2	5	4	1	12
	Sub Total	**6**	**9**	**10**	**17**	**7**	**49**
D	**Students and Unemployed**						
	Student				1	33	34
	Pensioner	1					1
	Unemployed (non-harvester)	13	2	5	7	10	37
	Unemployed (harvester)	1		3			4
	Sub Total	**15**	**2**	**8**	**8**	**43**	**76**
	Total	**47**	**35**	**41**	**40**	**50**	**213**

Note: **A.** Casual Harvester: those who harvest others' *sawah* on an irregular basis when they are asked to do so; Professional Harvester: those who work daily with the *penebas*.
B. *Warung*: owners of small shop in the hamlet selling a variety of daily necessities; Shop: owners of cosmetics, clothes and fruits shops in the local market or in the city; *Jamu: Jamu* is a traditional Javanese tonic made of medicinal herbs. It is made at home and sold either in the local market or by making door-to-door visits to each house in a certain rural area; *Mlinjo* and *Emping*: *mlinjo* refer to fruits of *Gnetum gnemon* and *emping*, snacks made from *mlinjo*; Broker: rice traders and traders who buy chicken, *tikar* (a plaited mat) and coconut sugar from rural areas and sell them to other middlemen.
C. Entrepreneur: seamstress, owners of places making bricks and *emping*, and a weaver; Animal Husbandry: pig breeders; Non-agricultural labourer: workers making *emping*; Factory Workers: workers in weaving factory located in Sumber; Shopkeeper: waitress in the restaurant and clerks in shops in the city; White Collar Worker: teachers, civil servants and administrators in the private sector.
D. Unemployed (non-harvester): those who do not have a specific job nor participate in harvest work; Unemployed (harvester): those who do not have a specific job but participate in the harvest of their own *sawah*.

Table II-7 shows that trading is the most important source of income for women of all ages. The most common items are *jamu* (traditional Javanese tonic made of medicinal herbs) and *emping,* while those classified as market traders handle a variety of merchandise including chicken and duck eggs, rice, vegetables, home-made snacks, *tempe* (fermented soybean cake), the skin of *mlinjo* and so on. This shows that there has been no remarkable change in the items of trade over time. Most still trade in what their predecessors did before the 1970s. In the mode of trading, however, a few changes have taken place. On the one hand, more villagers specialise in one merchandise rather than handling diverse items. Of five categories of traders in table II-7, *warung* owners and some market traders handle diverse merchandise while others sell only one item. On the other hand, the mobility of women traders is much greater than for their predecessors whose activities centred mainly on the local market. Many of them bypass the local market and deal directly with traders and customers in the city and some of them do their trading activities outside Yogyakarta. [21] One of the impacts of their higher mobility is that their activity in agriculture is limited to the harvest of their own *sawah*. Of 57 women traders in table II-7, 7 attend the harvest of their own and others, 22 participate only in their own harvest, 17 do not attend the harvest, although their families have *sawah* to be harvested, and 11 traders whose families do not cultivate *sawah* do not participate in any kind of the harvest. This implies that harvest work and trading have become less and less compatible. Only 7 of 57 woman traders are ready to harvest for others while the rest are not. The participation rate in agricultural work in general and in agricultural wage labour in particular is almost zero in the case of those who are classified under the categories of entrepreneur, factory worker, shopkeeper, white collar worker and student.

As is the case in the development of the agricultural labour market of men, increasing work opportunities in non-agricultural sectors, the longer schooling periods for teenagers and the withdrawal of many villagers from agricultural work have eased pressure on the agricultural labour market of women. Planting is now considered to be a highly specialised task so that only two groups of women form two teams and monopolise most planting work. In the case of the harvest, the number of casual harvesters has decreased considerably and villagers born after the 1950s seldom participate in the harvest of others' *sawah*. This brings about a situation in which a rice trader in Kolojonggo complained to me that only five from Kolojonggo wanted to work with her, so that she had to recruit harvesters from hamlets located in the mountainous area of Sumber.

[21] A good example is the traders of *emping* and *jamu*. Three women traders of *emping* from Kolojonggo do their trade regularly with traders in Semarang. Three women traders of *jamu* have stools to sell their product in a local market outside Yogyakarta and they alternately stay either in Kolojonggo or in a town in Central Java. Other *jamu* traders circulate in a certain rural area, usually, in other *kecamatan* everyday.

Compared with the rise in daily wages of male agricultural labourers for the last two decades, that in harvest labour is less remarkable. The *bawon* which dropped to 1:13 in the 1970s has risen to 1:7, so that in 1993, a harvester could obtain 3.5-4 kg. of unhusked rice, or about Rp 1000 for four to five hours work. However, this amount was still about Rp 500 less than wages paid for other agricultural work. [22] Unlike the harvest, the return for a day's work of women planters, weeders and professional harvesters was almost similar to those for men. They could earn between Rp 1500 to Rp 2000 for a day's work. [23] This wage scale shows that the daily wage for women's agricultural work has risen at a similar pace with that of men's, although harvest labour is exceptional.

To summarise, there is no clear sign in Kolojonggo that work chances in the agricultural sector have declined since the introduction of the green revolution. Cropping intensification, expanding work opportunities in the non-agricultural sector, the longer periods of education for teenagers and the formation of a more rigid boundary between agricultural and non-agricultural work have helped to decrease pressure on the rural labour market. This lessening pressure is reflected in the daily wage that agricultural labourers earn. Except for harvest labour, the daily wage in the agricultural sector has risen, so that agricultural labourers in Kolojonggo obtained about 3 kg. of rice for a day's work in 1993, almost three times higher than in the early 1970s.

2.4. Differentiation of Peasants in terms of Landholdings

When asked to choose a period after independence when peasants could expand their landholdings, many villagers selected the 1970s, just after the introduction of the green revolution. The reason for this selection was unanimous: farming was more profitable at that time than it had previously been and is now. The record shows that the memory of villagers is generally to the point. It was in the 1970s that transactions of *sawah* and *pekarangan*, which had slowed down after independence became more active, although the amount being transacted was not as large as it had once been before independence. The cases of land

---

[22] The diversified ratio of *bawon* makes it possible for the harvesters who have close relation with the owner to be better paid than others. In their cases, the *bawon* reached up to 1:4, making their daily wage around 6 kg. of unhusked rice (Rp 1500). This amount was almost equal to the wage for other agricultural labour.

[23] In the case of planting, the wage was fixed not in terms of labour time but in terms of the size of *sawah*. In general it took around 3 hours for four women to plant 1000m² of *sawah* while Rp 5000-6000 was paid for this job. This made the return for an hour's planting about Rp 400 - Rp500 per person, the amount which was similar to an hourly return for male agricultural labour. In the case of weeding, no difference was shown in daily wage paid to men and women and all were paid between Rp 1500 - Rp 2000. The professional harvesters received their reward in proportion to the amount that they harvested, at the ratio of 1:12. However, as they were more skilful in using the *ani-ani* and were given more opportunities to work per day, usually about six hours, their daily return was higher than that of casual harvesters. In general, they could harvest up to 100 kg. of unhusked rice per day and earned up to 7.5 kg. of unhusked rice (Rp 1850).

transactions and the size of land liable to transactions between 1950 and 1993 are presented in Table II-8:

Table II.8: Cases of Land Transactions in Kolojonggo between 1950 and 1993a

Year	Cases		Total Size of Transactions	
	sawah	pekarangan	sawah	pekarangan
1950-59	8	2	1.0580	0.1620
1960-69	3	3	0.1975	0.0785
1970-79	10	18	0.9875	0.7670
1980-93[b]	20	22	2.3740	0.8750

Source: Records kept in the *kelurahan* office and interview data.
[a] The data in table II-8 include three kinds of transaction: the cases involving residents in Kolojonggo who sold land; residents in Kolojonggo who bought land; and people living outside Kolojonggo who received land from a resident of Kolojonggo and sold it.
[b] There was one case in 1980-93 where *sawah* and *pekarangan* were transacted together but included in the column 'sawah'.

Table II-8 shows a rapid increase in the frequency of land transactions after the 1970s. Eighteen cases of *pekarangan* transactions were reported in 1970-79 and the average size was 0.043 hectare. As many newly married couples could use their parents' land to build a house and the productive value of *pekarangan* has not changed much since 1970 [24] , it is not certain whether the increase in *pekarangan* transactions was due to growing demand or not. It can be assumed that *pekarangan* transactions might have been influenced by rapid increase of new households, so that *pekarangan* came to be viewed more as a limited resource rather than unlimited one. The increasing transactions of *sawah* may be ascribed to the higher profitability of rice cultivation after the introduction of the green revolution.

Of the villagers who were involved in land transactions in the 1970s, the activity of Pak Tio's household was the most notable. Pak Tio [25] was the *kadus* (hamlet head) of Kolojonggo from 1965 till 1978 and his two sons who lived together with him were heirs of about 2.5 hectares of *sawah*. Added to 1.2 hectares of his salary land, his household controlled 3.7 hectares of *sawah*, an amount which made his household one of the largest landholders in Sumber. From 1972 until 1978, his household was involved in eight land transactions and purchased 0.3855 hectare of *sawah* and 0.2260 hectare of *pekarangan* as table II-9 shows.

[24] Although a few villagers commented that the use of *pekarangan* was more intensive in former days than it is now, the pattern of using *pekarangan* does not seem to have undergone a major change during the last two or three decades. *Pekarangan* are planted mainly with perennials such as palm trees, bamboo and *mlinjo*, the products of which have been used for home consumption as in the case of coconuts and for sale as in the case of bamboo and fruits of *mlinjo*; secondary staple crops and vegetables are seldom planted. In this respect, the dominant usage of *pekarangan* has been to build a house.
[25] Names of villagers appearing in this chapter and in the following chapters are pseudonyms.

Table II.9: Land Purchased by Pak Tio's Household between 1972 and 1978

Year	*Sawah* (m^2)	*Pekarangan* (m^2)	Residence of Land Sellers
1972	0	1040	(migrant)
1973	715	0	In Sumber, outside Kolojonggo
1974	285	0	In Sumber, outside Kolojonggo
1974	0	260	Outside Sumber
1974	2085	0	Outside Sumber
1975	0	740	Outside Sumber
1976	770	0	Outside Sumber
1978	0	220	Outside Sumber
Total	3855	2260	

Source: As for Table II-8.

Table II-9 shows that Pak Tio's household purchased land almost every year from 1972 to 1978. The wealth to buy land came from 3.7 hectares of *sawah* under his control, which, although sharecropped, gave him profits enough to purchase land with ease. [26] The case of Pak Tio exemplifies one facet of changes that the green revolution brought to the structure of land tenure: increasing profit from agriculture was reinvested into the agricultural sector which promised markedly higher profitability than before. This caused the movement of large landholders to purchase *sawah*.

Increasing profit from *sawah*, however, did not apply only to large landholders but to all landholders, signifying that the green revolution did not bring any incentive for small and middle landholders to sell their land. Moreover, widening work opportunities in non-agricultural sectors helped potential land sellers to improve their economic capacity to retain their land. The composition of those who sold their land to Pak Tio shows this point. Of the eight land sellers, one was a household which sold *pekarangan* just before it moved outside Kolojonggo; five others were those who lived outside Sumber, had received a plot of land by inheritance and sold it; and the remaining two were those who lived in Sumber and sold their *sawah* to Pak Tio. The same pattern is also visible in the transactions of *sawah* in Kolojonggo in which Pak Tio's household was not involved in 1970-79. Of the six cases of *sawah* transactions (see table II-8), four *sawah* sellers were heirs of the deceased residents in Kolojonggo who lived outside Sumber. The remaining two *sawah* sellers were Pak Tio's son who sold part of his inherited land after the death of Pak Tio and a woman who sold inherited *sawah*. This indicates that no villagers in Kolojonggo who cultivated *sawah* by themselves sold it between 1970 and 1979.

---

[26] If it is assumed that 1 hectare of *sawah* produced 5 tons of unhusked rice and half of it went to the landowner, Pak Tio could secure more than 8 tons of unhusked rice every four or five month. Although the life style of his household was far more extravagant than others, these yields gave it enough profit to buy small size *sawah* or *pekarangan*, whose price reached around 15 kg. of unhusked rice per metre or 7.5 tons per 500m^2. Moreover, his wife also had an income as a primary school teacher.

The situation of land transactions in the 1970s shows two disparate impacts of the green revolution on the structure of land tenure: it gave incentive for large landholders to purchase more land while the improved economic position of small and middle landholders made them unwilling to put their land on sale. One result of the interplay of these two forces is reflected in the price of land. As table II-10 shows, land price, when converted into rice equivalent, rose sharply between 1963 and 1973. 1 m² of *sawah* and *pekarangan* which had been equivalent to less than 2 kg. of rice until the early 1960s was valued at more than 6 kg. of rice after the mid-1970s. A possible reason for the rise of land price is the unequal developments of supply and demand in the rural land market. Those who had the capability to buy land were ready to increase their holdings but improvement of economic situation of small and middle landholders decreased the supply of land to the market. This then pushed up the price of land.

Table II.10: Land Price in Sumber in 1951-93

Year	Sawah per m² (Rp)	Pekarangan per m² (Rp)	Average Rice Price per kg. (Rp)	Price of 1 m² of sawah in rice (kg.)	Price of 1 m² of pekarangan in rice (kg.)
1951-53	2.46 [6]	1.56 [4]	2.18	1.13	0.72
1954-56	4.49 [6]	3.78 [9]	2.55	1.76	1.48
1957-59	7.78 [26]	6.54 [23]	4.54	1.71	1.44
1960-62	23.46 [18]	23.12 [23]	17.93	1.31	1.29
1963-73			Not Available		
1974-76	905 [7]	1033 [14]	135	6.7	7.6
1977-79	1201 [22]	1099 [22]	173	6.9	6.4
1980-82	1690 [14]	1884 [14]	258	6.6	7.3
1983-84	2900 [15]	3483 [11]	303	9.6	11.5
1985-92			Not Available		
1992-93	6,000-8,000	7.000-10,000	600	10-13.3	11.7-16.7

Source: Records kept in the *kelurahan* office and interview data; Rice price is from official statistics of the Bureau of Statistics in Yogyakarta (KSY,various issues), except for that in 1992-93.
Note: Figure in bracket = number of transaction cases.

The discussion so far suggests that in the 1970s, large landholders made a move to accumulate more land while small and middle landholders were unwilling to sell their land. An impetus to this development was the higher profitability of rice cultivation generated by cropping intensification and increase in yields per hectare. In the period after the 1980s, however, these two trends have been reversed: small landholders are more and more willing to sell their *sawah* while large landholders are less and less willing to purchase it. To understand why this development has taken place is a difficult task since many variables have influenced the process. The following discussion examines only two of the factors lying behind this development.

Asked why he had not bought *sawah* since 1980, Pak Bari owning around 2 hectares of *sawah* gave a brief answer: 'for what ?'. Then, he continued his answer by giving a calculation as follows:

To buy 1000 m ^{2} of *sawah* : Rp 7,000,000

Return from 1000 m^2 of *sawah* per cropping:

1) in case of sharecropping: Rp 50,000

2) in case of self-cultivation: Rp 60,000 - 70,000

According to his calculation, it will take more than forty years for the profit from 1000 m^2 of *sawah* to offset the initial investment, if the rise of land price is not considered. His next comment shows what he had in mind when thinking about the problem of buying *sawah*: 'if I had 7 million Rupiah to buy 1000 m^2, it would be better to save it in the bank, which will give me 700,000 Rupiah per annum.' [27] The comment of Pak Bari summarises the present situation of agriculture: return from rice cultivation is not large enough to compensate for the initial capital outlaid. This discourages large landholders from investing profit from rice cultivation or from any other sources in buying more *sawah*.

Not all peasants adopt the same mode of evaluating rice cultivation as Pak Bari. Most small and middle landholders probably have never compared agricultural profit with interest rate. Whatever modes are employed, though, all villagers, irrespective of their size of landholdings and of whether they actually cultivate *sawah* or not, share the same view that agriculture is no longer a profitable business. The comment of a villager presented below is a good example of how these peasants think about their own work and the prospective of cultivating rice:

> I have cultivated half a hectare of *sawah*. If someone has this size of *sawah* in this area, he surely is considered as a large landowner. However, the fate of peasants has got more and more difficult. If my wife did not help me by working as a trader, I might not be able to educate my children up to high school level. .... Just look at Pak Sugeng (who happened to pass by while we were talking). He came from the city after acquiring food for pigs that he raises at home. ... The daily work of Pak Sugeng is to go to restaurants in the city to get left-over foods and to clean the places where pigs live. ... How much income does he obtain from it? He has four to five pigs at home. The price of pigs is about Rp 80,000 after 4 months and up to Rp 200,000 after 7 months. This means that he can secure at least Rp 80,000 per month, if he raises four pigs. He also gets extra income when a pig giv es birth to babies. ... My income? Last time, I sold all my paddy to the *penebas* at the price of Rp 450,000. If I harvested it by myself, it probably reached half million.

---

[27] The next question of mine was why he did not sell his land and save the money in the bank which would give him more than a million Rupiah every month. He talked about the duty of children to pass their parents' inheritance to their children and his stable income both from his work as a civil servant and from his *sawah*.

However, subtracting the cost of farming, the money that I could get was only Rp 300,000. A half hectare of *sawah* is the same as four pigs! The fate of peasants in Indonesia is really bad these days.

One possible answer to the question of why rice cultivation which was thought to be profitable at the initial stage of the green revolution is now thought not to be may lie in change in input for rice cultivation. If the ratio of production costs to output has increased, this would explain the drop in the profit margin of rice cultivation. During the last two decades, several changes in the practice of rice cultivation have caused increase in input, especially, monetary input: most farmers buy seeds from local markets, hire animals or tractors for ploughing and apply more fertilisers, while the agricultural wage has risen. The same period, however, has also seen the emergence of a new agricultural practice which promises substantial decrease in input: the frequency of ploughing decreased from two to one. [28] Traditionally the cost of ploughing occupied the largest share in the total input for rice cultivation if the peasants did not use their own labour. Franke reports that the cost of ploughing twice was one third of the total input in a Central Javanese village in 1969-70 (1973), the ratio which was also applied to a village in Kulon Progo district (Roosmalawati,1973). As a result, the change in the frequency of ploughing reduces the total input, probably, by about fifteen percent. On the other hand, the price of chemical fertilisers, compared with rice price, has become much cheaper[29] and yields per hectare have continuously grown with the release of new rice varieties and with more fertiliser application. No official figures are available for the ratio of input to output in the 1970s but a few researches suggest that it was more than 30 percent. [30] In 1990, the official statistics for Yogyakarta show the cost of production was 27.42 percent of the total output (KSY,1990) while it was about 33 percent in Kolojonggo in 1993 (see table II-4). [31] The comparison of the early 1970s with the 1990s then suggests that the ratio of input to output has not changed a lot in this period. Several factors causing an increase in input are likely to have been offset by others causing a decline.

[28] In 1993-94, no villagers in Kolojonggo ploughed twice, although all of them agreed that this had been standard in the 1970s and was directly connected to increase in yields.

[29] In Indonesia, the price of fertiliser has been evaluated in terms of *rumus tani* (formula of the farmer), namely, that the price of 1 kg. of milled rice would always be kept equal to that of 1 kg. of urea (Utrecht,1973:159) In terms of this formula, trends in the price of urea and rice have been favourable for peasants from the mid-1970s on. The ratio of 1 kg. of paddy price to 1 kg. of urea, which was less than 1 in the early 1970s, became more than 1 in the mid-1970s and more than 1.5 in the 1980s (Pearson, et al.,1991:11). In 1993, 1 kg. of rice was equivalent to slightly less than 2 kg. of urea in the local market.

[30] Roosmalawati (1973) and White (1977:461-62) report that the ratio of input to output was respectively 33 percent (in the case of 1 hectare) and 24 to 43 percent in the early 1970s in Kulon Progo while Franke (1973) gives us far higher percentage, namely, 51 to 54 percent in cultivating 1 hectare of *sawah*.

[31] This does not include land tax, labour cost for weeding and other miscellaneous works such as making seedbed, water management and fertilising. Although these are included, the total input in Kolojonggo does not exceed 40 percent of the total output.

Another possible reason for villagers' current pessimistic view of rice cultivation is the uneven rise of the rice price and of prices of other consumer goods. If price rises of other consumer goods have exceeded that of rice, the relative profitability of rice cultivation may have declined. For this, the data concerning rice producers' terms of trade in Yogyakarta are presented in Table II-11:

Table II.11: Rice Producers' Terms of Trade (TT) in Yogyakarta (1976 = 100)

Year	TT	Year	TT	Year	TT
1977	99	1982	87	1987	93
1978	92	1983	82	1988	101
1979	97	1984	81	1989	96
1980	94	1985	79	1990	96
1981	88	1986	87	1991	96

Source: *Indicator Ekonomi* (BPS, 1976-1992)

Table II-11 does not show much of a decline in rice producers' terms of trade for the last fifteen years. A slight downturn was visible in the mid-1980s, but this markedly improved in the late 1980s, so that, when the index of the rice producers' terms of trade in 1976 was fixed at 100, that in 1991 was 96. The statistical trend in rice producers' terms of trade may not directly reflect villagers' own calculation based on their experiences. [32] Nevertheless, it may be regarded as an indication of no rapid decline in the profitability of rice cultivation during the last two decades, at least in statistical terms.

Examinations of the change in the ratio of input to output and the rice producers' terms of trade urge us to see factors lying beyond rice production to understand why rice cultivation is now considered unprofitable. One of these may be the rise of wages in non-agricultural sectors, especially that in the construction sector where every male villager can be easily employed. The daily wage for construction labour varies according to each labourer' skill. In 1993, novices received Rp 2,500, the masons who had worked for two to three years between Rp 3,000 and Rp 4,000, and the skilled carpenters Rp 5,000. As construction

---

[32] Most peasants in Kolojonggo commented that the rice price has not risen as quickly as that of other consumer goods. A factor influencing villagers' evaluation of their terms of trade is changes in the pattern of consumption. Over the last two decades, many consumer goods have undergone a status change from the luxurious to the necessary; motorbike, television, electricity and education are good examples. In 1993, of 132 households in Kolojonggo, 43 had one or two motorbikes, 55 owned black and white or colour television, 107 were connected to electricity and many households had secondary school students. As a result, the share of rice in a household's budget was, in the cases of twenty-five sample households, much lower than the findings of Penny and Singarimbun in the early 1970s that rice accounted for about half of the consumption of a household which belonged to *cukupan* (the having or the possessing of enough) (Penny and Singarimbun,1973:3 &47; see also Sukamto (1962), cited in Penny and Singarimbun,1973:46). In 1993, the cost of educating two secondary school students exceeded that for rice consumption while the expense of using a motorbike and a television was similar to, or, in some cases, more than that for rice consumption. Increased spending on non-food items was also recognised by villagers. However, when they made comments on the share of profits from rice cultivation in their households' budget, diversified spending on non-food items was not included in their consideration. Rather, they emphasised the fact that profits from rice cultivation could cover a much larger part of the budget of a household in the 1970s than now.

work continued for six days a week, one's weekly income could reach between Rp 15,000 and Rp 30,000 and one's monthly income, between Rp 60,000 and Rp 120,000. [33] If 1000 m² of *sawah* can give its holders about Rp 25,000 of profit per month [34], the daily wage of a mason is equivalent roughly to that of peasants cultivating 0.4 hectare of their own *sawah*. When a comparison is made of peasants and white collar workers, the position of peasants is less favourable. For example, in 1993, high-school graduates who began to work as civil servants could earn around Rp 120,000, an income equivalent to that from 0.5 hectare of *sawah*, while the monthly income of a teacher having a university degree was more than Rp 150,000, equivalent to an income from 0.6 hectare of *sawah*. The relatively higher income paid to civil servants made it possible for the *lurah* inSumber who received 3.5 hectares of *sawah* as his salary to insist that his income was no more than that of a teacher. Although somewhat exaggerated,[35] his remarks show how the *kelurahan* officials who receive their salary in the form of *sawah* and who thus belong to the largest landholders in Sumber evaluate their own income in comparison with that of other white collar workers. To them, wage in the form of *sawah* is no longer as advantageous as it once was in the 1970s or before that time. [36] In this respect, villagers' negative evaluation of

[33] In terms of security, many villages commented that construction labour is not less precarious than agriculture. In the case of construction work, the risk comes when a certain project finishes and villagers do not find another work place. However, compared with the danger of crop failure, unemployment for a short period in construction work is not considered to be a serious disadvantage by villagers.

[34] It is not easy to calculate income from 1000 m² of *sawah*. If we use the data presented in table II-4, one can get about 200 kg. of rice from 1000 m² of *sawah* every four month, which makes one's monthly income 50 kg. of rice or Rp 30,000 (1 kg. of rice = Rp 600). This amount is much higher than the income that villagers get from the *penebas* by selling their paddy before the harvest. In 1993, the *penebas* generally paid Rp 100,000-120,000 for 1000m² of *sawah*. If the production cost (excluding harvest cost) which is about 20 percent of the total output is excluded, peasants will get Rp 80,000-Rp 96,000 or Rp 20,000-Rp 24,000 per month. For the convenience of discussion, Rp 25,000 is used as a standard monthly income from 1000 m² in the text.

[35] The *lurah* in Sumber considered his monetary income from salary land as Rp 350,000 per month, or Rp 10,000 per 1000 m². This calculation seems to underestimate his actual income, compared with the estimation made in footnote no. 35. When 1000 m² of *sawah* was sold at between Rp 100,000 and Rp 120,000 to the *penebas*, the *lurah* who rented his *sawah* on a sharecrop basis could secure half of it or Rp 12,500 to Rp 15,000 per month, an amount which is much higher than his own estimation. However, the *lurah* had several reasons for depreciating his income. First, the yields from *sawah* were much poorer when it was sharecropped than when he cultivated it. Second, the *penebas* usually paid less to the sharecroppers of the *lurah* than to other small and middle holders. This was because the size of *sawah* that the *lurah* rented on a sharecrop basis was 0.4 to 0.5 hectare, and, in bargaining this size of *sawah*, the *penebas* faced greater danger of overestimating the yields than he or she did for much smaller sized *sawah*. This higher degree of danger then prompted the *penebas* to bargain for the larger sized *sawah* at a cheaper price. For example, when 1000m² is priced at Rp 100,000, a much larger block of *sawah*, say, 5000m² is priced less than Rp 500,000. In this respect, the *lurah*'s estimation of his income may not be too different from what he actually earned, although somewhat exaggerated. If it is assumed that the *lurah* could earn Rp 350,000 per month from his salary land, his appraisal that his income was similar to that of a teacher was generally right. The teachers who had worked for twenty years could get more than Rp 300,000 in 1993.

[36] According to the *lurah*, his income from *sawah* in the 1970s was far higher than that of teachers who started their career at the same time with him, while his income was about twice as much as that of teachers about ten years ago.

agriculture seems to be based on their relativistic point of view in comparing income from *sawah* with that from other non-agricultural work rather than on absolute decrease in profitability of rice cultivation.

Other local factors contributing to villagers' pessimistic view of agriculture are the periodical failures of rice harvest and of their efforts to diversify crops. Crop failure has been caused by pest attacks from such pests as the *wereng* (brown planthopper) and *ulat* (caterpillar) or by attacks from rats and birds. Crop failure is not a new phenomenon in Kolojonggo but, according to village elders, the frequency of rice diseases has been much higher and the damage they inflict on paddy has been more severe since the introduction of new rice varieties. These repetitive pest attacks decrease profit in rice cultivation and, more importantly, discourage peasants from investing further efforts, time and money in rice production. The adaptive strategy thus developed by most peasants in Kolojonggo is 'to let the paddy grow by itself'. What they do is to transplant and plant seeds, and to wait until these are ripe enough to be harvested rather than to maximise material and non-material inputs, which also will maximise their loss in case of severe crop failure. The result of this strategy is the stagnation of yields. The yields per hectare have not improved since the early-1980s, fluctuating between 50 to 60 quintals per hectare in *kecamatan* Gamol. [37] As many peasants still remember the rapid rise in yields in the 1970s and in the early 1980s, this plateau in yields per hectare in the 1980s has contributed to their present pessimism.

On the other hand, the reluctance of the peasants to plant crops other than rice has decreased the profitability of farming. However, this attitude also has its rationale. In the 1980s, several attempts were made, under the guidance of agricultural officials from the Department of Agriculture, to plant secondary staples or vegetables. Unfortunately for the peasants in Kolojonggo, all these trials failed and those who participated in such programs had to bear the cost of failure, since the government which was ready to support the implementation of the program did not want to compensate for loss. The repetition of trials and failures then made rice cultivation appear to be the best option for the peasants. Even when the yields are not good due to bad weather or pest attacks, they can secure at least a small amount of rice for home consumption and, as their input into rice cultivation is minimal, the loss can also be minimal.

To summarise, villagers' pessimistic view of rice cultivation is likely to have been based more on a comparative evaluation of income from rice cultivation

---

[37] Below is the average yields per hectare (*gabah kering*) in *kecamatan* Gamol:

Year	1980	1981	1982	1983	1984	1985	1986	1987	1988	1989
Yields (qt./ha)	54.13	59.80	50.0	50.4	59.70	52.25	51.92	57.88	53.39	59.13

Source: *kecamatan* office

and from non-agricultural work than on the absolute decrease in profitability of rice cultivation. Whatever the actual basis of this perspective, the pessimistic perception of rice cultivation, coupled with rising land prices, has provided a condition in which investment of capital in the agricultural sector is not thought of as the best option in disposing one's wealth, especially by those who cultivate *sawah* not for consumption but for profit.

The developments in land transactions and the differentiation process in Kolojonggo where rice cultivation is no longer viewed as profitable will be discussed further. As a first step in this discussion, the landholdings of those who sold and purchased *sawah* after 1980 are presented in table II-12:

Table II.12: Cases of *Sawah* Transactions after 1980

		Sawah sellers' size of landholding before they sold *sawah* (ha)				Outsiders[a]
		< 0.2	< 0.5	< 1	> 1	(unknown)
	0					4
Sawah buyers'	< 0.2	1	1			4
size of	< 0.5	1				
landholding	< 1	1				3
before they	> 1				1	
bought *sawah*	Outsider[b]				1	
(ha)	*Kelurahan* Office	1	1		1	
	Total Case	4	2	2[c]	1	11
	Total Size (ha)	0.28	0.26	0.87	0.15	0.80

Source: As for Table II-8.
[a] People who lived outside Kolojonggo, received *sawah* from a resident of Kolojonggo by inheritance and sold it.
[b] A city dweller who bought *sawah* from a villager in Kolojonggo. Her size of landholding before she bought *sawah* is unknown.
[c] These two cases were carried out by a villager who sold his *sawah* to two persons.

Although the frequency and size of *sawah* transactions have doubled since 1980 (see table II-8), there is no indication in table II-12 that a rapid differentiation process has occurred in this period. Only one or two cases of *sawah* transaction have taken place each year and the average size of *sawah* involved in each case was 0.12 hectare. Moreover, purchasing of *sawah* by large landholders owning more than 0.5 hectare has not outclassed those by landless or small landholders. Villagers owning more than 0.5 hectare were involved only in five *sawah* transactions as buyers and the average size of *sawah* that they bought was 0.09 hectare. The fact that the largest size of *sawah* put on sale could not be sold in Sumber also points to the inactivity of large landholders to purchase *sawah*. When one villager in Kolojonggo put 0.87 hectare of *sawah* on sale, only 0.08 hectare was sold to a man in Kolojonggo while the other 0.79 hectare went to an outside resident of Sumber. Villagers owning less than 0.5 hectare were involved in 11 cases of transactions and the average size of their transaction was 0.06 hectare.

The second notable feature in table II-12 is that 11 out of 19 *sawah* sellers were those who lived outside Kolojonggo but received *sawah* by inheritance. All transactions were undertaken just after the death of parents. This trend seems due to the rising *sawah* price. Although the average size of *sawah* sold was just 0.07 hectare, return could be millions of Rupiah, or to borrow a popular comparison that villagers made, it was large enough to buy a new motorbike.

One interesting point to note is that five out of the eight *sawah* sellers living in Kolojonggo changed their status from landholders to the landless after having sold *sawah*. This could be interpreted as an indicator that the process of polarisation was resumed in the 1980s, since only one such case was reported from the 1950s till the end of the 1970s. However, what should be considered in interpreting these cases is that economic conditions and the value put on holding *sawah* since the 1980s have become different from what they were in previous decades. While agriculture was the only sector which provided stable sources of livelihood and *sawah* was the key to securing one's access to agricultural resources in former days, it has become, especially since the 1980s, just one of many sources of livelihood. Moreover, income from rice cultivation has been considered less profitable than that from non-agricultural work and, subsequently, the value of *sawah* is now being viewed more in terms of its exchange value than its productive value. In these circumstances, more villagers think of selling *sawah* as a viable option if the capital acquired from selling can be invested for higher income. Of the five households that were ready to accept their position as the landless, two sold their *sawah* to open a *warung*, one to build a house for his married son, one to cover his bankruptcy and the last one, consisting of a mother and a daughter, to maintain their livelihood. In this sense, only one of the five households belonged to the 'classical' example of peasant differentiation, namely, economic hardship forcing small landholders to sell their land for survival.

In brief, the period after 1980 has seen an increase in *sawah* transactions and in the number of landless households. The main forces underlying this trend are the rise in land prices, changing perceptions of rice cultivation and profitability, and widening economic opportunities in non-agricultural sectors. However, the increase in the landless has not taken place concurrently with the concentration of land among large landholders, as table II-13 shows:

Table II.13: Land Ownership and *Sawah* Cultivation in Kolojonggo in 1971 and 1993

Size	Ownership				*Sawah* Cultivating
(ha)	Households		Land (%)		Households[a]
	1971	1993	1971	1993	1993
0	39	66	0	0	59
< 0.1	14	18	5.1	7.9	19
< 0.2	17	25	13.7	23.6	22
< 0.3	14	8	19.0	13.0	15
< 0.4	7	8	13.5	18.6	8
< 0.5	2	1	5.0	3.0	1
< 0.6	3	1	9.3	3.6	2
< 0.7	2	1	6.9	4.5	4
< 0.8	0	2	0	9.1	1
< 0.9	0	0	0	0	0
< 1	0	0	0	0	0
> 1	2	2	27.4	16.6	1
Total	100	132	100	100	132

Source: As for Table II-8.
[a] The size of *sawah* each household actually cultivates, irrespective of the ownership-status of *sawah*.

Table II-13 shows that the polarised ownership of *sawah* in 1971 has not changed much by 1993. Sixty-six households do not own *sawah* while two households own more than 1 hectare. Compared with the situation in 1971, the number of landless households has increased by 27 in 1993. As regards the number of households owning less than 0.3 hectare of *sawah*, a slight increase is apparent, from 45 to 51 households. Two major factors accounting for change in the composition of landless and small landholders are the increase of households and inheritance. Land transactions also play a role in this process, so that five households classified as landholders in 1971 are classified as landless in 1993. The number of households owning more than 0.5 hectare of *sawah* has decreased from seven to six. Of the seven households classified in this group in 1971, two are still recorded in 1993 statistics, four inherited *sawah*, and one who held 0.61 hectare of pension land *(pengarem-arem)* passed away. In three cases of inheritance, each heir received around 0.2 hectare of *sawah*, while in one case, the division was large and three heirs received about 1.2 , 0.9 and 0.7 hectare of *sawah* respectively. Two of the heirs are classified as large holders in 1993, while one sold all his land. The two others who are newly included in this group in 1993 consist of the *kadus* who received 1.2 hectares of *sawah* as salary land and one household which added about 0.2 hectare of *sawah* by purchase to its previous holding of 0.43 hectare.

Not all landless households listed in table II-13 lack access to *sawah*, while not all landholders cultivate *sawah* by themselves. Of the 66 landless households, 27 cultivate *sawah* either by sharecropping or by renting it from others while five households give out all their holdings on a sharecrop basis. With this temporary transfer of usufruct over *sawah*, the number of households that cultivate *sawah* becomes 73 (see the column '*Sawah* Cultivating Households' in table II-13). Given that 39 villagers cultivate *sawah* as their primary occupation,[38] 34 villagers do so as their secondary occupation. This implies that expanding work opportunities in non-agricultural sectors have not prompted villagers to move out of the agricultural sector. Many of those who work in non-agricultural sectors cultivate *sawah* of their own, and, in a few cases, sharecrop others' *sawah* as their secondary occupation.

2.5. Summary

This chapter has looked at socio-economic developments in Kolojonggo since the introduction of the green revolution. Worth reiterating are the following points. First, as much research on Javanese villages shows, Kolojonggo has also extremely polarised ownership of land. Almost half of the villagers own no *sawah* while a few villagers possess more than 30 percent of the total *sawah* in Kolojonggo. Unlike what has been reported in other parts of Java (Billah et al.,1984:261-62; Amaluddin,1978:112; Kano,1990:49), however, the historical development of land tenure in Kolojonggo suggests there has been no acceleration in the process of polarisation since independence. On the contrary, the situation of polarisation has been alleviated during this period. As table II-14 shows, the share of landholders of less than 0.3 hectare increased from 10.1 percent in 1943 to 44.5 percent in 1993 whereas that of landholders of more than 0.5 hectare dropped from 61.7 percent in 1943 to 33.8 percent in 1993.

Table II.14: *Sawah* Owned by Three Groups of Landholders in 1943-93 (%)

Size	Year			
(ha)	1943	1960	1971	1993
< 0.3	10.1	34.9	37.8	44.5
< 0.5	28.1	16.4	18.5	21.6
> 0.5	61.7	48.7	43.6	33.8

Source: 1943 and 1960: Records kept in the *kelurahan* office and interview data (For more about the structure of land tenure in 1943 and 1960, see Appendix A); 1971 and 1993: Table II-13.

Various factors have interacted to bring about this development in the ownership of *sawah*. Seen from the perspective of small landholders, decreasing pressures from outside after independence such as abolition of heavy land tax, higher yields per hectare, and widening work opportunities in non-agricultural sectors have been, among others, important in enabling them to retain their small plots of *sawah*. Seen from large landholders' perspective, inheritance which fragments their landholdings among several heirs, higher education which diverts their interests to non-agricultural sectors, and, especially after the 1980s, the rise of land prices and pessimistic view of profitability in rice cultivation hampered

---

[38] The villagers included in this category are those classified as 'owner cultivation', 'owner cultivation & tenant', 'tenant', 'tenant and labourer' and 'owner cultivation and labourer' in table II-6.

the will to accumulate more *sawah*. Agricultural development in the last decades has also left a deep imprint on the way *sawah* is evaluated by villagers. If *sawah* had been viewed as a burden and then was transformed into the most precious source of livelihood, it is now considered by many as a commodity. *Sawah* has been a commodity since the 1920s, but until quite recently, it was a commodity whose exchange value was overwhelmed by its productive value: it could be exchanged but this remained as a possibility to most villagers. To them, *sawah* was a part of themselves before it was a commodity. This view of *sawah* has gradually changed. Some villagers now consider it primarily in terms of its exchange value, comparing its value according to the current interest rate and buying it in order to sell it for profit. This trend has not yet become extreme, so that many villagers, especially, those belonging to middle and old age, still think of *sawah* as something that should not be put up for sale. However, as more villagers start their career in non-agricultural sectors and land prices continue to rise, it is likely that the proverb repeated by village elders that 'those who start their business by selling inherited land (*warisan*) will never be successful', will no longer be taken seriously by the new generation.

Second, two decades after the introduction of the green revolution, the absolute poverty which dominated the life of many villagers has gradually disappeared to such an extent that no villagers now experience rice shortage for home consumption. Today, the primary economic concern of many villagers is to have more consumer goods such as colour televisions, motorbikes, cassette players, semi-transparent windows, tiled floors and so on. The improvement of villagers' economic conditions is also reflected in the longer schooling period of the youth. These days, it is exceptional to encounter a youth who does not proceed from junior high school to senior high school. Tertiary education is not yet available to most youth but almost every year in the 1990s, one or two high school graduates have continued to their study at university. Widening work opportunities in non-agricultural sectors have had a primary role in improving general economic conditions, making it possible for many villagers owning no *sawah* or holding just a small plot to get access to an income which is higher than that from agricultural work. The disappearance of absolute poverty, however, does not imply that the economic gap between the wealthy and the poor has narrowed. This gap is still wide, probably more so than before. The better way to describe the economic gap between the rich and the poor since the 1970s is, as Edmundson puts it, 'the rich are getting richer while the poor are getting richer' (1994:134).

Third, diversification of occupational structure, widening work opportunities in the city and the decreasing importance of agriculture in villagers' economic life have helped to erode the basis on which such traditional village leaders as village officials, hamlet heads and large landholders, exert their power. No patron-client relation is formed between large landholders, on the one hand,

and sharecroppers or agricultural labourers, on the other. The autonomy of the sharecroppers in managing the *sawah* under sharecropping agreement has been enhanced, their unpaid labour for the *sawah* owners has disappeared, and the labour shortage in agricultural sector allows agricultural labourers to have a stronger bargaining position vis-à-vis large landholders. The same situation also applies to village officials and hamlet heads, so that their authority to intervene in villagers' public and private life has been on the decline. This has been the case especially after a series of agricultural development programs, which directly encroached on villagers' right to manage their own *sawah*[39] , failed in the 1980s. The village officials who could not obtain compensation for the loss lost face and, accordingly, they had to give up one of the sources of their authority since the early 1970s, namely, their role in the development programs. After these failures, the direct interactions between officials and villagers have remained minimal and the role of the officials has become much closer to simple administrators who issue papers or collect taxes, although they still enjoy higher status than ordinary villagers. Those who have emerged to compete with the village officials for higher status are highly educated villagers having white collar jobs. However, no one has not yet become an authoritative figure in Kolojonggo. Nor is it likely that any one will be such a figure as long as the present economic and political situation continues. In this respect, the village life in Kolojonggo is characterised by a lack of a strong figure who has an authoritative power to involve himself or herself in public life.

Fourth, the last two decades have seen villagers' more intensive contact with the outside world. Rapid increase in villagers' daily mobility, the introduction of mass media and a longer period of schooling have facilitated the constant contact of villagers with people living outside village and have accelerated the flow of information. These changes have made it possible that in terms of villagers' perception and of their everyday interaction, the importance of the hamlet has decreased, while that of much broader boundaries such as Yogyakarta and Indonesia has increased. On the other hand, as more villagers have tried to follow up development in the outside world, changes in the city or at the national level have been introduced into village more rapidly by them.

---

[39] These included such programs as semi-compulsory cultivation of sugarcane, collectivisation of agricultural working processes by organising tens of farmers into a group (*kelompok tani*) and cultivation of secondary staples and vegetables. In the case of sugarcane, the profit that the land owners could secure after the harvest of sugarcane was far less than the amount they could obtain from rice cultivation. This resulted in conflicts between village officials who wanted to continue the program and the land owners who wanted to cultivate rice, although village officials had been successful in securing land for sugarcane cultivation in several parts of Sumber until the mid-1994. The programs of collectivising rice cultivation and of planting secondary staples and vegetables failed due to pest attacks. As a result, the *kelompok tani* in Kolojonggo and its neighbouring hamlets did not operate at all in 1993-94, although the group itself was not disorganised.

Plate 1: A bird's-eye View of kelurahan Sumber. The areas surrounded by trees are residential areas.

Plate 2: Female Harvesters with the *ani-ani*.

Chapter 3: From Bamboo *Langgar* to Brick *Masjid*: Islamic Development in Kolojonggo

Since the 1970s, studies of Islam in Indonesia have portrayed a dualistic process of Islamic development: its waning influence over political life and its waxing influence over non-political life. Passive reaction to and submissive acceptance of a series of government measures which can be interpreted as attempts to decrease the political power of Islamic groups[1] have been interpreted by outside observers as examples of the political retreat of Islam. On the other hand, several developments in non-political domains have shown the increasing commitment of Indonesians to Islam: participation in daily prayers, Friday prayers (*Jumatan*) and the fast in the fasting month has increased and more Indonesians have made the pilgrimage to Mecca (Johns,1987:224); publications and public discussion about Islam have flourished (Tamara,1986:5-8); and Islamic activities such as the public celebration of Muslim holidays, the payment of *zakat* alms and the Quranic recital have been carried out in what would have been an unthinkable fashion years earlier in rural Java (Hefner,1987a:545-6). This state is called Islamic revivalism (Horikoshi,1976:15), revitalisation (Hefner,1987a:550), renaissance (Tamara,1986), or reIslamisation (Nakamura,1993:181).

The widening influence of Islam in non-political fields can be interpreted as an adaptive reaction to political pressure from the government (McVey,1983:218). Facing the situation in which their political activities have been limited one by one by the government, Islamic organisations have changed their orientation from the political to the non-political domain. The emphasis put on the term *dakwah* or Islamic missionary activities by these organisations and Muslim intellectuals after the 1970s (Boland,1982:191-193; McVey,1983:218) reflects this shifting focus. An Islamic organisation, Muhammadiyah, in a manual, 'Outline of the struggle of Muhammadiyah' (*Khittah Perjuangan Muhammadiyah*), clarifies its orientation as follows:

> Muhammadiyah will not carry out its struggle in the field of practical politics (*politik praktis*). Muhammadiyah is not and will not be a political party. Basically, Muhammadiyah will not enter political organisations.

---

[1] For a series of government policies against Islamic political groups after 1965 and the reactions by these groups, see Johns (1987:217-220), McVey (1983), Noer (1983:195-198), and Wertheim (1980). These measures included the government's monopoly of the *Hajj*, the government's favourable treatment of *kepercayaan* or *kebatinan* groups, the Marriage Bill, nomination of a higher percentage of Christian ministers in the cabinet, imprisonment of Islamic leaders, and enforcement of the national ideology, *Pancasila*, as the basic ideology of all Islamic organisations.

[2] ... [This decision is] due to consciousness that the struggle in the field of [civil] society (*dalam bidang masyarakat*) is an extremely important and honourable work, no less important than that in the political field (Muhammadiyah,1968:202).[3]

The goal of *dakwah* is thought to be attained by promoting educational activities and intensifying religious education in all levels of school, organising small groups like neighbourhood groups as units of *dakwah* (*gerakan Jamaah*), intensifying the celebration of *pengajian* (religious learning courses) in villages, training young Muslims as cadres of *dakwah*, maximising the use of film, television and radio as media of *dakwah*, and promoting social activities such as founding hospitals and orphanages (Muhammadiyah,1978:316-332). Although Muhammadiyah is one of the two largest Islamic organisations in Indonesia, its re-orientation to non-political domains represents a new direction for the Islamic movement. Now, the primary goal of the *umat* Islam (Muslim community) is viewed not from the paradigm before 1965, that is, to establish an Islamic state, but to Islamise Indonesians, in other words, to invite non-Muslims to Islam and to guide Muslims to make their religiosity perfect (Muhammadiyah,1967:186).

In parallel with this national development, Islamic development in Kolojonggo and in *kelurahan* Sumber also gives an impression that the revitalisation, revivalism or renaissance of Islam in non-political domains has taken place during the last three decades. Islamic leaders in Sumber felt easier describing this change in numeric terms, comparing the present with the early 1970s: the number of *masjid* has increased from 3 to 23, so that 18 hamlets out of the total 19 hamlets in Sumber have at least one *masjid* of their own; participants from all over the *kecamatan* then hardly filled half of a playing ground for the collective prayer after the fasting month (*Salat Idul Fitri*) whereas two playing grounds of the same size are now too small to accommodate participants solely from Sumber; previously the amount of *zakat* from all hamlets in Sumber reached around 100 kg. of rice, whereas now, a hamlet can collect 300-500 kg.; previously a *kelurahan* could not sacrifice a sheep for *Idul Adha* whereas now, a hamlet can sacrifice an ox; and previously almost nothing was donated by villagers for religious purposes, whereas almost two million Rupiah can now be collected on the occasion of *Salat Idul Fitri*.

---

[2] Before 1960 when the Islamic party, Masyumi, was banned, and from 1960 till 1965, Muhammadiyah did not give up its aspiration to seize power in national politics. This aspiration was based on the conviction that one of the primary goals of Muhammadiyah, namely, to promote Islamic law in Indonesia, could not be achieved without seizing political power. At that time, the political struggle was considered as one of the two ways in which activities of Muhammadiyah should be directed and was called an indirect missionary activity (Muhammadiyah,1954:17-24).
[3] The decision of Muhammadiyah not to be involved in the field of practical politics has been reaffirmed in Muhammadiyah Congress (*Muktamar*) held in 1971, 1978, 1985 and 1990. For more about this, see Muhammadiyah 1971:236; 1978:328; 1985:406; 1991:19.

The figures from Kolojonggo are consistent with this pattern. A *masjid* was built in 1988, *zakat* and other alms collection have increased, an ox was sacrificed in 1994, *pengajian* is held at least once every two weeks and there has been a steady growth in the number of participants in the fast. According to the Islamic leaders in their forties or older, all of these changes would have been unimaginable in their youth.

The purpose of this chapter is to examine the process of Islamic development in Kolojonggo. Among various possible ways to look at this process, the focus will be put on how the core group of Islamic activists has been crystallised, in that traditionally Kolojonggo and Sumber did not have an organised group of their own to promote religious life among Muslim villagers. This situation was different from many other Javanese villages where the religious institution of *pesantren* with its leader, a *kiyai*, has played a crucial role in determining the course of religious development. [4] Due to the lack of traditionally established *pesantren* and *kiyai*, Islamic development was not possible in Kolojonggo until the formation of a social force to transform individualised efforts to promote Islamic activities into collective action.

3.1. Development of Islam under the Dutch Colonialism

> At that time [before independence], people were not so brave about reciting *sahadat* [5]. When they recited it, they thought they had to sacrifice something, that is, a throat of a chicken, for *sahadat* was regarded as a magical spell (*rapal*).

> Why do Muslims face the west when they pray ? This is because Syeh Abu Bakar lived to the west of Java and, in order to commemorate him, people started to pray facing the west.

These two quotations are from two village elders in Kolojonggo. Although short, these give us a clue to understand the situation of Islam in the colonial period. First of all, these show the degree of Islamic knowledge that was available to the villagers of that time. The recital of the *sahadat*, which is the most central doctrine of Islam and should be carried out several times a day, was equated with a spell having magical power. This equation is understandable, if seen in the context of the popular belief system of that time. [6] In this system, Arabic

---

[4] For more about *kiyai* and their relation to Islamic development, see Horikoshi (1976) and Mansurnoor (1990).

[5] *Sahadat* refers to two Arabic prayers of 'there is no God but Allah, and Muhammad is His Messenger'. The recital of these two phrases is thought to be a requirement for being a Muslim.

[6] In the popular belief system of the previous time, natural and human affairs were thought to be closely connected to the supernatural world in which not only Islamic supernatural beings but non-Islamic ones originating from Hindu-Buddhist and local traditions existed side by side without conflict. C. Geertz labels this as the *abangan* version of Islam characterised by syncretism. As Geertz says, in this system, Hindu goddesses rub elbows with Islamic prophets and both of these with local *dhanyang*

occupied a special position, so that the utterance of an Arabic phrase was believed to bring extraordinary power, when accompanied by other proper conditions. As the *sahadat* is in Arabic and many villagers did not know its exact position in Islam, they thought of it as a magical spell.

Misunderstanding of this sort was not only confined to the recital of the *sahadat* but was widespread in every field of Islamic teaching, so that many villagers did not have a clear concept of what is commanded, recommended or prohibited in Islam. Nor did they have any interest in knowing whether a certain concept or practice was based on Islamic teaching, especially on the Quran and Hadith. They interpreted and accepted Islamic ideas and practices as those had been passed on to them from the previous generation.

The era of ignorance (*jaman bodho*) under Dutch colonialism, as it is often designated by village elders, did not mean that no one was exposed to Islamic teachings. There was a man called *kaum* who had higher religious knowledge than ordinary villagers. The *kaum* should have been capable of reading Arabic script and memorising some Arabic prayers to guide rites of passage and a ritual called *kendhuri* (collective meal). In many cases, the *kaum* in each hamlet had a *langgar* (small prayer house) where skill in reading Arabic was taught to village children and a few religious occasions were collectively celebrated. In spite of this ability, the *kaum* was not someone who would be a cornerstone for later Islamic development. First of all, he was oriented more to and involved more in 'tradition' rather than 'Islam', both of which he supported. As a villager put it, his role was much closer to burning incense and making offerings than to sponsoring Islamic activities such as the fast, daily prayer, *Jumatan* and so on. Moreover, he could not understand Arabic nor was accustomed to the written tradition of Islam, which made it difficult for him to be severed from the way Islam had been interpreted and transmitted. Therefore, the germ which would bring later Islamic development was located in a different group of villagers, that is, the newly educated youth in the Dutch colonial period.

The late nineteenth and early twentieth century saw an increasing intervention by the Colonial government in village affairs under the Ethical Policy, which aimed to acculturate indigenous villagers to the Western mode of thought. Efforts were made to expose them to Western ideas, based on the belief that these would bring about a Netherlands Empire consisting of two geographically distant but spiritually close parts (Vredenbregt, 1962:101). One of the key measures to achieve this goal was to educate village children in Western-style schools. At first, only the children of village officials were given seats in these schools, which were later extended to all children in rural areas. Although the actual beneficiaries of the widening educational opportunity were mainly the children of village

(guardian spirits) and there is little sign that any of them are surprised at the others' presence (Geertz, 1960,40). For more about this belief system, see Chapters V and VI.

officials and large landholders, due to high educational cost and parents' indifference to education, this new policy was able to produce a few villagers who received an education in Western-style schools.

Formal education was not the sole factor that created a group of youth who were sensitive to their religious duties and had a different perspective from their predecessors from which to look at Islam. The creation of this group was made possible by the foundation of an Islamic reformist organisation, Muhammadiyah, in the city of Yogyakarta and its devotion to education. Before the 1930s when there was no primary school and after the 1930s when there was no secondary school in Sumber, some village children went to the city and enrolled in a school founded by Muhammadiyah. When the encounter was made between village children and the Muhammadiyah school, their education became a basis for a different understanding of Islam from traditionally practised one. [7]

Muhammadiyah has been one of the most popular and influential Islamic organisations in 20th century Indonesia. Founded by Ahmad Dahlan who was an Islamic court official [8], it aimed to purify faith contaminated by non-Islamic ideas and traditions, a trend of which can be labelled as reformism. [9] For this purpose, reformist Muslims rejected blind submission to the authority of *ulama* and *kiyai* (established scholars), and advocated a return to the Quran and Hadith and the re-establishment of human equality. They supported the concept of *ijtihad* [10] as a way to refute blind submission to *ulama*. To them, the gate of

---

[7] As the first Statute of Muhammadiyah put forward, one of the central activities of Muhammadiyah was education. From the outset, Muhammadiyah made every effort to build schools which adopted Western-style curriculum (Noer,1973:307). In 1932, this organisation operated 207 Western-style schools, many of which were located in Yogyakarta and Solo (Alfian,1989:189-190) and the number reached 466 in 1937 (ibid.:309). For the characteristics of Muhammadiyah education in the colonial period, see Nakamura (1993:84-89).

[8] For more about Dahlan's life history see Peacock (1978b:29-42) and Alfian (1989:144-152).

[9] Reformism was not an indigenous idea in Indonesia but an imported one from the Arab countries. The increasing number of Indonesian Muslims who made the pilgrimage to Mecca and their contact with the pioneer teacher of the Islamic reformism, Muhammad Abduh of Cairo, are considered as the major factors that facilitated the flow of reformist ideas into Indonesia (Peacock,1978b:23; Noer,1973:297; Alfian,1989:149).

[10] *Ijtihad* means rational interpretation of the Quran and Hadith by individual Muslims, the concept of which is opposed to *taklid* or acceptance of the already established *fatwa* (a binding ruling in religious matters)and practices as being final and having an authoritative character (Noer,1973:9-10). The nature of *ijtihad* that reformist Muslims supported was expressed in the efforts of Ahmad Dahlan to change the direction of prayer. Around 1896, Dahlan discovered that the *masjid* of Sultan in Yogyakarta was not facing Mecca as it was supposed to, signifying that for years Muslims had not been practising their prayers correctly. After this discovery, he took the initiative in painting slanted lines on the floor of that *masjid* in order to point out the right direction of Mecca. His behaviour enraged the other old-established religious functionaries of the Sultanate and they erased all lines. Not discouraged by this failure, Dahlan built his own *langgar* facing Mecca, which was also destroyed by other established leaders of Islam (Alfian,1989:146-7). This story shows what was meant by *ijtihad* to the founder of Muhammadiyah, that is, to rectify Islamic teachings which had been blurred or interpreted wrongly by the established Islamic scholars and to follow the Islamic teachings as were inscribed in the Quran and Hadith. In order to carry out *ijtihad*, Muhammadiyah founded a committee called *Majelis Tarjih*. There, the committee members made an inventory of opinions concerning a certain religious issue, compared one with another and favoured the opinion which in their view conformed with the Quran

ijtihad was not shut once and for all, as had been considered since the second and third centuries of Islam (Gibb,1953:97), but was still open. The advocacy of *ijtihad* by the reformist Muslims prompted a transformation in the nature of religious knowledge and in the way of its reproduction. While Islamic education meant, among the circle of the *ulama* and *kiyai*, 'the teaching of fixed and memorisable statements and formulas which could be adequately learned without any process of thinking as such' (Hodgson,1974 vol.2:438) [11] , the reformist Muslims put priority on the understanding of the scriptures. To them, the memorisation of the scriptures was a praiseworthy and recommended work, but not a prerequisite for Muslims to make an attempt to understand the scriptures. Even those who did not know written Arabic should try to understand the scriptures translated into vernacular language. This changing focus of the reformist Muslims facilitated the shift of religious knowledge from that which is mnemonically 'possessed' to material that can be consulted in books (Eickelman,1978:511), and precipitated the change in the basis of religious leadership from a long apprenticeship under an established man of learning to a claim of a strong Islamic commitment and of a capability to interpret what Islam 'really' is (ibid.:511-12).

The presence of Muhammadiyah, apart from a few villagers who entered the primary or secondary school founded by it, started to be felt in the late 1920s when two youths from the city carried out their missionary activities in a hamlet near Kolojonggo. To attract children's attention, they brought a bike which two men could ride at one time and taught free gymnastics and other acrobatic motions. Then they asked children to attend a religious gathering to learn how to read Arabic script and to listen to Islamic stories from the Quran and Hadith. Although these activities were irregular and did not last long enough to create a group to continue their work, their visits gave the children the chance to gain contact with reformist Islam which was different from what was practised in their village. Their visits represented the first contact between Muhammadiyah and the villagers in Sumber, which has continued ever since.

In the early 1930s, a branch of Muhammadiyah (*cabang*) was founded in *kecamatan* Gamol by a small number of Islamic activists, all of whom received an education in the Muhammadiyah school. It was the first organisation of those

and Hadith (Noer,1973:98). The final decision made by the committee was called *fatwa*. One of the purposes of establishing the *Majelis Tarjih* was to prevent Muhammadiyah from making the same kind of mistake that the established scholars were thought to have made, namely, blindly rejecting existing *fatwa* for the benefit of attacking blind acceptance of them.
[11] In an autobiography, an Indonesian Muslim, Muhamad Radjab, remembers his experience of learning the Quran in his childhood as follows: 'When I began to study the reciting of the Quran, I did not know that the sentences had a meaning. ... I did not know that, if it were translated into one's own language, one might be able to understand what God meant in those verses. However, though I recited the Quran seven times, because it had no meaning for me, God never said anything which I was able to understand' (Cited in and translated by Soebardi,1976:46). Noer (1973:310) and Geertz (1976:178) also note the importance of memorisation rather than of understanding in traditional ways of learning Islam.

who were sympathetic to reformist Islam, combining the reformist activists scattered around each village into one place. According to a villager who belonged to the founding members, this *cabang* was the only place at that time where his ideas on Islam met with sympathy from others and he could be assured that he was not alone. In this respect, this *cabang* promoted consciousness of the sameness and the comradeship among the precursors of reformist Islam.

The first phase by which the reformist activists spread their ideas to other villagers in Sumber was characterised by peace. No confrontations or debates between reformism-oriented villagers and those supporting traditionally practised Islam took place. One of the factors which might have contributed to this peaceful introduction of reformism was the method of missionary activities (*dakwah*) employed by the reformist villagers. In dealing with various practices which were embedded in traditionally practised Islam but could not be approved of by reformism such as making offerings, worshipping other supernatural beings than Allah, negligence of ritual prayers and so on, they did not resort to force or vehemence. Instead, they retained an accommodational view that these practices would change gradually as villagers' understanding of reformist Islam deepened. According to Pak Seno who is known as the first reformist villager in Sumber, this attitude was not a compromise of reformist Islam with non-reformist Islamic practices but an actualisation of what Islam and Muhammadiyah taught. To support his argument, he quoted a passage from the Hadith saying 'those who command others to do good, do it in a gentle way', while he emphasised the most important way of conducting *dakwah* in Muhammadiyah was tolerance. Everyone is responsible for their own religious behaviour and what one can do for others is indirect guidance rather than direct actions, as he put it:

> The role of religious leaders is the same as that of people selling medicine in the street or in the market. What we can do is just to give suggestions, inviting others to religious activities, so that they may receive *anugerah* (a gift from Allah). We cannot enforce anything on others, since, if a person's heart is locked by Allah, we cannot achieve anything even with forceful measures.

Another factor contributing to the peaceful introduction of reformist Islam was the absence of a local religious figure (*kiyai*) who had authoritative power to influence the way Islam was interpreted and practised. In other parts of Java where the *kiyai* had established authority, the introduction of reformist Islam had been influenced by his position to evaluate it. Given that one of the basic tenets of reformist Islam is to attack blind submission toward the established *kiyai*, however, the adoption of reformist Islam might not be done without strong resistance from the *kiyai* and subsequently from the masses under his influence. In Madura, for example, religious behaviour of reformist Muslims was considered to be heretical from the initial stage of the introduction of reformism. This situation has persisted until recently to the extent that a local *kiyai* urged his audience not to attend the funeral of a sympathiser of reformist Islam (Jordaan,1985:48-55).[12]

The accommodational attitude of reformist villagers concerning *dakwah* and the absence of an established *kiyai* in Sumber made it possible for reformist Islam to be introduced peacefully into Sumber and to co-exist side by side with traditionally practised Islam. This peaceful introduction, however, had a disadvantage for the development of reformist Islam. With the lack of open confrontations between traditionally practised Islam and reformist Islam, the chances that the distinctions between these two streams could be highlighted and the 'Islam-ness' of both could be questioned, criticised or legitimised were given only to a small group of villagers who had close personal contact with the reformist activists. To those living beyond this boundary, the distinctiveness of reformist Islam was not well understood. To most of them, Islam was still what they practised and learned from their predecessors.

3.2. Islamic Development after the Independence of Indonesia

The period from 1949 when the Dutch troops retreated from Indonesia to 1965 is referred to by old villagers not as an era of ignorance (*jaman bodho*) but one of poverty (*jaman miskin*), of hunger (*jaman ngeleh*) or of communists (*jaman komunis*). As these terms imply, villagers put a negative image on it, describing it as the time of poverty, sickness, political unrest and, by some of them, coercive oppression from the communists. There are reasons that this period is not depicted as *jaman bodho*. Mass education began to be available from the mid-1950s, so that most children from Kolojonggo born in the 1940s were enrolled in the primary school for at least two or three years. The enlivened political situation also helped to make villagers more aware than before. Almost all male villagers were involved in one of three political parties extending their branches in the *kelurahan*: the communist (PKI), the nationalist or government (PNI) and the Islamic party (Masyumi). As all of these parties tried to indoctrinate their cadres, no week passed without political meetings. There, the peasants learned such borrowed terms from the West as '*kapital*', '*kontradiksi*' (contradiction), '*konfrontasi*' (confrontation), '*imperialismo*', '*manifesto*' and so on.

In the battle for increasing their followers, the Masyumi, which most reformist activists supported, was not the winner. In Kolojonggo, only a few households showed their allegiance to this party, while the rest were politically divided into

---

[12] For the doctrinal debates between reformist oriented Muslims and established *kiyai* in the late Dutch colonial period, see Federspiel (1970). For the religious debates at the local level between those who are committed to reformist Islam and those who are not, see Bowen (1993).

two, PKI and PNI sympathisers. Even the local commitment to the Masyumi was grounded less on their religious conviction that the state should be governed in accordance with Islam than on their blood relation or friendship with the Masyumi activists. A villager who had been a member of the Masyumi in the 1950s remembered his affiliation to this party as follows:

> The selection of a party at that time was dependent on one's compatibility (*kecocokan*) with it. If someone felt comfortable with the members [in a certain party], ya, [the selection] was already finished, leaving registration. ... I had chances to hear what the communists were saying but I felt these did not fit exactly with me. They were clever, strong (*keras*) and talked about big topics, and all the villagers who liked to ridicule others, were arrogant and lived an extravagant life entered the PKI. ... If one of my sons-in-law had not persuaded me, I might have entered the PNI. He (my son-in-law), who was a teacher in the elementary school, was honest, worked hard, knew a lot. Moreover, I was a Muslim. Why should I, a Muslim, not enter the Islamic party? ... At that time, I sometimes went to religious sermons but, probably because my heart was not yet opened by God (*Tuhan*), I was not so diligent in carrying out religious commands. In spite of this, my neighbours always commented that my behaviour and speech were like a *santri*.[13] If I listen to this comment now, I may be ashamed of it. But, at that time, I felt I really was a pious Muslim in that I entered the Islamic party.

The pattern of seeking supporters by employing personal relations was also adopted by the PNI and PKI. However, the PNI and PKI were in a more advantageous position than Masyumi. The PNI drew support from the *kelurahan* officials and large landholders, who could use their dominant political and economic power to attract followers. Some of the villagers who were economically dependent on them, namely, those who sharecropped their land or worked as wage labourers for them, were incorporated in the PNI.

In the case of the PKI, the economic conditions in Kolojonggo after independence allowed its policy to be attractive to many of middle and small landholders and the landless. In the late colonial period, Kolojonggo was characterised by a rapid polarisation of villagers in terms of their land ownership. Land tax and the short cultivation period made it difficult for middle and small landholders to retain

---

[13] In Kolojonggo, the term *santri* generally retains its original meaning, namely, the students who live in the *pesantren* to learn religious teachings. In some cases, this term is used to designate a pious Muslim who follows Islamic teachings and practises ritual obligations. When used in this way, especially by those who are not involved in Islamic activities, however, the term *santri* conveys a negative meaning: those who have not practised Islamic rules or have not participated in Islamic activities but suddenly show their interest in Islam. As a result, the term *santri* is never used by religiously active villagers to designate other villagers since there is no one in Kolojonggo as well as in Sumber who has studied in a *pesantren* long enough to be called *santri*.

land, and some of them sold it to others. This situation went on to the extent that more than three-quarters of the total households in Kolojonggo consisted of landholders owning less than 0.3 hectare of *sawah* and the landless (see Chapter II and Appendix A). After independence, the heavy land tax was lifted and landholders were granted a right to use their land all year round. To hold land was no longer a burden. The benefits from these changes, however, were not distributed evenly to all villagers. Those who had sold their land in the colonial period could not enjoy the same degree of economic stability that they might have done with their original landholdings. This feeling of economic deprivation that the land sellers felt in relativistic terms changed into a real economic deterioration when the inflation rate soared and pest attacks resulted in massive crop failure from the late 1950s. Even a half hectare of *sawah*, which was enough to make one an upper-middle landholder, could not provide a stable rice supply for a family of five to six members. In these circumstances, the communists' policy to locate the uneven land distribution at the centre of their program met with enthusiastic response from small landholders and the landless. In the 1950s, the issue at stake was to equalise landholdings by way of redistributing land. When the land reform act, promulgated in 1960, made it impossible to redistribute land within the boundary of law [14] , the slogan of the communist activists became 'to return land to the original owner', namely to nullify all land transactions since the reorganisation in the 1920s [15] . As land distribution at the time of the reorganisation was remembered by some villagers, this policy of the PKI seems not to have been considered as a dream by them. Villagers' participation in collectivising agricultural work was high, a policy which was understood as the first step in preparing the process of returning land to the tillers.

The political confrontation between villagers in the Old Order Period was based largely on class relations. At one end were traditional elites consisting of large landowners who had accumulated land in the late colonial period and *kelurahan* officials who were also large landholders, while at the other end were many middle and small landowners and the landless. The presence of the Masyumi, however, added a religious element to this political confrontation. The Masyumi

---

[14] In densely populated areas such as Java, five hectares of *sawah* and six hectares of non-irrigated land (*tegal*) were fixed as the maximum holding by the land reform act of 1960 (Huizer,1972:32-33). As there was no landholder in Sumber with more than five hectares, the ceiling of five hectares did not leave any *sawah* in Sumber to be redistributed to those who were landless or small landowners. For more about economic conditions in Kolojonggo under the Old Order, see Appendix A.
[15] One of the packages of the reorganisation starting in the late 1910s in Yogyakarta and Surakarta was to redistribute the land to villagers and to grant them rights to use, dispose and inherit the land. In principle, all adult male villagers who were capable of performing obligations to the village community and to the state were eligible for an equal amount of *sawah* (Suhartono,1991:110; Takashi,1990:20). The size of the land for redistribution varied according to the situation in each village. In the case of Kolojonggo, it was about 4000 m² of *sawah* and about 2000 m² of *pekarangan*. For more about economic conditions in Kolojonggo during the late colonial period, see Appendix A.

members criticised the PKI as the party of unbelievers and equated affiliation to the PKI with a straight path to Hell. This claim was considered as political propaganda by the PKI activists who believed that they were as religious as the Masyumi members. The difference was that they upheld not Islam but the Javanese religion (*agama Jawa*). The Javanese religion as was understood by the PKI members does not seem to have deviated much from traditionally practised Islam. However, the elements which were clearly identified with Islam such as daily prayers were consciously suppressed by the supporters of *agama Jawa,* while 'things Javanese' (*asli Jawa*) were installed as a framework to interpret what they practised and believed, irrespective of whether these actually came from Islam or not.

The politicisation of villagers and the use of religious distinctions as a way to differentiate one group from another implied that the spread of reformist Islam in the Old Order period was dependent on the local strength of the Islamic party. In a hamlet called Dawe where the Masyumi was successful in attracting a significant number of followers, the first *masjid* in Sumber could be built with uncompromising support from them. The same situation did not apply to hamlets such as Kolojonggo where the expansion of the Masyumi was sluggish. There, the spread of reformist Islam was blocked by the communist activists who equated this with the expansion of the Masyumi. Even the spread of the tenets of reformist Islam to the Masyumi followers was slow. This was because the concept of 'Muslim-ness' was defined in political terms, so that one's affiliation with the Masyumi was considered as an absolute criterion to differentiate, according to the Masyumi followers' view, Muslims from non-Muslims. In these circumstances, what mattered to define 'Muslim-ness' was one's political affiliation rather than any outward manifestation of one's religiosity such as fulfilment of religious duties, while much stronger emphasis was placed on increasing the number of the Masyumi followers rather than on spreading reformist ideas to its followers.

The interdependence of religion with politics brought a harsh blow to the Islamic activists when the Masyumi was banned in 1960 due to its alleged involvement in the unsuccessful rebellion in Sumatra. After the prohibition, the direct involvement of the Masyumi members in village politics was impeded to the extent that a *kelurahan* official and a few members of village council affiliated with the Masyumi were forced to resign. Some Masyumi members continued their socio-political activities in the branch of the reformist organisation, Muhammadiyah, but, in a hamlet like Kolojonggo where the recruitment of the Masyumi members was based largely on personal relations, the demise of the Masyumi implied the victory of *agama Jawa* over Islam. When the former Masyumi members were brave enough to practise the fast in public, not only they but their family members were mocked as '*fanatik*' (fanatic) and were intimidated by the PKI followers. This situation continued in the first half of the 1960s, giving birth to a state in which, according to a villager who newly moved into Kolojonggo in 1964, there were only two Muslim households and several Christian households while the rest were communists in this hamlet.

When the story of an attempted coup by the PKI spread, the non-PKI activists had to escape from the village at night. When they were seized by the PKI activists, those caught, according to their reminiscences, faced being killed. They went to the city or the mountains and stayed there, waiting for a change of situation. This did not take long. Within a few days, the troops appeared and made a base on the main street to the city, signalling the moment when the PKI activists had to escape from the village. This, however, was not an easy task and most of them were caught, and a few of them were directly killed by the villagers whose family members had been killed by the communists. Those who were caught and given a chance to go to jail are said to have been fortunate. [16]

The 1965 affair totally changed the atmosphere of village life. Everyone was involved in the killing, at least emotionally, either as an assailant or a victim. One of the two winners of this turmoil, the Islamic group, could use this situation to promote Islam among other villagers. In Dawe, its newly built *masjid* was full of villagers who turned up to pray. It was the time when those belonging to the PKI had to show their religiosity, namely, that they were not like they had once been. Those not belonging to the PKI also had to go to the *masjid*, assuring others that they were still on the side of the winners. The same situation, however, did not occur in Kolojonggo where Muslim villagers had no place to go to show their religious devoutness and their full incorporation into the *umat* Islam. Many villagers related to the PKI just remained silent, while some of them chose Christianity as their new shelter. The lack of proper infrastructure in the form of personnel and place, therefore, let the best chance to promote Islam slip away. This was all the more true when the strained situation eased after a few years. The urgency to show one's religious identity disappeared. So did the opportunity to promote Islamic activities. The benefit that the Islamic activists obtained from this period was the removal of freedom to remain an atheist and to oppose religion. Even this benefit, however, was given and has been secured by the government which was successful in emphasising the danger of communist

---

[16] Contrary to the recollection of the former Masyumi members that the communist activists killed the Masyumi followers after the alleged coup, there seems to have been no Islamic activist who was actually killed by the communists in Kolojonggo. When I asked a few former Masyumi members to specify the name of those who were killed by the communists, they generally avoided my question. In the case of the communists who were killed after the coup, two names were commonly specified by a few villagers. In this respect, the death toll in Kolojonggo at that time seems to have been not as high as in some other parts in Java (See, Cribb,1990). One probable answer for this seems to have been the swift action of the hamlet chief of that time who is said to have detained all the communist activists in his house as soon as the news of the failure of the coup was heard.

revival and in urging villagers to confess one of the five officially recognised religions (Islam, Protestantism, Catholicism, Hinduism and Buddhism). [17]

The momentum which enabled the construction of *masjid* in Kolojonggo and other hamlets in Sumber or, to borrow the Islamic leaders' words, a change from an acknowledgment (*mengakui*) of one's religion to its practice (*melaksanakan*), came about later under the so-called New Order Government. After the installation of this government, a group of villagers armed with higher Islamic knowledge and committed to promoting Islamic activities led the acceleration of Islamic development. The process by which this group was created was not an unitary one in Sumber. There was no religious leader or leaders who had a dominant influence over others, helping in the creation of the core group of Islamic activists. Rather, each Islamic activist had their own distinctive experience in Islamic activities as leaders. As this diversity makes it difficult to pinpoint various forces that helped the crystallisation of a group of religious leaders, my discussion will be confined to looking at a few characteristics of this group in Sumber. In doing so, one of the forces which have played a central role in giving birth to this group, namely, education, will be highlighted.

It is not easy to delineate the villagers who belong to the group of Islamic leaders in Sumber. Although every Muslim is formally or informally affiliated with Muhammadiyah whose branch is the only formal Islamic organisation in Sumber, one's involvement in the activities of Muhammadiyah or one's position in its executive board cannot be used as a criterion of Islamic leadership. Many of those who organise religious activities at the hamlet or village level are not formal members of Muhammadiyah, although they consider themselves as belonging to it. A better way to delineate the group of Islamic leaders seems to focus on the position of a *khatib* (preacher) at the *Jumatan* (Friday sermon). The *khatib* are selected by the *masjid* council (*takmir masjid*) among those who actively participate in religious activities.

---

[17] Even in 1993-94, several cases were reported in the local newspaper in which the military commandant in Yogyakarta prohibited the circulation of books, calendars and other items which were alleged to be produced by the communist remnants to propagandise communism. One of these was a tool designed to massage one's back. As this tool happened to take the form of the sickle, a symbol which had represented the PKI before 1965, the military commandant prohibited its circulation. This command, however, did not seem to be implemented well, so that I could buy one in the city after I had read this story in the newspaper. An interesting thing happened after I brought this tool into Kolojonggo. Some of the villagers were aware of the news that this tool was prohibited. Whenever I brought this tool with me, they told me it was produced by the communists, wondering how I had been able to buy one. There were also some who gave me a comment that I was brave enough to buy and to bring this tool with me in public, an action which they dared not do. This case shows how successful the Indonesian government has been in maintaining a social atmosphere by manipulating symbols. The danger of communist revival is not considered to have disappeared and the story related to the communists seems to have spread quickly. This social atmosphere has been, even if indirect, conducive to a favourable condition for the development of Islam. As the communists have been identified with the anti-religious or atheists, no villagers have opposed religion in public, although they themselves have not participated in religious activities.

Kolojonggo and five other hamlets in Sumber had twenty-four *khatib* in 1993. In many cases the *khatib* delivered their sermon once in five weeks, while some of them gave it in two or three different *masjid*. Of these twenty-four *khatib*, two were in their twenties, seven in their thirties, ten in their forties and five in their fifties. This composition shows that those who were born after independence constituted the backbone of this group. On the other hand, as a group they had more experience of schooling than other villagers. Only two of them in their fifties were primary school graduates. Even this background, however, was not ordinary, compared with other villagers belonging to their generation. At the time when they were children, a three to five year education was already enough of a qualification for someone to be an official in the *kelurahan*. Of the remaining twenty-two *khatib*, two stopped their education at middle school level, while thirteen proceeded to senior high school and seven to university. This higher educational background enabled many of them to find white collar jobs, so that nineteen worked as teachers of non-Islamic subjects, civil servants or administrators in the private sectors. The remaining one was a university student, while the other four consisted of two farmers, one labourer in the construction sector and one gardener in the high school.

All the *khatib* could read Arabic fluently, but most of them could not understand Arabic. Only three of them said to me they could understand written Arabic, although this is likely to mean that they could interpret the meaning of some Arabic passages word by word rather than that they had a full command of written Arabic. Others commented that they had not received any intensive education in written Arabic. Nineteen *khatib* started to learn to read Arabic in the hamlet *langgar*, two from their father and/or grandfather, while three of them did not learn it in childhood. Most of the *khatib* who had learned Arabic in their childhood, however, were of the opinion that these learning experiences were not enough for them to read Arabic properly and their present skill was acquired later. When they were asked to specify how they obtained their present skill in reading Arabic, their answer included *pesantren* (one *khatib*), radio programs (two *khatib*), books (four *khatib*), regular secondary or tertiary schools (thirteen *khatib*) or special secondary schools called *madrasah* where seventy percent of curriculum is devoted to religious studies (four *khatib*). In the case of the three *khatib* who were said to understand written Arabic, they acquired this skill in the *madrasah*, in an Islamic university and in the *pesantren* respectively. After having finished formal education, the *khatib* continued their religious education mainly by way of *pengajian* (religious sermon), books, newspapers and other media. Of these, the role of books and newspapers seems to be important. All the *khatib* answered they consulted books to deliver their sermon at the *Jumatan,* while a few of them made clippings of articles in newspapers which were related to Islam. The important position of written materials as a source of religious knowledge might be attributed to the fact that no *khatib* maintained a close relation with someone whom they could consult on religious matters.

One of the interesting points in examining the personal background of the *khatib* is that only five of them received special religious education either in the *pesantren* or in the *madrasah,* while most were educated in government schools. Many of them also considered religious education in government schools under the New Order as one of the most important occasions in which they could acquire the skill to read Arabic, to learn the right way to practise Islam and to obtain Islamic knowledge. This evaluation was contrary to their appraisal of religious education under the Old Order, which was not considered to have been systematic enough to produce 'good' Muslims committed to practising Islamic teachings and to promoting Islamic activities. To understand this contrasting evaluation of religious education in the Old Order period and that in the New Order period, it is necessary to look at several educational reforms after 1965.

The New Order government seized power, suppressing the communists while being supported by Islamic groups. As a result, the demands of the Islamic groups, in particular, those which were not directly political, were readily accepted by the government. Religious education belonged to this category. In 1966, parents' right to decide whether their children would receive religious education or not was abolished and attendance at religious class became compulsory in all government schools from the primary to tertiary level (Noer,1983:192). It was also stipulated in 1966 that religious education in elementary school started from the first grade (Noer,1978:37). As the majority of village children dropped out before they reached the fourth grade at that time, this modification gave all village children a chance of contact with religious education. In addition to the widening opportunities to receive religious education, the method of teaching and its content also underwent changes. The curriculum for religious education was standardised and religious textbooks written in Indonesian were introduced, while new religious teachers who had received regular education to teach Islam were recruited.

Under the Old Order when no unitary curriculum and textbooks were available in government schools, religious education was largely dependent on the religious orientation of teachers. In the case of the primary school where most children from Kolojonggo and neighbouring hamlets were enrolled, religious education, according to the evaluation of some Islamic leaders, failed to emphasise one of the most important teachings that children should learn, namely, the duty to carry out the requirements of the faith. The majority of religious teachings was related to learn to memorise a few Arabic phrases and to listen to stories from the Quran and Hadith, whereas the urgency to practise regular prayers, the fast and recitation of the Quran was not repetitively taught. Lack of religious textbooks meant that the traditional way of knowing and learning Islam, namely, by way of verbal transmission and memorisation, was maintained, and the need to understand the meaning of the scriptures and to consult them could not be properly inculcated. Without due emphasis on the importance of the scriptures, the Islamic leaders argued that religious education could not produce Muslims who were detached from traditionally practised Islam. Seen from this perspective, the significance of the introduction and popularisation of religious textbooks written in Indonesian was that this opened a new way for Islam to be learned. For the first time in the Islamic history of Sumber, Islam started to be transmitted by way of written materials. Islam was not only what one heard from others but what was written in the books. [18] With this shift, to learn Islam by way of materials written in Indonesian was established as a legitimate way to approach Islam and, subsequently the qualification to be a religious leader began to change. As the background of the *khatib* in Sumber shows, it is not the ability to understand Arabic nor to memorise the Quranic verses which makes them religious leaders. What they have is a commitment to reading written materials on Islam, a propensity and an ability which can be acquired through their education in government schools. [19]

Changes in religious education and the expansion of secondary education to villagers from the 1970s (See Chapter II) do not mean that all of those who received an extended period of religious education in the New Order period became agents to lead Islamic development. However, it is clear that religious education increased the opportunities for villagers to be exposed to regular religious teachings from their childhood on and, by shifting the way of learning Islam, facilitated the creation of a group of religious leaders. One needs not spend an extended period of time in the *pesantren* learning to memorise the scriptures or to understand Arabic in order to claim to be a religious leader and to be considered so by villagers. What is required is one's commitment to learning Islamic teachings by reading written materials in Indonesian and one's ability to interpret what Islam is, an attitude and capability which might not be very different from those required to be a 'good' student in secular education. As the number of villagers who were responsive to the plea to promote religious

[18] Another crucial factor which has helped to shift the basis of learning Islam is that there were no *pesantren* (religious boarding school), which supported the 'traditional' mode of transmitting Islam, in the vicinity of Sumber. As a result, the only stream of Islam which was readily available to villagers was reformist Islam represented by Muhammadiyah, which, as noted earlier, puts emphasis on the understanding rather than the memorisation of the scriptures and which supports the same mode of learning Islam as is applied in government schools.

[19] The influence of western education on Islamic development has been evaluated negatively by a few scholars of Indonesian Islam, as Benda puts it, 'western education was the surest means of reducing and ultimately defeating the influence of Islam' (Benda,1972:89; see also Berg,1932:295-298; Johns, 1978:226). Unfortunately, there has been no research which deals directly with the impact of secular mass education on Islamic development in Indonesia, except for Hefner (1987a:543-44) who suggests its positive impact on Islamic development. The assumption that western secular education reduces the influence of Islam has been recently challenged by a few scholars studying Islam outside Indonesia. For more about this, see Eickelman (1992) and Horvatich (1994).

activities and who were qualified to be religious leaders increased, they became the basis for transforming individual efforts to vitalise Islamic activities into collective ones.

3.3. From Bamboo *Langgar* to Brick *Masjid*

In Kolojonggo, the first visible sign of a new phase in Islamic development was the construction of a *langgar* (small prayer house) in the mid-1970s. A small bamboo *langgar* had existed in the *kaum*'s house but it was destroyed at the time of his death in the early 1960s, so that no place was available for villagers to perform their collective prayers from that time on. Some went to the *langgar* or to a half-constructed *masjid* in neighbouring hamlets. After more than ten years without a prayer house, the present *kaum* initiated a plea to build a *langgar* in his own yard. A *langgar* generally is constructed and managed by an individual, but the *kaum* was not rich enough to sponsor the construction for himself. Some of his neighbours donated bamboo, brick, wood and other building materials as well as labour. As a result, this *langgar* had a more communal basis than others in other hamlets. When finished, it was a small building of around 5m x 3m, which could accommodate around 20 people at one time. However, even this small space was too big to be fully utilised. On ordinary days, it was only the *kaum*'s family and a few other neighbours who came by for their daily prayers. This did not disappoint the *kaum* and others who built this *langgar* since they never expected that it would be full. The major motive for building the *langgar* was not for ordinary days but for the special month in Islam, the fasting month. During this month, religious passion among village Muslims was heightened, so that more villagers used the *langgar*.

When the first fasting month in the newly built *langgar* was celebrated, around ten households hosted religious activities by paying for the cost of food for the collective ending of the fast (*buka pasa*). The participants from these households and school children from other households made it possible for the *langgar* to be full during the *tarawih* prayer and subsequent sermon. Sometimes, the outside yard of the *langgar* had to be used for women who came to pray when the two praying lines inside were occupied by men.

The fasting month in their childhood is remembered by the youth of the present day as a time of joy rather than one of painful endurance of hunger: they went to the paddy field after the end of the *tarawih* prayer to find *belut* (a kind of eel), cooked and ate them at the spot, chatted and slept together in the *langgar* until dawn, walked around the paddy field after the morning prayer and came back home to have a sleep as satisfactorily as possible. [20] Their reminiscences give the impression that they used the most sacred time in Islamic calendar for

---

[20] Before 1979, schools were closed during the fasting month. This system was abolished in 1979 and the school children have around two weeks' holiday in this month.

playing rather than for praying. However, the use of the *langgar* as a gathering place and the fasting month as time for fun played an important role in the later process of Islamic development. This allowed the crystallisation of peer group solidarity among children and youth centring on the religious place.

During ordinary months, the *langgar* was used as a gathering place for some of the village children. A regular course to learn Arabic was held in the *langgar* by Pak Pomo, a high school student in the late 1970s and later a university student, and a few friends of his. He started this course in the belief that the transformation of children's religious outlook was much easier than that of adult villagers and future Islamic development would be brighter when the old generation passed away and they were replaced by the young generation armed with Islamic ideas. At first, only a few children responded to his proposal and there were even times when children did not appear at all. No compulsion was permissible to make children attend this meeting and the interest of parents in their children's religious education was low. To cope with this setback and to attract more children, Pak Pomo took two measures. On the one hand, he combined children from Kolojonggo and those from another hamlet into one group. In this way, he could assure the presence of at least a few participants, which made the continuation of this meeting possible. On the other hand, he changed the date of this meeting to Saturday night in order to induce more participation from children. [21]

It is not certain whether a strong peer group solidarity was formed among those who regularly participated in this religious class or whether the participation of one child in a pre-existing peer group triggered the attendance of others belonging to the same group at this meeting. Whatever the case, Pak Pomo was successful in incorporating a group of children into this meeting. In turn, their regular participation enlivened this learning course and, as these children grew older, they constituted a solid group of youth who were ready to invigorate Islamic activities.

The presence of a group of youth, however, was not the only condition to accelerate Islamic development. As these youths were not in a position to mobilise economic resources nor to influence adult villagers, their future role in the developmental process of Islam could not be realised without proper commitment from adult villagers to religious activities. The medium which attracted adult villagers' attention to religious activities was *tahlilan* among men and *pengajian* among women.

---

[21] To the Javanese in general and to the youth in particular, Saturday night is a moment when they should do some special activities. In many cases, they go outside and wander around, looking for fun. By changing the date of the learning course to Saturday night, Pak Pomo could use this tradition to attract more children. As this meeting was held alternately in two different hamlets, the children and youth from Kolojonggo visited the other hamlet once every two weeks, which gave an extraordinary mood to the participants.

Tahlilan is a religious meeting where participants recite the Quranic passages collectively. To many villagers, it is considered as an occasion to send Arabic prayers to their deceased ancestors. To those who have more religious knowledge, its purpose is not only to send prayers to the deceased but, more importantly, to bring oneself close to Allah by aggrandising, praising and adoring His name. This different degree of understanding, however, does not seem to bother the reformist leaders much. The more crucial point is that *tahlilan* can be used as a medium for them to mobilise villagers for religious purposes. The fact that not all of the participants can actually read or memorise Arabic prayers also does not trouble them. The mere act of listening to the recitation of an Arabic prayer is, according to the reformist leaders, enough to acquire high religious merit (*ganjaran*).

One of the reasons *tahlilan* could be a medium to mobilise adult men to religious activities with ease was its closeness to the Javanese tradition. Traditionally the funeral was followed by a ritual called *kendhuri* [22] and *tahlilan*, which aimed, according to village elders, to ask forgiveness of Allah for the sins committed by the deceased in this world. This, in turn, was thought to bring well-being for the living since the dead ancestors were believed to give blessings to their living children. These acts of devotion for the deceased ancestors were confined not only to the post-funeral period. The Javanese cleaned the tombs of their dead parents or other relatives, brought flowers, burned incense and made offerings in the cemetery, and, sometimes, stayed awake or slept there until dawn, waiting for the coming of blessing from the dead in the form of a dream or whisper.

According to the reformist leaders in Sumber, the traditional mode of celebrating *tahlilan* after the funeral is permissible on the condition that its aim is to ask forgiveness of Allah for the dead. However, it cannot be approved of when its aim is to ask something of the dead. Reformist Islam teaches that the relation between parents and children is severed with the death of parents, so that the dead cannot give any blessing to the living. [23] This clear distinction in reformist ideology is not so clear-cut in actual life: no one knows exactly what others have in mind when they pray for the deceased. This ambiguity, therefore, has been

---

[22] *Kendhuri* (*slametan*) refers to the traditional ritual, which was celebrated at each passage of life and on other specific occasions. For more about *kendhuri*, see Chapter V.

[23] The reformist villagers in Kolojonggo have an opinion that prayers from living children can lessen the burden of their dead parents in the *alam kuburan* or the world after death, where the dead are tortured for their earlier sins in this world. They base this idea on a passage in the Hadith saying that, after the death of people, all but three deeds are discontinued: alms given while alive (*amal jariah*), useful knowledge and a pious child (*anak sholeh*). However, they do not agree with the traditional idea that the dead ancestors can give blessings to the living children. In this respect, the relation between the living and the dead conceived by the reformist villagers is unilateral. The living children can help the dead whereas the latter cannot help the former. This idea of the reformist villagers in Kolojonggo is different from that of the Gayo reformists (modernists) who maintain that the living children cannot aid the dead parents (Bowen, 1993:268-272).

one reason why *tahlilan* was so successful in mobilising ordinary villagers and, eventually, in expanding Islamic teachings to them.

The selection of the day for *tahlilan* also indicates that a severance between the traditional concept of seeking blessing from the dead and *tahlilan* is not clearly manifested. From the outset, it was held on the night that begins the Javanese day of Friday-*Kliwon* and Tuesday-*Kliwon* [24] . Traditionally it was these two nights when spirits and souls of the dead were believed to hover around the village most actively, so that many villagers, who wanted to seek blessing from the dead or to increase their magical power by way of spirits, selected these two nights as the best time to visit tombs or other sacred places. This selection, therefore, smoothly changed the visiting place of villagers from tombs or other sacred places to a space where Islamic prayers could be heard. A school teacher who was one of the central figures to initiate the new *tahlilan* tradition in Sumber described the ease of inviting other villagers to *tahlilan* as follows:

> When invited to learn about Islam in formal meetings, villagers were not willing to attend. There were so many excuses that they made. ... However, the situation was somewhat different in the case of *tahlilan*. I persuaded them to attend it, saying that prayer for the dead was a praise-worthy work both in Islam and in Javanese tradition, since both taught us to be faithful (*bakti*) to our dead parents. This invitation was rather readily accepted, even if they could not follow the recital of Arabic prayers.

After *tahlilan* became a regular meeting among villagers, a change was made in its mode. The reformist leaders added a section with a sermon after the recital of Arabic prayers. With this innovation, they could overcome the initial unwillingness of villagers to attend a religious meeting and their original intention to give villagers more chance to learn about Islam was implemented in the long run.

In the 1970s when the celebration of *tahlilan* was already firmly established in several hamlets in Sumber, Kolojonggo had no resources to start it by itself. The first basis for the development of the *tahlilan* celebration was imported from other hamlets when three adult villagers and some youth attended the *tahlilan* meeting held in neighbouring hamlets. As their invitation to *tahlilan* was accepted by some other villagers and they themselves were able to memorise the sequence of recitation and Arabic prayers, they began to hold their own independent *tahlilan* in the *langgar* in the early 1980s. The *kaum* became a guide to recite Arabic prayers and other attendants were asked to repeat what was recited by him. Several reformist leaders from neighbouring hamlets were invited to give the sermon after *tahlilan*.

---

[24] See Chapter VI, for more about this traditional system of calculating the day and the week.

The significance of the independent *tahlilan* in Kolojonggo lay in the fact that it was the first occasion when adult Muslim villagers gathered under the banner of Islam on a regular basis. As its purpose was religious, the participants were ready to and expected to talk about religious issues. Whereas religious topics had been discussed in a private manner by those concerned about it before the initiation of *tahlilan*, these topics started to be discussed in a public sphere after its initiation. This meant the birth of a collective power in Kolojonggo, even if in a nascent form. One of the topics discussed at that time was religious education for those who did not participate in *tahlilan* in general and for women in particular. The result of this discussion bore fruit in the form of *pengajian*[25] for women.

With the introduction of *pengajian* for women in the early 1980s, all Muslim villagers were given a place in religious activities. The children and youth were allocated to the Arabic learning course, the men to *tahlilan* and the women to *pengajian*. Although the number of participants at these meetings was not enough to carry out certain religious programs, they provided a place where religious problems were regularly discussed. This easy flow of thought eventually constituted the basis for the construction of a *masjid* a few years later.

Asked the reason for constructing a *masjid*, villagers gave the same answer as they used to explain the construction of a *langgar*: the fasting month. Increasing numbers of villagers who participated in religious activities naturally led to an increase of those who carried out the fast. Soon, the *langgar* became too small to accommodate this expansion and villagers had to divide the participants into two: the *langgar* for men and a private house for women. This division of place in terms of sex brought several inconveniences. As the *tarawih* prayer and sermon were offered separately in two places, they had difficulty coordinating religious activities and this eventually intensified their desire to have their own *masjid*.

On the other hand, the Islamic development in Sumber after the mid-1980s also influenced villagers in Kolojonggo: nine new *masjid* were built in three years from 1984 to 1986. This was remarkable progress, compared with the previous time when only three *masjid* were constructed over almost three decades.[26] This development triggered a series of discussions among the participants to *tahlilan* and *pengajian* and gave villagers an opportunity to scrutinise the process of

[25] *Pengajian* refers to all religious meetings whose major purpose is to learn about Islam, so that the religious course for children and the sermon after *tahlilan* are also called *pengajian*. However, when the term, *pengajian*, is used without a modifier, it generally refers to a meeting where a speaker conveys religious teachings to the participants. See Chapter IV, for more about *pengajian*.
[26] This remarkable increase in the 1980s was not only a distinctive feature in Sumber but was applicable to other *kelurahan* in the *kecamatan* Gamol or even to the Special Region of Yogyakarta. At the end of 1979, the *kecamatan* Gamol had 28 *masjid*, which increased to 50 in 1986 and to 73 in 1990. In the Special Region of Yogyakarta, the number of *masjid* doubled from 1779 in 1979 to 3849 in 1990 (KSY, various issues).

building a *masjid*. The report of a few villagers who closely examined this process in other hamlets brought a great hope. According to them, most of the funds to build a *masjid* were not directly mobilised from the inside but from the outside. What villagers had to provide was mainly man-power.

As the first step to build a *masjid*, an informal preparatory committee was organised in early 1987. The first work that this committee did was to search for the land where the *masjid* could be erected. Fortunately, a villager donated his land. As his house was located at the centre of the hamlet, his proposal was welcomed by the committee. However, an unexpected problem occurred. The donated land was located not far from the Protestant chapel (*kapel*), so that the *kelurahan* office recommended finding another place in order not to locate chapel and *masjid* on the same plot of land. [27] This did not drive the committee to despair. They started to search for another donor, who soon turned up. Although located on the western side of the hamlet, the donation was finally approved of by the committee.

The other job that this committee carried out was promoting religious activities among villagers. *Tahlilan* was regularly carried out and an irregular *pengajian* for women was changed into a regular one for a general audience. From 1987 till 1988, *pengajian* was held almost once every week. In these meetings, a donation was asked from the participants, whose number expanded rather rapidly. The records showed that the participants reached around fifty and sometimes eighty at a *pengajian* and around thirty to forty at a *tahlilan*. Although donations from villagers were mainly Rp 50 or Rp 100 coins, the regular celebration of religious meetings, increasing participation in these activities and the commitment of the increasing number of villagers to the idea of having a *masjid* made it possible for the committee to collect around half a million Rupiah within two years.

In 1988, the informal committee was changed into a formal one and the head of the *kecamatan* (*camat*) became its chief counsellor. From this time on, a massive campaign started to raise funds, the total sum of which was estimated at around three and half million Rupiah. As villagers had expected before, most funds were collected from outside Kolojonggo with the effort of the committee members to seek donors. The final moment in collecting funds was the most impressive one throughout the preparation period. Following the practice of other hamlets, the placement of the first stone for the new *masjid* was accompanied by a

---

[27] In 1969, the Indonesian government issued a regulation on the way to construct religious buildings. According to this regulation, the main body preparing a construction should submit the application to the regional government which is authorised to issue a permission. The regional government is ordered to consider the opinion of the chief official of the Department of Religion, the condition of the area where the new building will be constructed and the opinion of religious leaders in that area. In this consideration, two important factors are the closeness of the planned building with the existing ones and the composition of population in terms of religious affiliation (Proyek Perencanaan Peraturan Perundangan Keagamaan,1980/81).

large-scale *pengajian* (*pengajian akbar*). Hundreds of people gathered, most of whom were from outside Kolojonggo. Surprisingly enough, more than a million Rupiah was collected at this *pengajian*.

In the process of building a *masjid*, a small myth was created. Around thirty men worked throughout the whole construction period. Some of them gave up their jobs as labourers to help this construction. Food for the labourers was provided by several Muslim households in turn. With this unprecedented support, it took only forty days to build the 11m x 14m building. Many villagers who participated in this construction unanimously mentioned their own surprise at such an easy and voluntary process of mobilising labour. Everyone worked hard, as if this was to build their own house. Many villagers who had not participated in Islamic activities before also came voluntarily to donate their manpower. In this respect, it was a chance for the potentiality of Muslim villagers to be publicised and the possibility of creating the *umat* Islam was felt by the participants.

3.4. Islamic Development after the Construction of the *Masjid*

The construction of the *masjid* building was not finished in 1988, nor was it meant to be. Villagers planned to build only its main structure and other parts were designed to be completed in subsequent years. From that time on, community work was mobilised before the fasting month to make the incomplete structure of the *masjid* perfect: a toilet, a place for ablution and a brick fence were built, walls were painted, the verandah was renovated, a slate cover was made over the ablution place, a sound system was installed and so on. Even if the present appearance and facilities seem fine, the villagers have still more plans for the future. They want an electric generator to replace the well with tap water, a more spacious toilet and ablution place which men and women can use separately, a better sound system, fans and a library. Although these will be furnished some day, it is obvious that they will then make another plan to improve their *masjid*. To them, the *masjid*, although it is just a physical structure, is the symbol of their religiosity and of Islamic development in Kolojonggo. As their religiosity is viewed as something that should be ceaselessly improved, so is the *masjid*.

Compared with the rapid pace of building the *masjid*, the increase of Muslim villagers who use it has not been remarkable. On ordinary days, only a handful of villagers come for daily prayer. In 1993-94, there were around 20 villagers for *isaq* (night prayer) and around 10 for *subuh* (dawn prayer). To some villagers, this was not disappointing since even this number was a remarkable increase. Moreover, the *masjid* is not the only place where one can do his or her prayers. The house or any other place will do for this purpose. To those who regularly prayed in the *masjid*, however, this number was not satisfactory. They wished more villagers would come to the *masjid* to make it full. Their expectation was not just a dream but based on the experience during the first phase of the fasting month when hundreds of villagers visited the *masjid*. They hoped that the same situation would continue on ordinary days.

The participation in the collective prayers during the fasting month gives a clue to understand the present religious situation in Kolojonggo. For this purpose, a graph showing the number of participants in the collective prayers during the fasting month in 1994 is presented below.[28] As the collective prayer starts with the *tarawih* prayer in the evening before the beginning of the fasting month and ends with the *subuh* prayer on the last day of the fast, these two days have just one collective prayer.

Figure III-1: Number of Attendants at the Collective Prayer during the Fasting Month in 1994

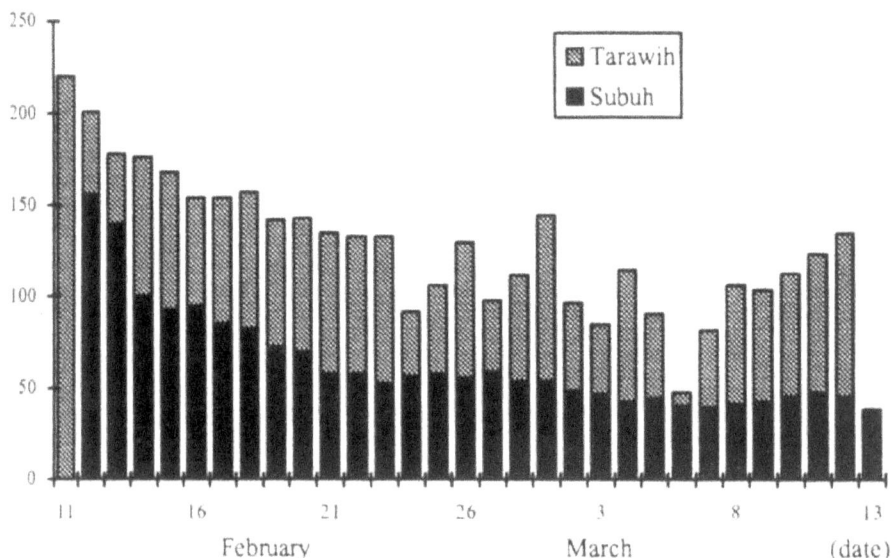

One of the notable features in Figure III-1 is the remarkable difference in the number of participants for the first and the last collective prayers. While it was around 220 for the first *tarawih* prayer, it was around 40 who attended the last *subuh* prayer. To understand what this difference signifies, the changing social atmosphere throughout the fasting month needs to be noted.

---

[28] During the *tarawih* prayer and sermon, I usually sat inside the *masjid* behind male villagers. As this made it difficult for me to count the number of female participants, many of whom sat in the *masjid* veranda, the number of female participants was calculated by a female youth, and her calculation was later combined with mine. When I could not attend the *tarawih* prayer, I asked a male youth to calculate the number of participants. As I did not attend the *subuh* prayer except for the last five days of the fasting month, the calculation was undertaken by a male youth. Numbers in Figure III-1 also include children who participated in the collective prayers.

The preparation for the fasting month started two or three months before its coming. A series of meetings were held to plan the community work, to organise a preparatory committee, to put each individual into the sub-sections of this committee, to fix the list of villagers who would supply food for the collective ending of the fast and to recruit the *khatib* who would give sermons after the *tarawih* and *subuh* prayers as well as for special *pengajian*. These meetings gave villagers who wanted to participate in the fast a chance to refresh their intention. They thought about their fast in the previous year and expected themselves to observe the coming fast better. Some of them practised the fast that they had not done in the previous year. Many public religious discourses also dealt with topics related to the fast. Due to this social atmosphere, the opening of the fasting month, beginning with the first *tarawih* prayer in the *masjid*, was enthusiastically received by villagers. Even those who had not frequently attended religious activities also visited the *masjid* for the opening of the fasting month. In this sense, the number, which reached around 220 in 1994 or around 50 percent of the total Muslims in Kolojonggo, signified the number of villagers who retained their interest in religious activities and who were responsive to the call from the Islamic activists.

As the fasting month went on, however, the first passion of villagers began to decline. Some villagers gave up their fast, the fixed list of *khatib* started to be revised due to their notice of absence, and the number of villagers who came to the *masjid* to end the fast together with others (*buka pasa*) decreased rapidly. Boredom began to replace the first strong will of villagers to complete their religious duty. As one villager put it, when one happened not to practise the fast one day, the temptation from the *satan* grew greater and greater. The fluctuating number of those who attended the *tarawih* prayer in the middle of the fasting month was a sign of this. On the 6th of March, it rained heavily and half of the villagers who had turned up the day before did not come to the *masjid*.

The number of participants in the *tarawih* prayer increased once again after the special *pengajian* was held on the 8th of March. Reanimated, villagers began to come to the *masjid* during the last phase of the fasting month. The same situation, however, was not applied to the *subuh* prayer. Compared with the *tarawih* prayer, the *subuh* prayer was said to be more difficult to carry out. First of all, it was done around 4 in the morning before the dawn. This means that one had to get up by at least 3 in the morning to have a meal (*saur*) and to take a bath for the prayer. Everyone who wanted to fast should do so, but to go to the *masjid* for prayer was, according to villagers, a totally different thing. Moreover, they had the option of performing their *subuh* prayer at home. [29] Due to this, many

---

[29] Islam teaches that the *tarawih* prayer can be done individually at home. However, villagers in Kolojonggo put strong emphasis on the collectivity of this prayer and many villagers considered it as a collective prayer by nature.

of those who participated in the *subuh* prayer at the beginning of the fasting month gave up going to the *masjid*. In this respect, the villagers who kept going to the *masjid* for the *subuh* prayer throughout the whole fasting month, whose number reached about 40 in 1994, represented the core group of reformist activists in Kolojonggo. Half of them were the youth while the other half consisted of old women and middle aged men.

In sum, the pattern of villagers' participation in the collective prayers is closely related to the composition of village Muslims in terms of their religious piety and of their commitment to Islam. The participation cannot be the sole criterion by which the religiosity of a certain Muslim can be judged. However, the weight that the reformist leaders and activists put on the importance of the collective prayer, their tendency to consider one's participation in these occasions as a key to evaluate religious orientation, and the positive correlation between one's participation in the collective prayers and other religious activities make it possible to use it as an indicator to understand the differentiation of religiosity among Muslim villagers.

Seen from this point of view, Muslim villagers in Kolojonggo are made up of three groups. The first is a small group of those who make every effort to harmonise their life with Islamic teachings. The youth who regularly attend the prayers in the *masjid* on ordinary days and some of the villagers who have a higher educational background and a white collar job constitute the majority of this group, to which are added a few old and middle-aged villagers who do not appear in the front line of religious activities but are active supporters. The second group consists of those who do not actively participate in religious activities but are ready to attend them on an irregular basis and are responsive to the call from the first group. Those who appeared at the first phase of the fast month but could not continue their visits to the *masjid* constitute most of this group. The third group is composed of those who do not respond to the plea from the first group nor attend any religious events even on an irregular basis. As the figures show, around half of Muslim villagers in Kolojonggo belong to this group.

Age is an important variable for understanding this grouping (see table III-1 below). As one grows older, one is more likely to belong to the third; while younger, to the first and second. Many of the youth in their late teens and twenties were generally ready to appear in the *masjid*. Even some of the youth who were notorious for their 'naughty' behaviour such as drinking and gambling, came to the meeting in the *masjid*, especially before and throughout the fasting month. The same pattern, however, did not apply to many of the adults, who felt uneasy at the idea of entering the *masjid*. As a result, they never appeared in the *masjid*, although their house was just next door to it.

Table III.1: Participation of Male Villagers Aged over 15 in the Collective Prayers in 1994[a]

Group	Year of Birth					Total
	- 1939	1940-49	1950-59	1960-69	1970-79	
A	4	5	3	6	10	28
B	3	6	12	18	15	54
C	21	11	11	15	9	67

[a] Comparable data on the participation of female villagers in the collective prayers were not collected. This was because, as I sat in front of female villagers in the *masjid*, it was almost impossible for me to check who came to the *masjid* and who did not.

Source: My observation of the *tarawih* prayers throughout the fasting month and of the *subuh* prayers for the last five days of the fasting month.
Group:
A: Male villagers who participated in the *tarawih* prayer regularly (although not continuously) and attended the *subuh* prayer at least once for the last five days;
B: Male villagers who participated in the *tarawih* prayer irregularly but at least once in the fasting month and did not attend the *subuh* prayer for the last five days;
C: Male villagers who did not participate in the *tarawih* prayer and did not attend the *subuh* prayer for the last five days.

The differentiation of villagers in terms of their religious outlook and of their participation in religious activities has existed since the late colonial period when reformist Islam began to influence some villagers. With the import of this ideology, villagers were given the opportunities to come in contact with an alternative mode of Islam to *the* Islam that their ancestors had passed down to them. At least for the supporters of reformist Islam, circumcision alone, for example, could not be a sufficient qualification to make someone a Muslim, as many villagers of that time considered. The accommodational attitude of the reformist villagers concerning missionary activities and their numeric inferiority, however, did not allow their religious distinction to be understood fully by villagers who did not have many opportunities of having contact with them. Lack of religious activities and lack of a *masjid* also decreased the chances that the different modes of religious behaviour between the reformist villagers and others were manifested in public life. The situation underwent changes in the Old Order period when villagers were clearly differentiated in terms of their political affiliation either to the Islamic party or to the other parties. In spite of the formation of a clear boundary, however, the differentiation was based more on personal relations than on differences in religious outlook. Anyone who joined Masyumi was considered to be a pious Muslim, and in this process, the different religious practices and orientations between reformist-oriented Masyumi members and those who were not did not come to the fore. Even those who did not know how to pray properly could be a member of Masyumi and be equated with other reformist activists.

By contrast with the situation in the Old Order, the accelerating Islamic development in the seventies and eighties has made it possible for the religious differences among villagers to be fully manifested in daily life. With the quantitative increase in the number of the villagers belonging to the group of Islamic activists and the expansion of religious activities, their distinctive religious behaviours and orientation are readily visible and easily contrasted with others who do not belong to this group: they appear in the *masjid* for prayer though irregularly, pay *zakat* and other alms, and attend *pengajian, tahlilan, Jumatan* and communal work to improve *masjid*.

'Islam KTP' is a common term used in the discourse of the reformist villagers to designate those who are not ready to respond to their plea to participate in Islamic activities. KTP (*Kartu Tanda Penduduk*) is an identification card of all Indonesians on which one's religious affiliation is written. Therefore, Islam KTP refers to a Muslim who belongs to the religion of Islam but does not carry out religious duties. On the other hand, the youth who are active in Islamic activities are called by others *anak masjid* or *bocah masjid(an)*(children of the *masjid*). This term originated from the fact that their everyday life is closely connected to the *masjid*. They perform *isaq* prayer together in the *masjid* and then play together in the *masjid*. No specific term has developed to designate all Muslim villagers who are active in Islamic activities, perhaps because the reformist villagers as a group do not develop the same sort of coherent relations outside the domains of religious activities. Only the youth have extended their relationship from the religious domain to non-religious domains. [30]

In a recent study of Islam in a Central Javanese village, Pranowo reports that religious differentiation noticed by outside observers is not what is actually perceived and used by villagers to divide themselves into different groups. This variation is viewed by villagers as a result of different emphasis on one of two possible religious trends, either the mystical and inner dimension or the outer dimension of religious life. Therefore, those who do not carry out their religious duties such as the fast or daily prayers are not considered as bad Muslims since one's inner state of religiosity, which is not visible from outside, cannot be evaluated by outward behaviour (Pranowo,1991:278-320).

The same argument does not apply to Kolojonggo. First of all, the major stream of Islam being practised in Kolojonggo and its vicinity is different from that in Pranowo's research area where Islamic development has not been initiated by reformist Islam but has been dominated by non-reformist Islam which places a heavy emphasis on the mystical dimension of religiosity. The inner aspect of religious life is not ignored by the reformist villagers in Kolojonggo but is

---

[30] In his study of reformist Islam, Irwan notes that the Muslims in a Central Javanese town categorise their community into different groups, based on their different attitude toward Islamic ideas and practices. The reformist leaders classify those who do not follow the Islamic values and customs as 'Islam KTP', while the latter call the religious leaders and the people surrounding them '*wong masjidan*' (mosque people) (Irwan,1994:89 & 97-98). Siegel also notices that the city dwellers in Surakarta, who counted themselves as Muslims for the purpose of burial at least, but in general followed syncretic Javanese religious practices, were called *Islam simpatis* (sympathetic to Islam) (Siegel,1986:60).

emphasised in a different manner. It is related to sincerity in one's religious activities: whether one's observance of religious duties is based on the sincerity of one's intention to follow Allah's command or is due to one's desire to show off. In this framework, the equation of the inner side of one's religious life with the mystical aspect is not formed, although it is not totally rejected.

The dominance of reformist ideology in the developmental process of Islam and its different interpretation concerning the inner aspect of religion make it impossible for a double standard for evaluating religious behaviours to be used in Kolojonggo, at least among the reformist Muslims. Instead, whether to perform daily prayers and the fast or not is thought of as the key to evaluate one's religiosity since, if one is pious and sincere enough to follow the path to Allah, he or she can not but carry out these duties (See Chapter IV). In this respect, outer manifestation of one's religious life is considered to be the reflection of one's inner religiosity and those who do not practise daily prayers nor the fast under ordinary circumstances are not regarded as pious Muslims (*Muslim sholeh*) by the reformist villagers (See also Bowen,1993:320).

In addition to daily prayers and the fast, the distinctive behavioural modes of the reformist villagers are also manifested in other domains of everyday life. They attend *pengajian, tahlilan, Jumatan* and other religious celebrations, donate religious alms, participate in the communal work to improve the *masjid* and do not gamble, drink alcohol, buy lottery tickets and eat dog. In this sense, villagers who are inactive in Islamic activities do not need to go to the *masjid* or *pengajian* to learn the difference between themselves and the reformist villagers, but they can do it simply by observing their neighbours. By repetitively seeing some of their neighbours' behaviour, they can perceive the differences between themselves and those who are active in Islamic activities and learn by heart who belongs to which group. As a result, when a *jagongan* [31] was celebrated and dozens of villagers came, those who gambled knew exactly who played for money and who did not, and took their seats besides their colleagues. Villagers could also enumerate who bought into the lottery and who did not, and who drank alcohol and who did not.

One's understanding of others' individual propensities, for example, whether one gambles or eats dog meat, has been developed from childhood. However, when more chances are given to look at this difference in terms of religion, the contrast is viewed not simply as that of individual taste or idiosyncrasy. Rather, it is interpreted and evaluated from a religious perspective both by those who try to practise Islamic teaching and those who do not. Now, one can say, 'one does this and does not do that, for one is a good Muslim'.

---

[31] *Jagongan* is a traditional gathering held in a new-born baby's house. Villagers come together and spend the night for several days after the birth of a baby.

In sum, the Islamic development after the 1970s in Kolojonggo, by providing more opportunities to look at different manifestations of religious behaviour in more diverse domains of everyday life, has accelerated the differentiation of villagers in terms of their religious outlook. This differentiation is clearly recognised by villagers and used as a framework to interpret villagers' private and social life.

3.5. Summary

Islamic development in Kolojonggo has been a process in which a group of villagers who are reflective upon their religious duties and who try to practise Islam has expanded. The increasing number of villagers who have received higher education since the 1970s was one of the factors which made it possible for this group to expand at an accelerating pace. With this quantitative expansion, the rural population has started to be differentiated rapidly in terms of religious outlook. If the germ of religious differentiation existed but was not clearly expressed in daily life before this time, it is now manifested explicitly in many aspects of social life. This naturally leads to a situation in which distinctive behavioural patterns of villagers are interpreted in terms of their commitment to Islam.

The accelerating Islamic development has brought about several related changes in village life. Armed with reformist ideology, some villagers have tried to look at and reinterpret things around them with a different perspective from others. With these efforts, the practices which have been taken for granted and considered to be natural are no longer treated as they once were. Two of the issues that the reformist villagers have challenged in this process have been those of tradition and of their relations with Christians. Therefore, the focus of the following chapters will be put on how village Muslims have dealt with tradition which reformist ideology does not clearly approve of and on what their attitude has been toward Christian neighbours. Before these two topics are dealt with, the efforts of the reformist villagers to Islamise everyday life will be presented in Chapter IV in order to understand the nature of the local-level Islam practised in Kolojonggo.

Plate 3: Improvement of the *masjid* before the coming of the fasting month in 1993.

Plate 4: View of the *masjid* in Kolojonggo just before the beginning of the fasting month in 1993.

Chapter 4: The Islamisation of Everyday Life

In reformist Islam, everyday life is the locus where ceaseless opportunities are given to human beings to carry out commands from Allah. As the Quran teaches that the purpose of Creation was none other than to let human beings worship Allah (li:56) [1], not only ritual prayers but all human behaviours should be directed at realising His will. In everyday life, human beings are also given innumerable opportunities to confirm the fact that everything in this world is the creation of Allah. If human beings are attentive enough to 'read' their surroundings, as the first order that Allah gave to the Prophet Muhammad was to 'read' (xcvi:1), things taken for granted due to their ordinariness will be sure to show His touch upon them. This emphasis on everyday life in reformist Islam is an urge to Islamise everyday life, that is, to behave in Islamic ways and to perceive things in an Islamic framework.

To Islamise everyday life is not just an abstract principle but is supported by a web of concrete rules. This web of rules, called Islamic law (*syariah Islam*), encompasses all domains of human life: from ways of praying, fasting and almsgiving to ways of seeking wealth, trading and banking; from ways to sleep, urinate and treat dreams to ways to deal with children, neighbours and relatives; and ways to deal with every phase of the human life cycle, from birth to death. In this respect, the conventional dichotomy that divides human life into the sacred and the profane or the religious and the secular has no significance in reformist Islam. Everything is sacred and religious.

According to the self-evaluation of the reformist villagers, *the* Islam traditionally practised in Kolojonggo was diverted from the ideal state of Islam seen from the reformists' point of view. Some Islamic teachings were over-emphasised, while others simplified or ignored. Circumcision, which does not have clear indications in the Quran, was regarded as a key to making someone a Muslim, so that 'to circumcise' was synonymous with *ngislamaken* (*mengIslamkan*) or 'to Islamise'. By contrast, daily prayer, regarded as the most essential duty of Muslims by the reformist villagers, was not strictly followed. Most villagers did not recognise its significance and only a few practised it. In the framework of traditional Islam, the status of a Muslim was something that could be retained without continuous renewal, whether it had been acquired by reciting *sahadat* (the profession of faith) or by circumcision.

---

[1] Roman numerals in the parenthesis indicate the Surah and the Arabic numerals, the verse(s) in the Quran. Any direct quotation from the Quran is from the translation of M. Pickthall (1930).

Born of the accelerating Islamic development, a group of reformist villagers in Kolojonggo has tried to put their ideals into practice. Their efforts can be rephrased as the Islamisation of everyday life, that is, to view things from an Islamic perspective and to practise what is commanded by Allah in all aspects of their life. This task, however, has not been an easy one, in that they are carrying it out in a society where reformist Islam is not the only way to perceive things and to provide norms of behaviour and where not all of its members are committed to reformist ideas. In spite of these difficulties, their efforts have begun to be visible in village life.

The aim of this chapter is to look at the efforts of the reformist villagers in Kolojonggo to Islamise their everyday life and to see how these efforts are manifested in their life. In the first part of this chapter, one of the most important religious activities of the reformist villagers, namely *pengajian,* will be examined. This is followed by a discussion of daily prayer and the fast, which will clarify the key concept underlying the efforts to Islamise everyday life: consciousness (*kesadaran*). The next part is related to Islamic laws in everyday life. It will be shown that Islamic laws, especially those belonging to the categories of *sunnah* (recommended) and *haram* (forbidden), have played a pivotal role in awakening Muslim consciousness by providing inexhaustible instances highlighting the contrast between the Islamic and the non-Islamic. In the last part of this chapter, some characteristics in the efforts of the reformist villagers to Islamise others' life will be examined.

4.1. Religious Activities of Muslim Villagers

It is not an exaggeration to say that the religious activities of the reformist villagers start from *pengajian* (religious meetings aiming mainly to listen to sermons) and end with it. Apart from the routine *pengajian* held at least once every two weeks, every special occasion in Islam such as the descent of the Quran (*Nuzulul al-Quran*), the end of the fasting month (*Syawal*), sacrifice (*Idul Adha*), the Prophet Muhammad's flight from Mecca to Medina (*Hijrah*), the Prophet's birthday (*Maulud*) and the Prophet's flight from Mecca to Jerusalem and His ascent to Heaven (*Israk-Miraj*) are commemorated by *pengajian*.

Due to the emphasis placed on it by the reformist Muslims, *pengajian* plays a role in connecting reformist intellectuals in the city to illiterate peasants in the rural villages. The *khatib* (preachers) who give their sermons in the hamlet *masjid* become the audience of *pengajian* in their schools or offices.[2] Those who deliver sermons in these schools and offices are the audience of *pengajian* where reformist intellectuals from Islamic universities or national Islamic organisations become the *khatib*. In this manner, the ideas of reformist intellectuals spread gradually from the city to the countryside.

---

[2] Most villagers who work as the *khatib* in *pengajian* in Sumber are either civil servants or teachers.

In Kolojonggo, the routine *pengajian* (*pengajian rutin*) started in the mid-1980s. At the initial stage, the participants were restricted to adult women. Later, men and children were included in the congregation and it started to be held in the *masjid* after its construction in 1988. The number of villagers attending the routine *pengajian* fluctuated in 1993-1994. Sometimes it reached thirty to forty while at other times, it was seventy to eighty. The frequency of celebration also varied. It was sometimes held weekly, sometimes fortnightly. The main reason for this variation was the difficulty of finding suitable *khatib* for *pengajian*. It often happened that those in charge of inviting a *khatib* could not recruit anyone, so that *pengajian* was postponed for a week.

To recruit a *khatib* was not an easy task, due to the qualifications that a *khatib* had to have. First, the *khatib* had to have enough religious knowledge to lead the sermon for an hour or so and he had to be fluent in reciting Arabic. Many of the school teachers and government employees living in the rural villages had this capability but only a few of them fulfilled the second requirement of the *khatib*: humour. As villagers of all ages sat together in one place and many had no education beyond primary school, those who could not hold the attention of the audience with humour were seldom invited. It sometimes happened that the sermons of the *khatib* who were known for their boring speech attracted only a few participants. As a result, the organising body of the *pengajian* was quite cautious in selecting the *khatib*.

A variety of religious issues connected to Islam were dealt with in *pengajian*, many of which were closely related to the villagers' life. For example, the *Hajj*, which is one of the Five Pillars of Islam, was seldom discussed in the *pengajian* except for a brief comment on it during the pilgrimage season. On the other hand, the personal experiences of the *khatib* and their interpretations of these experiences were frequently mentioned in sermons. The passage below provides an example of a *pengajian* held in Kolojonggo. The *khatib*, Pak Bibit, was a high school teacher living in a nearby village.

> At the end of the *maghrib* and *isaq* prayer, the loud speaker on top of the *masjid* announced the time of the Wednesday night *pengajian* and the name of the *khatib*. As the time for the *pengajian* was eight in the evening, those who came to the *masjid* to perform their *isaq* prayer did not return home but stayed there. Unlike other meetings in a Javanese village where the guests begin to appear much later than the planned opening time, most of villagers came to the *masjid* before eight. Female villagers and their children sat on the northern side of the main hall while males sat on the southern side. Half of the western side was occupied by female youth and the other half, by their male counterparts. Most female villagers wore *kerudung*, which covered some of their hair and ears, while a few wore white robes for daily prayer (*rukuh*) covering

all parts of their body except for the face. Many adult men and youth wore rimless caps (*peci)*. When Pak Bibit arrived at ten past eight, all seats in the *masjid* alongside the walls were already filled with villagers.

The chairman of the *pengajian* opened the meeting by asking participants to recite an Arabic prayer together. Then he introduced Pak Bibit, who sat just besides him. Reciting a longer Arabic prayer by himself, Pak Bibit asked forgiveness for being late, adding a comment that to keep the exact time is one of the most precious teachings in Islam. The sermon began with a brief remark on the private television station which had recently started transmission. He mentioned that many programs on that television channel were produced in Western Countries and would bring negative effects on the education of children. He asked the parents to take more care of their children's exposure to the ideas from the West.

The main topic of that night's *pengajian* was dreams. He quoted a passage from the Hadith, saying 'there is no sign of the prophecy except for *al-Mubasiroh*, especially when the Day of Judgement is approaching' and explained what *al-Mubasiroh* means.

> What is *al-Mubasiroh* ? It means a good dream. This shows that even a dream is regulated in Islam. Why? Because many people love to interpret their dreams. From former days until now, people have their own ways of interpreting dreams. When one dreams that one's tooth falls out, this is interpreted to foretell the death of one's brother. To be bitten by a snake is supposed to forecast one's marriage. ... As these examples show, people usually interpret dreams in accordance with their own will.

The next parts of his sermon were rather unsystematic. His remark on the connection between good dreaams and the Day of Judgement led him to talk about the Day of Judgement, which was followed by a speech concerning various symptoms foretelling its coming. As one of its signs is moral decay, he digressed to mention the abuse of the family planning program by the youth and their indecent sexual life. This reminded him of the marriage story between a Muslim female and a Christian male which he had experienced as a government official in the Department of Religion. His story went on and on until cups of tea and snacks began to be distributed to the attendants around quarter past nine, signalling to him that it was time to finish the sermon. Soon, he returned to the original topic and gave a brief interpretation on the passage in the Hadith that he had introduced before: when the Day of Judgement is approaching, the dreams of pious Muslims (*mukmin*) will not deceive. The last part of his sermon was devoted to the way Muslims should treat dreams:

If you dream a good dream, for example, dreaming of peasants harvesting a lot, utter a prayer of *Alhamdulillah* and tell it to others. However, if you dream a bad dream, for example, the dream of being chased by *wewe* (a kind of evil spirit), let's recite the prayer of *Audzubillahimminnassyaitonirrojin* and we don't need to tell it to others. ... We should also spit three times to the left while reciting the above prayer.

A few minutes later, Pak Bibit finished his sermon and the question-and-answer section came. According to the Islamic leaders, this section introduced into this village in 1993 was a recent innovation made by the reformist organisation, Muhammadiyah. It was aimed at inducing more participation from those attending the *pengajian*. For a few months after the introduction, this section did not seem to be successful. Only a few villagers asked questions while the majority remained silent. That night, a middle-aged woman asked an interesting question: what is the Islamic law about eating an egg after it starts to hatch. [3] A moment's thought was enough for him to give her a *fatwa*: it is permitted to eat an egg if the form of a chicken is not yet visible in it. However, when the shape of a chicken is already formed in an egg, it cannot be eaten. This is because Islam prohibits Muslims from eating meat of animals which are not slaughtered in the name of Allah and the chicken in an egg cannot be slaughtered in the prescribed way.

As no more questions were asked, Pak Bibit finished his sermon. The next session was to hear reports from the youth in charge of collecting funds for *Idul Adha*[4] and the announcement of the winner of the *arisan*.[5]

---

[3] At first sight, this seems to be a question for the question's sake and far from the villagers' everyday life. However, this was not the case. A few months before this *pengajian*, the government donated a electrical incubator to hatch out eggs. For unknown reasons, only about twenty percent of the total eggs were successfully hatched, posing the problem of disposing of the eggs which were not hatched. A few male villagers who had a belief that these eggs could be used as an ingredient of traditional medicine (*jamu*) made a deliberate visit to the house where the incubator was located, while some villagers boiled and ate them. In this context, her question in the *pengajian* was closely connected to her own or some other villagers' experience and curiosity. As this case shows, many of the questions asked in the *pengajian* were directly related to their daily life. These could be roughly classified in three categories: about purely religious matters such as prayer, ablution and so on; about Islamic law concerning traditional customs or other individual behaviour such as using incense and wearing golden ornaments; and about issues related to social life, such as giving meat from the sacrificed animal to Christian neighbours.

[4] After the end of *Idul Adha* (day for sacrifice) in 1993, the *takmir masjid* (the *masjid* council)initiated a program to collect money for *Idul Adha* in 1994. This plan was based on the idea that a Muslim who pays a part of the total sum to buy a sacrificed animal also carries out the recommended duty of sacrifice. Around forty villagers participated in this program and collected around Rp 100,000 for a year, the sum of which was slightly short of buying a sheep. This money was used to buy mutton on the day of *Idul Adha* in 1994.

[5] *Arisan* is a rotary credit system. The participants pool a fixed sum of money together and one or two of them receive the whole money thus collected. It finishes when all the participants have

After that, the *pengajian* ended with collective recital of an Arabic prayer. Although it was around ten in the evening, Pak Bibit did not go home directly. With a few male villagers and youths, he chatted for around an hour concerning religious activities in Kolojonggo as well as other issues related to Islam. It was already half past eleven when the last villager left the *masjid*, turning off the lamp and closing the door.

Although somewhat discursive, the sermon of Pak Bibit was one of the most popular ones in Kolojonggo. As he inserted many personal experiences and his interpretations of them, his *pengajian* was not like a formal religious class in schools but more like story telling. Laughter was one of the important elements in his sermon. This characteristic of his was shared by most of the *khatib* who gave regular sermons in Kolojonggo. They avoided being excessively scholastic, but used their personal experiences as similes to convey their ideas to the audience. As they were born and lived in the rural area, their experiences easily appealed to ordinary villagers and could hold their attention.

Compared with religious programs for adult villagers, the *pengajian* for children were more dynamic and experimental. Efforts were constantly made to renew the *pengajian* and to add new programs to it. The two hour *pengajian* per week was divided into two. The first half was devoted to learning to read Arabic, the skill which the reformist villagers regard as one of the most important duties of a Muslim, while the second half was to learn the recommended behaviour of Muslims, short Arabic prayers and anecdotes about the Prophets. Four to six youths became teachers and the primary school children were the main participants, although a few pre-school children and junior school students were also present.

All the participants in the children's *pengajian* were divided into several groups in accordance with their ability to read Arabic: a preliminary course to learn Arabic script, a secondary course to learn to read Arabic phrases and an advanced course to learn how to read the Quran. Except for the advanced course, the others used a six-volume text which could be easily bought in the market. The teaching was done on the premise that children did not review their previous learning at home. A progress report was made for each child on which the volume and page that they had learned the previous weeks and the teacher's evaluation were written, so that the teacher could check the lesson that a child had learned before. As a result, progress was slow. Each week only two or three new pages were added. In this way, it took two to three months or longer to complete one volume. In the beginner's course, one teacher dealt with one child at a time. The pronunciation of each character was taught to the child, who was asked to repeat it. In the secondary course, one teacher taught two or three children at one time

received their due amount of money. As the majority of attendants at *pengajian*, especially women, participated in *arisan*, it encouraged their regular attendance at *pengajian*.

while in the advanced course, the group was the main unit for study. A child read a certain phrase of the Quran, which was repeated by the teacher and other students.

After the meeting with a teacher which lasted for around 10 minutes, children were given free time for play. Playing with others for a short while, children were called again for the next session, consisting of story-telling, a short sermon, collective exercise of Arabic prayer, sing-along, reading poems and so on. In the case of the sing-along, the original text of a song was replaced with that related to Islam. Below is a new text of *'Burung Kakak Tua'*, one of the most popular children's songs in Indonesia:

> *Tuhan Saya Au'llah*[6] (My God is Allah)
>
> *Au'llah Tuhan Saya* (Allah is My God)
>
> *Tuhan Bukan Au'llah* (God who is not Allah)
>
> *Bukan Tuhan Saya* (is not my God)[7]

Compared with other well-developed organisations in the city claiming that six months or less is enough for them to teach a child to read the Quran, the progress of children in Kolojonggo was slow. Even a year was not enough for ordinary children to master a six-volume textbook, which was considered as the prerequisite to start reading the Quran. Children's lack of passion for learning Arabic, lack of any effective teaching method and lack of time seemed to be responsible for that.

The efficiency of the *pengajian*, however, did not bother the teachers. They were of the opinion that accelerating the pace of learning was not the primary goal of the *pengajian*. The more important points were to mobilise children regularly to religious activities and to let them get accustomed to a religious environment. The childhood experience of the teachers confirmed the relevance of this approach. They learned to read Arabic with less well-developed textbooks and teaching methods and their progress was much slower than the present children. There was even a teacher who said that he had spent almost six years in the course before he could begin to read the Quran. Despite this, they did learn to read the Quran in the long run and were more active in religious activities than others who had been quicker to read. As the remarks of the teachers show, the role of the *pengajian* for children was not just to teach how to read Arabic but to build a bridge to connect children with religious activities and to solidify the bond between the teachers and children who would replace the teacher's position

---

[6] The need to pronounce Arabic correctly is emphasised to children. In the *pengajian* for children, Islamic God is pronounced as 'Au'llah' with deep vocal sound rather than usual Indonesian term 'Allah'.
[7] The original text goes as follows: *Burung Kakak Tua/Hinggap di Jendela/ Nenek Sudah Tua/ Giginya Tinggal Dua.*

in the future. When this bond was established and children came to be conscious of the need to read the Quran, learning to read Arabic was said to be only a matter of time. Even a week was enough for someone to learn to read the Quran.

The routine *pengajian* alone was not sufficient to maintain the bond between children and Islam on the one hand and between children and the Islamic activists on the other, since children's interest in Islam was not retained with ease. They were quickly bored at the *pengajian*, as was easily recognised by the gradual decrease in the number of participants in it. To overcome this setback, the teachers organised special activities. In 1993-1994, they held three special meetings for children. As no meetings were held for children in village life, these occasions were enthusiastically received by children. Almost all Muslim children appeared, although it started around eight and finished around ten in the evening. In these meetings, several children came to the fore to recite Arabic passages from the Quran and to sing a song while the teachers prepared a short drama. The effectiveness of this measure to mobilise children was quickly proved. After these meetings, the number of participants in the routine *pengajian* increased dramatically.

Like those for adult villagers and children, the routine religious activity for the youth was called *pengajian* and held regularly once a week. Differing from other *pengajian*, that for the youth did not have any fixed format, and the organisers made programs rather spontaneously. In 1993-1994, these included recitation of the Quran from the first to the last page, courses to learn to play musical instruments and to sing songs called *Qosidah*, courses in how to give a sermon, and meetings with the youth from other villages or from the city. The participants in the *pengajian* for the youth were confined mainly to the *anak masjid* and the youth outside this group seldom attended it.

The *anak masjid* constituted the core group to make the acceleration of Islamic development in Kolojonggo possible. They were the main body planning, organising and carrying out all religious activities with the help of a few adult villagers. According to my estimation, the *anak masjid* consisted of nineteen youths aged between 15 and 25, about one fourth of the total Muslim youth in this age group, while three unmarried villagers in their late twenties could also be added to the *anak masjid*.[8] My estimation largely coincided with the opinions of some youths who were not included in this group when they were asked to enumerate the youths who belonged to the *anak masjid*.

Everyday life of the *anak masjid* could not be separated from religion. Apart from daily prayer, they were involved in a variety of religious activities both within and outside the hamlet. Observing these activities merely for a month is

[8] Seven of the *anak masjid* were high school students, two of them were university students, two of them were unemployed after their graduation from high school and the rest worked in the manufacturing, constructing and service sectors.

enough to appreciate how closely their life was connected to Islam or, in other words, how they Islamised their life. As an example, the monthly schedule of Mas Sigit, an unofficial leader of the *anak masjid*, is presented below:

Table IV.1: Religious Activities of an Islamic Activist

	Weekly (w) or Fortnightly (f) Activities	Monthly Activities
Sun	*Pengajian* in the *kelurahan* office[a] (w)	
	Pengajian for pre-school children[b] (w)	
Mon	Distribution of alms (f)	BAZIS[c] meeting in the *kelurahan* office
		Tahlilan I (Tuesday-*Kliwon*)
Tue		
Wed	*Pengajian* for adult (w or f)	
Thu	*Pengajian* for youth (w)	*Tahlilan* II (Friday-*Kliwon*)
Fri		BAZIS meeting in Kolojonggo
Sat	*Pengajian* for school children (w)	

[a] The branch of Muhammadiyah in Sumber started its weekly *pengajian* in the *kelurahan* office from the late 1970s on. Compared with those at the hamlet level, *pengajian* in the *kelurahan* office had one difference. The organising body of the Sunday *pengajian* tried hard to invite the *khatib* from outside Sumber and preferably from the city, so that the *khatib* invited to this *pengajian* were usually those who had not delivered a sermon in the hamlet *masjid*.

[b] In 1994, the *anak masjid* opened another *pengajian* for pre-school children, separated from that for primary school children.

[c] BAZIS is the abbreviation of *Badan Amil Zakat, Infaq dan Shadaqah* or Committee to coordinate almsgiving activities. This organisation was founded by an initiative of the government in the early 1990s and the branch of BAZIS in Sumber was established in 1992. This body was responsible for collecting voluntary donations from Muslim villagers and carried out several activities to improve the economic condition of Muslim villagers and to assist poor Muslims. Apart from being incorporated with BAZIS activities at the *kelurahan* level, Muslim villagers in Kolojonggo made their own program to help their neighbours. In 1993-1994, BAZIS in Kolojonggo distributed rice to the old and poor villagers, subsidised part of school fees for children of poor families and gave out religious necessities such as books and praying clothes to children.

Table IV-1 shows that Mas Sigit attended religious meetings more than four or five times a week. However, the above table just shows the official side of his religious activities. Apart from participating in these meetings, he spent extra time preparing for them. For example, he called at dozens of households to collect alms for the BAZIS meeting and visited Islamic leaders to invite them as the *khatib* in the *pengajian*. The preparation for the special occasions in the Islamic calender also required his time. When three large-scale gatherings for children were organised, he spent two to three weeks each time in rehearsing the drama which would be staged at these meetings. In the fasting month, he stayed in the *masjid* all evening and sometimes until dawn. For *Maulud, Israk-Miraj* and *Hijrah*, he went to several *pengajian* held in the neighbouring villages while he prepared for the same kind of *pengajian* in Kolojonggo. *Tahlilan* was another occasion in which he spent many of his evenings, since he also attended irregular *tahlilan* held after the death of Muslim villagers. [9]

The participation of other *anak masjid* in religious activities was almost the same as Mas Sigit. The male youth, in particular, attended *pengajian, tahlilan* and other religious meetings, and in the fasting month, slept together in the *masjid*. The common activities of the *anak masjid* was not confined to religious ones. In the evenings when there were no religious activities, they played together in the *masjid* or in the house of one of their members. The close relationship both in the religious and non-religious domains made possible strong peer group solidarity among the *anak masjid*. Their solidarity, however, was not always advantageous for them to carry out religious programs among their age group. As their group had a clear boundary, those placed outside of it felt uneasy mixing with them.

The *anak masjid* were quite conscious of the fact that their religious activities were too exclusive to incorporate the youth outside the boundary of their group. In order to overcome this limitation, they organised several special occasions, aiming to incorporate as many Muslim youth as possible. They visited the *masjid* in other villages to discuss religious issues with the youth there and made several recreational visits to tourist destinations. In the latter case, participation was open only to the Muslim youth, signifying that these visits were parallel with other religious activities, although religious elements were not clearly visible in them. These special activities incorporating other Muslim youth had the same purpose as those for children, namely, to consolidate the relationship between Muslims rather than to deepen their knowledge of Islam.

Since the *masjid* was constructed in the late 1980s, the Muslim community in Kolojonggo has seen an increase and diversification of religious activities. All Muslim villagers are allocated to certain routine activities such as *pengajian* and *tahlilan* while celebrations of the special Islamic days and of the fasting month play a role in breaking down the ordinariness of routine religious activities. One of the impacts of this development is that more opportunities have been given to the children born after the 1980s to be raised in a different religious environment from their parent. While the adult villagers as children accompanied their parents to tombs to ask blessings from the deceased, visited *dhukun* for healing or wandered around *sawah* eating offerings made to the goddess of rice, children now go to the *pengajian* with their mother, eavesdrop on the Arabic recitation in *tahlilan*, see their parents donate to BAZIS and witness the last breath of a sacrificed bull or sheep in the front yard of the *masjid*. This

---

[9] The duration of *tahlilan* after the death of a Muslim villager was dependent on the family of the deceased. Sometimes, it was celebrated in parallel with the cycle of *kendhuri*, that is, one, three, seven and thirty-five days after death while in others, it lasted throughout the first week after death. In several cases, it was held just once on the night of death. Whatever the case, Mas Sigit attended all of these *tahlilan*.

development does not imply that the religious atmosphere has been totally changed to the extent that traditional religious elements which are perceived to be incongruous with reformist Islam have been uprooted. These still constitute a part of village life (see Chapter V and VI). Rather, the importance of the expansion of Islamic activities has been that these provide the younger generation with more opportunities from their childhood on to be in constant contact with an alternative mode of religious life to the traditional one. Unlike adult villagers who spent their childhood walking several kilometres to watch *wayang* (shadow play) and sleeping there until the end of the performance, the children of these days go to the *masjid* with their mother and sleep there, hearing Arabic prayers and religious sermons as lullabies.

4.2. *Salat* and the Fast

In Kolojonggo, all ritual prayers, whether they are optional or obligatory, are called *salat*. When the term *salat* is used by itself, it customarily designates daily prayer while other prayers are designated by a specific modifier such as *salat Id, salat Istikha, salat jenazah* and so on. Daily *salat* is one of the Five Pillars of Muslims, called *rukun Islam*; others include the recitation of *sahadat*, the fast, almsgiving and pilgrimage to Mecca.

In contrast to traditionally practised Islam, reformist Islam puts absolute priority on daily *salat*. No one can be a pious Muslim (*Muslim sholeh*) without practising it. Daily *salat* was frequently compared to provisions or travelling funds (*sangu*) for the Hereafter: whether one practises *salat* or not will be the most important criterion to decide one's future placement either in Paradise or Hell. The reformist leaders were unanimously of the opinion that someone who did every good deed in this world except *salat* would be unable to enter Paradise, as a villager put it: 'if there is a Muslim who carries out *salat* but is stingy, he or she will enter Hell, but not for so long. If there is a person who does not perform *salat* but is generous, he or she will enter Hell for good.'[10] The performance of daily *salat* was used by the reformist villagers as a criterion to judge the religiosity of Muslims and, by a few, to differentiate pious Muslims from unbelievers (*kafir*). This is because one's outer self (*lahir*) is the delegate of one's inner self (*utusan batin*), so that one's outward behaviour cannot cover what is in one's heart (*hati*) (See also Bowen,1993:320; cf. Pranowo,1991). This emphasis placed on *salat* then allows the practice of daily *salat* to beemployed as a basis for making a conjecture about the non-religious behaviour of those the reformist villagers newly meet. Below is an example of this trend among the reformist villagers:

[10] Asked questions about whether people, who happened to be born in non-Islamic countries but lived an ethical life in the way recommended in Islam, would enter Paradise, all reformist leaders interviewed answered that these people might not enter Paradise. However, they did not take a dogmatic but a reserved attitude toward the question. After replying to a 'Yes-or-No' question, many of them commented that their answer was based on their interpretation of the Quran and Hadith and it was only Allah who would decide the future of all human beings in the last instance.

For the first six months, I conducted research with my Indonesian friend whom I had met in the city before I settled in Kolojonggo. He was, at least to me, a 'good' and a well-informed Muslim. He performed daily *salat* although not regularly, attended the Friday sermon regularly, carried out the fast throughout the whole fasting month, tried hard not to violate what was forbidden by Islam such as drinking alcohol and had more radical Islamic views about socio-religious issues than other villagers; he supported the dispatch of a voluntary Muslim army from Indonesia to Bosnia; he was an enthusiastic supporter of the Islamic party in Indonesia (PPP); he expressed his deep concern about the expansion of Christianity in Yogyakarta and so on. In terms of religious knowledge, he memorised more Arabic prayers and knew more about religious teachings than most of the *anak masjid*. In spite of these, his interests in and devotion to Islam were not clearly visible in the eyes of the Muslim villagers. For about half a year of his stay in Kolojonggo, his visits to the hamlet *masjid* were confined to a few occasions when I visited it. He sometimes prayed daily *salat* but in our room, while he went to the *masjid* near his own house in the city to attend the *Jumatan* and to participate in the *tarawih* prayer. After he had left Kolojonggo and as my relation with the *anak masjid* grew closer, I was surprised to find he was regarded as a bad Muslim by them. Some of them firmly believed he was accustomed to drinking alcohol, gambling, going to discotheques, visiting prostitutes and so on. This negative evaluation may be ascribed to various factors.[11] However, as some of them frankly told me, the most important factor for the *anak masjid* to reach this conclusion was that he did not visit the hamlet *masjid* for daily *salat*. As there was no other way for them to know whether he prayed *salat* in our room or not, his rare visits to the *masjid* were equated with his negligence in daily *salat*, which allowed them to construct a negative image of him. As this case shows, performance of daily *salat* was used by the reformist villagers as a basis to evaluate both the religious and non-religious orientations of others.

Muslims are ordered to perform *salat* five times a day. The name, timing and *roka'at*[12] of each *salat* are as follows:

---

[11] One of these might be his readiness to be a friend of a foreign researcher or, possibly at the initial stage of my stay in Kolojonggo, a foreign tourist. Villagers had a negative view of Indonesians who were ready to mix with foreign tourists, believing that these Indonesians were willing to drink alcohol and were sexually promiscuous.

[12] *Roka'at* refers to essential unit of prayer, from the standing position, through bowing and prostration, to the sitting position.

Name	Beginning	End	*Roka'at*
Subuh	Dawn	before *Duhur*	2
Duhur	Noon	before *Asar*	4
Asar	Around 3 PM	before *Maghrib*	4
Maghrib	Sunset	before *Isaq*	3
Isaq	Around 7 PM	before *Subuh*	4

One should do a certain *salat* by a fixed time. For example, one cannot perform *subuh* after noon, the time reserved only for *duhur*. Due to this, daily *salat* is compared to one's life. As life is given just once, so is the chance of each daily *salat* in one's life time. If a person skips *subuh* on one day, he or she will lose the chance to do it forever. This nature of daily *salat* makes it a necessity to carry it out on time.

The simple but the most correct answer as to why Muslims do *salat* is because Allah commanded them to do so. The replies that the reformist villagers made to the subsequent question of why Allah did so were not unitary. Some talked about the value of *salat* for this world and the Hereafter: Allah revealed that *salat* would make their wishes come true with ease and give them a place in Paradise. Others attached additional meanings to it: *salat* is a moment of remembrance, that is, to remember Allah, His grace to human beings, His greatness and the connectedness between Him and human beings. *Salat* was also interpreted as an occasion of repentance: as human beings keep committing intentional or unintentional sins in their daily life, they ask forgiveness, by performing *salat,* for their sins to Allah who has the right to grant it. There were also some who viewed *salat* in relation to human desire (*nafsu*). The difficulty of practising regular *salat* was equated with temptation by *satan* who distanced human beings from the right path. *Salat* was then conceptualised as a moment where the religious devotion of Muslims and their victory over *satan* was displayed. Still others talked about the relationship between human beings reflected in *salat*, often called the horizontal side of *salat* to distinguish it from the vertical one between human beings and Allah. The last movement of *salat*, which is to utter a greeting (*salam*) while turning the upper body to right and left, was interpreted as a sign that one cannot live a life without others to the right and left of oneself. Therefore, this movement was considered to be a gesture of inviting other human beings into fraternity (*ukhuwah*) and solidarity. The diverse interpretations of *salat* have one common theme: it is conceptualised as a moment where one's self-consciousness should be awake to the extent that one is conscious of one's connection with Allah and fellow human beings and aware of whether one's behaviour and thoughts are congruent with Islamic teachings or not.

If *salat* provides moments where one's consciousness as a Muslim can be heightened, the fast plays the same role for one month in the year. Villagers' interpretations of the fast were similar to those of *salat*: a chance to obtain high religious merit; an opportunity to cleanse oneself of previous sins and to ask forgiveness; a fight against one's physical desire (*nafsu*) or *satan*; and an occasion to experience and sympathise with the state of people who suffer from poverty. Whatever meanings were attached to it, the most crucial point in practising the fast was considered to keep one's consciousness awake. This is because the mere act of abstaining from eating cannot make the fast perfect, but one has to monitor continuously whether one's behaviour and thought are congruent to Islamic teachings or not. For example, to see, speak, feel and perform anything bad or forbidden was said to make the fast invalid. As a result, one should not be angry with others, vilify others, have lust for sex, and so on. This does not mean, however, that one has to void one's mind and body from any kind of desire (*nafsu*). Rather, what is intended in these rules is that one has to be conscious of the fact that he or she practises the fast and that desire should be controlled with this consciousness, as Mas Harto said:

> As an imperfect human being, I cannot restrain myself from sudden desire and from seeing and hearing what is forbidden by Allah. When I happened to see a girl wearing a mini skirt passing by, I sometimes looked at her once again, an action which might cancel the effect of my fasting. ... Because I am a man, I cannot suppress desire to look at a beautiful woman. What is more important to me is to be conscious of the fact that I violate the rules of the fast and to rebuke myself. As long as my consciousness is awake and I do not follow my desire further, I believe, Allah will forgive me and accept my fasting.

In this example, the primary goal of Mas Harto in practising the fast was not to be free from any human desires. According to him, desires could not be eradicated from human nature. It was not unusual that sexual desire was aroused in his mind on seeing a woman even in the fast month. Thus, Mas Harto believed that the appearance of desire in his mind, for example the desire to see a beautiful woman once again, did not invalidate the fast. Instead, what would invalidate his fasting was the next step after he found his desire was aroused: whether he did anything further to satisfy his desire either in imagination or in reality. If he did nothing further, his fasting would not be cancelled. In explaining this delicate difference between the valid and invalid fast, the emphasis of Mas Harto is placed on whether he keeps his consciousness awake to the extent that he keeps watching over his behaviour and thought or not. If he can do so, his fasting might be accepted by Allah, whereas if not, his endurance of thirst and hunger is simply for nothing.

Overall, *salat* and the fast are interpreted by the reformist villagers as the media to awaken their consciousness that their life is connected to and dependent on Allah and that their behaviour and thought should conform to commands from

Allah. However, these two occasions are not enough to keep that consciousness. When they finish *salat* and get through the fasting month, their heightened consciousness can easily be overwhelmed by daily life. Therefore, the goal of the reformist villagers in Islamising everyday life is to keep a heightened Muslim consciousness in ordinary life. This goal is achieved by incorporating a variety of Islamic laws which dichotomise things into the Islamic and the non-Islamic. Repeatedly inculcated, these laws can become junctures in everyday life which allow Muslims to be conscious of whether their behaviour and thought are congruent with Islamic teachings. In the section below, Islamic law at work will be examined. This discussion, however, includes only those which were frequently emphasised by the reformist villagers.

4.3. Islamic Law and Everyday Life

Islamic law categorises human behaviour into five classes: obligatory (*wajib*); recommended (*sunnat* or *sunnah*); neutral (*mubah*); not recommended but not forbidden (*makruh*); forbidden (*haram*). Villagers frequently used the dichotomy of sin (*dosa*) and religious merit (*ganjaran* or *pahala*) to explain these categories: *wajib* is that behaviour which will bring *ganjaran* if carried out and will be *dosa* if neglected; *sunnah* is that which will bring *ganjaran* if carried out, but will not be a *dosa* if neglected; *mubah* is that which brings neither *ganjaran* nor *dosa*; *makruh* is that which will bring *ganjaran* if not performed but will not be a *dosa* if practised; and *haram* is that which will not bring *ganjaran* if not performed but will be a *dosa* if practised.

Islamic law was one of the main themes in *pengajian*, although not all five categories were dealt with equally. In the 1980s, *wajib* behaviour was the most frequently discussed topic, since basic and elementary teachings were needed for village Muslims who had not had enough opportunities to be exposed to Islam teachings. In 1993-94, the focus was on *haram* and *sunnah*, although the teachings connected to *wajib* were not ignored.

When asked about the concept of *haram*, many Muslims gave the example of food. Pork, meat of dog and cat [13], and blood were cited as items of forbidden food and the act of eating them was called *haram*. The process of preparing food was also said to make a certain food *haram*. The meat of animals which were not slaughtered in the name of Allah but killed in another manner was categorised

---

[13] Several verses in the Quran (e.g., ii:173 and v:3) categorise pork as forbidden but the Quran does not make any clear remark on meat of dog and cat. Muslim villagers in Kolojonggo, however, categorised meat of such animals as dog, cat and tiger (because they have canine teeth), snake and frog (because they live in two different worlds), and owl and hawk (because they eat with their feet), as forbidden. They based their ideas of forbidden meat on the Hadith. Some of them knew that there was disagreement among Islamic scholars (*ulama*) as to, for example, whether dog meat should be categorised as forbidden or not. However, they suggested that, when they were not sure of the Islamic law related to eating dog meat, it was better for them not to do so. This is because, if there is something the identity of which is ambiguous, Islam teaches that Muslims should not do it.

as forbidden. Among these animals, dog received much more attention from the reformist villagers. Unlike cats, dogs together with pigs are categorised as dirty animals (*najis*). Muslims should cleanse their bodies when they have any physical contact with a dog or pig. Other reasons for the dog's special position were that many villagers raised dogs [14]; dog meat could be purchased more easily than pork; and dog meat was eaten by villagers who believed in other religions or did not take their duties as Muslims seriously. In this social environment, the reformist villagers were very cautious in dealing with dogs and their reaction sometimes seemed excessive to an outsider. The following example typifies their attitude:

> Mas Sargino was working in a construction site as an assistant supplying a mixture of cement, ash and water to the masons. The owner of the house where he worked kept two dogs, which did not stop wandering around the work site. It happened on one hot afternoon that a dog approached a big bucket filled with water and sniffed it. On seeing this, Mas Sargino yelled at it and chased it away. The bucket was quite big, so that in order to fill it, he had to go four or five times to the nearby well around 30 metres from his work place. In spite of this, he quickly threw out the water in that bucket and did extra work to refill it.

As the water in that bucket was only used to mix the cement and the dog did not seem to lick it, Mas Sargino's action was a bit strange. When asked why he did so, he said briefly, 'to guard himself' (*menjaga diri*). He did not say from what he wanted to guard himself, but it is reasonable to assume that as dog belongs to *najis*, he wanted to guard himself from *najis* by not using the water it had contaminated.

Mas Sargino's attitude is not unusual among the reformist villagers. For example, in one case when a dog happened to break into the *masjid* for a short while, a dozen of the youth spent their whole morning cleaning the *masjid* of *najis*. The reformist villagers tried to avoid any kind of physical contact with dogs, so that when a dog approached them, they made every effort to escape from it or to chase it away. This sometimes brought about awkward situations since many households kept a dog. One of these occurred when the reformist villagers visited a neighbour's house. When the dog in that house approached them, they could not take any direct action to drive it away since that was regarded as an action that would insult the host. The measure that they took was just to change their

---

[14] Most reformist villagers suggested that to raise dogs is not forbidden in Islam on the condition that certain rules are strictly observed. These rules include: the purpose of raising dogs should not be to sell them for profit but to guard the house; one should control one's dogs so that they may not disturb neighbours; one should keep dogs out of his or her house; and one should make a separate place for dogs outside the house. According to the reformist villagers, it is not easy to observe these rules, so that it is better for them not to raise dogs.

sitting position little by little, so that they could escape from the sniff of the dog.

Apart from food, other topics which were frequently discussed in the *pengajian* included gambling and drinking, both of which belong to the category of *haram*. Recently, these two issues have become more important than food items, for these activities have been gaining in popularity.

Gambling in this village had a long tradition. A few village elders mentioned it had existed since their childhood. As the general economic situation improved, the amount of money used in gambling also escalated. In 1993-94, it was around Rp 500 for one game and tens of thousand Rupiah were used for one night's play. The primary difficulty in tackling the issue of gambling was the abundance of venues for playing cards. Wherever opportunities presented themselves for dozens of villagers to gather until late night, whether it be in a house, a guard post or even a cemetery, villagers played cards. As villagers did night watch every night and *jagongan* were quite frequently held, a venue for gambling could be found easily by someone who wanted to gamble. Due to the abundance of venues for gambling and the publicity, most villagers knew exactly who gambled and who did not.

Compared with gambling, drinking is quite a new phenomenon since alcohol was only introduced into this village around a decade ago. Due to this short history, drinking was mainly confined to the younger generation. To some of the youth, the only obstacle to drinking alcohol was its high price. A bottle of whisky cost around Rp 2000 to 4000 or the equivalent of the daily wage of a labourer, a sum they could not easily afford. The high cost created a custom that some drank alcohol collectively. Several youth pooled their money, bought one or two bottles and drank together. This collective action made it possible for the drinkers to behave in a braver manner, so that it sometimes happened that those who were drunk made a fuss in public by fighting, singing and so on.

In the *pengajian*, gambling and drinking were described as temptation by *satan*. The reformist leaders believed that drinking was the most serious sin in Islam, since drunken men had a higher potential to commit other sins such as adultery, robbery, murder and so on. The *pengajian* as well as other religious meetings dealing with gambling and drinking gave the impression that public discussions about these two issues were not aimed at decreasing the number of gamblers and drinkers among Muslim villagers. Above all, those who customarily drank and played cards never appeared in those meetings. As they did not attend the *pengajian*, they had no chance to listen to the sermons against drinking and gambling. On the other hand, these discussions were also not designed to encourage the attendants of the *pengajian* to make efforts to guide the gamblers and drinkers in the right direction. The villagers who attended the *pengajian* were not brave enough to advise their neighbours or family members not to drink and not to play cards. In spite of this lack of direct connection between the discussions on drinking and gambling and actual practices of drinking and gambling, these sermons had a significant but indirect impact on the religious life of those who did not drink nor gamble.

When drinking and gambling were discussed among villagers in general, Islam was not the only reference point from which these practices were evaluated. Government officials, teachers and Christians had their own viewpoint: they criticised alcoholism and gambling primarily because these were closely related to negative social phenomena such as crime and poverty. Therefore, to them, the issues of drinking and gambling were mainly social rather than religious problems. By contrast, the reformist villagers viewed drinking and gambling from the perspective of Islam. To them, drinking and gambling had to be prohibited because they were forbidden by Allah while other negative aspects of alcoholism and gambling were regarded as the reasons why Allah forbade them. By emphasising Islam as a reference point to look at a particular phenomenon, what the reformist villagers did consciously and unconsciously was to resist the secularisation of religious issues and to re-position them in an Islamic perspective.

As the cases of drinking and gambling show, one of the processes of Islamising everyday life is to use an Islamic perspective to look at certain social events. Islamic laws categorised as *sunnah* provide an Islamic perspective as an alternative to non-Islamic ones such as tradition, social norms, justice, humanity and so on. Below is a simple example of how *sunnah* can be utilised to reinterpret generally accepted social norms. This list was obtained from several *pengajian* delivered by a few *khatib*:

1) To wash hands

2) To recite *Basmillah* before eating

3) To use right hand

4) To take dishes placed close to oneself and not to take those far from one's seat

5) Not to touch food which one does not like

6) Not to eat more as soon as one feels full

7) To recite *Alhamdulillah* after eating

If the second, the third and the seventh are omitted, this list can be easily mistaken for the manual of table etiquette for children. With the emphasis put on them by the reformist villagers, however, this simple list becomes one of the Islamic laws commanded by Allah and to practise it is regarded as a part of *ibadah* or an act of devotion in its broadest sense.

Unlike the Quran which contains words of Allah, the Hadith is the collection of exemplary behaviours and comments of the Prophet Muhammad. As the Prophet lived the same life as other human beings, the contents of the Hadith cover all domains of social life. Of the recommended behavioural norms (*sunnah*) in the Hadith, what was often delivered in the *pengajian* included: how to bathe, to wear clothes, to urinate, to greet others, to receive guests, to enter houses or cemeteries, and to live a harmonious social life. Although some of these look trivial to an outsider, the attitude of the reformist villagers to observing what they knew as *sunnah* was sincere and serious. Below is one of my encounters with an unexpected manifestation of Islamic law at work:

> I went to the hospital with some of the *anak masjid* to visit one of their parents who was being treated for diabetes. Shortly after we had arrived, the time for *maghrib* prayer came and they decided to go out for a prayer. One of them then approached me and asked me to exchange his brand new shoes for the sandals that I was wearing. He seemed worried that his shoes might get wet in the ablution place. When I took off one of my sandals and waited for him to give me one of his, he spoke to me in a somewhat loud voice. 'No, not this one.' At first, I thought I had misunderstood his intentions. However, I was soon told that I had to take off my right sandal first. My puzzlement concerning why he was so sensitive about this matter disappeared after I was informed that Muslims were recommended to put on shoes from the right side first.[15]

In addition to recommended behavioural norms, a variety of moral issues extracted from the Quran and Hadith was also frequently emphasised in the *pengajian*. The following is an example of how these moral issues were dealt with. Pak Iman, a high school teacher, cited a passage from the Quran as an introduction to his sermon:

> It was by the mercy of Allah that thou wast lenient with them, for if thou hadst been stern and fierce of heart they would have dispersed from round about thee. ... (iii:159)

He, then, explained what the character of 'stern and fierce of heart' meant:

> The Quranic passage cited above commands us that we should distance ourselves from the characteristics stemming from a stern and fierce heart.

---

[15] For several weeks after this incident, one of my research topics was to observe the behaviour of villagers who went into the *masjid*, since I had come to know that a set of rules, which seemed to be quite complex to me, was applied in entering the *masjid*: people should take off their left sandal first and put their left foot on the floor or over the sandal, and then, they should take off the right one and enter the *masjid* with the right foot first. Most of the *anak masjid* observed this rule, while most of villagers in their forties or older did not follow it, including two *kaum* from Kolojonggo and from its neighbouring hamlet who always took off their left sandal and then directly put their left foot on the *masjid* floor. It seems that the younger the villagers were, the more they kept this rule.

> These include, among others, jealousy, envy, to love to complain, to disturb and to oppose others, stinginess, over-confidence, coercion and so on. Someone who has these characteristics is described as someone suffering from heart disease (*penyakit hati*).[16]

The heart disease that Pak Iman mentioned was not a disease that was discovered by recent Islamic development. This was what had been discussed from generation to generation long before. In the traditional society, the stories in the shadow play (*wayang*) and collective recitation of text[17] after the birth of a baby played a role in inculcating these moral principles to the younger generation. Today, the reformist villagers began to view the same moral issues from a different perspective. They were urged to be kind to others, to be harmonious with their neighbours, to help others, to respect parents and to seek after knowledge because of Allah rather than because these would bring harmonious and prosperous life. As Allah commanded Muslims to greet their neighbours, to clean their surroundings, to educate their children, to be introspective, not to be arrogant, not to be jealous, to be responsible, not to talk about others and not to be stingy, each, as a Muslim, should do so. With this shift of perspective, the moral principles which had previously been treated without being referred to Islam were attributed to Islam and 'because of Allah' (*karena Allah*) became the rationale to explain and interpret moral principles and individual behaviours. As one villager put it, the reason why a certain behaviour is considered to be good is not because this is admitted to be good by neighbours, by ancestors or by the state but by Allah.

So far, the efforts of the reformist villagers to Islamise their behaviour and to take an Islamic perspective as an alternative to other possible points of view such as tradition, social norms, justice or humanity have been discussed. As is the case in daily *salat* and the fast, these efforts play a role in expanding the junctures where Muslim consciousness can be heightened. For example, the scenes of gambling or drinking, which may not have any religious significance to some villagers, can be moments to remind the reformist villagers of the contrast between the Islamic and the non-Islamic ways of behaviour and to make them conscious of their identity as Muslims. In this way, the more Islamic laws or

---

[16] The latter part of the sermon was about how to cure heart disease :

Even if one goes to hospital, this sort of heart disease is not curable. Why? Because it starts from one's indifference to the commands from Allah. As one is not faithful to and does not remember the words of Allah, one is given such a disease. Then, who can treat this disease? It is we ourselves. According to al-Gazali, five kinds of medicine are available to treat it: to read the Quran, to empty one's stomach [by regular fasting], to do *dzikir* at night, to do optional *salat* after midnight and to mix with those who are pious.

[17] According to village elders, one of the aims of celebrating *jagongan* after the birth of a baby was to recite books containing ethical norms to the new-born baby. In former days, it also happened that the elders frequently recited songs containing traditional ethics and customs to the baby while they were taking care of it.

Islamic perspective, whether these are the alternatives to other conventional ways of behaviour or new to villagers, are introduced, the more junctures are given villagers to keep their consciousness as Muslims alive.

4.4. The Islamisation of others' everyday life

Compared with the emphasis on the Islamisation of their everyday life, the reformist villagers placed far less emphasis on the Islamisation of the life of those who did not participate in religious activities and who sometimes violated Islamic laws, an activity which can also be called *dakwah* (missionary activities). In 1993 and 1994, no routine *pengajian* and the Sunday morning *pengajian* in the *kelurahan* office included *dakwah* as their main themes. Even the term, *dakwah*, was seldom heard in these *pengajian* and only a few *khatib* mentioned *dakwah* as passing remarks. These give the impression that missionary activities of the reformist villagers in Sumber were largely confined to those who were already ready to hear *pengajian* or to participate in Islamic activities.

The reformist villagers were aware of the fact that the participants in routine religious activities had been confined to a limited number of villagers. In spite of this recognition, however, their efforts to embrace the villagers who did not show interest in religious activities were not remarkable. One of the methods that they employed was to deliver invitation cards to almost all Muslim households whenever a certain religious activity was to be held, although this does not seem to have been effective enough to mobilise a wider circle of Muslim villagers. Another method was to celebrate special religious activities. In 1993, *pengajian akbar* (great *pengajian*) commemorating the special Islamic days such as the descent of the Quran and the end of the fasting month, a visit to the *pesantren* and visits to the *masjid* in other villages were organised to attract those who seldom participated in routine religious activities. The success of these special activities, if measured by the increase in participants, was different according to age. The special *pengajian* for children were enthusiastically received, so that almost all Muslim children in Kolojonggo attended these occasions. In the case of the youth, only a slight increase was visible, so that around ten to twenty youths outside the boundary of the *anak masjid* appeared when they visited the *masjid* in other villages. An increase was also visible when *pengajian akbar* were held. Some of the villagers who usually did not attend routine religious activities visited the *masjid* for these special ones. In spite of this increase, however, the special activities could not achieve one of the original goals, namely, to attract villagers to routine religious activities. Those who attended the special activities confined their participation only to the special ones and most of them did not appear in the *masjid* for the routine ones. In this respect, the celebration of special activities helped the creation of a group of Muslim villagers who attended the special ones but not the routine ones.

The reformist villagers' reluctance to employ more direct measures of *dakwah* such as, for example, to visit religiously inactive villagers to persuade them to participate in religious activities or to suggest to them not to carry out prohibited behaviour, contrasts with their enthusiasm to Islamise their everyday life. This inertia, however, does not seem to have posed a serious problem for the reformist villagers to evaluate their own religious activities. Most of them were of the opinion that, by organising the special activities, they already satisfied their duty as Muslims vis-à-vis other Muslims and that more direct methods for *dakwah* lay beyond their responsibility. One of the Islamic teachings cited frequently by the reformist villagers to support this attitude was that 'there is no compulsion in Islam'. Everyone is responsible for one's own religiosity and one will not bear responsibility for what others do. Some of them extended the relation between Allah and human beings to explain their relation with other villagers. As Allah does not lose anything when human beings do not carry out His commands, they do not suffer any loss when others do not perform their religious duties. There were also some who took a deterministic attitude. According to them, Muslims are to be divided into two groups, a minority of those who are pious and the majority who are not. This division is already determined (*ditakdirkan*) by Allah and cannot be changed by human beings. Therefore, whether people who have been inactive in religious activities and have violated religious laws will change their behaviour or not is dependent on Allah's will rather than on the efforts of human beings. If one's heart is closed by Allah, any measures designed by human beings will not be able to open it. This attitude can go to the extreme, allowing the reformist villagers to take an extremely relativistic position: none of them are certain whether their practice of Islam and their understanding of Islamic teachings are truly Islamic, or, to put it differently, whether they will be placed in Paradise when the Day of Judgement comes. This uncertainty is then used to rationalise their inertia in carrying out missionary activities. If they are not certain of their own behaviour, the priority should be placed on making their own religious practices perfect while they cannot order others to follow the way that they believe is right.

This lack of emphasis on the use of direct methods of *dakwah* seems to be influenced by the guideline stipulated by Muhammadiyah. *The formulae of belief and Ideal in the life of Muhammadiyah members*, for example, guides the aim of Muhammadiyah as follows: 'Muhammadiyah strives for upholding a pure Islamic mode of behaviour (*akidah*) ... without ignoring the principle of tolerance, conforming to the teachings of Islam' (Muhammdiyah, 1969:218). The principle of tolerance in Muhammadiyah teaches that one should appreciate and respect others' position, not to criticise (*cela-mencela*) them and not to force a certain understanding on others (Muhammadiyah, 1963:433-34). This does not imply that Muhammadiyah members should ignore errors and mistakes in the community. However, the right attitude encouraged by Muhammadiyah to deal with these seems to be too tolerant: 'one should not be happy (*tidak senang*) to see deviations from the right way and should have a desire (*ingin*) to change these' (ibid.:440). The principles of *dakwah* proposed by Muhammadiyah based on the principle of tolerance urge then that one should be open of mind, increase companions (*kawan*), widen their relations with other groups and not isolate themselves from the community (ibid.: 434), none of which recommend any direct involvement of Muhammadiyah followers in others' life.

The reformist villagers' attitude of *dakwah* has also been based on dominant norms governing Javanese social life, two of which are the dichotomy of *halus-kasar* and *rukun*. *Halus* means pure, refined, polished, polite, exquisite, ethereal, subtle civilised, smooth, while *kasar* is the opposite of *halus*: impolite, rough and uncivilised (Geertz,1976:232). In social interactions, *halus* ways of behaviour imply restraint and control of one's expression of emotions: although one is happy, angry or annoyed, one should not show these feelings and should maintain emotional calmness. *Kasar* ways of behaviour mean the opposite of *halus* ways: one is quick-tempered, easily shows emotional changes, speaks loudly and in some cases, says what one wants to say. Seen from this *halus-kasar* dichotomy, a recommended way to deal with the situation where one's opinion contradicts others' is to keep silent and to wait until others' ideas are criticised on a mass scale and its holders abandon these by themselves.

When the *halus* ways of behaviour dominate social life, this gives birth to a situation called, *rukun* (harmony). *Rukun* signifies 'a state of agreement, of unanimity in a group concerning its means and purposes, at least in outer behaviour', and thus in practice, it refers to 'the absence of overt interpersonal conflict' (Geertz,1961:149). [18] In this sense, *rukun* is not an abstract concept urging that all human beings should love each other. On the contrary, it presumes that by nature, human beings are egoistic and liable to be in conflict with others. In an atmosphere where the *halus* ways of behaviour and *rukun* dominate social life, the reformist villagers can not take direct and radical measures to carry out their *dakwah* in orderto correct what is considered to be non-Islamic behaviour and to incorporate religiously inactive villagers into religious activities. If one is dissatisfied with others' religious practices, their reaction should be to suppress the expression of this dissatisfaction and, as one villager put it, to let these be for the sake of *rukun*.

---

[18] According to Guinness (1986:131-39), the concept of *rukun* includes not only the negative connotation of social harmony but the positive side of it. *Rukun* as it is practised and conceived, therefore, includes three elements: mutual assistance and reciprocal obligations; respect for senior kin who hold special responsibilities for the welfare of junior kin; and emotional detachment and avoidance of open conflict between them to preserve an appearance of *rukun*. In Kolojonggo, the first two meanings of *rukun* pointed out by Guinness were also used by villagers to explain their participation in community labour, donation of money for the deceased's family, contributions for ritual celebrations and so on. However, the dominant usage of the term *rukun* was to refer to the situation where no conflicts are recognisable from the outside, especially when this concept was related to the *halus-kasar* dichotomy.

The way the reformist villagers discussed religious duty to parents, children and other close family members was somewhat different from the ways they talked about duty to religiously inactive villagers. The term, 'to be obliged to' (*diwajibaken*) was used to explain the duty of parents to guide their children's religious life, in contrast to the use of such terms as 'to suggest' (*mituturi*), 'to invite' (*ngajak*) and 'to remind' (*ngelingaken*) in describing one's religious duty to non-family members. This different treatment might be based on an Islamic teaching that the religiosity of one's children is directly related to one's well-being in the Hereafter. According to the reformist villagers, all the relations between the living and the dead are severed except for three. One of these is the relation between the living children and the deceased parents where the former can send prayers for the latter. This prayer is said to lessen the degree of torture that the deceased suffer in the Hereafter (*alam kuburan*). In this respect, to have children pious enough to pray for their deceased parents is considered one of the blessings that the parents can obtain in this world.

In spite of this scriptural reference encouraging parents to intervene in the religious life of their children, the reformist villagers' actual behaviour in dealing with the religious life of their children was not different from that in dealing with other villagers. They generally confined their duty to giving examples to children. Whether children would follow these examples or not was thought to be dependent on the children's dispositions and the will of Allah. When one's religious activities or religiosity were evaluated by others, it did not seem to be an important fact, at least in public, whether one had been successful in educating one's children or not. In one case where an unmarried high-school-aged daughter of a villager who was an active supporter of Islamic activities and who was sometimes invited as a *khatib* to the *pengajian* became pregnant, this did not seem to damage his reputation. Even after this incident, he kept being invited to the *pengajian* as a *khatib* while no villagers ascribed this incident to his failure to educate his daughter.

This attitude of the reformist villagers in dealing with their children's religious life can also be applied to that of the religiously active children in dealing with their family members. In several cases where children participated actively in religious activities while their parents or siblings did not, the children did not make any efforts to change their religious behaviour. Some of the *anak masjid* whose parents or siblings never appeared in the *masjid* or carried out religiously forbidden behaviour such as drinking or gambling, did not seem to be bothered by these, but considered these as private matters for their family members. In the passages below, a story told by Mas Dono, one of the *anak masjid*, is presented which typifies the attitude of the reformist villagers in dealing with religiously inactive family members and those who violate what is religiously forbidden.

My mother sometimes picked tree leaves from the neighbours' garden in order to use them as ingredients in the vegetable soup. In the hamlet life, people normally do not ask permission to pick these leaves from the tree owners, but take them whenever they need them. In the strict sense, this action is a theft categorised as *haram*, although this generally is not considered so in the community. One night, I saw we were having vegetable soup for dinner. As I was not sure whether the leaves were from neighbours' garden, I asked my mother where she had got the leaves. Obviously, she picked them from the neighbours' garden, probably without getting permission from the owner. Hearing this, I did not want to eat the leaves in the soup. I knew this might hurt my mother's feelings and to hurt parents' feelings was not a recommended behaviour for Muslims. However, as I knew that the leaves had been obtained in a prohibited way, to eat them made me commit a sin. I just avoided eating these leaves, attempting not to show my real thoughts, although what I actually wanted to do was to make my mother recognise my uneasiness and change her behaviour. This state of affair lasted for quite some time. Whenever I was sure that the leaves did not belong to our house, I refrained from eating. Eventually, my mother seemed to have realised why I did not eat the leaves in the soup, although I have no idea how she came to know the reason. She might realise this by seeing the way I ate or someone might have informed her of my uneasiness in eating her leaves. Whatever the reasons, she stopped taking the leaves from her neighbours' garden.

In this case, Mas Dono, seeing his mother violating an Islamic law, did not choose a direct way to correct his mother's behaviour such as informing her that her behaviour was religiously forbidden. Instead, he selected an indirect measure to convey his message, although he was not sure whether his message would be delivered to her and whether this would bring any result or not. This attitude of Mas Dono exemplifies the *halus* way of behaviour to which the reformist villagers resort to carry out their missionary activities. They do not employ the most effective way to achieve a certain goal in *dakwah* but confine their role to giving examples or suggestions. Even the way chosen to do so is one which might offend others as little as possible. This extremely cautious attitude in carrying out *dakwah* has made it possible that no tension and friction have been built up and manifested in public between the reformist villagers and religiously inactive villagers. However, this attitude of 'they-are-they and we-are-we insularity' (Geertz,1990:83) means that there are not many chances for the difference between these two groups in terms of their religious practices and orientations to become narrower. On the contrary, as the reformist villagers intensify their efforts to Islamise their life, the difference has been felt more clearly in much wider domains of social life than it was.

4.5. Summary

In Islam, Muslims are ordered to be conscious of the connectedness between themselves and Allah or, as one Achenese Muslim expressed it, of the rope binding themselves with Allah, the rope which neither rots in the rain nor cracks in the sun (Siegel,1969:115). With their consciousness awakened, Muslims can remember Allah, His mercy and His love to themselves and be thankful to Him for their existence. The earthly life of human beings, however, makes it hard for them to be always conscious of this 'rope'. They easily forget that their life does not exist without the mercy of Allah. As media to overcome this state of oblivion, Muslims are enjoined to practise *salat* five times daily and one month's fasting in a year. These moments provide them with chances to reflect upon the bond between themselves and Allah and to reaffirm the connectedness between themselves and Allah.

To those who feel that daily *salat* and the fast are not enough to keep them conscious of this connection and to make their life closer to Allah, Islamic traditions have offered additional options. As the followers of Sufism have done, they can seclude themselves from the mundane life and spend their time meditating on and remembering (*dzikir*) Allah. In this way, they can Islamise their life, that is, to think and to practise what is related to Islam. Not all Muslims, however, can pursue this way nor are they recommended to. For them, the starting point of Islamising their life is not to isolate themselves from this world but to stick to it.

The efforts of the reformist villagers in Kolojonggo to Islamise their life have followed two lines. On the one hand, they try to increase religious activities. All Islamic days are celebrated and religious meetings are regularly held on ordinary days. As the example of a young reformist villager shows, some of them are involved in a certain religious activity almost every day. On the other hand, they make efforts to increase the junctures in daily life in which their reflexivity as a Muslim can be awakened. This is carried out by replacing non-Islamic perspective on certain social as well as personal affairs with Islamic one. By taking an Islamic perspective, the reformist villagers are given more chances to be conscious of the contrast between the Islamic and the non-Islamic and to prompt themselves to be aware of their thought and behaviour, namely, whether these are congruent to Islam or not. In this way, they do not need to go to isolated places to Islamise their life. They keep their position firmly in the society and try to Islamise their life by transforming their social and personal life into the Islamic one.

In Chapters III and IV, the developmental process of Islam in Kolojonggo and the efforts of the reformist villagers to Islamise their life have been discussed. The following Chapters will be devoted to examining some of the changes which have taken place as Islamic development has accelerated in Kolojonggo. Among these, the focus will be on the relationship between reformist Islam and tradition and between reformist villagers and Christians which have been most fundamentally influenced by the Islamic development.

Plate 5: Salat Idul Fitri in Sumber

Plate 6: Sacrifice of a Sheep for *Idul Adha* in Kolojonggo

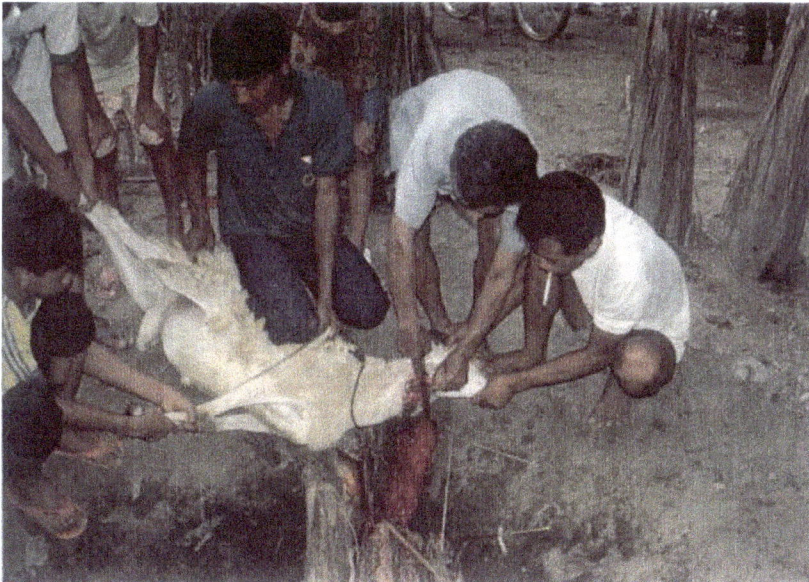

Chapter 5: The Islamisation of Village Tradition

In Kolojonggo, the customs and rituals reported by C. Geertz, R. Jay and Koentjaraningrat in the 1950s are still practised: it is not unusual to see a lamp lit in front of a new-born baby's house; marriages are most frequently held in the Javanese month of *Besar*; flowers and coins are thrown away while the funeral procession parades to the cemetery; incense is burned and offerings are made at tombs; and *kendhuri* are held at each point of passage in an individual's life.

The persistence of these customs and rituals comes as a surprise, considering that Islamic development in Kolojonggo has been led by reformist Islam, while reformist Islam in Indonesia has been said to oppose these practices strongly (Abdul-Samad,1991:65-66; Federspiel,1970:67-83; Geertz,1956:147; Irwan,1994:80; Nakamura,1976:277; Noer,1973:95; Peacock,1978a; Umar Hasyim,1990:1-6). The reasons for this opposition are twofold: these practices have no scriptural basis in the Quran and Hadith and are connected to magical power, negating the Oneness of Allah (*Tauhid*). Seen from this perspective, the persistence of these practices indicates that Muslim villagers in Kolojonggo are far from the right path to Allah and that, by performing these practices, they commit the worst sin in Islam, *syirik* (the negation of the Oneness of Allah)

This contrast raises a few questions: do the reformist villagers in Kolojonggo have the same understanding of traditional practices as reformist intellectuals?; If they have the same opinion, why have their efforts to Islamise all aspects of their life not included the issue of traditional practices and how do they explain their participation in these practices which jeopardise their whole religious life?; If the reformist villagers have a different view of traditional practices from reformist intellectuals, what is their perspective and how do they make them fit reformist Islam?

To answer these questions, this chapter will focus on the ways the reformist villagers in Kolojonggo have dealt with traditional practices which are thought by reformist intellectuals to be incongruent with reformist Islam. No unitary perspective is shared by the reformist villagers, but different individuals have different ideas about different practices. In spite of this diversity, however, two tendencies are clearly visible among the reformist villagers, namely to reinterpret traditional practices and their meanings in Islamic terms and to incorporate Islamic symbols in traditional practices in order to accommodate them better to the new socio-religious situation. In the first part of this chapter, a ritual called *kendhuri* or *slametan* which lies at the centre of all the ritual practices will be the focus; this will be followed by a discussion of some of the rites of passage.

5.1. The Process of *Kendhuri* [1]

After darkness falls on the village, several messengers visit their neighbours, informing villagers of a celebration of *kendhuri* in a certain household. As their coming is already expected, their visit is not a surprise. Taking a seat and exchanging brief greetings with the male head of a household, the messenger conveys the news of *kendhuri* and the intention of the host to invite him. This formal meeting does not last long, just two to three minutes. Soon after his message is delivered, the messenger asks permission to leave for the next house.

A person who is invited wears semi-formal Javanese clothes: a cap (*peci*), a *batik* shirt and a *sarung* or trousers. However, he does not head for the host's house immediately. He waits for his neighbours to come outside or visits them. Although not informed, everyone knows who will go to the *kendhuri* since invitations to the *kendhuri* of a certain household are delivered to the same group of villagers all the time.

The host and his few other close relatives and neighbours stand at the gate, waiting for the guests. They also wear semi-formal Javanese clothes. Whenever a group of guests appears, they smile and shake hands one by one. Then the guests are requested to go into the living room where the *kendhuri* is to be held. Upon entering the room, the guests disperse. Some go further inside the room, away from the door, while others settle down near the door. Except for the hamlet head (*kepala dusun* or *kadus*) who is in his mid 40s, the old villagers who already have a married child usually sit away from the door, near the spot reserved for the officiant of the *kendhuri*, *kaum* [2] . The relatively younger guests find their seats near the door or outside the room when it is crowded. Those who arrive late but are eligible to take inside seats are asked several times to do so by others who have come earlier. As there is usually a space inside the room, it is not difficult to accommodate them. If no space is available, those sitting near the door make room for them, causing a little disturbance. Those who are relatively young but have prestigious occupations such as teacher or civil servant generally do not want to sit inside, although they are usually asked to do so. They prefer to be with other villagers of the same age.

The guests sit down on the floor with their legs crossed. As they lean against the wall, they naturally face those sitting on the opposite side. While waiting

---

[1] Villagers said there is no terminological difference between *kendhuri (kendhuren)* and *slametan* (cf. Hefner,1985:105). As they preferred the former to the latter, the term *kendhuri* will be used here. '*Kendhuri*' is a word derived from Persian, '*kanduri*', meaning 'feast' while '*slametan*' comes from Arabic, '*salama*', meaning 'safe' (Jones,1978:column 42&80). The fact that the term, *kendhuri*, originated from Persian was not known to villagers and they considered it as a word from Javanese, whereas the Arabic origin of '*slametan*' was well known to them.

[2] '*Kaum*' is a title for the officiant of traditional rituals. Installed not by an election but by a consensus of Muslim villagers, he carries out this role until he withdraws from it. It is not a paid position but a small amount of money is usually given to him by the host who uses his service. Every hamlet has its own *kaum*.

for other guests, they talk freely amongst each other. It is not unusual to hear laughter and loud voices. When the room is almost filled, the *kaum* appears. His coming indicates that the *kendhuri* is about to begin.

When no more guests are expected, the ritual foods parceled in a bamboo box (*besek*) are delivered from the outside; in some cases, *besek* are already placed at the centre of the room before the coming of the guests. One *besek* is given to each person. If someone has been invited but does not come, his close neighbour is supposed to take a *besek* for him. Therefore, two or even three *besek* are allocated to those present. For several minutes, the room is once again in an uproar over the number of *besek* to be taken home. In loud voices, the guests keep checking the list of those absent and dispense *besek* to the right persons.

Confirming that each guest has received the due number of *besek*, a representative of the host, usually an old man known for his linguistic skill and closely linked to the host by blood, neighbourhood or friendship, opens the *kendhuri*. His opening remark (*ujub*) generally consists of two parts. First, he asks forgiveness for would-be mistakes in his speech and thanks the guests for coming. Second, he makes the purpose of the *kendhuri* public, for example, a celebration of a birth, and requests the participation of the guests in the coming ritual prayers. Then, he introduces the *kaum* who will take charge of the second phase of the *kendhuri*. Taking his turn, the *kaum* reiterates the intention of the host and recites Arabic prayers. While his prayer is going on, some of the Muslim guests place their flat hands on or over their laps, turn their palms upward and close their eyes. Whenever there is a short pause between the Arabic prayers, they chant '*amin*'. Not all of those present, however, take this position. Some of them sit in silence, focusing their eyes on the mat or the wall. Others whisper to those sitting next to them. They just wait for the end of the Arabic chants which continue for three or four minutes. Rubbing the face with two bare hands signifies the completion of the *kendhuri*. All the guests get up quickly and return home, taking their *besek*.[3]

5.2. Various Occasions to Celebrate *Kendhuri*

Geertz classified *kendhuri* into four categories: life-cycle *kendhuri* which were given at each point of passage in the individual life such as pregnancy, birth, circumcision, marriage and death; calendrical *kendhuri* which were celebrated

[3] Unlike the Protestant dwellers in a slum squatter community in Yogyakarta city where *kendhuri* was not celebrated (Guinness,1986:110), both Protestant and Catholic villagers in Kolojonggo hold *kendhuri*. No remarkable differences are visible in the pattern of the opening remarks between Muslim and Christian villagers except for two features: if the host is a Muslim, the representative and the ritual officiant are Muslims, whereas if Christian, they are Christians; and the ritual prayer of Muslims is uttered in Arabic whereas that of Christians, in high Javanese. Christians have their own ritual officiant, sometimes called *kaum Kristen*. However, the position of the Christian *kaum* is less formalised than that of the Muslim *kaum*. The title of *kaum* is never used to designate the Christian *kaum* in daily interactions whereas the Muslim *kaum* is generally called *Pak kaum*.

in connection with the yearly Muslim calendar; village *kendhuri* concerned with defining and celebrating one of the basic territorial units of Javanese social structure, the village; and intermittent *kendhuri* which were given from time to time for special occasions such as change of residence, change of name, embarking on a journey, bad dreams and so on (Geertz, 1976:38-85). According to the memory of village elders in Kolojonggo, these four categories of *kendhuri* were celebrated in former days, although not all of those listed by Geertz were held in Kolojonggo. For example, villagers did not celebrate the *kendhuri* on the first day of *Sura*, on the birthday of the Prophet Muhammad and on the day of *Miraj*, while the *kendhuri* in the month of *Ruwah* (*Nyadran*), during the fasting month (*Maleman*) and after the fasting month (*Syawalan*) were given.

The occasions for which villagers actually celebrate *kendhuri* are different from what they consider to be the ideal or to have been observed in former days. Some of them are simplified while others are not celebrated at all. The *kendhuri* during the pregnancy of the first baby which are said to have been celebrated three times in former days, namely, at three months (*telung sasinan*), at seven months (*tingkepan* or *mitoni)* and at nine months (*procotan*), are now held only once, usually at seven months. In some cases, a *kendhuri* is not given even at seven months but is replaced with the delivery of a dish of foods only to a few close neighbours of the pregnant woman (*bancakan*). *Kendhuri* after birth also show the same pattern. Three *kendhuri* which are said to have been previously held, namely, on the day of the birth (*brokohan*), after five days (*pasaran*) and after thirty five days (*selapanan*), are simplified into one, so that it is generally *selapanan* at which the *kendhuri* is given. In the case of circumcision and marriage, the frequency of *kendhuri* follows the ideal pattern, namely, once for each occasion. *Kendhuri* after death which are said to have been given traditionally on the day of death, on the 3rd, 7th, 40th, 100th days, at 1 year, 2 years [4] and 1000 days after death, are also in the process of simplification. Of these seven or eight occasions, two or three are generally skipped. The most frequently simplified *kendhuri* are one either on the 3rd or 7th days, one either on the 40th or 100th days, one either 1 year or 2 years after death.

Unlike life-cycle *kendhuri,* the communal *kendhuri* was abolished in the late 1970s when a new hamlet head was elected and the calendrical *kendhuri* was also ended in the 1980s. In the case of the intermittent *kendhuri,* most of the occasions which are said to have been celebrated by *kendhuri* in former days, are not celebrated

---

[4] Villagers had different ideas concerning whether two years after death should be given a *kendhuri* or not. Those who supported the view that *kendhuri* should not be celebrated two years after death sticked to the idea that the total number of *kendhuri* after death should be seven. The reason why it should be seven was not well understood by villagers. They just said seven times of *kendhuri* was the custom inherited from their ancestors. According to a villager regarded by others as a *dhukun* (traditional medical and magical practitioner, see Chapter VI for more about this concept), the celebration of seven times of *kendhuri* after death was because the essence of human body consists of seven different elements and seven occasions of *kendhuri* coincide with the dismantlement of these elements.

today, although this type of *kendhuri* has not disappeared totally. In 1993-1994, three *kendhuri* belonging to this category were held in Kolojonggo, one after a villager moved into a new house and two others, after recovery from sickness. When referring to these occasions, villagers preferred the term *syukuran* to *kendhuri*, although the mode of celebrating *syukuran* may not be different from that of *kendhuri*. [5] The abolition of other types of *kendhuri* and the use of the term, *syukuran,* rather than *kendhuri* to designate the intermittent *kendhuri* means that the term, *kendhuri*, refers exclusively to life-cycle *kendhuri*.

The simplification in the mode of celebrating life-cycle *kendhuri*, however, has not gone so far as, at least until now, to question a more fundamental issue: whether to celebrate it or not. Although there were a few who consciously mentioned the futility of it, most villagers including those who criticised it celebrated life-cycle *kendhuri* as a host and attended it as guests. [6] The way the simplification of *kendhuri* was dealt with in the opening remarks of the *kendhuri* also shows this point. When one of *kendhuri* after death was to be omitted, the representative of the host always made a remark that the *kendhuri* being celebrated, for example, on the 3rd day after the death, was both for the 3rd and 7th day after death. In this respect, villagers still stick to the traditional pattern of celebrating *kendhuri,* at least in the conceptual domain.

In brief, villagers in Kolojonggo celebrate *kendhuri* at each point of passage in the individual's life although, compared with the ideal pattern which is said to have been practised in former days, the frequency of celebration is simplified. The next question is, then, whether the interpretation of *kendhuri* supported by villagers in former days is still relevant to understand the reformist villagers' attitude.

---

[5] *Syukuran* may take different forms from *kendhuri*. In two cases where a youth celebrated *syukuran* for entering university, only a short remark was made by a representative of the host at the opening of the meeting, saying that the *syukuran* was to express thanks to Allah for permitting the host to enter university. After that, meals were served and the guests, close friends of the host who came both from Kolojonggo and neighbouring hamlets, spent the rest of the *syukuran* chatting, playing games and, in one case, by singing songs. No *besek* were given to the guests afterward.

[6] Several villagers mentioned that, as far as they remembered, only two life-cycle *kendhuri* had not been celebrated in Kolojonggo: one at the time of marriage of Pak Nadi's daughter and the other at the 1000th day anniversary after the death of Pak Wanto's mother. It seems, however, that the absence of *kendhuri* in both cases was not caused by the dissatisfaction of Pak Nadi and Pak Wanto with the celebration of *kendhuri*. When interviewed, both Pak Nadi and Wanto, who were described by some other villagers as brave enough not to have celebrated *kendhuri*, emphasised that the reason they had not held *kendhuri* was circumstantial, namely, they had been in a situation which had not let them celebrate it, rather than ideological, that is, they wanted to express their objection to the celebration of *kendhuri*. Their reply seems generally to the point since they celebrated *kendhuri* for other occasions after they had skipped life-cycle *kendhuri* before. The fact that these cases are still remembered by villagers shows that life-cycle *kendhuri* have rarely been skipped and the celebration of *kendhuri* is still considered as an essential part of village life.

5.3. Islamic Development and *Kendhuri*

Villagers had two 'official' versions as to why they celebrated *kendhuri*. These were official since villagers used one or both of them when they were asked to comment on *kendhuri* and the representative of the host used one or both of them as his rhetoric in the opening speech. According to the first version, *kendhuri* is an occasion in which the host prays for *slamet*, a state 'in which events will run their fixed course smoothly and nothing untoward will happen to anyone' (Koentjaraningrat,1960:95) and the neighbours, who play a part to achieve this state, are invited. This interpretation is similar to that of the Javanese of the 1950s except for one crucial fact. If all sorts of supernatural beings of different origin such as local spirits, dead ancestors, Hindu deities and Islamic prophets were previously invoked to bring *slamet* in the opening remarks of *kendhuri* (Geertz,1976:11; Jay,1969:209), it is now only the name of Allah which can be heard in the actual celebration of *kendhuri*. The same is true when villagers were asked to point out to whom this ritual was directed and of whom they asked a *slamet*. They only talked about Allah, although the terms they used were diverse. Some used 'Allah' while others, '*Tuhan*', '*Pangeran*' or '*Kang Maha Kuwasa*'. Whatever the selection of the term may be, the official version of the meaning of *kendhuri* gives an impression that the space allocated to supernatural beings of heterogenous origins is entirely filled with the Islamic God, Allah. [7] The introductory remark of the *kaum* in a *kendhuri* for a wedding shows this point:

> To the respectable elders and all of those present
>
> *Asalamu'alaikum warrohmatulloi wabarokatu*. (May God give you peace and prosperity, mercy and blessing)
>
> I hope that peace and welfare (*kawilujengan*) from Allah
>
> will be bestowed to all of those present
>
> And I am delivering my feelings of thanks to Allah
>
> who has already given us health and welfare to such a degree that we can be here.
>
> There is nothing for which I'd like to ask your assistance

---

[7] As will be mentioned in the latter part of this chapter, not all villagers possessed the same views. There were some villagers who seemed to adhere to the previous interpretation of *kendhuri*, namely, that it was dedicated to supernatural beings of diverse origins. However, most of those supporting this view did not want to express their idea to me but reiterated that a *kendhuri* was directed solely to Allah. One of the clues which made me understand that not a few villagers still supported this view was the incense burning during the celebration of *kendhuri*, an action which was considered by all villagers as a medium to invoke spirits. Some of those who put forward the view that a *kendhuri* was directed to Allah burned incense in their own *kendhuri*. However, in contrast with the previous time when incense would be burned in the room where *kendhuri* was celebrated, now it is done in the inner part of house or outside of it. As a result, if someone just sits down in the room where the official *kendhuri* is going on, it is impossible to know whether the host is burning incense or not.

except to ask you to help Pak Joyo and his family to send their prayers of blessing [to Allah]

I hope all the wishes of Pak Joyo in celebrating *kendhuri* will be fulfilled and what he has done and will do will be accepted by Allah.

With this intention in our mind, let's all ask Allah

so that everything may be peaceful and smooth (*wilujeng*)

For the purpose of comparison, the ritual prayers in a *brokohan*, which is held on the day of a baby's birth, are shown below. It is guided not by the *kaum* but by the *dhukun bayi*[8] whose major role is to give a massage to a new-born baby and to guide a few rituals such as *brokohan, tetesan* and *tingkepan*.[9]

In a *brokohan*, the *dhukun bayi* began the ritual by briefly talking about the baby for whom this ritual was performed; the time of its birth, its weight and the process of giving birth. Then she explained the meaning of the prepared foods.

Here plates of rice for *brokohan* have been prepared.

There are two *ambengan* (lump of rice taking the shape of mountain)

The first one is to make perfect [the journey of] *kakang kawah* and *adhi ari-ari*[10] , in order for them to reach the Southern Sea.

The second one is given to *dhanyang*[11] living outside this village.

It is made complete by *jenang abang, jenang putih, jenang palang, jenang baru-baru, jenang pliring,*[12]

All of which render meals for *dhanyang* inside this village.

---

[8] In former days when women gave birth to a baby in her own house, the *dhukun bayi* played the role of mid-wife. She is now deprived of this role since all women go to the modern clinic to give birth to a baby.

[9] *Tetesan* is a ritual enactment of female circumcision. A yellow herb called *kunir* (turmeric) is placed over the vagina of the baby and then removed by the *dhukun bayi*. *Tingkepan* is a ritual occurring at seven months of pregnancy of the first baby. In the one *tingkepan* that I attended, the future parents of a baby were bathed together by the *dhukun bayi* and their close relatives from both sides. After that, a scene of delivery was enacted. The *dhukun bayi* slid two young coconuts down inside the *sarung* of the future mother, one by one, while her mother and mother-in-law took them at the bottom. On each coconut were drawn pictures of Arjuna and Sembadra, both of whom symbolise the ideal types of male and female in the *wayang* story.

[10] *Kakang kawah* refers to the amniotic fluid and *adhi ari-ari*, the placenta. They are said to be the siblings of a baby.

[11] *Dhanyang* refers to the guardian spirit occupying a certain place such as house, tree, river, village and so on.

[12] *Jenang* is a porridge made from rice flour. The brown Javanese sugar (*gula Jawa*) and coconut are added to make different kinds of *jenang*: when *gula Jawa* is mixed, it is called *jenang abang*; when coconut milk is added, called *jenang putih*; when the added *gula Jawa* takes the shape of a cross, it is called *jenang palang*; when the *jenang* is made from *katul* (rice sifting) and sliced coconuts are scattered, it is called *jenang baru-baru*; and when the half of the *jenang* is brown and the other is white, it is *jenang pliring*. These five *jenang* are said to symbolise five different directions in this world: the north, the east, the south, the west and the centre.

I hope that all of those present will witness what I will surrender.

I will surrender [the following ritual prayer] to *Kang Maha Gesang* (the Being controlling life) in this village.

After this introductory speech, her ritual prayer began:

Bismillahirrahmanirrahim (In the name of Allah, the Merciful and the Compassionate)

I intend to cast a spell, [the name of] my spell is *Pulasari*.

All I offer is food, whatever condition it may be.

Flowers of *Gandaarum*, flowers of *Gandaarum* are [composed of],

Kanthil (name of a flower)is [for the baby] to behave harmoniously with and in accordance with (*kumanthil-kanthil*) the state of being,

(*Ke*)*Nanga* is [for the baby] to grow up, being protected (*winong*),

Mawar is [for the baby] to be disinfected (*tawar*) [from what is bad],

And *mlati* is [for the baby] to follow the right way (*sejati*).

With this, I ask blessing (*berkah pangestu*) from *Kang Murba Gesang* (the Being governing life).

Bismillahirrahmanirrahim.

I intend to cast a spell, [the name of] my spell is *Singasari*.

I wish everything to be regular and constant, as perfect as possible.

Kiyai Tawang, [that is] *kiyai* of love, *kiyai* of love, [that is] *kiyai* of protection,

May his soul (*sukma*) give permission to realise the requests of my granddaughter Sumirah (the mother of the new born baby) and her family.

For my faults in the guidance [of this ritual] and the preparation of the food, *wajib* (an obligatory gift) was prepared.

The *wajib* is 125 [Rupiah],

100 [Rupiah] is for acquiring a livelihood of food and clothes,

25 [Rupiah] for the fortune (*rezeki*) of my granddaughter Sumirah and her family.

The remarkable difference between the guidance of the *kaum* and that of the *dhukun bayi* is the object of their prayers. Whilst the former directs his prayer only to Allah whom he envisages as having a final authority to accept his prayer, the latter does so to several invisible beings such as local spirits living both inside and outside the village (*dhanyang),* an unidentified deity who controls life (*Kang Maha Gesang*), the goddess living in the Southern Sea, an unidentified deity of love and protection, and the Islamic God, Allah. [13] On the other hand, the *dhukun bayi* puts emphasis on the meaning of the ritual foods, which is totally lacking in the case of the *kaum*. Her emphasis is in the same vein as the point made by Geertz's informant, who said, 'at a *slametan* all kinds of invisible beings come and sit with us and they also eat the food. That is why the food and not the prayer is the heart of *slametan*' (Geertz,1976,15). To the *kaum*, it is not the food but the prayer that lies at the heart of *kendhuri*.

The exclusion of 'non-Islamic' supernatural beings from the rhetoric of *kendhuri* reflects the penetration of reformist Islam into Muslim villagers. As Allah is envisaged as the only Being who has the power to realise the state of *slamet* and requests by Muslims, other supernatural beings are excluded from the invitation list of *kendhuri*, at least, officially. This change, however, does not seem to be enough to legitimise the practice of *kendhuri* in Islamic terms. Although the exclusion of all supernatural beings other than Allah in ritual invocations makes it possible to equate *kendhuri* as a mode of prayer to Allah, this cannot explain why Muslims should use it for this purpose. On the other hand, *kendhuri* is a ritual which is unanimously said to originate from Hindu-Buddhist tradition, not from an Islamic one. [14] In a situation where Islamic ways of praying prescribed by the Quran and Hadith are known to villagers, there is no reason why they stick to a ritual which is thought to be related to non-Islamic traditions.

Many villagers talked about the strength of tradition to explain the persistence of *kendhuri*. As it had been practised from the era of their ancestors (*jaman nenek moyang*), it would not disappear with ease. Some of them used the term '*tradisi*', an Indonesian equivalent of tradition, to explain the maintenance of *kendhuri*. As the term, *tradisi* retains a positive connotation in the national discourse, the equation of *kendhuri* with *tradisi* implies indirectly that *kendhuri* is something that should be preserved. Therefore, to them, the classification of *kendhuri* as *tradisi Jawa* is already a sufficient condition to explain and rationalise the maintenance of *kendhuri*. Since *kendhuri* belongs to *tradisi*, they need not abolish

---

[13] Villagers could not remember exactly when non-Islamic deities were excluded from the official rhetoric of *kendhuri*. According to the *kaum*, he did not refer to the names of non-Islamic supernatural beings from the outset of his career as a *kaum* in the early 1970s. It is not certain whether his memory was correct or not since some of the villagers in their thirties who had been their teens in the early 1970s remembered the invocation of a variety of supernatural beings at the beginning of Arabic prayers. In the case of a neighbouring hamlet of Kolojonggo, the traditional style of ritual invocation continued until quite recently before the *kaum* died in the 1980s. The newly installed *kaum* in that hamlet did not follow the traditional pattern of invoking various supernatural beings but only recited a few Arabic passages as the *kaum* in Kolojonggo did.

[14] It is beyond the scope of this chapter to discuss whether *kendhuri* originated from Arab countries or from the indigenous religious tradition. What is important for the present discussion is that all villagers in Kolojonggo admit its Hindu-Buddhist origin. In the academic circle, the Hindu-Buddhist origin of *kendhuri* has not been challenged until recently when Woodward argues its Islamic origin (Woodward, 1988 &1989).

it by force but should cherish it as the old Hindu-Buddhist temples have to be preserved not only by the Hindu-Buddhists but by all Indonesians.

This justification, however, does not satisfy everyone. Some of the reformist villagers have attempted to impart new meanings to *kendhuri* in such a way that it does not contradict their religious teachings. Upon being asked why Islamised Java had not eliminated its previous Hindu-Buddhist tradition such as *kendhuri*, they told the story of Sunan Kalijaga, one of the nine central figures (*wali sanga*) who are said to have been responsible for the conversion of the Javanese to Islam.[15] According to their version, the inhabitants had religions of Buddhism, Hinduism, animism or a mixture of these when Islam entered Java in the 15th century. Seeing this situation, Sunan Kalijaga decided to use the old tradition as a container which would be filled with new contents rather than to take stronger measures. According to some, behind this decision of Sunan Kalijaga lay his consideration of *mafsadah-maslahat* (disadvantage-advantage): he measured the advantages and disadvantages of keeping tradition and reached a decision that to maintain tradition which would facilitate the conversion of all Javanese to Islam was more advantageous than to purge traditions which would hamper the conversion process.[16] A villager who was a civil servant, summarised the work of the *wali sanga* in this way:

> Their (*wali sanga*) duty was to extend Islam. For this, they did not prohibit all kinds of non-Islamic traditions that had existed before the coming of Islam. What they did at first was to modify some part of it, so that Islam could be easily accepted by the masses. For example, if there was a man worshipping a tree by burning incense and making offerings, they just proposed to change the ritual prayer rather than eliminating these customs. As a result, Islamic prayer gained its foothold in Java.

Other traditional practices such as *gamelan*, *wayang* and *tembang* are also interpreted in this framework. The more important point is that traditions have been coloured by Islam rather than the fact that they still retain their traditional appearance. A high school teacher related two Javanese art forms to the effort of Sunan Kalijaga:

[15] For more about the textual literature on the *wali* of Java and visits to the tombs of the *wali* (*ziarah*), see Fox (1989).

[16] According to the reformist villagers, to measure advantage (*maslahat*) and disadvantage (*mafsadah*) is one of the essential methods to issue a *fatwa*, a religious decision, and to examine the relevance of Islamic teachings. For example, the reason why Muslims are forbidden from drinking alcohol can be understood within the framework of advantage and disadvantage, namely, the advantage that one can get from drinking alcohol such as psychological stability or maintenance of bodily temperature in cold atmosphere is less than its disadvantages such as temporary loss of one's reason, surrender to desires and economic waste.

It is true that *gamelan* (a traditional Javanese music) was the tradition of Hindu-Buddhism. But the *wali sanga* used it as a way of spreading Islam to the commoners since they knew that the Javanese liked to listen to the music. Sunan Kalijaga placed a set of *gamelan* in front of the *masjid*. Whenever villagers came to listen to this delicious (*enak*) music, he asked them to read the *sahadat* (the profession of faith) first. Then they were invited to the *masjid*. It worked. It was not difficult for him to make villagers enter the *masjid*. ... *Wayang*, originating from the Hindu kingdom, had the same fate. For example, one of the most important and powerful (*sakti*) weapons in the story of *wayang* is named *kalimasada*. It is a transformed pronunciation of '*kalimat sahadat*', or two passages of *sahadat*, the core of Islam. [17]

Kendhuri is not an exception. It is rather a typical example used to project their ideas onto traditions of non-Islamic origin. Sunan Kalijaga, seeing that *kendhuri* was widespread and cherished among the Javanese, adopted it rather than got rid of it forcefully. However, he could not tolerate one element in it because of its explicit contrast to Islamic teaching, namely, the ritual prayer. As a result, he replaced the old Hindu-Buddhist chants with an Arabic one. [18] As one informant put it, 'to whom one's wish is directed is the most important criterion to divide the Islamic from the non-Islamic.' Even the name of *kendhuri*, according to Pak Rup, a primary school teacher, was also the creative invention of Sunan Kalijaga rather than mere imitation of the Hindu-Buddhist tradition. He suggested that the word '*kendhuren*' stems from '**kendh**u*ng r**u***kon* **nge**re**n**cangi' which, he interpreted as 'let's help each other by giving out something', one of the highly appreciated values in Islamic teaching. [19]

[17] According to Supomo(n.d.:15-23), *kalimasada* has its origin in *kalimahosadha* (the name of Yudhisthira's weapon) of the *Bharatayuddha* and accordingly, had been known to the Javanese long before the coming of Islam to Java. It was only in the 19th century when a new meaning was attached to *kalimahosadha* and the equation of *kalimahosadha* with *kalimat sahadat* found its way into Javanese literature.

[18] The opinion of the reformist villagers that Sunan Kalijaga replaced the non-Islamic ritual prayers with Arabic ones in *kendhuri* does not seem to be correct since, as the case of Kolojonggo and those reported by Geertz and Jay show, the invocation of non-Islamic entities in ritual prayers was not abolished until quite recently. In this respect, their interpretation of Sunan Kalijaga seems to be a good example of what Hobsbawm and Ranger called 'the invention of tradition' (1983). In this recent invention of Sunan Kalijaga, he is described as a sage seeking after the best way to spread Islam and implement Islamic laws, whose strength came not from spiritual equanimity but from religious wisdom to measure advantage and disadvantage of tradition. In this respect, Sunan Kalijaga is a projection of the reformist villagers who try to solve the conflict between Islamic doctrine and traditional practices. See Geertz (1968:25-29) for more about the conventional image of Sunan Kalijaga supported by Javanese rural villagers.

[19] *Kendhung* means 'line up' or 'be ready to', *rukon* 'unanimous' or 'harmonious' and *ngerencangi* 'serve'. Put together, '*kendhung rukon ngerencangi*' means 'be ready unanimously to serve [others]'. Compared with this literal interpretation, Pak Rup's interpretation has an additional passage, 'by giving out something'. As this addition contains what he wanted to convey, it is not omitted in the text. This kind of language play to guess the origin of a certain word is called *kirata basa*. It gives someone a chance to interpret a word by emphasising certain aspects that he or she wants to stress. Pak Rup gave other

This lexical analysis of *kendhuri* provides us a chance to understand the creative succession of Sunan Kalijaga by some of the reformist villagers and the second version of explaining the purpose of *kendhuri*, that is, *sadhakah* (*sodakoh, sadhaqa, sedhekah, sidhekah*). According to the manual on BAZIS written by the village youth, *sadhakah* means to give something to others, expecting blessings from Allah in return. In the context of village life, it is interpreted to mean a distribution of food and other daily necessities to the poor from the capable without expecting return payment from the poor but from Allah.

In Kolojonggo, the term *sadhakah* is unlikely to have a long history in the official discourse of *kendhuri*. [20] Only one among three villagers who were frequently assigned the role of the opening speaker used it as a repertoire for his speech. In a *kendhuri* celebrating the 7th day of Pak Budi's death, for example, Pak Mangun delivered his speech in the following way:

> ... If there is a *sadhakah* this evening, it is for [the sending of] our prayer [to him]. While Kiyai Budi's soul is facing Gusti Allah [interrogation after death], that is, for seven days, I wish his wrong deeds and sins in this world may be forgiven. And [his dead soul is] distanced from tortures in Hell and in the grave and offered a lofty place. ... May the giving-out of *sadhakah* for remembering Kiyai Budi on the seventh day after his death, be used as an intermediary (*lantaran*) to Gusti Allah, The Greatest. May this request be realised!

In a *kendhuri*, as Pak Mangun said, what the host expects from the guests is their participation in his prayer to Allah. To enable his prayer to be accepted by Allah more easily, the host distributes food or wealth to others. To ask something of Allah is a recommended act of Muslims. When accompanied by other recommended behaviour such as giving out one's wealth, this way of praying to Allah is a highly praiseworthy deed. With the notion of *sadhakah*, therefore, the celebration of *kendhuri* can be considered as *amal* (religious behaviour) which will bring high religious merit (*ganjaran*).

---

examples of it: *telasi, kanthil* and *kenanga*, three essential flowers in the offerings. According to him, the origin of *telasi* is *tesih isi* or 'still filled', that of *kanthil, kumanthil-kanthil*, 'to love', and that of *kenanga* (noun), *kenango* (imperative form of the verb, *kenang*) or 'to remind'. Put together, these three flowers carry a message that, when one still lives in this world (one still fills this world), one should love and remember one's deceased parents. With this interpretation, Pak Rup tried to illustrate that these three flowers were used originally not as media to make contact with supernatural beings but as media to convey a moral principle which is recommended by Islam.

[20] This does not mean that this equation has not been known in other parts of Java. In the Javanese dictionary published in 1939, *kendhoeren, slametan* and *sidhekah* are regarded as synonyms (Poerwadarminta,1939:567). Koentjaraningrat also uses the term, *sedhekah*, but confines its usage only to designating the series of the *kendhuri* after death without explaining the terminological difference between *sedhekah* and *kendhuri* (Koentjaraningrat,1985a:364-5). On the other hand, Bachtiar reports that the equation of *sedekah* with *kendhuri* was made by Muslims who tried to make it more suitable to Islam (1985:280).

At first sight, to relate the concept of *sadhakah* with *kendhuri* does not seem to be plausible since the flow of resources in a *kendhuri* is unlikely to be fit exactly to the implication of *sadhakah,* namely, a one-sided flow of resources. First, the host does not prepare food in a *kendhuri* relying only on his or her own resources, but receives contributions from others which, in 1993, reached about Rp 4000 from neighbours and more than Rp 5000 from close relatives. In most cases, the total amount of these contributions is large enough to cover the cost of celebrating the *kendhuri*.[21] Second, all villagers in the exchange network of *kendhuri* expect that their contribution will be reciprocated in the future when they become the host. Third, the same amount of contribution that the host receives from the contributors will be reciprocated in the future, irrespective of their economic differences. If a contribution is large enough to cover the cost of a *kendhuri,* economic resources are reciprocated in the long run, and economic inequality among villagers is not considered, it is not reasonable to say that the concept of *sadhakah* implying a one-sided flow of wealth from the capable to the poor can be applied to *kendhuri*. In order to solve this problem, it is necessary to see the different nature of flows of resources throughout the *kendhuri*.

Four different flows of resources take place centring on the *kendhuri*. First, those who receive contributions from others should reciprocate them when the contributors hold a *kendhuri*. As the occasions of celebrating *kendhuri* are different in each household, the flow of resources is not equal in terms of quantity. In spite of this imbalance, however, long-term exchange is conceptualised as a balanced reciprocity, probably due to the fact that the reason for this imbalance is beyond the control of villagers, such as birth and death.

The second is the exchange of contribution and food parcel. From morning till mid-afternoon, contributors visit the host's house, bringing either a white envelope containing money or a wooden carrier filled with foodstuffs. After they return home, a parcel of food is delivered to their house. The third is the exchange of labour and of a food parcel. In order to prepare food distributed to the contributors and to the guests at a *kendhuri,* the host needs women-power from a large number of villagers. For this, the host's family asks assistance of neighbours and of close relatives and, as a compensation for their labour, a parcel of food is delivered to the house of those who supply their labour. The governing rule of the second and third exchange is strict reciprocity. Those who do not contribute nor work do not receive the home-delivered food parcel whereas

---

[21] The cost of celebrating a *kendhuri* depends on the quality of food distributed to the contributors and to the guests and on the number of the guests in the *kendhuri*. Roughly, it was around Rp 300,000 in 1993-94 (equivalent to around 500 kg. of husked rice) to celebrate a *kendhuri* where around 100 *besek* were prepared. This meant that about 60 to 70 contributions were enough to cover the cost. For the cost of celebrating a *kendhuri*, contributions and exchange system centring on *kendhuri* in Tenggar region, see Hefner (1985:216-238)

those who both contribute and work receive two parcels. [22] Villagers are conscious of this nature of exchange, so that the word designating the delivered food parcel is not *sadhakah* but *balasan* (reply) or *ganti lelah* (substitution of one's tiredness). As reciprocity has to be observed strictly, all visitors who come to the host's house are monitored and the hostess is alert to watch over the working process of her neighbours.

The fourth flow of resources is what actually happens during the celebration of a *kendhuri*. The host invites all villagers living in his *kendhuri* circle [23] and a *besek* is distributed to them irrespective of whether those who are invited attend it or not. This strict egalitarianism in the invitation rule means that those who do not contribute are also invited and given a *besek*. Let's take an example. Pak Mandyo had a *kendhuri* for celebrating his son's circumcision. During the daytime, his family received contributions from 75 visitors. Among them, 13 were those from outside his *kendhuri* circle while 62 visitors were from inside it. For the *kendhuri*, his family prepared 90 *besek*, slightly more than their expectation of the number of guests. They did so in order to prevent an accidental shortage of *besek*, even if this was unlikely to happen. That night, 85 *besek* were distributed and 5 were left. The discrepancy between 85 and 62 was the difference between the number of households in his *kendhuri* circle and that of the contributors living in it.

Two categories of households belonged to these 23 households. First, the recently married couples living with their parents and the old villagers living with their child's family were included in it. Although the parents may have contributed and the child may not or the other way round, two *besek* were allocated for that house. Second, it included the households belonging to the poorest in the hamlet. Female-headed households were a typical example of this category. They could not afford the high standard of the contribution which exceeded their average daily earnings by two or three times. To the ordinary households consisting of

[22] Not all of those who help cooking get a food parcel. Its delivery is dependent on whether one receives an invitation from the host's family and on the time and intensity of their work. Those who help preparing food for a while after they hand in a contribution are not eligible for a food parcel. Generally, it is those staying half a day (4-5 hours) or more in the kitchen who are liable to get one.

[23] *Kendhuri* circle (*wilayah kendhuri*) refers to an area within which the host invites guests for a *kendhuri*. This area spreads in four directions from the host's house although it does not form the exact shape of a circle. Each household has a slightly different *kendhuri* circle of its own. It seems that the present set of *kendhuri* circles was formed during the Dutch colonial time when the lowest unit of administration was not the *dusun* but the *kebekelan*, whose extent was smaller than that of the *dusun*. Many *kendhuri* circles of the present households overlap with the boundary of the *kebekelan* rather than that of the *dusun*. According to some villagers, the *kendhuri* circle of the Dutch colonial period has been maintained until now with minor modifications. Due to the increase in households living in a certain *kendhuri* circle from that time on, the number of households belonging to it has also increased from around twenty to thirty in the Dutch colonial period to sixty to a hundred these days. The different size of a *kendhuri* circle is dependent primarily on the location of a certain household. When a house is placed at the centre of the hamlet, its *kendhuri* circle is the widest, including up to a hundred households. When a house is located at the eastern or western side of the hamlet near *sawah*, its *kendhuri* circle includes about sixty households.

at least a spouse, it is unimaginable not to contribute to a neighbour's *kendhuri*. Although one may resort to debt, one will appear at the host's house to pay a ritual obligation. This is their way of achieving a sense of full membership in the hamlet, without feeling ashamed in one's interaction with neighbours. In this context, not to reciprocate the ritual contribution means that one admits to other villagers one is in a poor economic position.

In sum, two different logics governing the flow of resources in *kendhuri* make it possible to understand how the concept of *sadhakah* can be applied to *kendhuri*. The first principle of reciprocity in *kendhuri* ends conceptually with the delivery of the daytime food parcels to the contributors of material resources and labours. In the actual celebration of a *kendhuri,* then, comes the second principle of a one-sided flow of resources in the form of *besek,* irrespective of whether the actual cost of preparing *besek* comes from the contributors or not. That some villagers do not contribute to the host is another factor that allows the concept of *sadhakah* to be easily applied to *kendhuri*. Whatever the actual reasons for this, those who do not contribute are considered to be too poor to do so by others. In this sense, the distribution of food in a *kendhuri* fits the concept of *sadhakah*, namely, the flow of food from the capable to the poor without expectation of its repayment.

5.4. Islamising the Meaning of Ritual Foods

These days, a variety of ritual foods are parceled in *besek* before the coming of the guests and distributed to them just before the beginning of the introductory speech. The *besek*, however, does not have a long history. It entered the village sometime in the 1980s. Prior to that time, the ritual foods were arranged at the centre of the room until the end of ritual prayers. Then, several young guests divided these foods in banana leaves and distributed them to the guests. In spite of this change in the mode of distribution, most of the *kendhuri* foods have remained unchanged. As has been the case with the meaning of *kendhuri*, some reformist villagers have also tried to reinterpret these ritual foods by giving them new contextual meanings. Among the various ritual foods, two kinds of food which are essential for every occurrence of *kendhuri* are highlighted: a lump of rice and the chicken.

The process of cooking rice for a *kendhuri* is in two stages. At first, rice is boiled in a big bowl. Then, the half-cooked rice is transferred to a utensil called a *kukusan* and steamed. As the *kukusan* takes the form of a cone, the resulting rice also takes the same shape. This cone-shaped rice is given the new name of *tumpeng*.

The chicken used for a *kendhuri* should be a full-grown rooster. A hen is not permitted. After being slaughtered, the rooster is plucked and its body is cut in two. All the inner organs are removed, washed and reinserted in the body, and various condiments and herbs are added. Then, the divided body is tied with two or three bamboo strings. First, each leg is folded and tied with a bamboo string so that the back sides of the upper and the lower feet can be in tight contact with one another. The next step is to tie the two wings to the body. A third string is used to fix the head to the body. For this, a villager passes the string through two holes in the nose, connecting the head to the neck. The last job is to boil it in a big bowl with various kinds of condiments and herbs. After it is cooked for around 2-3 hours, the rooster is called *ingkung*.

Asked why these two ritual foods had their special forms, many villagers talked about the convenience of cooking. In the case of the rooster, the strings tying the two feet and wings to the body are to prevent the added condiments from coming out while being boiled. As these strings hold the halved body tightly, this explanation is quite relevant. In the case of the rice cone, the reason is also simple. The *kukusan* itself is cone-shaped, which makes it inevitable for the *tumpeng* to take this form. When asked further questions about other possible meanings, many villagers did not have any idea; this was what their ancestors had done and they were just following (*ikut-ikutan*) what they had learned from them. A few village elders interpreted it within the framework of the traditional belief system. According to them, a mountain is the place where the dead souls reside with other invisible beings after they are freed from this world. By making the *tumpeng*, therefore, the host can make easy contact with those who will eventually bring the state of *slamet*. Some reformist villagers also had their own versions. Compared with the village elders, they expressed their ideas openly and confidently. A civil servant proposed his idea as follows:

> We cannot imagine a *kendhuri* without the *tumpeng*. Why is it essential among such a variety of foods? Just look at the Quran. There is a passage in it that the world created by Allah was not balanced at first. (He tried to refer to the exact verse of the Quran but he could not remember it.) ... As a result, Allah made mountains. *Tumpeng*, taking the shape of a mountain, symbolises a world made by Allah. [24]

According to another informant, each grain of rice in the *tumpeng* symbolises a human being. As a collectivity of human beings, the *tumpeng* is the symbol of this world. But this explanation is not persuasive since it does not explain why it takes the form of mountain. So a further explanation is added. The *tumpeng*, taking the form of a cone, has only one peak. As a metaphor, it delivers a message that Allah is one and human beings cannot be the same as Him.

---

[24] It seems that there is no verse in the Quran which clearly contains this idea. On the creation of mountain, there are two verses: 'And He hath cast into the earth firm hills that it quake not with you' (xvi:15) & 'And He it is who spread out the earth and placed therein firm hills and flowing streams' (xiii:3). The adjective 'firm' in these two verses seems to be the basis for Pak Sandiyo's idea.

On the other hand, the *ingkung* symbolises a human being. A hen or any other kind of animal is not permitted for making the *ingkung* but only a rooster. In Java, the rooster (*jago*) has a special meaning. The *jago* is regarded as the strongest and the cleverest of all chickens or, sometimes, of all animals. In everyday language, the *jago* signifies someone who is the best in a certain field. To say 'he is a *jago* in mathematics' means that he is the most brilliant at mathematics. In this context, it is not so difficult to understand the connection of *jago* to human beings, the best and the cleverest among all creatures of Allah.

When the ritual foods are arranged at the centre of the room, the *ingkung* is placed to face the *tumpeng*, surrounded by various foods made from vegetables and other ingredients. This geometric arrangement of the food is said to take after the cosmos. The *tumpeng* symbolises Allah, the *ingkung* human beings, and other small items of food all the products that Allah gave to human beings. The specific ways of preparing the *ingkung* reveal the relation of a human being to his or her Creator. A precise look at the *ingkung* shows that the shape of a tied chicken resembles that of human beings praying to Allah, a position called *sujud*; the upper and lower part of the feet are folded, the folded wings are tightened to the body, the chin is in touch with the neck and the head is placed at the centre of body. In sum, the arrangement of *kendhuri* foods can be interpreted as representing a human being praying to his or her Creator, surrounded by other creatures bestowed upon him or her by Allah. The purpose of praying is provided by three other ritual foods. These are *apem*, *kolak* and *ketan,* all of which are said to have originated from Arabic. *Kolak* is from *kolakqun* or speech, *apem* from *afuun* or to ask forgiveness and *ketan* from *kotokan* or mistake.[25] Together, they create a message, 'to utter words (prayers) asking forgiveness (of Allah) for all sorts of faults (that the host has committed)', one of the highly recommended deeds that Muslims are asked to do.

5.5. Syncretism and Tradition

Although some reformist villagers' reinterpretation of *kendhuri* is dominant due to their central role in Islamic activities, their ideas are not shared by all villagers or even by all reformist villagers. One of the reasons the plurality of views persists is the abstract nature of Islamic teachings in the Quran and Hadith. If these two ultimate sources are specific enough to contain passages on the validity of *kendhuri*, for example, 'do not celebrate *kendhuri* and do not make an *ingkung'*, the diverse opinions might not have been sustained in the face of the surge of reformist Islam. Scriptural ambiguity gives villagers relative freedom to interpret abstract religious teachings in accordance with their specific orientations and dispositions.

---

[25] The pronunciation of these three Arabic terms written in the text are taken from villagers. The right pronunciations of them are *qola* instead of *kolakqun, afwun* instead of *afuun* and *khatha'* instead of *kotokan.*

Overall, the attitudes of villagers toward *kendhuri* can be categorised into four, although these are not mutually exclusive and villagers may take different attitudes at different times and different contexts.

The first is what the *dhukun bayi* represents in her guidance of the *brokohan*: the traditional interpretation of *kendhuri* is still relevant. To those who take this position, supernatural beings are considered to intervene actively in human affairs and the *kendhuri* is a way to neutralise their bad effects, if any, and to attain the state of *slamet*. Although not a few villagers, especially those in their middle and old age, support this interpretation, it has been marginalised in village life. It is marginal because its supporters do not want to clarify their idea to others and, at the official level, they accept the view that *kendhuri* is directed solely to Allah. Nor do they express their ideas in action. In contrast to former days when the odour of the burning incense filled the room where the *kendhuri* was held (Geertz,1976:12), those who want to burn incense now do so in a place where the guests in *kendhuri* cannot recognise it, for example, outside the house or in the kitchen.

The second is an accommodational and flexible attitude to the *kendhuri*. Those who support this position try to impart new meanings to *kendhuri* so that it may be harmonious with Islamic teaching. This does not mean, however, that they have kept every part of *kendhuri* intact. Those elements which cannot be harmonised with Islamic ideas such as invocation of supernatural beings in the opening remarks, burning incense and making offerings have been removed by them.

The third is a purist attitude proposed by reformist intellectuals in the city. Those who advocate this position insist that *kendhuri* should be removed from village life for it has no scriptural reference in the Quran and Hadith and it originated from the Hindu-Buddhist tradition. [26] Most of those supporting this position are young and unmarried reformist villagers who are not yet officially invited to *kendhuri*. In spite of the clarity of their ideas, it is not certain whether they will put their ideas into practice when they are invited to *kendhuri* in the future. Refusing to participate in the *kendhuri* of their neighbours is so radical in village life as to be interpreted as a gesture to sever their relations with others. Therefore, it is more likely that they will take either the second or the fourth position, when they have to legitimise their behaviour to attend *kendhuri* in the future.

---

[26] Mas Bambang supporting the third position pointed out an aspect of *kendhuri* which makes the equation of *kendhuri* with a mode of praying to Allah impossible: the presence of Christian guests in Muslims' *kendhuri*. If *kendhuri* was an occasion on which the host expressed his or her gratitude to Allah and the guests were invited to participate in the prayer, Mas Bambang argued, Christian guests could not properly perform their roles. On the contrary, what Christian guests could do was to pray to their own God, an action which is *syirik* (polytheistic belief) in Islam. As long as Christians were invited to *kendhuri*, therefore, it could not be considered as a form of praying to Allah and, in this respect, the celebration of *kendhuri* could not be an Islamic activity.

The fourth position is to detach religious meaning from *kendhuri* and to emphasise the relation between villagers expressed in it. According to those who support this position, all villagers, irrespective of their religious and economic differences, are invited to and attend their neighbour's *kendhuri* and, in this sense, it is a ritual which actualises the social norm of harmony (*rukun*). With this shift of emphasis, ritual prayer or specific kinds of food are not thought to be at the heart of *kendhuri* nor to be preserved strictly. Instead, it is permissible, for example, to replace ritual prayer in *kendhuri* with a short prayer performed in other secular meetings[27] and to substitute bread which is favoured by villagers for boiled rice (*tumpeng*) which is not welcomed.[28] However, what cannot be replaced is the principle that all villagers living in the same neighbourhood or in the same *kendhuri* circle should be invited. Although those who support this position have not yet invented an alternative form of *kendhuri*, their position can be developed as radically as that of the third position, since *kendhuri* is thought to be just one mode of consolidating *rukun* among villagers and, if it is evaluated as not the best way, they will try to replace it with another form.[29]

Despite these differences in interpreting *kendhuri*, one common point is shared by almost all Muslim villagers: it is a ritual directed to Allah.[30] This commonality gives us a chance to reappraise the concept of syncretism which has long been used by scholars to characterise the religious orientation of Javanese villagers.[31] Syncretism refers to a religious framework where Islamic, Hindu-Buddhist, and animistic or indigenous religious elements are mixed together without causing a feeling of unease at the others' presence. In this framework, villagers do not differentiate one element from another and they have not given any

[27] In secular meetings, a short time in which every participant is asked to pray according to their own religious conviction is provided as a part of an opening procedure.

[28] These days, the *kendhuri* foods, especially those contained in *besek* are not welcomed by villagers. As these foods are cooked a few hours before the celebration of *kendhuri*, they are already cold when the *besek* is taken home, thus less delicious. In most cases, villagers give away the cooked rice in *besek* to chickens or other animals.

[29] Most Christian villagers supported the fourth view, commenting that *kendhuri* is a mode of expressing one's love to neighbours. In dealing with the non-Christian origin of *kendhuri*, Christians showed a more pluralistic attitude than the reformist villagers. They were willing to admit the Hindu-Buddhist origin of *kendhuri* and Islamic influences in it, while these admissions do not seem to have posed any problem for them to celebrate it. They were of the opinion that what was more important in celebrating *kendhuri* was not its form but its meaning. If the goal of *kendhuri* was toexpress one's love to neighbours, its non-Christian origin did not matter at all.

[30] The exception is only a few villagers who expressed their opinion clearly that all supernatural beings should be invoked in *kendhuri*. In one case, an old villager who was considered to be a *dhukun* by others argued that the sole invocation of the name of Allah in *kendhuri* would nullify its efficacy, namely, to bring the state of *slamet* to the host. This is because, according to him, *kendhuri* was based on 'Javanese knowledge' (*ilmu Jawa*), and 'Javanese knowledge' consisted of indigenous Javanese elements (*asal Jawa*) which put priority on one's contact with indigenous supernatural beings. Except for those who were considered as *dhukun*, I did not meet anyone either from Kolojonggo or from other parts of Yogyakarta who expressed their support of this idea to me.

[31] Syncretism has been supported by many scholars as a key to understanding the religious orientation of Javanese villagers. For more about this, see Benda,1958; Berg,1932; Drewes,1955; Geertz,1976; Jay,1963; Koentjaraningrat,1985a; Mulder,1983; Noer,1973; Supatmo,1943; Zoetmulder,1967.

thought to the question of the relations between these elements (Supatmo, 1943:4) and of their origins. *Kendhuri* is one of the finest examples of the syncretic tradition. In the ritual prayer of *kendhuri* as reported by Geertz and Jay (Geertz, 1976; Jay, 1969:209), supernatural beings of different origin were invoked and *kendhuri* foods were dedicated to each of them without discrimination. [32]

As Hefner points out (1987a:535), the lack of attention paid by scholars to the nature of the religious outlook in rural Java after Geertz, Jay and Koentjaraningrat provided a comprehensive picture of it [33], makes it difficult to understand the process of change that has taken place in *kendhuri*, a change which provides an indicator of the religious orientation of the present Javanese villagers. Although the shortage of comparative data makes it impossible to generalise [34], the case of Kolojonggo provides a chance to look at both continuity and change in the mode and interpretation of *kendhuri*. On the one hand, the way *kendhuri* is celebrated is not clearly different from what it once was. Villagers are invited, foods are distributed, the representative speaks in place of the host, ritual prayers are recited and many of the occasions for which *kendhuri* were given are retained. There are also villagers supporting the view that *kendhuri* is dedicated to supernatural beings who intervene in human affairs. On the other hand, ritual prayer rather than ritual food is now considered by many to be the core of *kendhuri* and its content has changed. Supernatural beings of both Islamic and non-Islamic origin are not invoked and only the name of Allah is heard. The more important point to show the change is that almost all villagers agree to the idea that *kendhuri* is dedicated only to Allah, whether this admission is nominal or not. To the accommodational villagers who try to Islamise *kendhuri* rather

---

[32] The ritual prayer reported by Jay goes as follows (1969:209):

> 'Giving honor to Mohammed the Prophet, to Adam and Eve, and to Dewi Sri, the rice goddess.' As more locally specific spirits are invoked - the Iron Smiths of Java, Earth and Water, the village Place Spirit, its Founding Ancestor, its First Clearer of the Land, the collective village ancestors - the litany gradually becomes more extended: ' Giving honor and food to the Place Spirit who guards the village of Tamansari together with the four sacred directions and the fifth [referring to the four cardinal directions and the centre, a directional complex of much mystical strength] all day and all night, we beg pardon so that there will be no troubles at all.

[33] One of the reasons that may explain this lack of attention is that the scholarly discussions on the religious orientation of the villagers in rural Java have centred on Geertz's book, *The Religion of Java*, and, in doing so, the focus has been placed on whether the trichotomy proposed in *The Religion of Java* is relevant and on whether this trichotomy can be applied to understand socio-political behaviour rather than on whether syncretism was or still is relevant to understanding the religious orientation of Javanese villagers.

[34] Bråton (1989) shows there are three different ways villagers in Central Java interpret *kendhuri*: a) a ritual to restore states of *slamet*, among other things by pleasing disturbing spirits; b) a ceremony of gratitude to Allah; and c) a modern, secular celebration. Although Bråton does not mention the official position of those who support the first view, he makes a remark that they do not express their belief clearly to others but try to dissociate themselves with what is considered to be non-Islamic such as incense and offerings. In this respect, the development reported by Bråton is comparable to that in Kolojonggo. See also Bowen (1993:174-81), for three distinct ways of interpreting *kendhuri* (celebrated for agricultural purposes) among Muslims in Gayo.

than to remove it, the influence of Islam is visible not only in the direction of ritual prayer but in the goal of *kendhuri*. If the reason for celebrating *kendhuri* for the villagers in the 1950s was to attain a state of *slamet*, its goal is now thought by them not only to achieve *slamet* but to actualise the Islamic virtue of *sadhakah*. This implies a semantic change in the way the celebration of *kendhuri* is interpreted. If *slamet* implies a homeostasis where 'nothing is going to happen' (*gak ana apa-apa*) (Geertz,1976:14) or 'there will be no troubles at all' (*mboten wonten alangan punapa*) (Jay,1969:179), *sadhakah* is a concept implying active involvement of human beings in seeking religious merit (*ganjaran*) and blessing (*berkah*) from Allah.

In sum, the syncretism which dominated villagers' interpretation of *kendhuri* in the 1950s has been gradually pushed to the margin in Kolojonggo. Now it is Islam which provides a basis on which *kendhuri* is interpreted and villagers' participation in it is explained. The degree that Islam is assimilated to villagers is different. However, the dominance of Islam is accepted by all of them, so that those who support the syncretic point of view are conscious of the difference between the Islamic and non-Islamic modes of interpreting *kendhuri* and show their official allegiance to the former.

The situation in Kolojonggo may represent one possible way a new Islamic tradition can emerge from a syncretic background. The initial stage in this process is to question and reinterpret village traditions and to recontextualise them in Islamic terms rather than to isolate and purge them from village life. This process seems inevitable since the efforts of villagers to Islamise village tradition have not been made in a cultural vacuum but in a local religious milieu in which the syncretic character of *kendhuri* had not been a matter of conscious questioning. An answer of Pak Leo to the question of why he did not give up celebrating *kendhuri* in spite of his objection to it is appropriate to understand the long-lasting impact of the previous local milieu on villagers. To this question, he answered, '[if I do not celebrate *kendhuri*] I do not feel good' (*kurang enak*). He, then, explained the state of '*kurang enak*' by giving a few examples, one of which was: 'it [that I do not celebrate *kendhuri*] is as if I excrete (*buang air besar*) in the toilet.' What he meant by this comparison was that he who had been accustomed to excreting in the nearby creek could not feel the same degree of satisfaction if he did so in a toilet, although the result was the same. As Pak Leo said, many villagers feel something is missing if they do not hold a *kendhuri* for the occasions which have been customarily celebrated with it. They, although ready to condemn the traditional ideas behind *kendhuri*, are children of a *kendhuri*-based religious culture (Bowen,1993:234). This, however, does not rule out the possibility that an alternative mode to *kendhuri* will be created in the future. Borrowing the terms of Pak Leo, as more people get accustomed to using the toilet, it will create a situation in which going to the creek is perceived to be unsatisfactory.

In Kolojonggo, a few symptoms are visible which show a new direction of change in village tradition. These are taking place mainly in life-cycle rituals whose forms are more flexible than that of *kendhuri* and which, in this respect, have a higher capability to incorporate new elements. In the following section, the efforts of some Muslim villagers to create a new Islamic tradition in life-cycle rituals will be discussed.

5.6. Constructing a New Islamic Tradition

Traditionally, *kendhuri* was not the only ritual celebrated at each point of passage in one's life but was accompanied by other optional ones. At seven months of pregnancy, villagers celebrated *tingkepan*, after birth, *tedhaksiti* [35] , upon circumcision, *supitan*, on engagement, *srah-srahan* and on marriage, *mantenan*. These days, two somewhat contradictory trends are visible in the way these life-cycle rituals are celebrated. On the one hand, the rituals at pregnancy and birth are in the process of simplification, so that *tingkepan* and *tedhaksiti* have seldom been celebrated recently. On the other hand, the wedding ceremony has become bigger in scale. In most wedding ceremonies, hundreds of guests are invited and conspicuous consumption becomes one of the most essential parts of it. In the case of *supitan*, both trends overlap, so that a few wealthy families celebrate it on a much greater scale while most villagers do it with or even without *kendhuri*. In this respect, the life-cycle ritual which is considered to be important and in which the most elaborate resources are mobilised is the wedding ceremony. It provides the best medium by which a person or a family can express their socio-economic status, modernity and religious orientation. [36]

A case of a villager who tried to separate himself from others in celebrating a ritual for pregnancy will be presented first. This case shows what the reformist

---

[35] *Tedhaksiti* is a ritual held at seven months after birth celebrating the baby's first contact with the earth.

[36] *Kendhuri* is also an occasion where villagers can display their socio-economic status. However, the chances that the celebration of *kendhuri* canenhance the social status of the host are less than the wedding ceremony. First, most households consisting at least of a couple hold *kendhuri*, so that the celebration of *kendhuri* is more a minimum requirement to be considered as a member of a community than a sign to show one's distinctive socio-economic position. Second, the procedures of *kendhuri* are inflexible, making it difficult for the host to insert a section which may assert his or her distinctiveness from others. For example, the host can improve the quality of *kendhuri* food. However, the food items that should be included in *kendhuri* are less flexible than those for the wedding, so that one's *kendhuri* food cannot be remarkably different from others'. Third, the guests for *kendhuri* are invited from a fixed *kendhuri* circle, making it impossible, unlike the wedding ceremony, for the host to increase the number of guests arbitrarily or to invite them selectively. As a result, those who want to use *kendhuri* as a chance to assert their socio-economic difference should use more radical measures, one of which is not to receive contributions from others. However, this method, which surely gives the host a reputation for generosity, does not seem to be so attractive to villagers. In 1993-94, only one such case took place in Kolojonggo. Even the *lurah* in Sumber received contributions from other villagers for a *kendhuri* in his house,and selected the wedding ceremony of his son as a chance to display his socio-economic status by inviting a large number of guests and by conspicuous consumption.

villagers' major concern about village tradition is and the way they try to modify it.

When his wife was seven months pregnant with his first child, Pak Sis had to face a problem: his father asked him to celebrate a *kendhuri* while he did not want to do so. He had a conviction that traditional rituals such as *kendhuri* should, if possible, disappear from the life of Muslims and, as a young leader of the *umat* Islam in Kolojonggo, he alluded to his ideas in several religious meetings. As a result, he wanted to use this occasion to put what he had proposed to others into practice. However, he could not ignore the fact that his father was a *kaum* who guided *kendhuri* and that he lived together with his father. Due to this position, no other villagers thought the *kendhuri* would be skipped. Some villagers even said to me that it would be the best chance for me to witness the celebration of *tingkepan*, the conjecture grounded on villagers' conception that the *kaum* upheld the traditional side of religious life. It was not certain how the process of negotiation between Pak Sis and his father had been going on since both of them did not want to comment on this, but the news of the *kendhuri* in the *kaum*'s place spread a few days before its celebration. When I met him on the day of the *kendhuri*, however, Pak Sis denied the fact, at least to me, that he would celebrate a *kendhuri* related to his wife's seven months of pregnancy. Instead, he kept insisting what he intended to celebrate was a *syukuran* which had no connection with seven months of pregnancy. According to him, *syukuran*, namely, an occasion that one expresses thanks to Allah, could be held at any time during the pregnancy. Until that moment, I thought the term, *syukuran*, was just a different way of designating *kendhuri* and I interpreted this as an effort of Pak Sis to differentiate himself from the traditional terminology and to associate himself with an Islamic term. [37] It turned out later when the *kendhuri* finished in the *kaum*'s house that my guess was wrong. Just before I went home, Pak Sis informed me that the *syukuran* would be held shortly afterwards. When I re-visited the *kaum*'s place, I could see several villagers sitting inside the *langgar* (prayer house) in the front yard of the *kaum*'s house. All of them were close neighbours of the *kaum* who had attended the *kendhuri* before. In contrast to the *kendhuri*, Pak Sis also sat in the *langgar*. [38] Soon, it turned out that not all invited guests in the *syukuran* were those who had been invited to the *kendhuri*. Villagers living outside of the *kaum*'s *kendhuri* circle also

[37] Villagers believe that the term, *syukuran*, originates from Arabic whereas the term, *kendhuri*, from Javanese, although the origin of *kendhuri* is Persian (see footnote, no.1 in this chapter).
[38] In *kendhuri*, the host does not sit together with other guests inside the room where it is held. In the *kendhuri* celebrated in the *kaum*'s house, Pak Sis stood at the gate to greet the guests but he did not enter the room for *kendhuri*, whereas his father, the *kaum*, was present, not as a host but as an officiant of it.

came and two of them were from neighbouring hamlets. When all the guests arrived, the total of whom were around thirty, one of them who took the role of the representative of Pak Sis, explained the purpose of the *syukuran*, namely, Pak Sis and his family wished to thank Allah for the pregnancy and asked others to assist them in expressing their feeling of gratitude to Allah by way of reciting the Quran. The opening of the *syukuran* was quite similar to that of the *kendhuri* which had been celebrated a little while ago, but a difference was also visible in the selection of the representative. The representative who made the opening remarks in the *syukuran* was from the generation of Pak Sis, differing from the *kendhuri* where an elderly villager had taken this role. After a short speech, the representative asked the *kaum*, who was also present in the *syukuran*, to guide the recitation of Arabic prayers. Without mentioning anything, the *kaum* directly uttered, *al-fatihah*, the name of the first Surah in the Quran. With this, all participants started to recite *al-fatihah*. After chanting this Surah three times, the guests began to recite the Surah of Maria (*Surat Maryam*) in the Quran individually, the Surah which was requested to be read by Pak Sis. For almost half an hour, the *langgar* was full of different voices reciting different parts of this Surah. Some who finished reciting it chanted another Surah while others repeated it several times. Feeling that the guests were a bit tired of recitation, the *kaum* clapped his hands and chanted a few Arabic passages, signalling that the latter part of the *syukuran* would follow the sequence of the *tahlilan*. A few more Arabic passages were collectively chanted until the whole section finished with the recitation of *al-fatihah* once again. As was usual in *tahlilan*, the end of the recitation was followed by a short sermon delivered by one of the two guests coming from the neighbouring hamlet. The last part of the *syukuran* was devoted to eating together. As an expression of thanks to the participants in the *syukuran*, according to the representative, Pak Sis prepared a meal for them. Soon after they finished eating, the guests left the house of the *kaum*.

This case shows several elements which Pak Sis wanted to incorporate in the *syukuran*. First, his denial that the celebration of the *syukuran* was for the seventh month of pregnancy reflected his idea that the new tradition should be severed from the traditional rule of holding celebrations at a certain fixed time. He made public his idea by asking his representative in the *syukuran* not to specify his wife's seven months of pregnancy. As a result, the representative made a remark that the *syukuran* was related to the pregnancy of Pak Sis' wife, suggesting that it could have been held at any time during the pregnancy. This was different from what had been done in the *kendhuri* by the representative who clearly mentioned the *kendhuri* was for celebrating seven months of pregnancy. Second, the invitation rule in the *syukuran* was not the same as that in the *kendhuri*. Rather than inviting all villagers living in the *kendhuri* circle of the *kaum*, Pak Sis invited only those with whom he had close friendship. It was not an accident then that most of those invited were the villagers who usually attended the *tahlilan* since it was one of the media by which Pak Sis maintained close relations with others. This pattern of invitation suggests that the new tradition in the mind of Pak Sis can not be harmonious with the *kendhuri* where no discrimination is permitted in invitation and even Christians are invited. On the contrary, the new tradition should be selective, based on religious difference or even the religious orientation of villagers. This is because, if the new tradition is Islamic, no villagers having a different religion should be included, although immediate neighbours. Third, the elements that he incorporated in the *syukuran*, namely Arabic recitation and sermon, were recognised as Islamic by all villagers. In this sense, the new tradition should be grounded on the elements which everyone agrees to be Islamic.

The case of the *syukuran* exemplifies a way a traditional practice can be replaced with a new form by those who are dissatisfied with its relation with non-Islamic tradition. In his effort to create a new tradition, Pak Sis was not an innovator who made something from nothing. The two elements that he employed, sermon and Arabic recitation, have recently been used by some villagers as a part of the life-cycle ritual, especially in the wedding ceremony.

In Java, the marriage between Muslims is officialised by an official of the Department of Religion. This process of officialisation, called *ijab*, can be done either in the government office or in the private house. In both cases, the procedures of *ijab* are almost the same. The bridegroom recites *sahadat Islam* and gives a token of marriage (*mas kawin*) to the bride under the guidance of a government official who informs the newly wedded couple of Islamic rules regulating marriage and divorce, recites Arabic prayers and delivers a short sermon. If these procedures were the whole of the wedding ceremony, the space reserved for non-Islamic traditions in marriage would be minimal. However, the *ijab* is just part of the whole complex of the wedding ceremony. After finishing the *ijab*, the newly wedded couple return to the bride's house where the marriage is celebrated once again in accordance with local custom. The guide of this latter part of marriage, which was thought to be more important than the former in the 1950s (Geertz,1976:56) and still is in the sense that more resources and guests are involved, is not a government official but a specialist called *dhukun manten*. In former days the roles of the *dhukun manten* in the wedding ceremonyincluded making and locating offerings in due places, conducting rituals and chanting spells, all of which displayed the syncretic nature of the wedding (ibid.:58-60).

Most ritual enactments at the wedding ceremony in Kolojonggo are similar to what is described by Geertz [39] and these are also guided by the *dhukun manten*. However, the emphasis that villagers put on these rituals has changed. Today, no rituals are regarded as an essential part of the wedding, no single ritual is performed uniformly at all weddings and villagers do not show any interest in their meanings. In this respect, it is more appropriate to consider them as entertainments and, sometimes, an art group such as *kroncong* singers (popular music originating from Portuguese songs), *dhagelan* group (comedians) and dance group are invited to perform during the wedding. On the other hand, the role of the *dhukun manten* is reduced to the technical side of rituals, namely, to inform the bride and the groom what they should do and when. The *dhukun manten* is also deprived of her previous roles of chanting magical spells and making offerings.

The facts that spells are not cast and offerings are not made [40] imply that no clear sign of syncretism is visible in the complex of the wedding ceremony. Instead, the major trend which characterises the wedding ceremony these days is 'secularisation', namely to disassociate the wedding ceremony from religious meaning and to associate it with a cult expressing social-economic status. This is reflected in the major interests of villagers to see the wedding ceremony. What they could remember concerning the wedding ceremonies in the past or what they immediately talked about after they attended the wedding were not ritual enactment but foods and the number of guests, two factors which determined the scale of a certain wedding. The more guests were invited and the more foods were served, the greater economic resources and the more chances to insert certain ritual enactments or entertainments. [41]

The second trend in the wedding ceremony, although it has not been yet popularised, is the opposite of the first one, namely to incorporate Islamic symbols in the wedding complex. [42] The elements to which villagers have recourse for

[39] These include the bride and the groom's throwing of betel nuts to one another, breaking of an egg by the bride on the foot of the groom, their standing on the double ox yoke and the groom's pouring of money into the hem of the sarung of the bride. See Geertz (1976:58-60)

[40] In a few weddings, offerings did not disappear totally and the host made one or two offerings in the house. However, it never happened that offerings were made in a place where guests would be able to recognise them or outside the bride's house, except for one case. In the rare occasion when a Catholic villager married off his daughter, the *dhukun bayi* was invited to make sixteen offerings inside the house and twenty-four outside it, including at seven different springs in his neighbouring houses, crossroads, a creek and big trees.

[41] The usual pattern of the wedding ceremony was to alternate between the serving of food and a certain program. The maximum number of serving food was four and in that case, the host could include four different agenda (one before the serving of the first food).

[42] The same trend is also visible in the wedding celebrated by Christians. In this case, the symbol that they use in the wedding is a hymn. Of the seven cases of Christian wedding that I attended, only in one case was a section included where a group of Christian youth came forward and sang a hymn. One Muslim guest told me later that this new section was not appropriate to the wedding ceremony where not only Christians but Muslims were invited. His evaluation reflected the negative attitude of the reformist villagers to Christian activities since, as will be shown below, Muslims also try to incorporate

this purpose coincide with what Pak Sis used in the *syukuran*: the recitation of passages from the Quran and a sermon. [43] Quite recently, one element has been added: to open the wedding ceremony with the recitation of Arabic prayers. This option is not a new one but has long been known to villagers. However, an idiosyncratic condition of Kolojonggo has prevented the use of it for the wedding ceremony, namely, the existence of a Christian Master of Ceremony.

The MC has the most important and appreciated role in the wedding, so that the MC-ship is only given to qualified men. One should possess a good command of the polite form of Javanese (*krama*), be middle aged and have a nice-looking face and white skin which symbolises one's distance from manual labor. Pak Suroyo, a primary school teacher, monopolised this role in Kolojonggo for around a decade. If he were a Muslim, his monopoly would continue until he is past middle age. However, he was a Christian, and therefore was not suitable, according to some villagers, to guide the wedding ceremony in an Islamic way. Their demand was not complicated, just to have an Arabic greeting at the beginning of the ceremony with '*Assalamualaikum waromatullohi wabarokatu*' (May God give you peace and prosperity, mercy and blessing). [44] This simple insertion, however, was not trifling to the reformist villagers, as one put it:

> How lovely to say, '*Assalamualaikum wa. wr.*', when you meet others? Compare it with other conventional greetings such as good morning (*selamat pagi*) or good evening (*selamat sore*)! Don't they imply that we don't need to be in a state of well-being in the afternoon? These greetings emphasise only the moment when we meet others and thus are not permanent. But, how about the Islamic one? We give blessings to others not for a restricted span of time: it is forever.

The lack of a qualified person for the MC role might have been one reason why it was hard for those who questioned the religion of Pak Suroyo to find someone to replace him. Even if they found someone, however, it would not be an easy task to deprive him of this role. Unless this replacement was done with good

---

Islamic symbols in the wedding where Christians are invited. See Chapter VIII for more about this attitude of Muslims vis-à-vis Christians.

[43] In the weddings held in other villages, the Islamic symbols were more diverse than those in Kolojonggo. These included: the Islamic song, *samroh*, rather than the traditional Javanese song, *tembang*, was played before and throughout the wedding ceremony; the serving men in the reception and the bridegroom wore a *peci* and a shirt which is called '*baju santri*' (shirt worn by students in Islamic boarding school); and the serving women and the bride wore *jilbab*.

[44] It seems that the Arabic prayer *Assalamualaikum wa.wr.* started to be used only recently in Kolojonggo. Not many Muslim villagers uttered *Assalamualaikum wa.wr.* and those who recited this prayer did so only in a few limited situations such as when they entered the place where religious meeting was held and just before they started a speech in public meetings. When entering others' house, all Muslim villagers in Kolojonggo used *kula nyuwun* (I ask permission). This short history allows *Assalamualaikum wa.wr.* tobe employed as a way to assert one's Islamic identity and makes it impossible for non-Muslims (including myself) to use it for greeting Muslims. For the controversies concerning non-Muslims' use of *Assalamualaikum wa.wr.* and the legislation prohibiting non-Muslims from uttering this prayer in Malaysia, see Peletz (1993:81-95).

reason stemming from Pak Suroyo himself, it would easily stir up gossip, which would eventually damage Pak Suroyo's reputation. Despite these difficulties, a new MC has recently emerged in Kolojonggo: Pak Mardi. At first sight, he failed to fulfil all the appropriate qualifications to be a MC: he worked as a labourer on construction sites, he was thin, his skin was dark and his command of Javanese was imperfect, as proved in the wedding ceremony when he stammered several times. Despite these shortcomings, he was a Muslim, with experience in guiding minor meetings. The transfer of MC-ship was also facilitated by the fact that he was a close neighbour of the host, which partially justified the replacement without humiliating Pak Suroyo in a direct way. Finally, the bride had a cousin who was braver than others in expressing his religious ideas and who urged her family to nominate Pak Mardi to be a MC. In village social life, this attitude could easily be labelled as arrogance (*sombong*) but her cousin's higher educational background as a student in the most prestigious university made it easier for him to behave in this way, lessening negative reactions from both his family and by his neighbours.

The wedding ceremony that Pak Mardi guided exemplifies what some village Muslims conceive an Islamised rite of passage to be. He opened the ceremony with an Arabic prayer. But he did not stop there. He continued his remarks in a mode in which the introductory statements of religious meetings are delivered: we utter praise and thanks to Allah, the Powerful (*Maha Kuwasa*) who has given us well-being and health so that we can come to this wedding. Then, he briefly delivered words of thanks to the guests for their coming, as is usual in the opening remarks of the wedding ceremony. This was followed by the recitation of passages from the Quran, a section which had been introduced to this village quite recently. Two young men came to the fore. They wore a *peci*, white shirts and black trousers, a fashion which is identified as that of the *santri* by villagers. One read two Arabic passages from the Quran while the other read their Indonesian translation. When asking prayers of blessing from the guests for the future spouse, Pak Mardi deviated once again from Pak Suroyo's usual way of guidance. When Pak Suroyo guided this section, he used an inclusive way by asking the guests to pray according to their own beliefs and by giving them a short and silent pause to pray. In the case of Pak Mardi, no pause was allowed:

> As an opening of this ceremony, I asked prayers of blessing from the guests. For Muslims who are present here, I will guide the prayer of the *Basmillah*. I ask the guests to follow my prayer either aloud or internally [in their heart].

Then he recited it with the use of a microphone, getting rid of any opportunities for followers of other religions to utter their own prayers. Even if this looks trivial, the way of extracting prayer from the attendants of a certain meeting is the key to understanding whether a certain gathering has a secular or religious nature. All the meetings where villagers are invited irrespective of their religions are opened in a way that Pak Suroyo employs whereas the religious meetings both in the *masjid* or in a private house follow the way of Pak Mardi. In this respect, Pak Mardi violated the implicit but obvious custom by converting the multi-religious nature of the wedding, shown in the religious diversity of the guests, into an Islamic one. The remaining sessions, *ijab* and reception, proceeded as usual except for the fact that the *mas kawin* was the Quran, a villager delivered a short sermon and chanted long Arabic prayers and the ceremony finished with a collective recitation of an Arabic prayer of '*Alhamdulillah*' for which Pak Mardi also used the microphone.

Where Islamic models of rites of passage are not known, one of the options chosen by the villagers who are dissatisfied with the traditional ways of celebrating them is to create a new tradition. This has been done in Kolojonggo by incorporating elements which are considered Islamic by all villagers. The elements thus selected are the recitation of Arabic passages and a short sermon. The incorporation of Islamic elements into rites of passage, however, does not result in the total abandonment of village traditions. The *syukuran* was celebrated side by side with the *kendhuri*, its old counterpart, while the recitation of the Quranic passages and the sermon in the wedding ceremony did not need a sacrifice of other elements. Although the way villagers put their ideas into practice is not radical and is, in one sense, syncretic, what is significant is that the inclusion of these elements into life-cycle ritual is already enough for it to be viewed as Islamic both by those who try to create the new tradition and those who stick to the old one. This is because only a few villagers have ever adopted these elements as a part of rituals and, in this sense, their identity as 'things Islamic' has not yet been diluted. This assures that the process of creating a new tradition will be an on-going one. New Islamic symbols will be continuously incorporated while those which were once considered to represent 'things Islamic' will be routinised and lose their religious meaning.

5.7. Summary

In spite of a long history of conversion to Islam, a variety of practices originating from the local and Islamic tradition have co-existed in Javanese villages, making village traditions. The ways this co-existence is viewed have been different at different times and places. There was a time when villagers did not question the 'Islam-ness' of certain practices, judging from their scriptural basis in the Quran and Hadith, and thus local and Islamic practices existed side by side without conflict. Time has passed and reformist Islam has come to the countryside bringing a framework to separate 'things Islamic' from 'things non-Islamic'. As more and more villagers are committed to this stream of Islam, the traditional practices which were taken for granted are questioned and re-evaluated from this framework.

In Kolojonggo, two different attitudes to define 'things Islamic' are prominent in the circle of the reformist villagers. There is a puristic group who follow the position of reformist intellectuals in the city, namely by disapproving of anything which has no scriptural reference in the Quran and Hadith and by denouncing this as non-Islamic tradition. Their ideas, however, remain mainly ideals. The option that they can choose, namely, not to celebrate the practices categorised as 'non-Islamic' and to object to participating in these, is too radical to be practised in village life. The fact that most of those who support this position belong to the younger generation who are not the main body celebrating these practices also means their ideas are not expressed clearly in public life. The second group of the reformist villagers takes an accommodational position to locate traditional practices in the context of Islam by imparting new meanings to them. They try to interpret *kendhuri* in connection with Islamic concept of *sadhakah* and recontextualise the meaning of ritual foods in Islamic terms. To them, the argument that the traditional practices are 'non-Islamic' because they do not have scriptural basis in the Quran and Hadith is not exactly to the point, although this is not wrong. The Quran and Hadith do not give a clear guidance to everything that may happen in human society and those which are not directly referred to in the scriptures should be interpreted by human beings. Seen from this perspective, the attitude of classifying all traditional practices into 'non-Islamic' ignores the contextual meanings put on these practices which are persuasive enough to make them Islamic. The ways these reformist villagers deal with traditional practices show that the process by which an Islamic tradition emerges from the syncretic background is far more complicated than what is customarily portrayed. It is not simply a process of imposing a certain criterion on traditional practices and removing them, but rather a process of questioning their relevance, abandoning what can not be accommodated, reinterpreting what can be harmonious with Islam and recontextualising them in Islamic terms. With these efforts, the dichotomy of 'things Islamic' and 'things non-Islamic' is established as an axis to evaluate local tradition and villagers try consciously not to be identified with the adherents of 'things non-Islamic', in whichever manner this term is defined.

Plate 7: The contents of a *besek*. Two brown yams (*ketela*) at the upper centre are *kolak*; road break at the lower centre is *apem*; and banana leaf is *ketan* (glutinous rice).

Plate 8: *Ingkung*

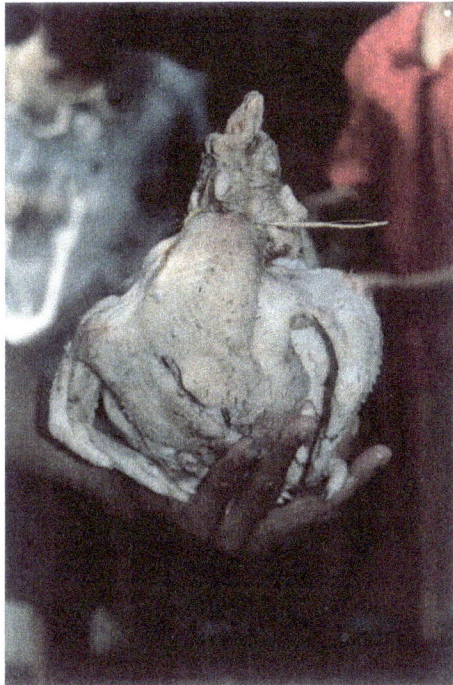

Plate 9: The celebration of a *kendhuri*. The *kaum* is the third on the left sitting along the wall.

Plate 10: The recitation of the Quran during a wedding ceremony

Chapter 6: Reformist Islam and Supernatural Beings

To the reformist villagers in Kolojonggo, attempts to confine Islamic teaching to religious life are not acceptable, since the division between the religious and non-religious is meaningless in Islam. Every facet of life should be directed at actualising what is commanded to human beings by Allah. In order to appreciate how this idea has been put into practice in Kolojonggo, the preceding chapters have examined the effort of the reformist villagers to Islamise every aspect of their life. In Chapter IV, their struggle to adopt Islamic teachings as working principles in everyday social and private life was discussed. In Chapter V, we have seen their endeavour to impose new contextual meanings on *kendhuri* and to incorporate new elements into life-cycle ritual to make a new Islamic tradition. In the same vein, this chapter will deal with belief in supernatural beings, a belief which was deeply embedded in life, constituting one of the core elements of the traditional syncretic worldview (Geertz,1976; Koentjaraningrat,1985a; Supatmo,1943). The focus of this chapter will be put on the fate of traditional supernatural beings and their spokespersons, *dhukun*, in a situation where reformist Islam has gradually become a major religious tenet in village life, and on the emergence of new ways to use supernatural power as alternatives to the traditional ways. For this purpose, a brief summary of the previous situation connected to belief in supernatural beings will be presented first.

6.1. Previous Situation of Belief in Supernatural Beings [1]

Various kinds of supernatural beings were thought to live side by side with villagers in rural Java. These can be classified into three in terms of their origin: Allah and souls of the dead prophets and holy men from Islam, gods and goddesses from Hinduism; souls of the dead and spirits residing in various places, probably of local origin. Villagers' attitude to each category of supernatural beings seems to have been slightly different, as was reflected in the terminology

---

[1] Two points need to be mentioned about this section. First, of a variety of traditional beliefs and practices related to supernatural beings, only limited materials are presented here, which are pertinent to further discussion in the next sections. In this sense, the picture that I present is selective. Second, the materials on which this section is based were collected from villagers who were alive at the time of my field research. Although they were older than sixty and retained much of their previous mode of thought, it is not plausible to say that they have not been influenced at all by the changing society. However, as their ideas were in parallel with those described by other scholars in the 1950s (Geertz,1976; Jay,1969; Koentjaraningrat,1985a; Supatmo,1943), they were considered to be 'old fashioned' (*kuna*) by other villagers and they were the only group of villagers who were accessible for this research, the method of mine to adopt their ideas as a baseline to understand the previous situation might be justified, even if partially. The number of villagers that I interviewed for this section was eleven. All of them were male and they were regarded as *dhukun* (for more about this concept, see below) by others. Of these eleven, two were from Kolojonggo, seven were from other hamlets in Sumber and the remaining two were from neighbouring *kelurahan*.

used to designate them. The titles for kings or high officials, such as *gusti, kanjeng* and *sunan* were applied to Islamic supernatural beings while the kinship terms such as *eyang, kyai, nyai* or *mbah* were used for others (Koentjaraningrat, 1985b:289). However, this distinction was unlikely to mean that a superior status was bestowed on Islamic supernatural beings. They were not compared with each other and villagers never bothered to think about a power relation, for example, between Allah and *dhanyang* (guardian spirits) (Supatmo,1943:4). In this respect, the supernatural world was a loosely connected confederation of supernatural beings, where a clearly defined hierarchy was not elaborated.

Sharing the same living space with villagers [2] , these supernatural beings were supposed to have partial responsibility for human affairs. They were thought to cause volcanic eruptions, floods, drought, eclipses, disease, poverty, fortune and other happenings (Supatmo,1943:4-11). In this way, they provided part of a meaningful framework to interpret the world for those who believed in them. As Geertz says, they were 'the triumph of culture over nature, human and non human' (1976:28). However, this did not mean that Javanese villagers lacked a capability to analyse natural forces or were not careful to see the immediate cause and effect of certain events. Rather, the tendency of Javanese villagers to pursue deeper explanations lying beyond the perceivable relation between cause and effect allowed supernatural beings to be included as a part of an explanatory scheme. If one person's house was damaged by fire or by a falling tree while that of his neighbour was not, the difference should be accounted for. If one person's stall was full of customers whereas neighbouring stalls were not, if one person's rice field was attacked by mice whereas others were not, if one person was infected by a contagious disease while others in the same house were not, explanations should be sought in order to rationalise the uneven results of certain phenomena. The mode of explanation seeking after deeper meanings beyond the perceivable cause and effect is well expressed in a story told by a villager regarding his previous experience of a fire:

> One of the tactics of the Dutch troops during the war of independence was to burn down all houses in order to sweep away the guerrillas and to destroy their infrastructure. .... It actually happened in this village. Since most of the houses were made from sugarcane leaves and wood, the fire spread rapidly. ... When the fire approached my house, however, it died down suddenly. As there were many trees in the yard, it was a real surprise to me. Another fire came, but it also disappeared, a situation which was repeated several times. ... It was only when I came of age that I understood the reason. My father told me this was due to the *pager*

---

[2] Trees, houses, wells, paddy fields, stones, rivers, swamps, forests, mountains, oceans and other natural objects were thought to be the places where supernatural beings resided.

omah (supernatural protection) which my grandfather had made surrounding the house and the *pusaka* (heirloom) which he possessed.

As this case shows, supernatural beings were available to give answers to the questions, which careful observation of certain phenomena could not provide. They transformed contingency into inevitability for those who were not satisfied with the explanation, 'by accident', alone.

As villagers had rules and tactics to live with their fellow human beings, they had knowledge and rules to deal with supernatural beings. This was called *ilmu* or *ngelmu*.[3] *Ilmu* was used to communicate with supernatural beings, to prevent their vicious intervention, if any, and to make use of their power. Every villager had some sort of *ilmu* which was passed on verbally. However, more powerful *ilmu* could be acquired either by accident[4], by inheritance, by achievement or by all of these means. Among these, achievement was the most common way. Although a person had a biological tie with someone known for his[5] high standard of *ilmu*, he had to make his own efforts to develop what he inherited. Otherwise, the efficacy of inherited *ilmu* was thought to be lost.

The best and in some sense, the only, way to acquire *ilmu* by achievement was to practise asceticism (*tapa*) such as fasting, not sleeping, not speaking, avoiding specific foods, suppressing the desire to breathe, enduring physical pains and so on. These exercises were believed to make the ascetic's inner self clean, which was a necessary condition for *ilmu* to enter his body. Among these various methods of asceticism, the fast (*pasa*) was regarded as the most basic. Only when the ascetic was accustomed to the fast, would he add other methods to his repertoire, for example, he might keep walking or immersing himself in cold water while practising the fast. Due to its importance, complex rules and regulations of carrying out the fast were developed.[6]

Generally, the villagers who decided to pursue *ilmu* sought assistance from others known for their high standard of *ilmu*, although independent pursuit without a teacher (*guru*) was not unknown. They visited their *guru* on a regular

[3] The term *ngelmu* is the association of *ilmu* and *ng-* which acts as an active verbal prefix, emphasising the practical side of *ilmu* rather than the knowledge for the sake of knowledge (Weiss,1977:264). Even if *ngelmu* is grammatically a verb, it was also used as a noun (Supatmo,1943:14).
[4] The acquisition of *ilmu* by accident happened when certain spirit entered the body of human beings. Compared with *ilmu* obtained from asceticism, it was thought to be more powerful but temporary (Supatmo,1943:17; Geertz,1976:99-103). When the state of possession ceased, the possessed was thought to lose his or her *ilmu*. For a recent description about a possessed *dhukun*, see Keeler (1987:119-124).
[5] As almost all of those who pursued *ilmu* and all the interviewees whose explanation this section is dependent on were male, the pronoun 'his' or 'him' rather than 'her' will be used.
[6] Different rules of restricting foods and of fixing the places, the beginning and closing date and time, the length and magical spells make each fast different. Some of the examples of the fast are: *pasa ngebleng* (all kind of food are prohibited); *pasa mutih* (rice and pure water without salt and sugar are permitted); *pasa ngrowot* (only vegetables and cassava are permitted); *pasa ngasrep* (cold foods and drinks are permitted); *pasa ngluweng* (complete fasting under the ground); and *pasa patigeni* (complete fasting in a dark room).

basis and learned methods of ascetic practice (*lelakon*)[7] , taboos connected to *lelakon* (*pantangan*)[8] , magical spells (*mel*)[9] and a system of numerological divination (*petungan* or counting)[10] . Their visits decreased rapidly when they were dissatisfied with the *guru* or got tired of their slow progress. It was at this stage that they tried to find another *guru* who was likely to give a different dimension of *ilmu*. This process of seeking a *guru* went on and on until they finally met someone who suited them or they stopped the quest, satisfied with what they had already attained.

In this traditional way of learning, the *guru* did not show all his repertoire to his pupils at one time as the teachers in modern educational system do by giving out a curriculum at the outset of study. Nor did he have any systematic way of teaching what he knew to his pupils. As the pupils did not know exactly what their *guru* possessed, the *ilmu* that the pupils asked of their teacher was none other than that directly related to their interests. They did not and could not give priority to *ilmu* in which they had no interest.

According to village elders, when they were young, most male villagers pursued *ilmu* at some stage of their life. However, not all of them continued their quest to an advanced stage. Only a few could keep their interest and proceed further with it. One of the important factors in maintaining their interest was indirect support from others. As one person kept pursuing *ilmu*, his fame would spread little by little until it eventually attracted others who were in need of his assistance. They came to his place to learn *ilmu*, to recover from disease, to discover lost items, to track down a thief, to increase their wealth, to enhance

---

[7] *Lelakon* or *lakon* means every kind of exercise to which one resorts to acquire *ilmu*. Apart from the most popular mode of *lelakon*, namely, the fast, there are countless other ways, some of which are: not to sleep, not to speak and to restrict one's breath.

[8] Some of the examples of *pantangan* are not to have sexual relations, not to eat specific foods (before or after the commencement of *lelakon*), and not to select a certain day for practice.

[9] *Mel, rapal* or *mantra* is the communication code which a person utters when he wants to make contact with supernatural beings. In most cases, *mel* is composed of words from Arabic and Javanese. Below is an example of *mel*: *Bismillah Alaikum Allah Bilghaib, Kawula nyuwun ijin Narantaka dalem ngaturi manjing wonten badan kawula jabang bayi* [insert the name of someone who pursues this *ilmu*], *kangge latihan manjingaken, ingkang estu, ingkang leres, ingkang keras, kanthi wilujeng.* The first part of this spell, *Bismillah Alaikum Allah Bilghaib*, seems to be Arabic, even if its meaning was not known even to the practitioner who taught this *mel* to me. The next Javanese part can be translated as follows: I ask a permission to allow *Narantaka* (name of *ilmu*) to enter my body, the name of my *jabang bayi* is [the name], [I do it] for exercising the insertion [of *Narantaka* to my body], with sincerity, with accuracy and with ardour. May everything be well!

[10] In the *petungan* system, hours, days, months and years are given with specific characters (*watak*) and numbers (*neptu*). In the case of calculating days which is most frequently used, a day is the combination of two different sequences of day, one from the 7-day system, from Monday to Sunday and the other from the 5-day system of *Pon, Wage, Kliwon, Legi* and *Pahing*. Being combined, each day is the association of one from the 7-day system and the other from the 5-day system such as Monday-*Pon*, Tuesday-*Wage*, Wednesday-*Kliwon* and so on. As a result, a certain combination can only be repeated after 35 days, when all possible associations are exhausted. 12 different days in these two systems are given their own specific numbers (*neptu*) ranging from 3 to 9, so that the 35 possible combinations have specific numbers ranging from 7 (Tuesday-*Wage*) to 18 (Saturday-*Pahing*). For more about this system, see Geertz (1976:30-35).

their authority over others and so on. Whatever the reasons, their visits gave him an incentive to practise asceticism to obtain higher *ilmu* or to maintain what he had already attained. After gaining widespread fame, he started to be called '*dhukun*', '*wong pinter*' (clever man), '*tiang sepuh*' or '*wong tuwa*' [11] by his clients and *guru* by his pupils.

The ideational system of the *dhukun* had a lot in common with that of the *priyayi* as it is described by Geertz: emphasis on emotional calmness, centrality of feeling (*rasa*) and pursuit of spiritual power through withdrawal from worldly life (1976:312-326). However, compared with the *priyayi*, their ideas were more concrete and expressed in personalised forms. If the *priyayi*'s ultimate aim of mystical pursuit was described as a search for reality or for the reflection of God in one's self (Geertz,1976:314), that of the *dhukun* was frequently explained as a search for the missing brothers called *kakang kawah* (amniotic fluid) and *adhi ari-ari* (umbilical cord) [12], for *bapak guru sejati* (the true teacher) or for *simbah* (ancestor), who were thought to make all the wishes of a human being possible. As ascetic practice had a subjective nature, the experiences of those who reached this last stage were also dependent on their own subjectivity. Some saw the missing brothers, *bapak guru sejati* or *simbah* with their very eyes while others just heard their voices. A villager explained his experience as follows:

> The *bapak guru* whom I met had exactly the same face as I have. Therefore, the situation in our encounter was just like when you stand in front of a mirror and see yourself. When I met him, I asked myself, 'this is myself and that is also myself, then, which one is the genuine one?' But the *bapak guru* kept silent, which made me realise that he was the one whom I had sought after for such a long time.

The philosophy of the concrete that the *dhukun* pursued was indifferent to doctrines. Their primary goal was not to make a metaphysical system but to deal with situations which concerned them, so that possible inner contradictions in their ideas did not bother them. This attitude was reflected in the ways they used their *ilmu*. There was no absolute way, for example, to cure a certain disease. If one method did not work, another should be tried, whose relation with the

---

[11] *Tiang sepuh* quoted by Geertz and *wong tuwa* reported by Keeler have the same meaning: old person. The difference is only the level of language. *Tiang sepuh* belongs to *krama* while *wong tuwa*, *ngoko* (Geertz,1976:96; Keeler,1987:114). In Kolojonggo, the most frequently used term is either *dhukun* or *wong pinter*. As the term *dhukun* has some derogatory meaning, the *dhukun* themselves as well as those who maintain close relations with them never use it. Only those who want to express their animosity use it.

[12] The *kakang kawah* and *adhi ari-ari* are thought to be twin brothers of every human being as their names imply: *kakang* means elder brother and *adhi*, younger brother. These three beings are said to exist together in the womb of a pregnant woman. After birth, they are separated. Some say that *kakang kawah* and *adhi ari-ari* live in the Southern Sea, waiting for the time of reunion after the death of their brother, while others are of the opinion that they are hovering over villages. Whatever their place of living, they are believed to have power to assist their visible brother when the latter successfully gets through the last stage of his ascetic exercise.

former might not be clear. These trials could continue until the most suitable one was discovered. For example, Pak Arjo had different ways of diagnosing and curing a disease, which he used in the following way:

> When someone asks me to cure his or her disease, I diagnose it with this calculation: *jogan* (floor), *catur* (speech), *sawah* (paddy field), *kali* (river).[13] ... If he or she does not recover and returns to my place, I'll use the second way. I'll cut a branch of a tree and use the calculation of *mari* (recover), *mulya* (sublime), *seneng* (glad). After it, I'll ask *dhanyang* with a magical spell. ... Apart from *dhanyang*, assistance can also be sought from ancestors (*leluhur*). ... If these do not work, I'll make use of another one, namely, *Allah-Ngendiko* (says)-*Mundhut* (take)-*Nyawa* (soul) while asking Allah for the right method of treating that disease.

The existence of the *dhukun*, their continuous communication with villagers and the efficacy of their practice were conditions that allowed the reproduction of belief in supernatural beings. The popularity of ascetic exercise among ordinary male villagers assured the position of the *dhukun* and the maintenance of the system that he supported. In spite of individual variations, many ordinary villagers went to the river to immerse themselves in water, especially, every night of Friday-*Kliwon* and Tuesday-*Kliwon* when spirits were said to be the most active. They stayed awake at the tomb of their dead ancestors in the Javanese months of *Ruwah* and *Sura*. They began to restrict food intake when their day of birth (*neton*)[14] approached.

In sum, supernatural beings, with their influential grip over villagers, provided for those who believed in their existence a set of answers to the questions posed by vague and otherwise incomprehensible experiences (Geertz,1976,17&28). They also provided a reservoir from which villagers could draw appropriate measures to cope with difficulties and to satisfy their wishes. In this traditional system, the *dhukun* was the medium to connect villagers with supernatural beings and, in doing so, he played the role of an ideologue who supported, elaborated and perpetuated this system.

---

[13] In this calculation, he may use the *neton* of the patient, the *neptu* of the time and the date when the patient visits his place or of the time and the date when the first symptom of a disease appears. (see footnote no. 10 for *neptu* and no. 14, for *neton*) After he gets a certain number from this calculation, he divides this by 4. When the remaining number is 1, it signifies the disease is related to *jogan*, if it is 2, it is interpreted to be connected to *catur* and so forth. For example, if the patient comes to his place on Sunday-*Pahing* which has the *neptu* of 13, the calculation falls on *jogan* in that, after 13 is divided by 4, the remaining number is 1. It is almost impossible to make a generalisation about how he interprets different results from different ways of calculation. Intuition, context and mood of the moment when he meets the patient seem to influence his treatment of a disease a lot.

[14] When the Javanese are asked when they were born, the usual answer is not the date of their birthday but the day of their birth. As the Javanese day is a combination of the seven day and five day systems, one meets one's day of birth once every 35 days. When one was born, for example, on *Senin-Kliwon*, this day becomes one's *neton*.

6.2. Reformist Attack and Supernatural Beings [15]

In *kendhuri*, non-Islamic supernatural entities have lost their positions. It is only the name of Allah that is heard in its introductory speech. This gives the impression that supernatural beings have failed to retain their earlier privilege to intrude into village affairs. This impression is reinforced, when we look at the mundane life of villagers. In public, conversations about supernatural beings are not frequently heard and ascetic practices are seldom visible. If they happen to be the subjects of casual talking, conversations about them are usually done in a caricatured manner. When there was a lunar eclipse, for example, many villagers made comments on it as if they had once lived in a pre-enlightened era: 'at that time, we used to come outside, hitting the *kenthongan* (a drum made from a hollowed-out log) and yelling, 'the moon is eaten by the *Buta'* (a kind of supernatural being who has a giant body), so that it might return the moon to us.[16]

One of the factors which have brought this change is the development of reformist Islam which opposes traditional belief and practices connected to supernatural beings. As one villager put it, a shift has taken place from the situation in which '*syirik* was not known to villagers' to the state in which '*syirik* matters a lot'. *Syirik* is the same as *shirk* in Arabic. The word, *shirk*, has a literal meaning of 'sharing'; man is forbidden to share his or her worship of Allah with that of any other creatures, and to ascribe partners to Allah as sharers of His Divinity (Netton,1992:231). According to the reformist villagers, *syirik* is the worst sin in Islam. It is the only one which cannot be forgiven by Allah whereas other great sins (*dosa besar*) such as killing, telling a lie, disobedience to one's parents and adultery can be forgiven on the condition that one's repentance is true and one does not repeat the sin. In the discourse of village Muslims, the commonly used definition of *syirik* was belief in and reliance on supernatural power of things and persons, as Pak Hardi put it:

[15] In the above section, Allah was included in the term 'supernatural beings', since villagers did not differentiate Allah clearly from other supernatural beings. However, the term 'supernatural beings' in the sections below does not include Allah. This is because the term 'supernatural beings', which is the English equivalent of an Indonesian term, *makluk halus*, is now used by villagers as a concept separated from Allah. This semantic modification reflects the change that has taken place in the way villagers perceive Allah and supernatural beings, the proper topic of this and the next sections.
[16] Bråten gives a different way Central Javanese villagers dealt with the lunar eclipse: some of villagers at his research site celebrated a lunar eclipse *slametan* in a secret and disguised manner. It was secret since Bråten was not informed of it by his landlord who participated in it. It was disguised since he got an explanation, after he went to the place of the *slametan*, that it was given not for the lunar eclipse but for the initiation of a new house. He interpreted this experience as supporting his argument that Muslim villagers strive to make their own religious identity ambiguous (Bråten,1989). This is different from the way villagers in Kolojonggo dealt with the lunar eclipse. What I observed was a special ritual prayer in the *masjid* after the regular *isaq* prayer. A short sermon on the meaning of the lunar eclipse and the way of praying at the time of eclipse was delivered to the villagers. Apart from this, I did not observe any special event that night, although this might not guarantee that the *slametan* was not given in a secret and disguised manner in Kolojonggo.

The most serious *syirik* is to think that Allah has a son and a wife or to make pictures or statues of Him. To follow a mystical teacher, to ask help from the *dhukun*, to make offerings and to possess amulets (*jimat*) also belong to this category. Some of the Islamic leaders (*kiyai*) outside the circle of Muhammadiyah still have an understanding that short [Arabic] passages wrapped in a white cloth (*mori*) or written on the surface of an agate (*akik*) or bracelet, will bring protection, invulnerability and fortune to its holder. This is a wrong understanding, which will make someone go astray. ... One day, a man visited my place with the Quran of a small size, called *Al-Quran Istanbul*, which he had bought in a market for Rp 1500. ... A story goes that the soldiers brought this book with them during the war of independence [against the Dutch], believing it would make them invulnerable to bullets. I will provide the correct interpretation of this story: it will bring us fortune, invulnerability and so on, not when we carry it in our pocket or under our *peci* but when we learn and practise it.

Even if Pak Hardi did not comment on supernatural beings, it is not so difficult to assume that belief in them may belong to the category of *syirik*. However, this is not the case. On the contrary, not to believe in them is what is categorised as non-Islamic. This paradox stems from the concept of *jinn* which is separated from satan in Islamic ontology.

According to the Quran[17], God created a being called a *jinn*, apart from angels (*malaikat*), satan (*syaitan*) and human beings. Angels were created from light (*cahaya*), the *jinn* and satan from pure fire and human beings, from dried clay (xv: 26-7).[18] The purpose of Allah in creating the *jinn* and human beings was the same, that is, to let them worship Him (li:56). Although much remains vague, the nature of the *jinn* is described as parallel to that of human beings: the *jinn* were created to have the heart to understand, eyes to see and ears to hear (vii:179) and to have sexual desires (lv:72-4).[19] As is the case among human beings, the *jinn* are in two categories, those who have surrendered themselves to God and those who [did not and] are unjust (lxxii:14). With this freedom to choose their own way, the *jinn* are responsible for their own behaviour which will determine their future place either in Paradise or Hell (xi:119; lxxii:15). Despite these

---

[17] The following quotations from the Quran are selected with the help of several references: Ali Chasan,1980; Bjorkman,1953; Rahman,1980; Umar Hasyim,1980. However, interpretations of these quotations are my responsibility, unless the sources are cited.
[18] Roman numerals in the parenthesis indicate the Surah and the Arabic numerals, the verse(s) in the Quran. Most of the quotations from the Quran in this chapter use the translation of M. Pickthall (1930).
[19] That the *jinn* have sexual desire is based on the exegesis of several verses done by Umar Hasyim (1980:42): Wherein (are found) the good and beautiful. ... Fair ones, close-guarded in pavilions ... *Whom neither man nor jinn will have touched* before them (lv:72-4, italics mine). These passages, according to Umar Hasyim, make it possible for us to infer that the *jinn* also have sexual relations with their opposite sex.

similarities, the realm the *jinn* inhabit is separate from that of human beings, so that the world of the *jinn* is not directly perceivable to human senses. However, several verses in the Quran imply this separateness is incomplete. 'And indeed individuals of humankind used to invoke the protection of individuals of the *jinn*' (lxxii:6) or 'the *jinn* know well that they [human beings] will be brought before (Him)' (xxxvii,158). These verses make it possible for us to infer that human beings can perceive the existence of the *jinn* and the *jinn* know the situation in human society. Otherwise, there is no possibility that human beings could worship the *jinn* and the *jinn* could condemn the sinful behaviour of human beings.

The concept of the *jinn* that the reformist leaders possess does not deviate from the Quranic references, as is seen in this story told by a former junior high school teacher:

> The *jinn* and human beings were created to live in different worlds, even if the boundary is liable to be transgressed. Among the *jinn*, there are those who believe in Islam and those who do not. ... In the *masjid* of my hamlet, it happened that the tap in the place for ablution opened by itself after all villagers finished their ablution and entered the *masjid*. While praying, they could feel that someone was following their movements, although they could not see who he or she was. This situation was repeated for several days, stirring up lots of rumours. However, the answer was quite simple. It was the *jinn* who prayed side by side with villagers. We don't know exactly why the *jinn* came to our place, but since they are also commanded to pray, it is not such a strange story at all.

The significance of the Islamic concept of the *jinn* is such that traditional supernatural beings do not need to give up their previous ontological position to acquire new Islamic identity, if they accept some modifications.[20] On the one hand, they should admit that the term *jinn* is a name representing them. If previously the term *jinn* (or *jim*) was for a specific kind of supernatural being, it should now be the generic term to embrace all kinds of supernatural beings other than satan and angels. On the other hand, they must acknowledge their inferior position vis-à-vis the newly encountered Creator of them, Allah. If these changes are admitted, the ontological basis of traditional supernatural beings subsumed under the rubric of the term *jinn* becomes much stronger than before. If Muslim villagers were allowed to doubt the existence of supernatural beings, no space is now reserved for scepticism since the Quran reveals that Allah created the invisible *jinn* and the division between their world and human world is not

---

[20] The souls of the dead are an exception. It is because reformist Islam teaches that all relations between those who live in this world and those who have already died are severed. The dead souls, which were believed to visit this world frequently, are no longer able to do so.

absolute. Careful observation is enough to confirm the existence of supernatural beings as a villager said: 'it is possible that the experience of supernatural beings is hallucination but, if many people have seen them, they are certainly the *jinn*.' Acquisition of a stable position in the belief system of Muslim villagers, however, does not guarantee that supernatural beings retain their previous relationships with human beings. Rather, these relationships should also be redefined.

The reformist villagers suggested that one's attempt to make contact with the *jinn* does not belong to *syirik*, in that it is the duty of every Muslim to search for knowledge. There were even some who attached credit to this attempt since it would make one's belief in Allah strong, getting rid of any scepticism as to the truth of His words. However, most reformists reserved this attempt not for all Muslims but for a few, since it could bring negative effects, especially to those whose religious piety was not strong enough to resist the temptation of the *jinn*. The following conversation between Pak Wiknyo and me over this problem shows the concern of the reformist villagers about this issue. When Mas Kuri and his friends talked in the *masjid* about the experience of a man who had made contact with the *jinn*, Pak Wiknyo intervened, scolding me because I had asked Mas Kuri to take me to that man.

> **Pak Wiknyo** : Do not ask others to take you to the place of someone who can contact the *jinn*! It is a sin (*dosa*) for you as well as those who introduce you to him since it is quite clear that he does not practise the right way of Islam. Even if you give me several million Rupiah, I definitely won't comply with your request.
>
> **My question** : Is it forbidden by Allah to be in contact with the *jinn*?
>
> **Pak Wiknyo** : In principle, no.
>
> **My question** : Then, why is it a sin if one tries to make contact with them?
>
> **Pak Wiknyo** : If there is a man who is simply satisfied with the mere act of meeting the *jinn*, it is not a problem at all. However, it is impossible in reality. When the *dhukun* begins his trial to know them, he may have the same idea, that is, to know is enough. However, after making contact with them, he cannot resist the temptation to use them. ... Do you know why Allah created satan? They were created to entice human beings and to cause them to commit what is forbidden by Allah.
>
> **My question** : What I am talking about is not satan but the *jinn*. I've heard that there are *jinn* who are pious to Allah.
>
> **Pak Wiknyo** : That is true, as is written in the Quran. However, the pious *jinn* never try to be in contact with human beings. It is only the heathen *jinn* (*jinn kafir*) who are happy to be summoned by us and are willing to make friends with us. As these beings are not on the side of

Allah, those who try to know them are also on the opposite side of Him. Why do we make efforts to know the *jinn*, the behaviour of which is not recommended by Allah? Our life is too short to realise what is ordered by Him.

As Pak Wiknyo unconsciously showed in his conversation, the term *jinn* is used almost synonymously with satan in the everyday language of the reformist villagers. It is because, they argue, the *jinn* who are ready to be friends with human beings are *kafir* (heathen) and bad-mannered (*kurang ajar*) rather than pious. As they are *kafir*, it is quite natural that their role is similar to that of satan.

The Quranic verses about the relation between the *jinn* and satan seem rather ambiguous. In some cases, they differentiate the *jinn* from satan while in others they do not. The Creation story in the Quran shows that Iblis originally belonged in the category of an angel:' ... Fall ye [angels] prostrate before Adam! And they fell prostrate, all save Iblis, who was not of those who make prostration. ... (Iblis) said: I am better than him' (vii:11-12). This arrogance caused Iblis to be expelled from Heaven. He was cursed by Allah, even if the execution was postponed by Him until the Day of Judgement. 'He (Iblis) said [to Allah]: Now, because [Thou] hast sent me astray, verily I shall lurk in ambush for them on Thy Right Path' (vii:16). The role that Iblis begged of Allah was granted and Iblis was destined to lure humans beings to deviate from the road which Allah commanded to them. Iblis acted in his role first to Adam and his wife. The Quran explains the scene of the first temptation in human history as follows: 'Then satanwhispered to them that he might manifest unto them that which was hidden from them of their shame' (vii:20, emphasis mine). This verse shows that Iblis and satan are the same entity. It was Iblis, called satan, who whispered to Adam and his wife that Allah forbade them the tree, only lest they should become angels or immortals.

In contrast to this equation of Iblis with satan, another verse in the Quran informs us that Iblis belongs to the *jinn*: 'And when We said unto the angels: Fall prostrate before Adam, and they fell prostrate, all save Iblis. He was of the *jinn*, so he rebelled against his Lord's command' (xviii:51; emphasis mine). This equation of Iblis with the *jinn* seems inconsistent with that of Iblis with satan in the quotation above (viz. vii:20).

Apart from this vagueness in the Quran, personal experiences of the reformist villagers might be the reason why exact separation between the *jinn* and satan is not observed. Many of them were born and raised in a situation where villagers did not differentiate Allah clearly from supernatural beings, relied on them to achieve certain aims, made offerings to them and, sometimes, worshipped them, all of which could be directly classified as *syirik*. As a result, it may not be such a big mistake for them to equate supernatural beings, namely, *jinn*, with satan, who is a declared enemy of human beings (xxxv:6) and who has the role of luring human beings to deviate from the path commanded by Allah.

When supernatural beings are subsumed under the term *jinn* which is frequently equated with satan, one of their characteristics cannot be retained. Formerly, the natures of supernatural beings were not defined in an absolute way: they could be both benevolent and malevolent, depending on the human side. [21] If one's wish was vicious, the supernatural beings whom he would be in contact with were thought to be malignant whereas, if one had a virtuous goal, for example, to cure disease, the beings who would assist this request were believed to be benevolent. In the same vein, *ilmu*, the weapon of human beings to deal with supernatural beings, was not divided into good and bad or white and black since its nature would be decided in accordance with the development of one's degree of dignity (*derajat*) as a villager put it: one's admission that his *ilmu* was white or he sought after only *ilmu putih* (white *ilmu*) could not be a sign that he actually practised *ilmu putih*. Instead, if someone reached a high degree of dignity, the *ilmu* that he practised would naturally be categorised as white.

In contrast to this relativistic attitude, the reformist villagers have urged an absolute evaluation of supernatural beings. In their thought, all supernatural beings are vicious in so far as they are ready to be in touch with human beings. The same evaluation also applies to the act of seeking assistance from supernatural beings. To ask something of supernatural beings is now considered to be sin. The reason is quite simple: the being with whom they make contact is vicious. *Ilmu* is also judged by this absolute yardstick. Irrespective of whether the practice of certain *ilmu* brings positive outcomes or not, for example, to cure illness, to find lost things and to help someone obtain a prestigious job, it is now categorised as black when it is done with the help of supernatural beings. There is no more 'white' left in *ilmu*.

To summarise, traditional supernatural beings can find their ontological position in Islam. They are fit for the category of the *jinn*, whose existence is fully approved of by Islamic ontology. However, their acceptance of this new position means that they have to give up one of the characteristics that the Javanese villagers had given to them, namely, benevolence. The reformist villagers have been at the forefront to eradicate the benevolent character from supernatural beings by equating them with satan. In their thought, mere contact with supernatural beings is supposed to be a sign that one's religiosity is not strong. If this effort of the reformist villagers had been successful, supernatural beings might have admitted their evil nature, abandoning their influential position and accepting a marginalised position in village life. Until now, however, this ideal

---

[21] There were a few exceptions such as *dhanyang* who was thought not to harm people and *thuyul* (a kind of supernatural being who steals others' wealth for the patron) who was believed to be always vicious.

of the reformist villagers has not yet been reached in Kolojonggo. Supernatural beings still imprint their presence upon villagers, resisting attacks from the reformist villagers.

6.3. The Position of Supernatural Beings

In spite of the bad reputation inflicted on them both by reformist Islam and by the coming of demystified society [22], supernatural beings still constitute a part of village life. They have been able to imprint their existence on the villagers' belief system, expressing their willingness to assist them. The lack of public conversation about them makes it difficult for outsiders to appraise the present state of belief in supernatural beings in villagers' worldview. A rare chance to understand it, however, came from an unexpected quarter: a traditional art called *jathilan* or *jaranan*.

The *jathilan* is a collective group dance where the performers ride bamboo horses and experience a state of trance in the course of dancing. Formerly, it was mainly performed by a professional itinerant troupe (Geertz,1976,296-7; see also Koentjaraningrat,1985a:211). However, the pendulum has swung from the professional to the amateur and from streets and markets to villages. It is now ordinary villagers living in rural areas who organise their own troupes and perform it sporadically whenever a request is made to them.

Several factors seem to be responsible for the recent popularity of the *jathilan* group amongst rural villagers. First, the government has encouraged villagers to participate in a program to preserve traditional art. [23] Second, as the general economic situation has improved, more villagers have tended to celebrate certain private occasions such as circumcision, entrance to university and getting a job, by sponsoring an art performance. This is not a new trend since *wayang* (shadow play) performances were held for the same purpose. However, the cost of *wayang*, which is about ten times higher than other folk arts such as a *gamelan orchestra*, *slawatan, kethoprak* and *jathilan*, makes its celebration difficult. [24] Third, the

[22] Demystification in the text means the surge of the positivist paradigm, science and technology which dominates modern Western society. This paradigm has eroded many of the domains where spiritual belief played its role as a legitimate factor of explanation, as the cases of disease and natural phenomena of earthquake, drought, volcanic eruption, flood, etc., indicate. It has also collided with the previous mode of explanation which sought a rationale beyond the phenomenological relatedness of observable cause and effect.

[23] The visits of the *camat* (head of the sub-district office), *kelurahan* officials and *lurah* to the first official performance of several *jathilan* groups in Sumber show government's commitment to the preservation of traditional art forms.

[24] Villagers said that it cost more than 1 million Rupiah to invite a group to perform *wayang*, while the cost could be reduced to as little as Rp 100,000 when they invited an art group of *gamelan* (Javanese traditional orchestra), *slawatan* (recitation of traditional Javanese poetry, whose story is connected to the life history of the Prophet Muhammad) or *jathilan*. In the case of *kethoprak* (the Javanese drama depicting historical or pseudo-historical events), the cost reached around Rp 300,000-400,000 in 1993. In contrast to *wayang*, whose performers should be invited from a different sub-district, villagers had easy access to other art groups since every hamlet had one or more of them. For example, Kolojonggo

jathilan is more dynamic than other traditional arts and appeals easily to youngsters who have much time to idle away, freed as they are from productive labor. Fourth, it is relatively easy and inexpensive to form a *jathilan* group. Three or four kinds of musical instruments, 8 bamboo horses, 2 *topeng* (wooden masks) and costumes for 8-12 performers are the minimum requisites to establish a new group. Whatever the exact reason, the popularity of *jathilan* has been extraordinary. In 1993-94, five hamlets among nineteen in Sumber founded their own *jathilan* groups.

Before the beginning of the performance, eight horses are placed at the center of an open ground, making two rows. Offerings to supernatural beings are placed near where *gamelan* musicians take their seats, facing the horses. When the music starts, eight performers come out of the house and kneel beside the horses. Each of them grips a wooden stick with their right hand and holds the neck of the horse with their left one. The changing rhythm of music signals the commencement of the performance. All the performers stand up and begin their dances, locating the bamboo horse between their thighs as if they were riding a horse. Different footsteps and diverse motions of hands and head bring variations to their dance. Within a few minutes, the riders are divided into two parties and enact a war scene. [25] They are drawn into a series of combats in which they strike one another with their bamboo sticks. This act reaches its end when one rider leads an abrupt assault on the opposite party, which is followed by all the other performers. Clashing together, they fall down on the ground. It is at this moment of chaos that supernatural beings are said to enter the performers' bodies. Possession is recognised by their paralysed bodies.

A massage makes the performers recover from their paralysis. After recovery, the movements of the performers are thought to be controlled by supernatural beings. Some show their extraordinary capacities by biting off the outer shell of a coconut with their teeth, by chewing pieces of glass, by holding a chicken in their mouths and sometimes by walking on coals with bare feet. Others behave in an uninhibited fashion, by chasing after girls, climbing a tree, making exaggerated facial and bodily expressions and so on.The more incredible their feats or passions are, the greater the applause they receive from the audience. As the play continues, some members of the audience who are grasped and pushed down on the ground by the riders are also possessed. They join the original performers and dance in a state of possession. The performance goes on

had *gamelan, jathilan* and *kethoprak* groups while its neighbouring hamlet had *slawatan* and *kethoprak* groups.
[25] According to the leader of the *jathilan* group in Kolojonggo, its story originated from the kingdom of Demak: a princess of Demak kingdom whose wedding was close at hand was kidnapped by its enemy. In order to get her back, the king organised a group of soldiers. While they did military drills, they became too much absorbed in them and forgot the fact that they were doing exercises. As a result, they fought one another as if they had met a real enemy.

until the last dancer is freed from possession by a *pawang*[26] , which normally takes around an hour and half. Therefore, a *jathilan* group can play four or five times a day, from 10 in the morning till 5 or 6 in the afternoon, attracting huge audiences.

It was Pak Silo who initiated a plea for establishing a *jathilan* group in Kolojonggo. At first, his move originated from his personal desire to strengthen his weak position among villagers. He and his wife were university graduates, a condition sufficient to give them high social status in village life. However, they were not born in this village, which caused them to be treated, according to their own evaluation, improperly for their high qualifications. [27] To compensate for this weakness, Pak Silo has attempted to organise art groups since he moved into this village. He established a *kethoprak* group andthen, a *gamelan group*, over which he lost control after the groups got started. The *jathilan* was the next item that he relied on for the same purpose. As his personal motive implies, it was not his commitment to the traditional belief system and *ilmu* which lay behind his initiative in establishing a *jathilan* group. On the contrary, he was proud of his modernity stemming from his education and had never showed interest in supernatural beings before he set out to found the group.

When he announced his intention to launch a *jathilan* group, it was greeted enthusiastically by the younger generation, already acquainted with this art form. At the first preparatory meeting, villagers from their early teens to their early thirties were present *en masse*. From that time on, they collected donations from villagers, made costumes and *topeng* and practised *gamelan* music and the horse dance under a temporary *pawang* whom Pak Silo invited from the neighbouring *kecamatan*.

When the *jathilan* became a hot public issue before and shortly after its foundation, scepticism dominated discussion about the state of possession during the horse dance. Many villagers, especially those in their twenties and thirties, considered it to be a fake originating from collective hallucination or from the alcohol that the performers drank before the beginning of a performance, both of which made them brave enough to behave in an abnormal manner. Pak Sri enumerated several points which caused him to suspect possession was not supernatural:

---

[26] The *pawang* is the guide of the *jathilan*. During the performance, he monitors whether the whole situation is in order and, with his magical power, makes the possessed regain consciousness.

[27] Whether one was born in this village or not is not the sole factor determining one's status in village life. To understand the case of Pak Silo, his personality which was considered to be arrogant (*sombong*) by villagers should be taken into account. It is a custom in village life that one should not display what one is or has, if he or she does not want to be considered *sombong*. If one speaks frankly about what one is or has, he or she can be easily considered to be *sombong*. The personality of Pak Silo which makes him speak frankly of what he knows and show off his educational background has brought him a bad reputation.

The performers who were said to be possessed (*dadi*) knew exactly who the pretty girls were and they only chased after them. If they had been really possessed, how could they do so? ... Only a few among the performers were said to be possessed. If they were in the same situation while dancing, why were all of them not possessed? It is said that those who are in bodily contact with the possessed man and pushed down on the ground by him will also be possessed. However, I've never seen any of the assistants of the *jathilan* group [28] possessed, although they stumbled over the possessed performers accidentally. ... There are so many things which make me doubt the actuality of possession. Seeing the performers whom I know well, I get an impression that they pretend to be possessed with the help of alcohol which might lessen their feelings of shame in public.

After the *jathilan* group did their regular performance, more youngsters were involved in it, and their experiences of possession spread to other villagers, a side effect which was not anticipated by Pak Silo and other members began to appear among villagers, namely, the disappearance of sceptical or 'I-doubt-it' attitudes. Most villagers believed that possession during the performance was real and that it was triggered by supernatural beings, although no consensus was reached on the identity of the supernatural beings who were responsible for it.

The reformist villagers were certain that the responsibility lay in the heathen *jinn* or satan, whose duty was to entice human beings. As the performers did not use reason (*akal*), emptied their heads and followed their physical desires (*nafsu*), all of which were not recommended behaviour for Muslims, they argued that Muslims should distance themselves from the *jathilan*, as they fought against the temptation of satan. Others who were less active in Islamic activities used the neutral term, 'invisible being' (*makluk halus*), to explain the possessing beings, while their specific names were not agreed upon. Even the main body of the *jathilan* group in Kolojonggo did not have any conclusive idea of them. Its members generally thought of them as supernatural beings residing in certain places such as a cemetery, river, tree, or the yard where they performed. This lack of consensus among the *jathilan* members arose from the fact that no one in its organising body had deep knowledge of supernatural beings and that they failed to incorporate someone who was famous for his *ilmu* as an ideologue of

---

[28] The *jathilan* group consists of two sub-groups. One group consists of the performers and the other, of those who control the performance. The major duty of the second group is to make a barrier around the playground to block the possessed performers when they suddenly dash into the audience. As they do this job with their bodies, it is quite usual for them to be in close contact with the possessed performers. It seldom happens, however, that these guards are possessed while dealing with the performers.

their group. Accordingly, they took their experience of possession for granted rather than tried to explain it systematically.

The same situation did not apply in the *jathilan* group in Pasekan, a hamlet on the southern side of Kolojonggo. Soon after its foundation, the *jathilan* group in Kolojonggo achieved remarkable popularity in this area, which naturally caused the youth in Pasekan to decide to have their own group. In this process, they were lucky enough to include Pak Atin, the famous *wong pinter* living in Pasekan, as a *pawang* of their group. As a result, the *jathilan* members in Pasekan shared a more systematic explanation for their own performance which originated with Pak Atin. Asked about supernatural beings in the *jathilan*, Pak Atin replied as follows:

> Before the day of the performance, various supernatural beings visit my house, disclosing their wishes of me, such as for specific drinks, foods, flowers or something else. If they are satisfied with what is offered to them [the offering made by the host of the *jathilan*], no serious problem occurs during the performance. They observe the agreement made between me and themselves. If they are not satisfied, however, it takes longer for me to control the situation. As it is my side that breaks the agreement first, I have to fight with these beings who are angry at this maltreatment. ... Therefore, which supernatural beings are responsible for a specific performance can be decided only when they visit my place, registering themselves with me. They are sometimes those living in the area where the performance will be celebrated, while in other cases, they are the souls of the deceased.

Ordinary members of this group had the same ideas as Pak Atin. They knew more about the reasons and the process of possession, the methods for expelling invisible beings and other extraordinary things happening during the performance than their counterparts in Kolojonggo. A high school student had a clearer idea than Pak Silo about why the performers in the *jathilan* group of Kolojonggo did not speak when they were possessed:

> It is because they [the *jathilan* group in Kolojonggo] made a permanent contract with a *dhemit* [29] who will safeguard the performance from possible interference from other supernatural beings. As a result, interferences from an unexpected *roh* (dead soul) who wishes to talk through the mouth of the possessed performers have not occurred unlike cases in our group. ... Until now, they are quite fortunate since *roh* who have higher *ilmu* than their guardian *dhemit* do not visit their performance place. If it happened, it would be a catastrophe for them.

---

[29] The term *dhemit* is sometimes used to refer all supernatural beings, while in others, it is considered as a kind of spirit which lives in a specific place such as a house, a tree, a well and so on.

The *ilmu* of the *pawang* [in Kolojonggo] is not strong enough to control this accident. What he did was just to make a pact with the *dhemit* and to keep that relation.

There is an interesting point to be made about the development of the *jathilan* group in Kolojonggo. Its initiator was not a man who had close relations with supernatural beings such as a *dhukun* but one who stood somewhat against it. His original intention was also far from that of reviving a traditional belief system. The youth reacted enthusiastically to it not because they were curious about supernatural beings and wanted explanations for the experiences beyond their reason, an attitude demonstrated by their lack of interest in understanding the rationale behind possession. Instead, they pursued it as fun and enjoyed the severance from daily life which emphasises refined ways of behaviour. However, despite this naiveté, the effect of the *jathilan* has been remarkable. It has reaffirmed the existence of supernatural beings. Moreover, the supernatural beings they support are not an abstract and moralistic image of supernatural beings as the reformist villagers hold, but concrete and vivid images which were common before the surge of reformist Islam. [30] In brief, the *jathilan* has strengthened the traditional identity of supernatural beings, helping them to resist an attack from reformist Islam which has tried to equate them with the *jinn* and satan.

I had another chance to look at the present position of supernatural beings when the *anak masjid* performed three dramas for children, commemorating the birth of the Prophet Muhammad and the end of Fasting Month, and consolidating the brotherhood among Muslims. A brief summary of these three dramas is as follows:

[The first drama]

Parjo, the only child of a poor peasant, hated his life in the village and yearned for a new life in the city. In spite of the objection of his father, he left his house and headed for the city, making a promise that he would fetch his father when he became rich. In the city, he seduced the daughter of a rich businessman and succeeded in marrying her, hiding his village background from her family. One day, two street musicians from his village happened to visit his house to ask for money. Not recognising them, Parjo treated them harshly and expelled them from the door. They returned to their village and told this story to Parjo's father who had

---

[30] Traditional supernatural beings were concrete and vivid in the sense that their characters were thought to take after those of human beings. A few examples are: *gendruwo,* a giant with big red eyes; *peri,* a charming woman with a hole at her back and appearing only to those who frequently flirt with women; *thikthikan,* a male making a sound of *thikthik* while walking; *pocongan,* a living corpse wrapped in white cloths with a tie over its head; *wewe,* a female who has an ability to make someone invisible when the latter steals something; *thuyul,* a child stealing money from others; and *dewi Sri,* a beautiful woman controlling paddy and *Niyai Lara Kidul,* a charming woman living in the Southern sea and inviting people to her palace.

been eager to meet his son. Hearing the news that his son had become rich, he headed for his son's house. However, Parjo pretended not to know his father. In front of his wife, he denied his father and drove him out of his house, cursing and beating him. It was not long before Parjo was seized with an unknown disease, which could not be cured by the doctor. As the last resort, his wife fetched the *dhukun*. Using his heirloom (*pusaka*) and uttering magical formula, the *dhukun* began to diagnose his disease.

> *Dhukun*: If the situation is like this, I am not brave enough to treat it. My magical spell is not strong. Serious, really serious! This is not ordinary sickness. His disease originated from his inner self since he was disobedient (*berani*) to his parent.

> Parjo's Wife: Oh, it is certain that the old man who came before is the father of Parjo.

> *Dhukun*: Right, as is written in my *pusaka*.

> Parjo: I don't believe in an obscene *dhukun* (*dhukun cabul*) like you. My sickness might be from sprain.

> *Dhukun*: Listen to my words! If one is disobedient (*berani*) to his parents, his fate is like this. There is no way to cure this disease except for the help of the man whom you have hurt. In fact, you are cursed (*kualat*) due to your behaviour. Cursed!

> Parjo: What? Being cursed! Please, help me, Pak *Dhukun*. I ask forgiveness.

The drama ended happily. The *dhukun* brought Parjo's father, who at last forgave his son.

[The second drama]

Murni was a daughter of a poor peasant who could not afford her education nor wanted to do so. She had to go to the house of Wanti whose father was rich to borrow books and other materials. There, Murni was mocked by Wanti. Although she returned home with a broken heart, her parents did not bother about it much. Then, there came the final exam. Murni was fortunate to pass it whereas Wanti was not. Hearing that his daughter failed the exam, Wanti's father became furious and swore at his wife and Wanti. This caused Wanti to became hysterical, which could not be treated by doctors. Then she was taken to the *dhukun* who could not cure it, either. At last, her family took Wanti to the *pesantren*. Hearing the story, the *kiyai* asked his pupil to bring the Quran and a glass of water. He recited some verses in front of the glass of water and ordered Wanti to drink it, which made it possible for her to recover her consciousness. Then, the *kiyai* gave advice to Wanti and her family about the importance of educating children and of adopting the teaching of Allah in everyday life. After returning from the *pesantren*, Wanti visited Murni's house to apologise for her arrogant behaviour.

[The third drama]

Every day Harto gambled and spent money. One day, returning from gambling, he asked his father to sell the house and paddy field to pay his debt and for more gambling, arguing that the property would be his upon his parents' death. Being pressed by Harto, his father died from stress. Not regretting what he did to his father, Harto coaxed his mother and two sisters to give up their right of inheritance. As they rejected his proposal, he expelled them from their house and sold the paddy fields. As a result of his bad behaviour, he was cursed (*kualat*) by his dead father, which caused his two legs to be paralysed. When he begged money from the passers-by in the street, he met three girls whom he had known before. Seeing Harto's pitiful situation, they started to mock him. Filled with shame, Harto fled from them. His mother, returning home with two daughters, heard the story of Harto and tried to find him. When they met at last, Harto regretted truly what he had done before. The three girls who had ridiculed him also asked forgiveness of him for their wrong behaviour.

Originally, these stories were intended to convey several Islamic ideas on the duties of Muslims: obedience to their parents (drama 1); the importance of the right education and the danger of being arrogant (*sombong*) (drama 2); and prohibition against gambling, the importance of repentance of one's sins and readiness to forgive each other for wrong deeds (drama 3). However, the selections of the motifs which enabled the dramas to proceed to their conclusions, namely, *dhukun*, *kiyai* and *kualat* (cursing from the dead father) were not congruent with the messages that they were intended to convey. In other words, they resorted to non-Islamic elements to transmit Islamic teachings. [31]

This raises a question as to why non-Islamic motifs were used to express Islamic lessons in religious events. In considering this question, it should be emphasised that the non-Islamic motifs were inserted into the dramas extemporaneously rather than intentionally. The *anak masjid* who created these stories did not have any intention, for example, of displaying the efficacy of the *dhukun*'s

---

[31] In the case of the *dhukun* and *kualat* (cursing), their non-(reformist) Islamic identities are clear whereas the identity of the *kiyai* is not. *Kiyai* is a title for a learned scholar in Islam. However, the practice of the *kiyai* in the second drama, that is, the use of pure water to cure the disease, is not fully compatible with reformist ideology. Although not totally rejected by the reformist villagers, this practice is not considered to be recommended for reformist Muslims. In this sense, the motif of *kiyai* can be said to be non-(reformist) Islamic.

practice. In everyday life, they do not show any interest in supernatural beings nor do they want to follow *ilmu*. Rather, they attack the practice of the *dhukun* and villagers' dependence on them.

The inclusion of non-Islamic elements can be interpreted as an indicator that the Muslim youth are not wholly freed from the influence of the traditional worldview. As Islamic development in Kolojonggo is quite recent, they have grown up and spent much of their time in a social environment which was oriented less to reformist Islam but in which supernatural beings played an important part. As a result, their reformist orientation has been inculcated by exposure to education rather than acquired through their socialisation process. This has given birth to a state in which they can, at the conscious level, harmonise their thought and behaviour with reformist ideology, while the traditional worldview is still a part of their disposition as Durkheim puts it:

> In each one of us, in differing degrees, is contained the person we were yesterday, and indeed, in the nature of things it is even true that our past *personae* predominate in us, since the present is necessarily insignificant when compared with the long period of the past because of which we have emerged in the form we have today. It is just that we don't directly feel the influence of these past selves precisely because they are so deeply rooted within us. They constitute the unconscious part of ourselves. ... ... with the most recent acquisitions of civilisation we are vividly aware of them just because they are recent and consequently have not had time to be assimilated into our collective unconscious. [32]

This does not mean that the *anak masjid* have the same syncretic religious outlook as many of their predecessors had, where Islamic and non-Islamic ideas were mixed together without conflict (Geertz, 1976:40). In the case of the *anak masjid*, the mixture is a rather stratified one: Islamic elements are dominant but other non-Islamic elements are not excluded as unthinkable. In brief, the cases of the *jathilan* and dramas show that supernatural beings have not been expelled from village life as a result of their encounter with reformist Islam. Although they have been placed in an unfavourable position, they have not lost their grip over villagers, at least, up to this point.

One crucial factor which has made it possible for supernatural beings to maintain their influence over villagers is that their efficacy has not been negated by most villagers. They are still believed to have the ability to assist villagers who desperately seek every means possible to solve their problems. There are many success stories about villagers who received assistance from supernatural beings

---

[32] Durkheim, E., *The Evolution of Educational Thought* (1977:11, London: Routledge & Kegan Paul). Cited in Bourdieu (1990:56).

and attained certain goals. Moreover, these praiseworthy services are done almost for nothing. Flowers, incense and small offerings of foods are enough to satisfy supernatural beings, supplemented by small gifts for the *dhukun*, if the assistance is sought by way of him. Within the limitless capabilities of supernatural beings, and in frequent demand by the villagers are: to find lost things, to cure sicknesses that cannot be treated properly in the hospital, to cause someone be selected for a vacant post, to increase wealth, to predict the number of the lottery [33] , and to attract the other sex. Below are two examples of villagers who sought the service of supernatural beings by way of the *dhukun*:

[case 1: position] Pak Bari, a person who has the largest *sawah* in Kolojonggo, decided to apply for a vacancy in the *kelurahan* office. It was his life's dream to be a government official, in that he wanted to convert his wealth into social status which can only be achieved by taking a position in government office. In the written test, he was ranked as the second among eight candidates. However, it was just the beginning. He had to compete with two others who also passed the same test. According to popular perceptions, success in the next selection process of interview is dependent on one's economic capability and one's connection with the interviewers. It was not so difficult for him to prepare 3 million Rupiah, guaranteed to be fully refundable. However, he was not so sure about his selection only with money since the other competitors were also capable of raising money. As the date for the interview approached, he came to be more and more anxious. With advice from his family, he at last made two long journeys to East and Central Java where, according to him, the most powerful (*sakti*) *dhukun* lived. There, he received an *ilmu* to attract the interviewers, consisting of a spell, a method of practising the fast and several prohibitions. He followed the ascetic exercise sincerely until the day of interview. However, he was not successful in being selected as a *kelurahan* official. Recounting this long story, Pak Bari briefly commented that his religiosity had not been strong at that time and, if an opportunity arose again, he would not follow the same course, but would only pray to God for the realisation of his dream.

[case 2: lost things] Pak Sodo lost his wallet in his work-place. At first, he thought that it had just fallen on the ground and would be returned to him the next day. Several days passed, but there was no news. He thought more about that day and at last recalled someone who might have stolen it. After this, he used several indirect measures to make the

---

[33] Unfortunately for some of the *dhukun* who specialised in guessing the four digits of the lottery, the national lottery was abolished in 1993 through mass protests initiated by Muslim university students. After this, the local newspaper carried several articles on the *dhukun* who had to change their specialties.

culprit return his wallet. A week passed but there was no sign that the culprit was impressed by his action. At last, he visited Pak Akir who was known as a *wong pinter*. Hearing what he said, Pak Akir raised his right hand and began to swing it over his head. After going round several times, his hand stopped at a certain point, indicating the direction of the thief's house. The direction pointed out by Pak Akir was the one where the house of the culprit was located. After this, it took a few more minutes for Pak Akir, waking from his silence, to begin to talk about the fate of his lost wallet: most of money was already spent but the thief intended to return it. As the thief was ashamed of his behaviour, it would take a few more days for him to return it. Listening to this advice, Pak Sodo decided to wait. It was not long before a note was delivered to him, on which was written the address of someone whom he did not know but who was said to have custody of his lost wallet.

As the above cases show, the efficacy of supernatural beings is not denied by villagers as an option for assistance. In this circumstance, the efforts of the reformist villagers focus on making an 'ethical person': one who, although admitting the power of supernatural beings, does not make use of them. The case of Pak Ibrahim, compared to Pak Sodo in case 2, exemplifies who the 'ethical person' is:

> Pak Ibrahim's sister-in-law lost his bike at a street stall. As the theft happened in a street, it was quite difficult for him to track down the thief. A few days after this theft, he mentioned why he did not take any further action to find it: 'I thought a lot about this problem. Sometimes, I was eager to visit someone [*dhukun*] who would be able to help me to find my lost bike or I was almost ready to do some *lelakon* to disturb the thief and get my bike back. But soon, I changed my mind. I knew it was not the right way to do so. ... Instead, I just added additional prayers at the end of my regular ones, asking Allah that my bike would be brought back. If my prayers are accepted by Allah, the thief will return it to me. If not, it is the intention of Allah to let my bike be lost, which I cannot do anything about.'

The focus of this section was put on the position of supernatural beings in present village life. As the cases of *jathilan* and three dramas performed by the *anak masjid* demonstrate, supernatural beings still retain their grip over villagers and are not excluded as 'unthinkable'. One of the factors which help supernatural beings maintain a position in village life is their ability to intrude in human affairs, the efficacy of which is admitted by almost all villagers. In this situation, the emphasis of the reformist villagers is put on making an ethical person, whose religious piety is strong enough, to resist temptation to ask assistance of supernatural beings.

Recently in Kolojonggo, the efficacy of supernatural beings which reformist Islam has not been able to deny, has started to be challenged from an unexpected side: the rise of villagers who pursue *ilmu* in different ways from that of the *dhukun*.[34] Their presence may bring a more fatal result to belief in supernatural beings than the surge of reformist Islam since their basic tenet is to bypass supernatural beings in order to seek *ilmu*. In the section below, the diversification of those who seek *ilmu* and their specific ideational systems will be discussed.

6.4. The Diversification of Villagers Seeking *Ilmu*

In the face of Islamic development which has imposed the concepts of *jinn* and *satan* on traditional supernatural beings and which has condemned villagers' contact with them, the *dhukun* have reacted in two different ways. Some have chosen not to adapt themselves to the new environment by emphasising their specific identity while others have endeavoured to blur their identity by accepting some of the basic dogmas of Islam. Below is the summary of a meeting with Pak Wiro who took the former position:

> We were talking about the meaning of *wiwitan* (a traditional ritual celebrating the harvest), which he explained as a ritual dedicated to the *dewi Sri* who is believed to control rice. He proposed that this sort of belief did not belong to Islam but to 'the original Javanese' (*asli Jawa*), which meant to him anything which is not connected to 'things Arabic'. Then, he argued the superiority of 'things Javanese' over 'things Arabic': if one wanted to achieve something, he or she should resort to 'things Javanese'. His idea was expressed clearly when he heard that the Arabic prayer of *Basmillah* was used in my village. Hearing this, he commented, 'the request of the host cannot be reached with *Basmillah*. It is meaningless to celebrate the *kendhuri* with *Basmillah* and the host spends money for nothing.'

The attitude of Pak Wiro is somewhat extreme since he expressed his anti-Islamic view clearly. Others belonging to this non-compromising group choose a more refined way: not to refer to anything connected to Islam. It might not be an accident among the *dhukun* that the older one is and the less one's contact with the outside world, the greater the possibility is that one will take this position.

---

[34] In Yogyakarta city as well as in other parts of Java, different ways of pursuing *ilmu* from that of the *dhukun* have existed as a long tradition. In this respect, it may be wrong to say that these ways have not been known to villagers in Sumber. However, until recently, there was no villager who was attracted to these different ways of pursuing *ilmu* and who became the followers of these. The five villagers in Sumber who taught these different ways to others were all in their thirties and early forties, and, when asked where they had learned these ways, they identified Yogyakarta city or places outside Yogyakarta. In this sense, it may be said that the coexistence of diverse ways of pursuing *ilmu* is a recent phenomenon in Sumber, although not in other parts of Java. It seems that changing socio-religious situations have prompted some villagers to be attracted to these different ways of pursuing *ilmu*.

The changing social atmosphere does not matter a lot to them and in this sense, their influence over villagers has decreased dramatically.

Other *dhukun,* many of whom are in middle age, have confronted the changing world more directly. The strategy that they have employed is to affiliate themselves closely with Islam, which is achieved by imposing Islamic identity on supernatural beings and by giving supernatural beings a position of intermediary (*utusan* or *perantara*) between themselves and Allah. This implies that equal treatment of all supernatural beings is given up and Allah [35] is accorded the highest position. Pak Tin explained the changing atlas of supernatural beings as follows:

> As human beings have different appearances, those of supernatural beings are different. The same is true of religion. Each supernatural being has a different religion. There are those who have the religion of Islam, Christianity, Hinduism or Buddhism. ... In former days, *Kanjeng Ratu Kidul* (same as *Niyai Lara Kidul*) did not have a religion. At the moment, however, *Kanjeng* has the religion of Islam. *Kanjeng* can read all kinds of Islamic Holy Books and write Arabic.

The influence of the national ideology of *Pancasila* is shown in Pak Tin's idea. As all citizens are required to believe in one of the five official religions recognised through *Pancasila*, so, too, are all supernatural beings. Consequently, Pak Tin as a Muslim is in contact with Islamic supernatural beings or the *jinn* which are pious to Allah, the fact signifying that he does not deviate from Islamic teaching.

Apart from this modification, most practices which were once employed by the *dhukun* in former days such as burning incense, making offerings, recitation of spells, emphasis on the fast and use of *petungan*, have not changed much. In some sense, it is almost impossible for the *dhukun* to abandon these practices in so far as they make contact with supernatural beings, since these are the media without which they cannot communicate with the latter and no alternatives have yet been invented. The mode that the *dhukun* use to rationalise the efficacy of their practices by way of supernatural beings has also maintained. They retain the optimistic vision that all kinds of good requests from the human side will be granted immediately by supernatural beings, who now subsume the role of messengers from Allah, if these are done in the proper manner and by way of the right persons. The right persons are those who have performed ascetic practices to purify their inner and outer self, a state which makes easy communication with Allah possible.

---

[35] The *dhukun* who belong to this category prefer the term *Tuhan yang Maha Esa, Kang Maha Kuwasa* and *Pangeran* to Allah when they have to refer to a monotheistic God.

The modifications that the *dhukun* have made do not seem to be effective enough to save them from open criticism. Irrespective of the changes that the *dhukun* have made, the reformist villagers still think of them as those who practise *syirik* and whose role is to cause villagers to go astray from the right path to Allah. At the heart of this criticism lies the continuing contact of the *dhukun* with supernatural beings who are equated with the heathen *jinn* or satan. Their use of incense, magical spells and offerings which are considered to be non-Islamic by most villagers, is another factor which makes it difficult for the *dhukun* to escape criticism.

The second group of those who pursue *ilmu* has not yet been given a proper name by villagers. Sometimes, a borrowed English term *mistik* (mystic), *wong kepercayaan* (literally, people having a belief) or *wong kebatinan* (literally, people pursuing spirituality) is used by some villagers but these terms have not yet been popularised. [36] It is not easy to make generalisations concerning the orientation of the *mistik* due to the internal variations amongst them but two aspects which they have in common as a group make them distinctive from the *dhukun*.

First, the *mistik* disapprove of connections with supernatural beings as a way to pursue *ilmu*. Instead, their ultimate goal is said to make direct contact with God without any intermediaries. The existence of supernatural beings is not denied but their role is thought to be negative, namely, to make the *mistik* go astray. This is because their degree of perfection (*derajat*) is lower than human beings and consequently, they cannot help the *mistik* reach a certain goal. The separation from supernatural beings allows the *mistik* to exclude the key symbols related to the *dhukun* from their practices: making offerings, burning incense and chanting spells. Despite these differences, however, several elements still connect the *dhukun* and the *mistik* together. Both of them emphasise the spiritual side of human religiosity, meditation is considered to be one of the best ways to reach their goal and, in the process of reaching their goal, they are thought to acquire an ability to feel and to do things that an ordinary person cannot do. [37]

The second feature which distinguishes the *mistik* from the *dhukun* is the religious relativism of the former. In contrast to the *dhukun* who identify themselves as Muslims and equate supernatural beings with Islamic ones, the *mistik* do not give priority to any of the five official religions in Indonesia. To them, what

[36] In the section below, the term *mistik* will be used to designate this group. Although this usage is somewhat misleading and villagers have different ideas to understand the term *mistik*, it is adopted for the sake of convenience.

[37] Although the main reason why ordinary villagers are attracted to the *mistik* is *ilmu*, the *mistik* deny the pursuit of *ilmu* as their major goal. Instead, they suggest that their goal is to approach God and, if possible, to achieve union with God. To most of them, *ilmu* are just side effects of their mystical pursuit, while, to some, these are rewards from God.

matters is not which God - for example, the God in Islam, Christianity or Hindu-Buddhism - created human beings but that 'God' created human beings and gave human beings a potential to unite with 'Him'. As a result, it is not uncommon that Muslim, Christian and Hindu-Buddhist students are guided by the same *mistik*. This is permissible since, whatever the religion of each follower, they have a commonality, namely, that they are the creatures of 'God' and given the same potential by 'God'. [38] In accordance with this religious relativism, the term Allah is seldom used by the *mistik*. Instead, they used the term *Tuhan* or in some cases, *Pangeran* (literally, prince or lord).

These two characteristics seem to originate with the efforts of the *mistik* to separate themselves from negative images imposed on the *dhukun*, namely, as heretic. By denying their association with supernatural beings, by refuting some of the practices upheld by the *dhukun* and by emphasising direct spiritual contact with 'God', the *mistik* try to show that they are compatible with the 'orthodox religion' defined in Indonesia as belief in one God. This characteristic of the *mistik* allows them to be less vulnerable to the criticism from the reformist villagers than the *dhukun*. The most probable source of attack from the reformist villagers is the religious relativism of the *mistik*, namely, to which 'God' their spiritual pursuit is directed and from which 'God' they acquire a certain spiritual strength: if followers of different religions can acquire the same result, this would imply that all religions and the God in every religion are the same, an argument which cannot be accepted by the reformist villagers. Facing this criticism, the *mistik* have a reliable weapon to protect themselves: *Pancasila*. As *Pancasila* guarantees freedom to believe in one of the five religions, they give their followers freedom to pursue 'God' in accordance with their own religious conviction. What they emphasise is that, as the state recommends her citizens to believe in One God, so they ask their followers not to forget the spiritual side of their religiosity and the connectedness between human beings and 'God' in whichever religion they believe. The incorporation of *Pancasila* as the basis of their ideology gives the *mistik* a certain immunity from criticism. In so far as *Pancasila* remains an ideology that cannot be refuted by the reformist villagers, so do the *mistik* escape criticism.

The third group of those who pursue *ilmu* is more 'Islamic' than the *dhukun* and the *mistik*. Supernatural beings are not included, ascetic exercise is not stressed while Islamic elements such as Arabic recitation, obligatory and optional prayers constitute an essential part of their practice. No specific term has been developed

---

[38] In one case, a *mistik* argued that one's affiliation to a certain religion was not at all important since we did not know which religion, for example, of the five official religions in Indonesia, was the right one. According to him, the more important point was that one truly believed in 'God' (*Tuhan*) as our Creator and tried to approach 'Him'. This attitude was extreme among the *mistik* who generally put religion in a higher place than their own practices and equated the latter as a way to make perfect one's devotion to a certain religion.

for them, implying that its introduction has been as recent as the *mistik*. Those who belong to this group will be called 'the seekers of *ilmu ghaib*'. I adopt this term since the young villagers call what is pursed by this group *ilmu ghaib*.

The starting point of the seekers of *ilmu ghaib* is similar to that of the *dhukun*: there exist phenomena categorised as *ghaib* (mysterious or invisible) which cannot be understood or proven by ordinary senses: for example, a thing or a person can be moved without any physical contact. After discovering the existence of the *ghaib*, their next step is to understand its significance for human beings: there is a Being lying beyond the *ghaib*. The rationale on which they rely to explain the identity of this Being separates them from the *dhukun*. The Being behind the *ghaib* is Allah. They are sure of this since they have the Quran, the revelation from Allah. [39]

The next step of the seekers of *ilmu ghaib* after appreciating the significance of the *ghaib* is not just to be satisfied with this understanding but to take advantage of it. They ask Allah to make something mysterious happen to themselves. [40] In order for this to happen, one has to maximise one's ritual prayers to Allah and the recitation of Arabic passages. In addition to these acts, physical exercises, meditations, *dzikir* and breath control are frequently emphasised, while the fast is not strongly recommended. [41] Although some of the methods that they adopt to pursue *ilmu ghaib* overlap with what is emphasised by the reformist villagers as duties of Muslims, the way these Islamic elements are used is different. They put extra emphasis on the selection of the Quranic passage, time and place for prayers and recitations. This is one reason why a *guru* is thought to be necessary in pursuing *ilmu ghaib*. Each *guru* has different ways to select these requirements which they obtained in their earlier career in pursuing *ilmu ghaib* and which provide the shortcut to learn it for the novices.

In a neighbouring hamlet of Kolojonggo lived a seeker of *ilmu ghaib* who had a wide reputation in this area. He was not only a *guru* of *ilmu ghaib* but one of the five speakers in the *Jumatan*.Considering that the *khatib* is reserved only for those who have higher religious knowledge than others, this selection signifies that his religious piety was recognised by others. As this case shows, those who are famous for their *ilmu ghaib* can easily be included in the category of religious leader, in that they have high religious knowledge, are fluent in reading Arabic, are diligent in their everyday prayers and teach their disciples to follow their

[39] Two verses which were frequently quoted to support their idea were: And with Him are the keys of the invisible (*ghaib*) (vi:59); And Allah's is the Invisible (*ghaib*) of the heavens and the earth and unto Him the whole matter will be returned (xi:123).
[40] The act of requesting something from Allah is categorised as a recommended behaviour. It is because those who do not ask something from Allah easily become arrogant (*sombong*), forgetting their dependence on Him.
[41] They do not emphasise the fast as heavily as the *dhukun* do, although it is considered to be one way to facilitate the process of seeking *ilmu ghaib*. The fast which is approved of by the seekers of *ilmu ghaib* is the non-compulsory (*sunnah*) fast, which is also recommended to ordinary Muslims.

behaviour. The fact that their practices do not deviate directly from Islamic teaching makes the reformist villagers very cautious about commenting on them. When talking about *ilmu ghaib*, the reformist villagers frequently used the expression 'with the permission of Allah'. With the permission of Allah, everything may happen. However, this cautious attitude is unlikely to make them approve of pursuing *ilmu ghaib*. In contrast to their caution not to talk directly about a certain villager seeking *ilmu ghaib*, the reformist villagers enthusiastically enumerated the conditions under which the pursuit of *ilmu ghaib* could lead to *syirik*. The selection of certain passages for certain purposes and the arbitrary fixation of the occasions, places, and sequences of prayers and recitations were frequently cited examples. They argued that the Prophet Muhammad had not given any exegesis that, for example, recitation of a verse called *ayat Kursi* in the Quran five times is the fastest way to acquire high spiritual energy, *ayat Ibrahim* to strengthen physical power, *ayat Yusuf* to attract women, Surah of *Yasin* to make oneself invisible and so on. [42] The reluctance of the reformist villagers to involve themselves in *ilmu ghaib* also shows their partial disapproval of it. The teachings that they cited most frequently when asked to comment on *ilmu ghaib* were 'when there is something, the identity of which is ambiguous, it is better not to do it' and 'when the danger is greater than utility, it is better not to be entangled in it'. As the identity of the seekers of *ilmu ghaib* is ambiguous, it is better, according to them, not to involve themselves in it.

There are thus three different ways, or *aliran* (currents) as villagers call them, to seek *ilmu,* each of which has distinctive frameworks of viewing supernatural beings and of locating Islam in its ideational system. The introduction of the new *aliran* as alternatives to seek *ilmu* and to interpret supernatural phenomena has been related to the emergence of reformist Islam and *Pancasila*, two leading forces which have regulated the official side of villagers' religious life. As Islam and *Pancasila* locate a monotheistic God in an absolute position, so do the new *aliran*. In this respect, they are better adapted to the new socio-religious environment and are less vulnerable to the criticisms of the reformist villagers.

The new *aliran*, in whichever ways its relation with reformist Islam may be understood by villagers, challenges the efficacy of supernatural beings more directly than reformist Islam does. This is because all of those who pursue *ilmu* work in the same domain, entail similar results but resort to different frameworks to interpret them. It is said that all of those pursuing *ilmu* are able, applying their *ilmu*, to cure disease which cannot be treated by modern medical technology, to make one invulnerable to physical attack, to allow one to be attractive to others, to find lost things and so on. However, they explain these

---

[42] There is a rationale for selecting certain verses for certain purposes. For example, the ninth verse in the Surah of *Yasin* which goes, 'and we have set a bar before them and a bar behind them, and (thus) have covered them so that they see not' (xxxvi:9), is believed to make one invisible to others.

extraordinary powers in different terms. When finding a thief, for example, it is said that all of them can see the scene of theft in their mind. However, the *dhukun* ascribes it to assistance from supernatural beings, the *mistik*, to his developed spirituality, a potential given to human beings by 'God' in every religion, and the seekers of *ilmu ghaib*, to blessing from Allah. These different ways of explanation imply that the efficacy of *ilmu* which was ascribed to supernatural beings can now be attributed to a monotheistic 'God' or Allah. In this sense, the emergence of the new *aliran* in Kolojonggo opens a more effective way for spiritual power diffused to various supernatural beings to be monopolised by 'God' or Allah.

It is not certain whether this process of monopolisation will continue in the near future. What is certain, however, is that this process will be going on as reformist Islam and *Pancasila* remain two dominant ideological tenets in village life. As long as these two tenets urge villagers to show their allegiance to a monotheistic God and if they can get the same results from the new *aliran* as they obtain from the *dhukun*, it is unlikely that they will retain an interest in supernatural beings, the contact with whom is condemned as non-Islamic. If this happens, supernatural beings, even if not totally freed from their roles of explanation and assistance, will lose their previous identity and conform to Islamic concepts of the malignant *jinn* or satan.

6.5. Summary

The focus of this chapter has been on the position of supernatural beings and their spokesmen, *dhukun*, in village life. Supernatural beings have faced diverse challenges from different angles. The first of these is the positivist paradigm backed by science and technology. The positivist paradigm has discouraged villagers from searching for a deeper meaning beyond the observable cause and effect, while science and technology have shrunk the domains in which supernatural beings have privileges to be involved. This challenge, however, has not been successful in eroding the basis of belief in supernatural beings. First of all, science and technology cannot replace all of the roles that supernatural beings have played for villagers. For example, these cannot cure all diseases, cannot find lost things, cannot make one invulnerable to physical attack, cannot help one to be attractive to others and so on, all of which villagers still believe to be attainable with the help of supernatural beings. On the other hand, the surge of the positivist paradigm has not been able to create villagers who are brave enough to show their scepticism about the existence of supernatural beings and their power. This is related to the idiosyncrasy of Indonesia where the development of the positivist paradigm cannot proceed to its logical extreme, namely, denial of all supernatural phenomena including religion. *Pancasila* has effectively restrained the full development of the positivist paradigm and has urged it to show its allegiance to religion. As a result, its role has been confined to shrinking the domains where supernatural beings work, not refuting their efficacy and ontological position.

The second challenge that belief in supernatural beings has faced is reformist Islam, which has tried to reformulate the position of supernatural beings in accordance with Islamic theology. In this framework, supernatural beings with whom villagers make contact are equated with the *jinn*, beings created by Allah separate both from human beings and from satan. Although not all *jinn* are thought to be vicious, only the malevolent *jinn* are supposed to respond to requests from human beings. As a result, irrespective of whether their involvement in human affairs is benevolent or not, supernatural beings are supposed to be always malignant in so far as they are ready to make contact with human beings. This modification of the nature of supernatural beings by reformist Islam, however, does not challenge directly the efficacy of supernatural beings. They are still thought to have power to fulfil what is demanded by human beings. The difference is that the act of asking something of supernatural beings is now categorised as non-Islamic by reformist Islam.

The third challenge to belief in supernatural beings is related to how to define the being behind supernatural phenomena. In former days when the dominant position of the *dhukun* as agents to deal with the supernatural world was relatively well preserved in Kolojonggo, supernatural beings had the same degree of monopoly over supernatural power. With the emergence of the new *aliran,* however, the monopolistic position of supernatural beings has begun to be shaken. Villages are now given a different framework with which to interpret supernatural phenomena and to obtain supernatural power, namely, a monotheistic God. In this sense, the emergence of the competing *aliran* to the *dhukun* has much greater potential in eroding the efficacy of supernatural beings than the positivist paradigm and reformist Islam. If villagers can get the same result from a monotheistic God as they do from supernatural beings, there are no reasons why they should resort to the *dhukun* who are strongly criticised by reformist Islam.

In some parts of the world where traditional society is rapidly incorporated into capitalistic modern society, belief in supernatural beings has provided one of the mechanisms by which people interpret and conceptualise their new experiences (Nash,1979; Ong,1988; Taussig,1980). It is also suggested that, in Indonesia and Malaysia where so-called 'world religions' backed by the state are expanding their influence over the population, belief in supernatural beings is not on the wane but flourishes (Boon,1979; Peletz,1988). Observing the revitalisation of rituals related to supernatural beings, Boon argues that the Balinese society is in the process of *re*enchantment of the world rather than demystification (1979:288). The position of supernatural beings in Kolojonggo is somewhat different from their counterparts in Bali. Although not forced out of village life, they have not provided a framework with which villagers cope with the changing society. They are under attack both from reformist Islam and the new *aliran*, facing 'the process of religious rationalisation' in which the sense of sacredness is gathered up from the countless tree spirits and garden spells through which it was vaguely diffused, and is concentrated in a nucleate concept of the divine' (Geertz,1973:173-4; see also Weber,1963:22).

Compared with the rationalisation process suggested by Geertz, what makes this process in Kolojonggo distinctive is that it is not expedited by the replacement of traditional religion with world religion. Although reformist Islam reformulates the concept of supernatural beings, it has not been successful in depriving them of supernatural power and in concentrating it in a monotheistic God. Instead, what reformist Islam has done by imposing a moralistic dichotomy of good and bad on supernatural beings is to equate the power of supernatural beings with the bad. In comparison with that of reformist Islam, the role of the new *aliran* in the rationalisation process is more crucial in Kolojonggo. By working in the same domain as the *dhukun* but by using different paradigms to explain the same supernatural phenomenon, the new *aliran* opens a more effective way for supernatural power to be concentrated in a monotheistic God.

This distinctive rationalisation process seems to be one reason, among others, that the concept of God who is 'apart, above or outside of the concrete details of ordinary life' in a rationalised world religion as is suggested by Geertz (1973:171) is not the only nature that Allah has in Kolojonggo. In addition to this, Allah inherits part of the nature that supernatural beings have and remains a Being who involves Himself 'in an independent, segmental and immediate manner with almost any sort of actual event' (ibid.:172). This then makes it possible for villagers in Kolojonggo to ask the same questions of Allah as they did of supernatural beings, such as 'what should be done to gain more profit in the business?' as well as more abstract and more generally phrased questions such as 'who belongs to the category of the blessed?' In this way, the rationalisation process in Kolojonggo and subsequent concentration of supernatural power in Allah does not result in a widening distance between human beings and Allah. Allah is still thought to be a Being who is close to human beings and of whom villagers may ask the fulfilment of their wishes related to the odds and ends of everyday life.

Plate 11: Moment of chaos in a *jathilan* performance.

Plate 12: The last scene in the drama performed by Muslim youth (drama No. 1 in the text). From left to right: *dhukun*; Parjo's father; street musician from Parjo's village; Parjo; Parjo's wife.

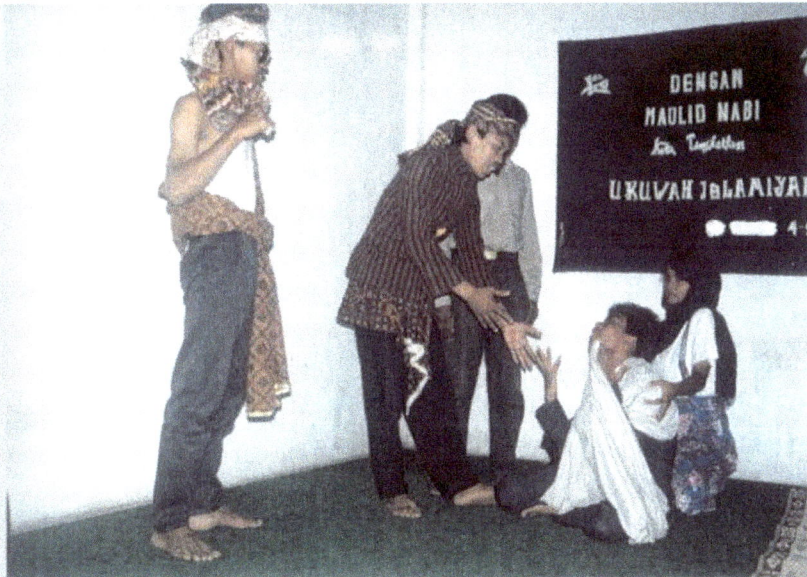

Chapter 7: Muslim and Christian Relations in Kolojonggo

In Kolojonggo, Wednesday evenings symbolise the co-existence of two religious communities. Both Muslim and Protestant villagers hold their weekly learning courses, the former in the *masjid,* and the latter in the house of a Protestant family. The evenings when Christians have a meeting in a house near the *masjid* give villagers an additional chance to appreciate their religious difference. A group of villagers from the same neighbourhood, walking and chatting together, arrives at the *masjid* and then separates, each group heading for a different place. On these occasions, it often happens that Muslims sitting inside the *masjid* and listening to the sermon about the Grace of Allah hear a hymn praising Jesus Christ.

The importance of one's religious identity, previously confined to the religious domain, has begun to extend into non-religious domains. This is most clearly manifested in the life of some youth whose peer group solidarity is limited to those of the same religion. They play, chat, eat, watch television and go to the market mainly with either Muslims or Christians. Another example of the increasing importance of religious identity in non-religious domains is the activities of BAZIS which collects religious alms solely from, and uses it only for, Muslims. BAZIS activities indicate that the consideration of villagers' economic welfare, conventionally thought to be the duty of community, kin group or a family, is now viewed as the responsibility of a religious community. These developments show that the previously fixed division between the religious and the non-religious is in the process of erosion.

The purpose of the present chapter, and the next chapter, is to examine the relations between Muslims and Christians in Kolojonggo at the point at which religious identity has gradually extended into non-religious domains. One thing that should be considered in this discussion is the effects of outside influences on these relations and the ways villagers perceive them. The first of these is the government's policy of suppressing any expression of open conflict, which has helped the concept of harmony (*rukun*) become an official idiom in village life. As a result, conflicting interests between Muslims and Christians have not been expressed in public but remained hidden, unseen from the outside. The second outside influence is that of Muslim intellectuals from Yogyakarta city. Their perspective on Christianity and Christianisation has flowed into rural areas through various channels, helping Muslim villagers to re-conceptualise their relations to Christians.

The first part of this chapter will look at the development of Christianity in Java and Yogyakarta after the independence of Indonesia, focusing on the statistical expansion of the Christian population. In the second part, the development of Christianity in Kolojonggo will be discussed. This will be followed by a discussion of Muslim villagers' growing consciousness of religious difference and expansion of the religious difference in non-religious domains.

7.1. Development of Christianity in Java and Yogyakarta: Some Statistical Considerations

Although indigenous Christian communities were present in several parts of Java in the 19th century [1] and Christian missionaries were allowed to work among the Javanese Muslims from the mid-19th century (Hefner,1993b:99-100), the numeric expansion of Christians in Java was not so remarkable in the Dutch Colonial period. The 1930 census shows that only 0.27 percent of the total population in Java embraced either Protestantism or Catholicism (Rauws et al.1935). The pace of Christian expansion accelerated in the Old Order Period. Between 1953 and 1964, the Roman Catholic Church doubled its followers in Java (Lembaga Penelitian dan Pembangunan Sosial,1968:table33), while membership growth of a few Protestant Churches in Java reached more than 20 percent per annum between 1960 and 1964 (Willis,1977:192).

The growth of Christians in Java before 1965, however, bears little comparison with that from 1965 to the early seventies. In this period, both the Protestant and Catholic Churches witnessed an extraordinary increase in new converts to Christianity. More than a million Javanese converted to Christianity between 1965 and 1971. Local level statistics show the same picture: the average increase in members among five denominations of the Protestant Church in Java reached 27.6 percent per annum in 1965-1967 and 13.7 percent in 1968-71, compared with 7.7 percent in 1960-64 (Willis,1971:110). The growth of the Catholic Church in Java reached 18.2 percent per annum in 1965-71 (Lembaga Penelitian Dan Pembangunan Sosial,1968). The high growth of the Christian population from 1965 to 1971 was not drastically interrupted in subsequent decades. The Christian Churches in Java gained almost two million Christians between 1971 and 1990. With this growth in the absolute number of Christians, the ratio of Christians to the total population has gradually increased as Figure VII-1 indicates:

[1] For the history and the characteristics of Christian communities in East Java in the 19th century, see Akkeren (1970) and Guillot (1985:9-50); For a Christian sect which spread to various parts of Central Java in the 19th century, see Guillot (1985).

Figure VII-1: Percentage of Christians in Java and Indonesia (1930-1990)

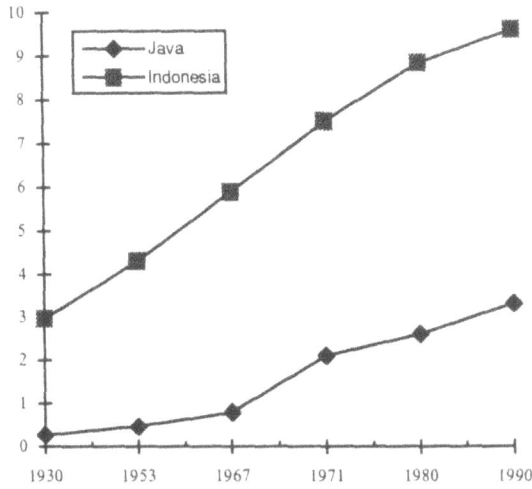

Source: 1930: Rauws et al. (1935); 1953 & 1967: Protestants from Cooley (1967); Catholics from Lembaga Penelitian Dan Pembangunan Sosial (1968); 1971, 1980 & 1990: Official Statistics based on national census.

Figure VII-2: Number of Christians in Java (1930-1990)

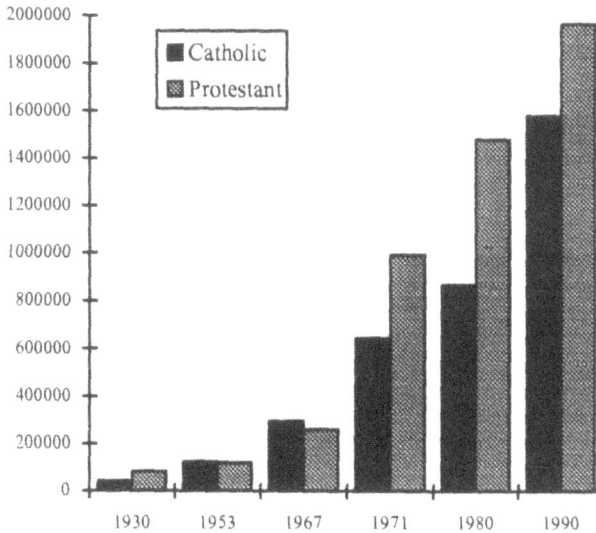

Source: As for Figure VII-1.

Table VII.1: Percentage of Christians in Java (City and District / Urban and Rural)

	1971			1980			1990		
	Cities	Districts	Total	Cities	Districts	Total	Urban	Rural	Total
Jakarta	8.0	-	8.0	9.3	-	9.3	10.9	-	10.9
West Java	7.8	0.6	1.1	8.0	0.5	1.1	4.6	0.4	1.8
Central Java	12.9	1.4	2.2	14.0	1.7	2.6	8.2	1.4	3.2
Yogyakarta	14.9	3.0	4.6	18.1	4.9	6.8	13.2	5.6	9.0
East Java	8.9	0.9	1.7	9.9	1.1	2.1	7.1	0.9	2.6
Java	9.9	1.0	2.1	10.9	1.2	2.6	7.5	1.0	3.3

Source: Census Data

The 1971 and subsequent census data on the number of religious followers show two interesting points related to the geographical deployment of Christians in Java. First, a higher ratio of Christians to the total population is found in municipalities (*kotamadya*) than in districts (*kabupaten*) where rural villages are located. As table VII-1 shows, the ratio of Christians in the municipalities reached 9.9 percent in 1971 and 10.9 percent in 1980 while that in the districts was 1.0 percent and 1.2 percent respectively. More reliable data showing the deployment of Christian populations in urban and rural areas can be obtained in the 1990 census since this census classified the urbanised parts in each district in the category of the urban.[2] In 1990, the ratio of Christians in urban areas was 7.5 percent while that in rural areas, 1.0 percent.

Second, the census data make clear that some districts in Java have been more open to the spread of Christianity than others. When the ratio of Christians to the total population in eighty-two districts in Java is compared, this becomes clearer, as Figure VII-3 portrays.

Figure VII-3 shows that in 1980, Central Java and Yogyakarta possessed a higher Christian ratio than East and West Java. One of the interesting features in Figure VII-3 is that four districts in Yogyakarta are ranked at the top among thirty three districts in Central Java and Yogyakarta.[3] To take a more precise look at this feature, a ratio of Christians in four districts of Yogyakarta and that in twenty-nine districts of Central Java is compared in table VII-2. As this table indicates, four districts in Yogyakarta had a ratio of Christians which was three times higher than districts in Central Java in 1971 and this gap widened in the 1970s, making the ratio more than four to one in 1980.

---

[2] The data on religious followers in each district were available in the 1971 and 1980 census whereas no comparable data were presented in the 1990 census, which differentiated the urban from the rural rather than the municipality from the district.

[3] The districts located outside of Yogyakarta with a higher Christian ratio than Gunung Kidul in Yogyakarta were Klaten and Semarang, whose ratio was 5.02 percent and 5.76 percent respectively in 1980.

Figure VII-3: Percentage of Christians in 82 Districts in Java, 1980

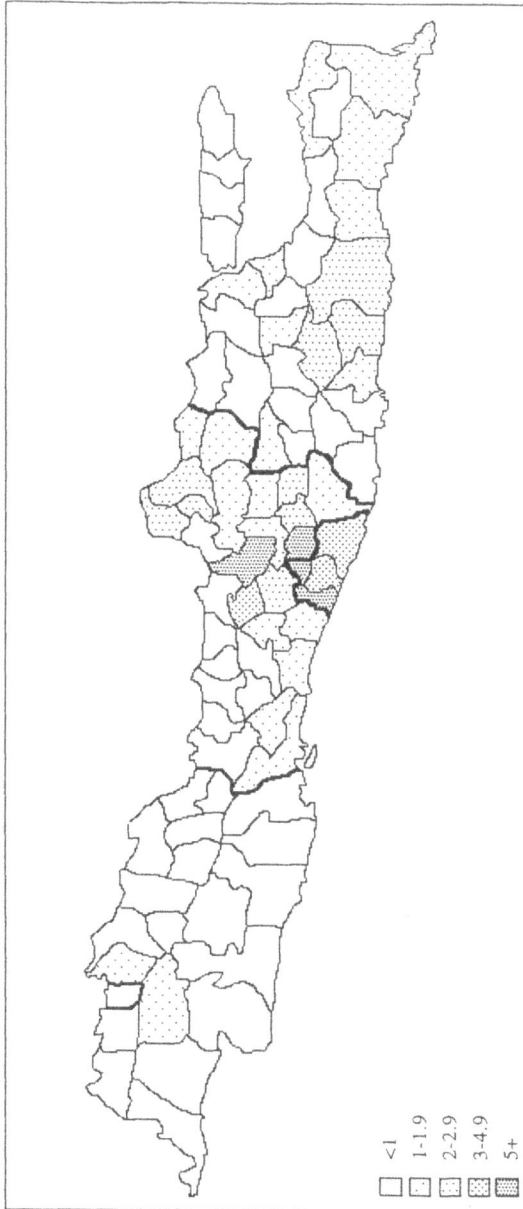

Source: 1980 Census.

Note: Percentage of Christians in Jakarta (9.3%) is not marked on this map.

Table VII.2: Percentage of Christians in Central Java and Yogyakarta

	Year		
	1971	1980	1991
29 districts in Central Java	0.9	1.1	n.a.
4 districts in Yogyakarta	3.0	4.9	5.2
Sleman	3.1	7.5	8.2
Bantul	2.8	3.4	3.3
Kulon Progo	5.6	5.7	5.8
Gunung Kidul	1.5	3.3	3.7

Source: 1971 and 1980 from Census Data; 1991 from Kantor Statistik Yogyakarta (1991).

One of the remarkable features in Table VII-2 is the rapid growth of the Christian population in the district of Sleman (and Gunung Kidul). The percentage of Christians in Sleman was much lower than that in Kulon Progo in 1970 but, in subsequent years, it surpassed the latter. The annual increase rate of Christians in Sleman was 11.9 percent in 1971-1980, which exceeded the increase of three other districts in Yogyakarta and of twenty-nine districts in Central Java. [4] Overall, the statistics show that of the eighty-two districts in Java, the highest ratio of Christians to the total population in 1980 and probably in 1990 [5] was found in the district of Sleman where Kolojonggo is located. [6]

In Yogyakarta, rapid expansion of Christianity and the presence of a higher ratio of Christians have given Muslims more opportunities of witnessing the process of Christianisation and of interacting with Christians than Muslims in other parts of Java. The other factor which makes Yogyakarta peculiar is that it hosts the headquarters of Muhammadiyah and many reformist intellectuals. These then have helped to create an environment in which the issue of Christianisation is discussed more seriously and frequently by Muslim intellectuals than in any other part of Java. For example, in the Muhammadiyah Congress held in 1990, the harmonious life among followers of different religions came to the fore. One

[4] The annual growth rate of Christians between 1971 and 1980 was 10.3 percent in Gunung Kidul, 3.2 percent in Bantul and 0.6 percent in Kulon Progo. Christians in twenty-nine districts of Central Java increased by 3.7 percent per annum in the same period. The only district in Java which had comparable growth rate to Sleman was Semarang, which recorded 11.1 percent annual growth rate in the same period.

[5] The 1990 census does not provide any data to compare the ratio of Christians at district level. However, it is plausible to assume that the ratio of Christians in Sleman, which was 8.4 percent in 1992, was the highest among 82 districts in Java.

[6] These data coincide exactly with the information that the Muhammadiyah pamphlet, which reported a joint conference of the Roman Catholic and Protestant Churches in 1963, describes. Christians denied that such a conference ever took place (Umar Hasyim,1991:271) while Boland, who summaries this Muhammadiyah pamphlet, also maintains that such a conference was not certainly held (Boland,1971:227). A part of this pamphlet goes as follows:

> They [Christians] chose the island of Java as a pilot project [for their scheme to Christianise the Indonesian people]; in Java they chose Central Java, in Central Java, in particular, the Special Administrative Area of Yogyakarta; and within this area of Yogyakarta they chose the district of Sleman to become the center of their activities, i.e. the area along the road to Kali Urang (Cited in Boland,1971:227).

of the resolutions of this Congress called for the government to take strong action against the violation of the government decree prohibiting the missionary activities toward Muslims. [7] Reformist intellectuals' concern about Christian missions is well expressed in an article officially published by Muhammadiyah, a part of which goes as follows:

> As we witness in Indonesia, Protestants and Catholics have spread their religion professionally. For two decades since the installation of the New Order Government, we have witnessed an extraordinary expansion of these two religions: the increase in the percentage of Christians [in the total population], [the foundation of] many churches and the spread of schools [established by Christians] into the rural villages. As is known, power of attraction in Christianity is not its teaching and Scripture, but [its capability to carry out] community service such as giving out foods and clothes to the poor, and assisting orphans, the decrepit, those experiencing disasters and so on (Muhammadiyah, 1991:104-105).

The concern of reformist intellectuals about Christianisation was not confined to their own circle but spread gradually to the countryside by way of the network of *pengajian*, publications, individual contact and so on. As a result, relations between Muslims and Christians in the rural areas of Yogyakarta have been constructed not only by local dynamics but by influences from Muslim intellectuals in the city. The frameworks that these intellectuals use to grasp the issue of Christianisation and Christianity constitute Muslim villagers' understanding of their relations with Christians.

7.2. Development of Christianity in Kolojonggo

In the late nineteenth century, a Christian sect called *Kristen Kerasulan*[8] founded by a Javanese, expanded its influence from its birth place, Central Java, to the western part of Yogyakarta. When one of its followers married a girl in Kolojonggo, the history of Christianity began. After moving in, he successfully persuaded his wife and parents-in-law to embrace this sect, although he did not succeed in converting other villagers. The second wave of Christianity began just after the introduction of *Kristen Kerasulan*. In the early 1920s, a villager working as a warder in the Dutch prison caught a disease which could not be

---

[7] In 1978, the Indonesian government issued a decree prohibiting the missionary activities directed toward those who already confess one of the five official religions. This decree will be discussed in Chapter VIII.

[8] Little is known about the historical development of *Kristen Kerasulan* and its theological position. The influence of this sect in Sumber and neighbouring villages was lost during the Dutch colonial period, so that no Christian villagers remember it clearly. Synthesising what is remembered by villagers, it seems that *Kristen Kerasulan* resorted heavily to mystical practices and indigenous esoteric knowledge (*ilmu Jawa*) to attract its followers. It is said that the name *Kerasulan* stemmed from the fact that the head of this sect called himself *Rasul* (prophet). In general, Christians have the opinion that *Kristen Kerasulan* was not a proper Christian sect, although it used *Kristen* (Christian) as a part of its name.

treated by the *dhukun*. His friendship with a Dutchman gave him a chance to be treated in the hospital run by Dutch missionaries in the city. His contact with Christian missionaries in the hospital and his eventual recovery from the disease, which was considered to be a miracle at that time, led him to Christianity and soon he converted to it. His next step was to call a missionary from the city to Kolojonggo in order to spread Christianity to his neighbours. His efforts were successful in attracting two more villagers to Christianity.

The next stage of Christian expansion in this area came from a Dutch-Javanese technician in the sugar factory located about four kilometres from Kolojonggo. Described as a highly religious man with a strong will to spread the Bible to villagers, he did not overlook the presence of a few Christians in Kolojonggo. Having contact with Christians in Kolojonggo and receiving financial assistance from the Protestant missionary society in the city, he constructed a small church in a hamlet near the sugar factory. [9] In 1926 this church baptised its first two members who were from Kolojonggo, an incident which signalled its massive expansion in the coming decades to embrace thousands of villagers under the name of *Gereja Kristen Jawa* (Javanese Christian Church). The first phase of this church's expansion was achieved by incorporating followers of *Kristen Kerasulan* rather than by finding new converts from the Muslim population. In doing so, however, the centre of church activities was diverted from Kolojonggo to the hamlets located to the west of the church where a substantial number of *Kristen Kerasulan* followerswere present. [10]

The geographical shift of church activities seems to have negatively affected the expansion of Christianity in Kolojonggo. From the 1930s till 1965, no other family in Kolojonggo was incorporated into this church, while two families embraced Roman Catholicism which arrived at Kolojonggo in the early 1950s. In addition to the distance from the church, some Christians attributed the sluggish expansion of the Protestant community to villagers' general indifference to religion, an incomplete infrastructure to carry out missionary activities, the occupation of the Japanese and the war of independence. Especially under the Old Order, the political position of the existing Christian community seems to have played a significant role in hindering the expansion of Christianity. All Christian families in Kolojonggo before 1965 were the supporters of the PNI, the ruling government party. This was probably due to the fact that some Christian families worked for the government where the PNI was predominant. The *kaduo* (hamlet head)

---

[9] According to Christian village elders, direct missionary activities by foreign missionaries vis-à-vis indigenous Javanese were not permitted in the Yogyakarta Sultanate throughout the colonial period. In this context, the presence of indigenous Christians seems to have been crucial for foreign missionaries to expand their activities in the rural area since, after the establishment of a church, the missionaries are said to have been tacitly permitted to visit the countryside and to carry out their missionary activities.
[10] The records show that conversions to Christianity before 1965 occurred mainly in the hamlets surrounding this church, signifying that its major proselytising activities were carried out in its immediate vicinity.

belonged to one of four Protestant families while the household heads of two Catholic families were respectively the *lurah* and an official in the *kelurahan* office. In the case of three other Protestant families, their close relations with the Protestant *kadus* were probably one of the reasons which made them affiliate with the PNI. [11] Considering that the PKI had a stronghold in Kolojonggo, it was likely that the affiliation of all Christian families to the PNI brought a negative impact on the expansion of Christianity, in that an equation of Christianity with the government made it impossible for someone to convert to Christianity without changing his or her political affiliation. Ironically, however, this very characteristic of the Christian community was one of the major incentives for some villagers to approach Christianity after 1965 when the PKI could no longer bring them safety.

When several million Javanese converted to Christianity in the post-1965 period, villagers in this area were no exception. According to the clerks in the Catholic and Protestant Churches to which Christians in Kolojonggo are affiliated, there was a flood of villagers who wanted to embrace Christianity in 1965-1968, making it impossible to keep precise records of the converts in that period. [12] In Kolojonggo, seven households, all of whom were involved in the PKI before 1965, converted to Protestantism.

The expansion of the Protestant community and the active involvement of the new converts in religious activities made it possible for them to construct a place of worship (*kapel*) in the mid-1970s. [13] Although small in scale and having no clergyman, part of the significance of this construction was that the whole process was undertaken without outside financial assistance. In this sense, it displayed the strength and solidarity of the Protestant community not only to other Christians but to Muslims who did not have their own *masjid* at that time.

For reasons that are not clear, the construction of the *kapel* did not become the catalyst for further expansion of the Protestant community. No household conversion was recorded in the 1970s while only a few individuals embraced Christianity. It was only with the coming of the 1980s that Christian expansion resumed. Seven households changed their religious affiliation from Islam to

---

[11] The Catholic and Protestant Parties which were established under the Old Order did not have branches in the *kecamatan* Gamol, so that Christian villagers had to choose among the PKI, PNI and Masyumi. As the PKI was considered to be anti-religious and the Masyumi, to be a Muslim party, it seems to have been quite natural that Christian villagers opted for the PNI.

[12] The records in the Protestant and Catholic Churches to which the Christian community in Kolojonggo is affiliated show that each Church baptised respectively 126 and 268 villagers between 1967 and 1968, although these data are said to have been based on an incomplete list. The average number of baptisms in these two Churches are respectively 15 and 34 per annum from 1951 to 1959 and 17 and 42 per annum from 1960 to 1965.

[13] Christians in Kolojonggo together with those living in several neighbouring hamlets constitute a *pepantan* (a Christian community which combines with an existing church temporarily until they can form their own church). As a result, the construction of the *kapel* in Kolojonggo was carried out not only by Christians in Kolojonggo but by those from its neighbouring hamlets.

Protestantism, joined by several members from two households. In 1993, the Protestant community in Kolojonggo included thirty households and the Catholic, seven households. [14] Among the thirty-seven households, eleven were mixed ones where Muslims and Christians lived together under the same roof. [15]

It was difficult to research what made villagers embrace Christianity. One of the reasons was that conversion to Christianity was a taboo topic. [16] New converts to Christianity were not willing to discuss it except for a brief comment while other Christians generally did not want to talk about who the new converts were, who, among Muslim villagers, were sympathetic to Christianity and who were participating in the Christian learning course preparing for baptism.

If they did talk about the reason for conversion, the new converts generally mentioned their feeling (*rasa*): since they had a good feeling about Christianity and found it to be compatible (*cocok*), they decided to accept it. Sociologically, one common feature is found among the new converts: a Christian family lives nearby in their immediate neighbourhood. However, the converts did not want to admit this fact. When asked about the sources by which they had come to know Christianity, they did not point out the person who had persuaded them to attend the Christian learning course, the prerequisite for conversion. Instead, they emphasised the independence of their decision. The same mode of explanation was used by those who had converted to Christianity a long time ago or had been born into Christian families when asked to explain other villagers' conversion to Christianity. They generally talked about the life style and behaviour of Christians and the solidarity of the Christian community as the primary sources through which non-Christians encountered Christianity. Below is the reply of a Christian villager, when asked why people converted to Christianity:

> The central thing which guides someone to Christianity is the life style (*pola hidup*) and behaviour (*tindak laku*) of Christians. Christians are not like 'a huge empty barrel which is lousy'. Christians love others and try

---

[14] Since the first Catholic appeared in the 1950s, the Catholic community in Kolojonggo has been successful in converting only one couple. In 1993, the seven households of the Catholic community consisted of three households which were the descendants of the two original converts, three households which had embraced Catholicism outside Kolojonggo and later moved into it and one household in which the couple were newly converted to Catholicism. Among these seven households, two households were mixed ones where parents were Catholics while some of their children were Muslims.

[15] Seen from the economic point of view, the thirty-seven Christian households did not have any characteristics which could distinguish themselves as a group from the other ninety-six Muslim households. The economic stratification, occupational structure and educational backgrounds of Christians were almost the same as Muslims. In many cases, Muslims and Christians were related each other by kinship ties except for the two families which had first embraced Christianity. All descendants of these families, whether they lived in this hamlet or not, were Christians.

[16] This tendency did not apply to Muslim villagers, as will be shown in the next chapter. However, Muslims' open remarks on conversion were made only to other Muslims while they also did not talk about this issue with Christians.

to actualise this love. This impresses non-Christians and becomes the major motive for them to make efforts to know more about Christianity.

The strong solidarity of the Christian community was not denied even by Muslims. Whenever a ceremony was held in a Christian family, Christian villagers, irrespective of their geographical proximity, came to give assistance. As the preparation process for a ceremony, especially cooking, was customarily done by neighbours or close relatives, the presence of Christian women who were neither close neighbours nor relatives of the host could be easily recognised by others. When a Christian died, the solidarity of the Christian community was even more clearly expressed. From the first to the last stage of burial, all the work was monopolised by Christians. They bathed the corpse, dressed it, carried the coffin to the cemetery and performed the last service at the cemetery, all of which provided no room for Muslims to be involved, apart from their participation as guests. The same situation, however, did not apply when a Muslim died. Not only Muslims but Christians actively participated in it. Sometimes, the participation of Christians in dealing with the death of a Muslim was more evident than that of Muslims. In several cases, it was a Christian villager with the Muslim *kaum* who entered the hole where the corpse would be placed, arranged the corpse to face Mecca, calculated the number of stones to support the corpse [17] and closed the hole with cement plates. In this respect, the evaluation of Christians that the solidarity of the Christian community is the key in attracting non-Christians to Christianity seems to be correct.

Apart from the solidarity of the Christian community, several clergymen enumerated various other factors as reasons for conversion to Christianity: Christians' emphasis on love rather than on rules and regulations; stress on one's personal experience and feeling rather than on mere memorisation; fanaticism of Muslims; the desire to be buried in a coffin; and witness of God through dreams or other experiences. Whatever the actual reasons for conversion, the Christians' own evaluation of conversion puts high emphasis on one's inner aspects rather than outer influences: attracted to Christianity by observing the behaviour of Christians, people are eager to know more about it and increasing knowledge enables them to convert to Christianity.

Studies about relations between Muslims and Christians in Java have shown that the official view of the government, namely, that harmony dominates the relations between followers of different religions, was not incorrect. Akkeren, who did his research in the early 1960s in an East Java community where Christians were in the majority, pointed out that discrimination based on religious difference was not felt in social interactions (1970:136). The same situation applied to a Yogyanese village in the 1950s. Muslims and Christians in this village

---

[17] According to the custom of Muslim villagers, the number of stones which support the corpse in order for it to face the west should be an odd number, usually five or seven.

created an atmosphere of peace in social life, respecting each other's religion (Soemarjo,1959:99). Research done in the 1970s in Central Java also noted that mutual respect between Muslims and Christians free of incidents suggesting conflict characterised their social interactions (Mohammad,1979/1980:177). Although the shortage of comparative data makes it difficult to make a generalisation, these studies show that religious difference was not a basis of social conflict, and religious distinction between Muslims and Christians was not felt strongly in non-religious domains.

It is likely that until recently, Muslim-Christian relations in Kolojonggo were dominated by harmony, as was symbolised by the reciprocal movements of foods and visits between Muslims and Christians. It is said that Christians were included in the Muslims' exchange network of food after the fasting month and were invited to *kendhuri* held after the fasting month. The food that Christians received at that time was reciprocated at Christmas when they sent food parcels to their Muslim neighbours while some Muslim villagers attended the Christmas celebration held in the *kapel*.

The acceleration of Islamic development in the 1980s, however, has brought a change. Islamic identity is expressed more clearly in everyday life and Islam becomes more and more a factor guiding individual and collective behaviour and providing a framework on things surrounding them. As a result, today, no food is reciprocated and no more visits are made between Muslims and Christians after the fasting month and at Christmas. [18]

---

[18] This change has been influenced by the *fatwa* issued by the Islamic organisation, *Majelis Ulama Indonesia*, in the early 1980s. According to this *fatwa*, Muslims are not permitted to participate in Christmas celebration since its nature is religious rather than social. When celebrating Christmas in the *kapel*, Christians in Kolojonggo delivered invitations to all executive members of the government organisations in the hamlet such as the youth organisation (*Karang Taruna*), the organisation for women (PKK) and the hamlet's social activities group (KKLKMD), irrespective of their religion. This was criticised by Muslims as a violation of Decree No. 70 issued in 1978 prohibiting the spread of a certain religion to those who already confess another religion. In spite of this invitation, no invited Muslims were present at the Christmas celebration in 1993. Muslim villagers' concern about this decree was proved once again when I made a complaint half in a joke to a few Muslims that an invitation card to *pengajian* was never delivered to me for twenty months of my stay in Kolojonggo. All of them mentioned that they did not want to violate Decree No. 70 issued in 1978 (I was a Buddhist). One exception to this practice was a community ceremony, called *Syawalan* or *Halalbilhalal* which was celebrated after the fasting month. Although this ceremony was an extension of Islamic activities, all villagers irrespective of their religion were invited by Muslim organisers. They legitimised this invitation by referring to the fact that *Syawalan* is the tradition of Java as well as of Kolojonggo, so that, to invite Christians to it is not a violation of Decree No. 70 in 1978. At the 1994 celebration of *Syawalan*, it happened that most of the invited Christians did not attend it, except for a few who held the position of RT and RW head. This absence seems to have been triggered by an argument between Muslims and Christians concerning the place of celebration. The rumour went around that Christians insisted *Syawalan* in 1994 should be celebrated in a house of a Christian, a proposal which could not be accepted by Muslims. It is not certain whether the attempt by Christians to change the venue of *Syawalan* was a reaction to Muslim villagers' opposition to attending Christmas celebration or not. Whatever the reasons for this dispute and subsequent absence of most Christians at the *Syawalan* might be, however, this incident shows that the space shared by both Christians and Muslims has been getting narrower and narrower.

7.3. Clarification of the Boundary between Muslims and Christians

All the names of Muslim villagers in Kolojonggo are written in a notebook stored in the *masjid*. This book was made after the organisation of *takmir masjid* (*masjid* council) in 1989 and, from that time on, has been constantly revised. When someone moves in or out, gives birth to a child or passes away, these changes are added to it. In this sense, this book is comparable to the registration book of residents kept in the house of the *kadus*. In one respect, however, it carries more accurate data: on the religious affiliation of villagers. Unlike the official registration book which updates its information on the religious identity of each villager once in five or ten years, the book in the *masjid* does so as soon as a certain change occurs. When a villager's rumoured conversion turns out to be true, a red mark is added to his or her name, signifying a withdrawal from the *masjid* membership. As the invitation cards to certain Islamic activities are based on this registration book, a red mark implies that no invitation will be delivered to that person. In this respect, this book is the most updated religious atlas in Kolojonggo.

This updated book, however, is not always correct. It may contain data based on the speculation of the book-keepers, the *anak masjid*. The possibility of inaccurate updating was demonstrated when the distribution of *zakat* was completed in 1994. One day after it, Bu Wiro, who lived next door to the *masjid*, passed on Bu Utomo's complaint to the youth who were in charge of it that she did not receive her portion of *zakat* distribution. According to Bu Wiro, Bu Utomo, to support her argument that she had every right to receive a portion of *zakat*, maintained that she possessed praying clothes and memorised the motions of *salat*. The reason the Muslim youth had not allocated a portion of *zakat* to Bu Utomo was simple. Her name had a red mark in the registration book. The youth had a solid reason for this red mark: her daughter and son-in-law had converted to Christianity a few years ago. As Bu Utomo was totally dependent on her daughter and had never been to the *masjid*, her name was marked when her daughter and son-in-law got the same treatment.

As the case of Bu Utomo shows, the registration book in the *masjid* has played the role of identifying villagers by their religious affiliation. Religious difference had certainly existed and had been perceived by villagers in Kolojonggo even before the registration book was made. However, at that time, the boundary of the *umat* Islam was rather vague and arbitrary. No single criterion was available to draw a clear line and each resorted to their own criterion to define the *umat* Islam. In this respect, it was similar to what Anderson (1983) calls, 'an imagined community'.

The imaginary demarcation of the *umat* Islam is reflected in the way sacrificed animals and *zakat* were distributed in the 1980s. When the first sacrifice in

Kolojonggo was made in the mid-1980s by Pak Rono, two thirds of the mutton allotted for communal distribution was not apportioned equally to all Muslim households in Kolojonggo. [19] Instead, it was distributed only to the Muslims near his house. This uneven distribution brought about, from the present perspective of Muslims, an absurd situation, since Pak Rono distributed some of his portion to his close Christian neighbours. In principle, he did not violate the Islamic law which permitted him to dispose of his own portion as he wanted. However, the result was rather contrary to the idea underlying the command to distribute a sacrifice. Some Christians received a part of the sacrificed animal whereas many Muslims did not.

After talking about this story, Pak Rono excused this situation by commenting that villagers' religious knowledge was not great at that time and the amount of mutton was not enough to cover all the Muslim households in Kolojonggo. If the boundary of the *umat* Islam had been clearly conceptualised at that time by Pak Rono and other Muslims, however, this way of distribution would have been hard to implement. As this boundary was vague and was not repeatedly and consciously delineated, he could distribute his portion to his Christian neighbours, giving priority to the traditional duty of distributing food to one's close neighbours.

The first movement to coordinate *zakat* collection and distribution was started by the *kaum*'s family in 1983. [20] Twenty-one households responded to its request, donating 120 kg. of hulled rice. [21] It was then distributed evenly to thirty-three households, so that each received 3.5 kg. From that time on, the collection of *zakat* has increased steadily: 315 kg. of rice and Rp 20,750 (equivalent to 35 kg. of rice) were gathered in 1994. Apart from this quantitative increase in the amount of *zakat*, a remarkable change took place in its mode of distribution, amid the decade's history of *zakat* collection.

Asked how to distribute *zakat*, the Muslim youth in charge of it replied that all Muslim villagers who did not pay their *zakat* had a right to receive it. The rationale underlying this explanation, however, was not consistent. Some said that this mode aimed to incorporate all Muslims into the exchange network of *zakat*, which would help to consolidate fraternity (*ukuwah*) amongst Muslims. Others argued that this system would help to heighten the religious consciousness of villagers. Those who were capable but did not pay their *zakat* would feel

---

[19] According to the teaching of Islam as interpreted by the reformist villagers, one third of sacrificed animals should be allotted to its purchaser and two thirds to other Muslims who cannot afford to purchase one. For a different mode of distributing sacrificed animals, see Bowen (1993:276-7).

[20] Some Muslim villagers said that they had started to pay *zakat* in the 1970s. However, no organising body was formed at that time to take charge of *zakat* collection, so that villagers paid their *zakat* either to the *masjid* in a neighbouring hamlet or distributed their *zakat* individually to other Muslims.

[21] At that time, not every participating family paid the due amount of rice, namely 2.5 kg. of hulled rice per head. Only five families did so while the others paid just 2.5 kg. of rice for the whole family.

ashamed when they received a portion of rice collected from villagers who were poorer than themselves, and this feeling of shame would encourage them to participate in *zakat* payment the next year. One youth had a totally different idea. He postulated that all villagers had the intention of paying their *zakat* but economic difficulties hindered them, so that rice should be distributed to everyone who did not pay *zakat*. In spite of these differences, all of them shared the view that every Muslim should be included in the network of *zakat* either as a recipient or as a donor.

The attitude of the Muslim youth in considering *zakat* as a medium to draw all Muslim villagers into one network did not exist in the 1980s. At that time, a household's economic wealth was said to have been an important criterion for choosing the recipients of *zakat*. However, as an absolute yardstick to measure the economic situation of each villager was not available, the actual distribution was done on an arbitrary basis and many households who were poor did not receive their portions. In 1983, only thirty-three households received a portion while about forty Muslim households, including some of the poorest in Kolojonggo, were excluded from it. Islamic development in the 1980s increased the amount of *zakat* collection until 300 kg. of rice was collected in 1990, almost three times more than that in 1983. However, the expanding amount of *zakat* did not result in an increase in the absolute number of villagers who received it. Rather, each recipient got more rice than before. While 3.5 kg. of rice was given to thirty-three households in 1983, 8 kg. of rice was allocated to thirty-six households in 1990.

In 1991, a dramatic change took place in the mode of distributing *zakat* as the idea that *zakat* distribution should embrace all Muslim households replaced the previous arbitrary selection of recipients. Consequently, the number of recipients increased to sixty-one households in 1991. The expansion of the recipients was accompanied by varying the amount of rice being distributed. From 1991 onward, the rice was not allocated equally but varied between 5 kg. and 15 kg., depending on the economic situation of each recipient. With this modification, almost all Muslim households were included in the network of *zakat* in 1993 and 1994 either as donors or recipients. [22]

---

[22] In 1994, three households were excluded from the network of *zakat* among one hundred and seven Muslim households in Kolojonggo (including those households which have both Christians and Muslims). Two of them belonged to relatively rich households and the other was a household which objected to participating in social activities with other villagers. In this respect, the exclusion of these three households does not seem to contradict the idea that the *zakat* network embraces all Muslim households, demarcating the boundary between Muslims and Christians. In addition, the first two households regularly received an invitation from the *masjid* for the *pengajian* and a portion of sacrificed animals was distributed to them, signifying that they were considered to be the members of the *umat* Islam. In the case of the household belonging to the second category, the situation was rather different. Neither invitation to Islamic activities nor a portion of sacrificed animal was distributed to it. However, this exclusion was the result of the idiosyncratic character of that family since it severed all social relations with villagers.

As the changing mode of distributing *zakat* and sacrificed animals [23] illustrates, the boundary of the *umat* Islam in Kolojonggo has become more and more clearly defined and specific. The registration book of the *umat* Islam symbolises the culmination of this process, showing that no ambiguity is permissible in the religious affiliation of villagers. This change has been triggered by the acceleration of Islamic development which has helped Muslims to be more conscious of their own religious identity and that of others and has provided more religious activities reminding them of the boundary of the *umat* Islam. The presence of Christians has been another important factor. As will be shown in the next chapter, Christians are envisaged by Muslims to be obsessed with expanding their community at the expanse of the *umat* Islam. By clarifying the boundary of the *umat* Islam, therefore, Muslims try to draw a line between themselves and Christians, a line which should not be transgressed.

7.4. Expansion of Religious Difference in Non-Religious Domains

In Kolojonggo, the religious demarcation which has been consolidated in the religious domain is on the point of expanding to non-religious domains. The dichotomy of Muslims and Christians, which is sometimes referred to by the terms of *kita* (we) and *wong liya* or *tiang sanes* (other persons), is used as a framework for Muslims to interpret certain events in everyday life and to guide their behaviour. The comparison of two elections in 1978 and 1993 exemplifies the increasing importance of this dichotomy and the ways it works in the domain of secular life.

The hamlet headmanship (*kadus*) is directly connected to material benefit. The successful candidate receives approximately one and a quarter hectares of *sawah*, the size of which will make him or her one of the largest landowners in Kolojonggo. Apart from this material benefit, the headmanship guarantees high status in hamlet life. The *kadus* will be invited to all private and public occasions in hamlet life, will be given a chance to speak on these occasions and will be consulted whenever a problem occurs. In this respect, the *kadus* is at the center of all hamlet affairs.

The sudden death of the *kadus* in 1978 activated villagers in Kolojonggo. Free election, which was promised at that time, attracted many male villagers into competing for the headmanship. When the application period was closed, ten male villagers had registered their names as candidates. All applicants were aged between twenty-five and thirty-five and had jobs in the agricultural or construction sectors. Considering that the position of *kadus* was one of the most

---

[23] In 1994 when a bull was slaughtered at *Idul Adha*, its meat was distributed to all Muslim households in Kolojonggo, except for one (see footnote No. 22). In cases where a household was composed of two married spouses, two portions were distributed to it. As a result, around 140 portions were distributed to Muslim villagers, exceeding the total number of Muslim households.

preferred ones among villagers and competition was keen due to the abundance of candidates, it was natural that all possible resources were mobilised for the campaign.

All ten candidates worked hard to form their faction. The kin group was the most trustworthy resource of each candidate, as was revealed by the fact that no immediate kinsmen competed for the headmanship. [24] Apart from this, they used other personal relations to expand their faction. In some cases, verbal contracts were made between a candidate and his supporters about the benefits that the former would give to the latter after winning the election. Some borrowed money from others and used it as a bond between themselves and the creditor. Ascetic practices were another resource to which most candidates resorted. Many performed these by themselves while some visited the *dhukun* to get advice.

One of the interesting points in the campaign was that religion did not play a major role in building a faction. In many cases, the Christian candidates associated with the Muslim villagers and vice versa. The present Christian *kadus* who won the 1978 election, for example, had Muslims as his main opinion leaders, one of whom is now the most active supporter of Islamic activities. The fact that Christians did not resort to religion to create their faction was understandable since the Christian community had five candidates. In a situation where more than three-quarters of voters were Muslims, to use the religious element as a part of their campaign strategy might lose potential support of Muslims. As a result, it was the Muslim candidates who would be advantaged if religion became one of the key issues in the election. However, this was not the case and Muslim-Christian dichotomy was not highlighted throughout the campaign period. [25] The result of the election also shows that the religious identity of a candidate was not an important variable in deciding the voting pattern of villagers. The winner and the runner-up received about 90 and 70 votes from the total of about 250 voters while the other eight candidates got less than 20 respectively. This meant that the Christian candidates received more than two-thirds of the total votes since both the winner and runner-up were Christians and the other Christian candidates also received some votes.

---

[24] Two kinship ties existed among the ten candidates. Two of them had the same great-grandfather, while Pak Budi and Pak Dar were related by 'incomplete' affinal tie: Pak Budi was the step-son of his step-mother's younger brother, Pak Dar.

[25] When asked about the strategies in this election, all former candidates enumerated their kinship and friendship as a basis of building factions and no one commented on religious ties. The absence of any organised Islamic activities was one of the major reasons which had hindered the formation of friendship amongst Muslims based on religious activities and, consequently, made it impossible for the Muslim candidates to use religious difference as a resource to build a faction. One of the Muslim candidates whom I asked a more direct question about the role of religion in that election answered that, at that time, villagers had not been concerned with the question as to whether the *kadus* should be a Muslim or not.

Karang Taruna is the youth organisation founded by the government. Although its presidency is not a paid position, it is in demand among the youth: it is the only official organisation encompassing the young generation; and its president is invited to all official hamlet meetings, bringing high status to its holder.[26] In addition, many villagers' desire to hold a position in an organisation also explains its popularity.

In 1993, the president of *Karang Taruna* expressed his intention not to run for another three years' term. From the outset, there appeared two strong candidates for the presidentship, Ferdi and Sulis, both of whom had similar personal backgrounds: they were university students; belonged to the same age group; and had a position on the executive of *Karang Taruna,* Ferdi as a treasurer and Sulis as a vice-president. They had a good reputation among adult villagers and they actively participated in religious activities. Ferdi was one of the opinion leaders of the *anak masjid* whereas Sulis was an organiser of a Bible Study Group.

Several weeks before the election day, it was decided in the general meeting of *Karang Taruna* that the president would be selected not by direct vote from among its members but by an electoral board consisting of several hamlet leaders. As the candidates running for the presidency would also be selected at the board meeting, no candidates could be made official and no public campaign was possible before that time. In this situation, the most important factor for someone to be selected as a president was one's previous relations with the board members. The religious identity of the candidates was one of the crucial elements in forging such relations since the contact between the youth and middle aged board members was made most frequently at religious meetings.

Ferdi was quite aware of the fact that religion would be crucial in the coming election process. As time went on, his evaluation proved to be true. One rumour was that Pak Adi, who was not a member of the electoral board but had an excellent ability to convince others, openly sought support for Sulis from the Christian board members. Unfortunately, Ferdi had no trickster in his side. In terms of numbers, the composition of the electoral board was not disadvantageous

---

[26] One of the factors which added religious significance to the position of the president in *Karang Taruna* was a mutual suspicion between Christian and Muslim youth that the elected president from a certain religious group would not appreciate the religious activities of the other. The Christian complaint against the outgoing Muslim president of *Karang Taruna* was that he had fixed the time for its main activity, that is, to take coconuts from the trees owned by this organisation, on Sunday morning. Although this activity usually finished before nine in the morning when Sunday service started in the *kapel*, some Christian youth argued that the fixing of the time on Sunday morning was inappropriate for the communal activity of *Karang Taruna*. They also complained that its monthly or irregular meetings sometimes coincided with those of the Christian youth, due to the Muslim president's lack of consideration for Christians. The Muslim youth also suspected that if a Christian youth were selected as a president of *Karang Taruna*, he would not consider their religious activities in selecting the meeting day. As the Muslim youth used three or four evenings in a week for their religious activities, it might be difficult for a Christian to choose the day of *Karang Taruna* meeting without making it collide with Islamic ones. The outgoing Muslim president could do this job easily since he himself participated in all Islamic activities.

to him since it would consist of five Christians and six Muslims. However, what made him worried was the fact that all five Christian members were active in the church while three of six Muslim members did not frequently visit the *masjid*.

Deciding that the situation was not favourable to him, Ferdi, in company with his close friends, began to consider alternatives to giving the presidency to a Christian. At last, they found two options: first, to make the outgoing president remain in that post for another three years and second, to nominate a third person as president. Ferdi met the outgoing president but the latter reiterated his intention to resign. This forced him to accept the second option but it was not easy for him to find a proper person. According to Ferdi, the candidate had to be a Muslim, had to have a higher qualification than Sulis and had to be able to satisfy both Muslim and Christian board members. His choice was Pak Hartono, who was a primary school teacher and retained good relations with the board members. In order to make Pak Hartono a candidate, however, Ferdi had to overcome an obstacle: Pak Hartono was not a member of *Karang Taruna* due to his marital status [27] and as a corollary, he could not be a candidate for its president. This problem which did not appear easy to overcome did not pose a serious challenge to Ferdi. He discovered a way to change the conventional rule for membership to *Karang Taruna*:the manual of *Karang Taruna* issued by the government stipulated that everyone under the age of forty was eligible for membership. When this rule became known to other youth, no one could oppose the nomination of Pak Hartono as a candidate. After solving the problem, Ferdi visited Pak Hartono on the day before the election and gained agreement from the latter to be a candidate. As part of his plan, he asked the outgoing president, who would be included on the electoral board, to nominate Pak Hartono as a candidate.

The general meeting for the election was convened in the house of the *kadus*. Before it started, Ferdi passed the government version of membership rules to everyone attending. Apart from this, he made a short remark just before the electoral board meeting that he had had many difficulties working with a president of the same age and expected a more mature president for the next term of *Karang Taruna*.

The electoral board met in an isolated room. As one board member was not present that night, a senior female of *Karang Taruna* substituted for him. With this replacement, the board was composed of four Christians and seven Muslims. When the chairman of the board, the *kadus*, asked for nominations from others,

---

[27] Asked the membership rule for *Karang Taruna* until a few days before the election day, all members pointed out marital status as its main criterion. This rule had been strictly observed, so that unmarried villagers in their thirties were considered as members and invitations were delivered while those in their early twenties but already married were excluded from it. The married youth were categorised as honorary members.

the Christian RW[28] head nominated Sulis while the Muslim RW head put forward the name of Ferdi. With the nomination of the third person, there were three nominees. Each of them, then, briefly talked about the reasons for nominating. The next session was to hear the opinions of other board members one by one. All Christian members except for the *kadus* who reserved his opinion backed Sulis, five Muslims supported Ferdi and two Muslim members, the third candidate. This result placed the *kadus* in deep trouble. Although Ferdi had more supporters, this numeric dominance was not enough for him to be selected. They needed some kind of consensus but the *kadus* knew that the Christian members would not give up their preference easily. The moment of silence which fell over the room was broken when the outgoing president of *Karang Taruna* put forward the name of Pak Hartono. He repeated Ferdi's speech before the beginning of the election that a mature person was required for the presidency and emphasised that Pak Hartono was qualified to be a member of *Karang Taruna*. The *kadus* swiftly sought the opinions of the others. No objection was heard. Finally, he asked the opinion of the two RW heads. As they showed their consent, the *kadus* made it clear that Pak Hartono was selected as a president.

After they came out of the room, the *kadus* announced the result of the board meeting, adding that everyone should accept this decision although they had different opinions. In contrast with the previous progress of the meeting which had gone as expected by Ferdi, it finished unexpectedly. When the *kadus* asked Pak Hartono to give a speech of acceptance, no one answered. He had already gone home.

The different electoral processes in the two elections illustrate the increasing significance of religious identity in non-religious domains. The election of *Karang Taruna* implies that one's religious identity is now viewed as a factor that should be considered in selecting a person for an organisation with which both Muslims and Christians are associated. Although Ferdi did not mention it publicly, the main reason why he made efforts to prevent Sulis from being elected as a president was because Sulis was a Christian.[29]

---

[28] RW (*Rukun Warga*) refers to an administrative unit below hamlet (*dusun*). RW is composed of several RT (*Rukun Tetangga*), the lowest administrative unit encompassing twenty to forty households. The head of RW or RT is not a paid position, although their role includes administrative works, such as issuing certificates of residence, birth, death and so on. Kolojonggo consists of two RW and five RT.

[29] Ferdi's opposition to Sulis may be interpreted in a different way. We may ascribe this not to Sulis' religion but to Ferdi's personal rivalry with Sulis. Ferdi and Sulis belonged to the same age group, grew up together in Kolojonggo, shared similar personal background and were regarded as informal leaders of their age group. Although the personal rivalry between Sulis and Ferdi might play a certain role, it should be noted that this rivalry was expressed and the Muslim youth who were close to Ferdi interpreted this case in religious terms. When asked why Sulis was not suitable for a president in *Karang Taruna* and why Ferdi opposed Sulis, they suggested that this was not because Ferdi opposed Sulis personally but because Sulis was a Christian. In this respect, it can be said that religious difference was at the center of the *Karang Taruna* election, irrespective of whether it was the main reason for Ferdi's opposition to Sulis or not.

Public discourse in the *umat* Islam also emphasises Muslim identity as a factor to guide one's behaviour in non-religious life. For example, Muslims are now prompted to visit their sick neighbours, to participate in funeral procedures, to help the family of the deceased and to give economic assistance to their neighbours, primarily because they are Muslims. Pak Giran expressed this idea in a *Jumatan* as follows:

> When Muslim villagers are sick, we, as Muslims, have to visit them, so that we can gather again to carry out commands from Allah. I stress this duty, since there is a member (*warga*) in the *umat* Islam in Kolojonggo who is sick, namely, Bu Yogo. Her sickness is serious and, due to her family problem, that her daughter has a different religious belief, she is in a much worse condition. [30] ... Don't let our sisters and brothers (*sedherek kita*) [face hardships by themselves]! It is obligatory for Muslims to visit our sisters and brothers, to share their sufferings and to help them. These acts are what can be regarded as *ibadah*.

The next week, Pak Giran's ideas were re-emphasised by two speakers in the *Jumatan* and in the routine *pengajian*. One of them, Pak Tugi, pointed out the difficulty in coordinating the activities to assist Muslim villagers and proposed a more systematic plan to take care of their well-being: to select a representative from each RT who would be in charge of monitoring the conditions of Muslim villagers in each RT and of reporting it to the *masjid* council (*takmir masjid*), which would later mobilise the *umat* Islam to take certain measures. [31] Pak Tugi's proposal was not put into practice for the three months of my stay in Kolojonggo after his speech had been delivered. However, his ideas seemed to be sympathetically received by others and became a basis for them to mobilise a *gotong-royong* to improve a house belonging to Bu Nangun.

In a *takmir masjid* meeting where the *gotong-royong* to help Bu Nangun became an item on the agenda, a youth argued for repairing Bu Nangun's house as follows: her house was on the verge of collapse and rain leaked into her house but her cousin who owned the land where her house was erected did not pay any attention to it. He then emphasised the devotion of Bu Nangun to Islamic

---

[30] Asked why her Christian daughter made Bu Yogo's condition worse, Pak Giran replied that her daughter could help Bu Yogo only outwardly (*secara lahir*), for example, by cooking food, by house cleaning and by washing clothes, but could not help Bu Yogo spiritually (*secara batin*). The spiritual assistance was, according to Pak Giran, what Bu Yogo was urgently in need of and what she could obtain only from the *umat* Islam.

[31] The other villager who dealt with the same issue in the *pengajian* mentioned two reasons why Muslims should take care of other Muslims: first, one's visit to sick Muslims would strengthen fraternity among Muslim villagers and second, this would prevent followers of other religions (Christians) from making attempts to lure Muslims. 'If the followers of other religions take care of sick Muslims (although he did not mention the name of Bu Yogo, it was clear to the audience that he was talking about Bu Yogo)', he argued, 'they definitely have a hidden intention.' Then, he explained what the hidden intention was, 'They pretend to assist Muslims, but in their mind, they keep saying: We will take care of you (Muslims), but you have to follow us, namely, you have to follow our religion.'

activities and called for assistance from the *umat* Islam. In his speech, he did not identify her cousin but everyone knew who he was. There even was someone who commented, probably half in a joke, that the working party should not expect to be served snacks and drinks since Bu Nangun was too poor to buy them; the story suggested that her cousin would not prepare food for them. [32] Unfortunately, the bad guy in this discussion, the cousin of Bu Nangun, was not in a position to represent himself and excuse his negligence to his aunt. He was the Christian *kadus*. Therefore, the statement by the youth, by emphasising the misery of Bu Nangun and the neglect of her by her kinsman, indirectly highlighted the religious significance of the *gotong-royong*. This was not only to help a member of the *umat* Islam but to embrace a Muslim abandoned by her Christian kinsman. In other words, this was a chance to show that religious solidarity could be stronger than kinship ties.

In two subsequent *tahlilan*, funds to purchase building materials were collected [33] and the date of the *gotong-royong* was fixed for Friday afternoon after the *Jumatan*. Around thirty villagers gathered at the backyard of the *kadus'* house and renovated Bu Nangun's house for two days. As Bu Nangun talked of the mobilisation of *gotong-royong* to her cousin the day before its initiation, the working party was fortunate enough to be served with tea, snacks and meals. Although a few Christian families lived not far away from the *kadus'* house, the *kadus* was the only Christian who participated in the labour process throughout two day's *gotong-royong*. This signified the acknowledgment of other Christians that it was the *gotong-royong* organised by Muslims and they had no obligation to participate in it.

Every group in the hamlet, whether it be a family, a neighbourhood, an administrative unit (RT, RW or hamlet) or a voluntary association (religious groups or art groups), is entitled to make a plea for *gotong-royong*. However, two different logics are applied to it. First, the invitation to *gotong-royong* for private purposes is governed by the rule of reciprocity. When one asks assistance of others, he or she is expected to reciprocate others' requests for labour in the future, although the reciprocity is not strictly balanced. Second, where a communal body mobilises *gotong-royong* to improve roads, ditches, guard posts, *masjid* and so on, the invitation is strictly limited to those who will benefit from

---

[32] It is an unwritten rule that the host of *gotong-royong* should provide tea, snacks and meals to the participants.
[33] The total sum estimated to renovate Bu Nangun's house was about Rp 100,000 or equivalent to about 160 kg. of rice, which was not a small amount in the village economy. Most of the donors, who numbered about forty, contributed between Rp 1000 and Rp 2000 while a few gave between Rp 5000 and Rp 10000. It took a month for around Rp 100,000 to be collected. The swiftness of this donation process surprised even the organisers of the *gotong-royong* since the *umat* Islam in Kolojonggo had had no precedent for gathering that sum of money in a month. This success was considered by village Muslims as proof of the maturing religious piety of the *umat* Islam.

these works. In this sense, a clear division between the private and the communal has been observed in the pattern of mobilising *gotong-royong*.

Seen from this logic, to mobilise Muslims in order to improve the structure of the *masjid* is acceptable while to ask labour from Muslims for the purpose of improving a private house is not. This is because the benefit gained from this work is not shared by all participants nor will it be reciprocated in the future. Therefore, Bu Nangun's house could be improved by *gotong-royong* only when initiated by the *kadus* since she had not previously been involved in any network of *gotong-royong*. If initiated by the *kadus*, others would come with the idea that they reciprocated the labour of the *kadus* and their labour would be reciprocated by him in the future. In this context, *gotong-royong* initiated by Muslim villagers to improve Bu Nangun's house deviated from the usual logic.

However, one condition can transform this abnormality into normality. If the benefit of this labour is conceptualised as falling on Muslims as a group, the communal labour outside the boundary of the *masjid* can be reconciled with the logic of *gotong-royong*. This conceptual change was what happened in the plea to initiate *gotong-royong* to renovate Bu Nangun's house. The participants believed that the benefit of this labour would be ultimately shared by themselves as Muslims. As a hamlet can initiate *gotong-royong* for the benefit of the whole community, so can Muslims initiate it for the benefit of Muslims. In brief, this example signals that religious identity is significant not only in the religious domain and that the daily life of a Muslim, which was previously perceived to be outside the boundary of religion, is becoming a concern of Muslims as a group.

Islamic development in Kolojonggo has been accompanied by the construction of a clear line demarcating the Muslim community from its Christian counterpart. As this demarcation is consolidated, it does not remain in one's conceptual scheme but begins to be utilised as a factor to guide one's actions both in the religious and the non-religious domains of life. The fact that one belongs to the *umat* Islam can now be used as a rationale for rejecting a certain candidate in an election and for giving assistance to fellow villagers.

This situation in Kolojonggo seems to be what is expected by the motto of 'agreement in difference' (*setuju dalam perbedaan*) popularised by Muslim intellectuals in the 1970s as the right guideline for regulating relations between followers of different religions. It defines the prerequisite to bring harmonious relations between followers of different religions as a certainty (*keyakinan*) of one's religious belief, not as a relativistic approach that sees every religion based on the same essence (*hakekah*) (Badan Penelitian dan Pengembangan Agama, 1983/1984:25-6). Only when one is convinced of the rightness of one's own religion and a clear consciousness of one's religious identity, is one thought able to proceed to the second part of this motto, that is, 'agreement' with followers of different religions.

It is not certain, however, how far this idea can be actualised in real life. The case of Kolojonggo shows that the transition from one part of the motto, 'difference', to the other part, 'agreement', is neither an easy nor an automatic process. Although no open conflicts have been found between Muslims and Christians, friction and antagonisms have built up as Islamic identity has been consolidated and Muslims become more conscious of the differences between themselves and Christians. The relations between Muslims and Christians in Kolojonggo where religious difference has become increasingly important in everyday life will be examined in the next chapter.

Plate 13: Bu Nangun's house before reconstruction.

Plate 14: Gotong-royong mobilised by Muslim villagers to build Bu Nangun's House.

Chapter 8: War of Words: The Muslim Villagers' View of Christians, Christianity and Christianisation [1]

The Preamble in the 1945 Constitution of independent Indonesia contains an ideological tenet called *Pancasila*, which is composed of five principles: Belief in One God, Humanity that is just and civilised, Unity of Indonesia, Democracy guided by the wisdom of representative deliberation, Social justice for all Indonesians. Since its installation as a state ideology, *Pancasila* has been the most commonly used rhetoric in political discourse and the governing principle of social life. In spite of this significance, *Pancasila* has remained an abstract doctrine which should be supplemented by concrete ideas, depending on the socio-economic and political considerations of each period.

The first principle, 'Belief in One God', has been a source of controversies since the independence of Indonesia. Each religious group has tried to exert its version of this principle on other religious groups and to implement it as official government policy. Two of the critical debates centring on this principle have been how to define 'One God' and how to interpret religious freedom included in it. There has been continuing ups and downs, but history shows that Islamic groups have been more successful in this struggle than other religious groups. Their definition of religion has been accepted by the government, so that only five religions, considered to be religions by Islamic groups, are officially recognised in Indonesia. On the other hand, the concept of religious freedom supported by Islamic groups was formulated as decrees in 1978, so that it is forbidden to carry out missionary activities among those who already confess another religion.

In spite of this success of Islamic groups and contrary to their expectations, the Christian population kept increasing in the New Order period (See Chapter VII), while Islamic groups have had no effective and direct measure to counteract this. Most importantly, they have no coercive power to put the law into practice without assistance from the government, which, fearing an open explosion of conflicts, has desisted. In this situation, the reaction of Muslims who are dissatisfied with the expansion of Christianity and the government's inertia has concentrated on exposing the nature of Christianity and of Christian missionary activities to the masses. They have published polemical books comparing Islam

---

[1] In this chapter, my discussion is focused only on the attitude of Muslim villagers toward Christians, Christianity and Christianisation. This does not mean that Christian villagers do not have ideas concerning Muslims, Islam and Muslims' view of Christians. For the consistency of the thesis, however, Christian villagers' view is not included in this chapter but will be discussed in Appendix B, titled 'The War of Words: Voices of the Christians'.

with Christianity, have written articles in magazines exposing tricks played by the missionaries [2], held *pengajian* to spread their ideas and founded an organisation to counter the expansion of Christianity. [3] It is not certain how effective these measures have been in decreasing Muslim conversion to Christianity. However, it is rather clearer that these have facilitated the flow of information on Christianisation amongst Muslim intellectuals, on the one hand, and from these intellectuals to the countryside, on the other.

The focus of this chapter is on the ways Christians, Christianity and Christianisation are viewed by the reformist villagers in Kolojonggo. In the first section, the negative image of Christians constructed by the reformist villagers will be discussed. This will be followed by a discussion of one of the key issues underlying Muslim and Christian relations in Kolojonggo, namely, conversion. The last section will deal with one of the key concepts with which Muslims villagers evaluate their own religion and Christianity: *akal*.

8.1. Harmony and Tension in Everyday Life

In Indonesia, it was rare for *Pancasila* not to become a subject of conversation when I first met Indonesians, especially those who had received a formal education under the New Order. After introducing themselves briefly to me, they began to talk about the racial, religious and cultural diversities of Indonesia. This was followed by a comment on the strength of *Pancasila* in combining all these diversities into one without conflict. These casual meetings could give an impression that the Indonesian government has been successful in indoctrinating her citizens with *Pancasila*. This success has not been achieved without intensive programs to expose *Pancasila* to her citizens. Not only students or civil servants but peasants and housewives have been mobilised to participate in a special course designed to learn *Pancasila*. There, they are taught that *Pancasila* condemns behaviour such as objection to the collective consensus of a meeting (*musyawarah*); enforcement of one's own will on others; extravagant life; idleness; giving priority to private interests over state interests and intolerance to followers of other religions. If someone were brave enough to query some of this nationally-accepted ideology, he or she would be branded as 'anti-*Pancasila*', someone who should be corrected by the spirit of *Pancasila*.

---

[2] Christianisation seems to have been one of the most frequently discussed issues in Islamic magazines, especially in the early 1990s. *Panji Masyarakat*, one of the most widely read magazines in the Islamic circle has presented special reports on Christianisation and relations between Muslims and Christians at least once a year since 1991. The issue of Christianisation has been more seriously dealt with in a monthly magazine called *Media Dakwah*. Apart from carrying more articles about Christianisation than *Panji Masyarakat*, *Media Dakwah* has had a special column from 1990 onward devoted entirely to the expansion of the Christian community and the tactics of Christian missionaries.

[3] In Yogyakarta, an organisation calling itself 'a foundation to guide converts to Islam', was founded in 1993. Apart from guiding converts, the aim of this organisation was to spread awareness of the danger of Christianisation to the masses and to inculcate cadres who would educate and guide Muslim villagers in rural areas who were facing the expansion of Christianity.

The same situation applies to villagers in Kolojonggo. Almost all adult villagers have attended the special course to learn *Pancasila* once [4] and several have received a certificate as coordinators to guide the P4 course in a lower administrative unit such as a hamlet, RW and RT. Intensive contact with *Pancasila* made it possible for them, especially those who worked as teachers and civil servants, to have a comprehensive understanding of it. They knew its historical foundations and the detailed guidelines (*butir*) for each principle, [5] and they readily incorporated it as rhetoric in private conversation. *Pancasila* was also a frequent topic in official religious discourse. Pak Timan in a *Jumatan* explained why the first principle of *Pancasila* had been accepted:

> We have to be conscious of the fact that the inhabitants of this world of Allah, in particular, those in Indonesia are not only Muslims. We are living in a differentiated nation consisting of different races, cultures and religions. Therefore, the land of Allah is not our monopoly but the possession of ours (*golongan kita*) and theirs (*golongan sanes*). We should recognise that they have their own religious conviction and values, which should be respected. This is why *Pancasila* and the 1945 Constitution promote harmony (*rukun*) and tolerance (*toleransi*) among followers of different religions.

The next part of his speech explained how Muslims should understand *rukun* and tolerance in religion stipulated by *Pancasila*:

> With these other groups, we will have both parallel and discrepant ideas. When ours is different from theirs, we are not permitted to be silent, just folding our hands. We should not be confused but hold our own identity tightly. We, Muslims, have to be certain that the only true religion is Islam, as is written in the Quran. ... [6] What *Pancasila* teaches is not that we do not need to have certainty as to the truth of Islam. What is taught is that we Muslims need not deride other religions and others do not derogate us, and we do not interfere in religious matters of others and others do not intervene in ours. This will then bring about the situation of 'agreement in difference'.

---

[4] In Indonesian, this course is called P4 (*Pedoman Penghayatan dan Pengamalan Pancasila*). The government established a special organisation to instruct in P4, called BP 7 (*Badan Pembinaan Pendidikan Pelaksanaan Pedoman Penghayatan Dan Pengamalan Pancasila*), which extends its branches to the district level.

[5] As an effort to systematise education in P4, the Indonesian government and the MPR (People's Assembly) stipulated detailed guidelines (*butir*) to make each of the five pillars in *Pancasila* concrete. For example, its first pillar, Belief in One God, has four guidelines: to believe in and show piety to One God, to respect followers of other religions and to cooperate with them, to respect others' freedom to carry out religious obligations and not to force any religion on others.

[6] He then recited Arabic verses from the Quran and its translation in Javanese, which has the meaning of 'the only religion on the side of Allah is Islam.'

The condition that Pak Timan refers to as bringing 'agreement in difference' is the Islamic interpretation of religious freedom in *Pancasila*: all Indonesians have freedom to carry out their religious duties in their own community, without violating the boundary of other religions. Just as Muslims confine their activities to Muslims, so should Christians.

Since the independence of Indonesia, whether a religious community should confine its religious activities to its own community has lain at the core of the debates between Muslims and non-Muslims, especially Christians. Christian leaders interpret religious freedom stipulated in *Pancasila* in its broadest sense. For them, it implies freedom to choose religion, to change one's religion and to manifest, either alone or in community with others and in public or private, one's religion in teaching, practice, worship and observance (Sudjabat, 1960:288). Therefore, religious freedom should include freedom to carry out missionary activities to those whom the Bible has not yet reached. This broad interpretation has not been acceptable to national Muslim leaders. For them, *Pancasila* cannot imply total religious freedom since no such freedom of choice is given to those who have already entered Islam (Singodimejo, 1969:73). In the eyes of Muslims, therefore, the interpretation of religious freedom implied by *Pancasila* should go as follows:

> Islamic groups are not permitted to force others to accept Islam. But this command of Allah signifies that non-Islamic groups are not allowed to force Muslims to become apostates or to leave Islam, whether it be done subtly through cheating or openly by building a church, monastery or temple (*klenteng*) in Islamic areas mainly occupied by Muslims (Singodimejo, 1969:73-4).

The controversy surrounding freedom to spread one's religion finished in favour of Islamic groups in 1978 when two decrees were issued by the Ministry of Religion, one of which (No.70) reads[7] :

> The spread of religion cannot be approved of when:
>
> 1) [it is] directed to a person or persons who already have another religion;

---

[7] The other decree issued in 1978 (No.77) gave the Department of Religion, which was under the influence of Muslims, the right to manage foreign Christian funds and to issue permits to foreign missionaries. Sect. 2 and 3 of Decree No. 77 read:

> Sect. 2 Assistance from foreign countries ... can be accepted only after acquiring agreement/recommendation from the Department of Religion and when it is channelled through the Department of Religion.

> Sect. 3 (a) ... restrictions apply to use of foreign personnel for developing and spreading religion.

2) [it is] done by resorting to enticement/distribution of materials of money, clothes, food/drink, medicines and so on to attract persons who already have another religion.

3) [it is] done by disseminating pamphlets, bulletins, magazines, books and other materials in areas/houses where the residents have a different religion;

4) [it is] done by making door to door visits on whatever pretext to those who already have a religion.

According to national Muslim leaders, this decree, if observed strictly by all religious communities, eliminates any possibility of massive Christian expansion in Java since all Javanese confessed one of the five official religions at the time that the decree was issued. The only possibility that a certain religious community can expand is through voluntary conversion. However, in a situation where no information on a certain religion can reach those who do not confess that religion, it is almost impossible for someone to change one's religion. Although it happens, it may be confined to only a small number of people.

No. 70 Decree 1978 is well known to villagers in Kolojonggo and they share the same mode of interpreting this as national Muslim leaders. One villager who worked in the sub-district office explained:

> According to the government law [No. 70 Decree 1978], non-interference (*tidak campur tangan*) in the internal affairs of other religious communities is the most important principle for living without conflict in a multi-religious society. The core of this policy is that, if someone is of a certain religion, others are not permitted to say anything about other religions to him or her. Therefore, it is possible to say that a Christian son violates the law when he talks about Christianity to his Muslim parents. ... To invite a Muslim for Christmas celebration is not permissible in this context since it is definitely a religious activity rather than a social one. Therefore, the invitation of Muslims by Christians is a violation of this law.

To the reformist villagers, religious non-interference is the only principle that can combine the diversified population under the banner of Indonesia. This is also what was commanded by Allah to mankind, as the Surah of 'The Disbelievers (*Al-Kaafiruun*)' in the Quran reveals;

> Say: O disbelievers!

> I worship not that which ye worship;

> Nor worship ye that which I worship.

> Nor will ye worship that which I worship.

Unto you your religion, and unto me my religion.

The last verse of this Surah was so popular among the reformist villagers that many of them memorised its Arabic pronunciation (*lakum dinukum waliyadin*) with ease. Another Quranic verse frequently quoted to emphasise the urgency of implementing this principle into social life is: 'And each one hath a goal toward which he turneth; so vie with one another in good works' (ii:148). To the reformist villagers, harmonious life between followers of different religions is not such a difficult task since the ideas in *Pancasila* and in the Quran show the right and easy way to achieve it and as both Indonesians and Muslims, they are ready to actualise it.

In contrast to the hope of the reformist villagers, the reality is, according to their own evaluation, gloomy and disappointing. There have been many incidents which were incongruent with the spirit of *Pancasila* and which, as a result, complicated the realisation of harmonious life. The reformist villagers attribute such happenings to Christians. As a proof of this, they refer to the rapid growth of the Christian population in Indonesia. If *Pancasila* and No. 70 Decree, which only permits a conversion based on one's free will, have been observed by Christians, there should be little, if any, growth in the Christian population.

This opinion is somewhat 'prejudiced', in the sense that Muslims attribute all sources of inter-religious conflicts to Christians. This 'prejudiced' view of inter-religious relations cannot be appreciated without understanding the negative image that the reformist villagers have constructed of Christians. In this framework, Christians are depicted as ignoring Muslim presence in village life, disturbing the religious life of Muslims and luring Muslims by unfair methods. Below are two examples of how this image is used by the reformist villagers to interpret certain social phenomena. The first was delivered in the *Jumatan*. The second one was spoken by the chairman of a youth committee preparing for the fasting month:

> As the Prophet did not give us an example, playing with fireworks in the fasting month cannot be permitted. This is also contrary to the regulation of the government which forbids it. Above all, this forms the best opportunity for someone (*sa'tunggaling tiang*) who is not friendly to Islam to distract the attention of our children from religious activities. ... Let's work hard, so that the atmosphere of this month is freed from the sound of fireworks.

> Shall we always be influenced by them (*golongan mereka*) or shall we possess our own strong devotion to Islam? This is dependent on our own will. A good example is food. In Islam, all problems connected to food are spelled out while in their religion (*agama mereka*), no rules are made to regulate food. As a result, their bad influences make us confused and

some of us have been lured by this temptation and drink alcohol. Only by strong and mature will on our part based on Islamic teaching will we free ourselves from the addiction to alcohol, which originated with them.
... I am saying this because we all are brothers, belonging to the same *umat* Islam.

The two speakers did not explicitly indicate who belonged to the category of the 'someone' or 'they', who had possessed the vicious intentions of disturbing Islamic activities and of confusing the *umat* Islam. However, it is quite obvious that these two words pointed to Christians. No Muslims, in the view of the reformist villagers, would want to obstruct Islamic teachings or would get benefit from it. Only Christians would be damaged if Muslims follow the right track of Islamic teaching.

The reformist villagers' negative image of Christians has been constructed by influence from the outside world and from their own everyday experiences. Many routes have been found to import the ready-made negative image of Christians into the village. *Pengajian* is one of the best media for this flow of information. In 1993-94, five *pengajian* were held in Sumber and one in Kolojonggo, where the speakers from the city were specialised in so-called *Kristologi*, a polemical critique of Christian theology. Other routes are the regular and special courses held in the city by Islamic organisations to teach how Christians use certain tactics to lure Muslims to Christianity. A few *anak masjid* in Kolojonggo attended these courses and the cassette tapes of these lectures circulated among Muslim villagers for several months. In addition to the public flow of information, other chances of personal contact were also abundant. Below is an example of an indirect flow of information and of what this is about:

> On returning home after photocopying two sheets of paper that I had just acquired in the *masjid*, I found two village youths who had handed over this material to me sitting in front of my house. As soon as they entered the house and sat down, one of them asked me whether I had made a copy of it or not. Hearing my affirmative reply, he apologised and then asked me to return the original copy as well as the photocopied one to him. He explained that Mas Guno who had originally circulated that paper requested that they find me so that I might return it to him. Although I regretted a lot that I had not written this material into my field notes, their desperate attitude urged me to hand it over to them. Looking at the relieved smile on their faces, I asked them to take me to Mas Guno's house, which they willingly agreed.

The letterhead of that paper showed that it was published by a Christian Group calling itself the Movement of Christian University Students (*Gerakan Mahasiswa Kristen*). It was composed of sixteen passages, all of which concerned the tactics to be used by Christian students to realise their mission. Unfortunately, I could not remember all of these passages but some of them went as follows: do not help Muslim friends; do not lend any study material such as reference books and lecture notes to them; try to conceal Christian identity when getting acquainted with new persons; do not sit with other Christians when attending lectures or visiting other public places; put forward the issues of emancipation of woman and human rights when talking to Muslims; and, especially for Christian girls, keep close contact with Muslim male students.

According to Mas Guno, this manual had been secretly circulated among Christian students. He obtained it by way of his close Muslim friend and brought it to the *masjid* to help other Muslims to understand the orientation of Christian activities in Indonesia, whose ultimate aim was, according to him, to destroy the *umat* Islam. He then talked enthusiastically about the attitude of tolerance taught by *Pancasila* and about how this message had been observed by Muslims and transgressed by Christians. At last, he explained the reason why he could not permit me to have a copy of it. He alluded to his concern that this paper would be made known to Christians in Kolojonggo through me, which would eventually incite them.

In addition to influences from the city, everyday life has also provided Muslim villagers with opportunities to construct a negative image of Christians. One thing that should be considered is that everyday life itself has not changed a lot. What has changed is the perspective of Muslims in looking at a certain phenomenon and the way they interpret it. For example, when conversion occurred a few decades ago, it was not interpreted as a result of a vicious tactic employed by Christians. When it occurs now, however, it is perceived as a proof of the offensive attitude of Christians toward the *umat* Islam. Marriage held in the fasting month is another example. When only a few Muslims participated in the fast, marriage in the fasting month did not arouse any concern. The frequency of the weddings in each month of the Javanese calendar shows that the fasting month was not regarded as a bad choice for marriage and no dramatic decrease in the frequency of marriages was recorded in the fasting month from 1979 to 1990. [8] However, the situation has now changed. In the two fasting months in 1993 and 1994, only one wedding was held in Kolojonggo, which was

[8] The frequency of the weddings in each month of the Javanese calendar between 1979 and 1990 in Sumber is as follows:

Month	Frequency	Month	Frequency	Month	Frequency
Sura	4	Jumadil Awal	50	Pasa	63
Sapar	49	Jumadil Akhir	68	Sawal	70
Maulud	82	Rejeb	94	Dulkaidah (Sela)	73
Bakdo Maulud	92	Ruwah	23	Besar	144

celebrated by a Christian family and this marriage was evaluated differently by the reformist villagers.

Pak Sastro had several good reasons to hold his daughter's wedding in the middle of the fasting month. First, his daughter was three or four months pregnant. Second, he could not tolerate an unmarried daughter giving birth to a baby, although his future son-in-law had made a promise to marry her. Third, his future son-in-law, who worked in Kalimantan, had to leave Kolojonggo before the end of the fasting month. After deciding to celebrate the wedding in the fasting month, he had to choose one of two options. On the one hand, he could hold the wedding on a small scale, skipping a reception to which lots of guest would be invited. However, he could not accept this option. In accordance with his status as a civil servant and the status of his daughter and his son-in-law as a university student and a university graduate, he did not want to miss a chance to hold a reception. Moreover, his own religion placed no restriction on a marriage in the fasting month.

When the news of this marriage spread to the hamlet, the *anak masjid* viewed it as a typical example of the intolerant attitude of Christians to Muslims and Islamic activities. It was offensive and provocative since a wedding reception cannot be held without food. As Pak Sastro's family had to ask for assistance from their Muslim neighbours and since all the work was closely related to food, whether it be to cook or to serve the food, it was quite obvious that a person's participation in the preparations escalated the possibility of cancelling the fast.

The nominal ideal of village life, harmony (*rukun*), made it difficult for the *anak masjid* to express their anger. In spite of this inhibition, however, they found a way to express it. They used the strategy of sabotage. With the excuse that he was busy working, the president of *Karang Taruna*, Mas Sri, who was a core member of the *anak masjid* and whose cooperation was urgently needed to mobilise the youth into work, did not convene a meeting to organise a working party for the wedding. This sabotage continued until three days before the marriage ceremony when a Christian youth visited the *masjid* late at night to meet with Mas Sri. This visit was an extraordinary one since it was the only occasion that I witnessed in 1993 and 1994 when a Christian entered the *masjid*. At that time, Mas Sri had already returned home after finishing his prayer, so that the Christian youth was asked to visit him at home. The next day, Mas Sri opened a meeting where a compromise was made to organise the working party. The time for the Muslims youth to work was set after six in the evening when the fast finished.

This case shows how Islamic development helps Muslims to see the same phenomenon from a different angle. This shift of perspective then helps them strengthen their negative image of Christians. Throughout the year, the fasting month provides many chances for the heightened religiosity of Muslims to be offended by actions of their Christian neighbours. For example, when Christians organised *gotong-royong* and served a meal to the participants, they smoked freely in the face of Muslim smokers and they made a noise by singing a hymn at night and by loud music, all of these were considered to exemplify the intolerant and offensive attitude of Christians to Muslims.

8.2. Conversion; Ideological War

One of the central issues which has had an impact on the production and reproduction of the Muslim villagers' image of Christians is that of conversion. Conversion is quite frequently discussed amongst Muslims and numerous stories of conversion are circulated. The Muslim version of the conversion from Islam to Christianity contains all negative features: seduction, fraud, selfishness, foul play and violation of law. In reverse, the conversion story of Christians to Islam emphasises positive features: truth, spiritual pursuit, rationality and tolerance.

This gives the impression that Muslims wage an ideological war against Christians over the issue of conversion. However, this aggressive attitude is directed more at their own community than at Christians. This is because, first of all, no public sphere is available where Muslims and Christians can meet to discuss this issue. Secondly, Christians are generally reluctant to be involved in any religious discussions with Muslims.

According to the reformist villagers, none of the factors which induce a Muslim to convert to Christianity are directly connected to sincerity or pursuit of the truth but stem from the factors external to the converts. The first is economic benefits. The term *Kristen Sari-mie* (the trademark of a brand of instant noodle) summarises how the reformist villagers perceive the new converts to Christianity just as they were referred to *Kristen beras* (rice Christians) in the 1960s. As the Church is believed to tempt Muslims by distributing boxes of *Sari-mie*, *Kristen Sari-mie* symbolises the poor Muslims who sell their faith in exchange for material benefit. At the village level, the conversion stories are not connected to *Sari-mie* but water buffalo, cow or bull. A villager, when passing along the village path by motorbike with me, pointed out a big cow and commented that the owner received her from the Catholic Church when his whole family converted to Christianity. According to the reformist villagers, merely giving out material goods is a rather naive tactic of the Church, compared with the one which is said to have been used in the city:

> Many Muslims living in the city slum converted to Christianity lured by economic benefits such as food and opportunities of work. However, these economic benefits did not last long after their conversion. Within a year or so, the Church withdrew all previous assistance since it was aware of the fact that the converts could not return to Islam again. Their re-conversion to Islam was impossible since Muslim neighbours of the

converts already knew their conversion and severed relations with the latter. As a result, the converts were forced to stay Christians, begging charity of the Church.

In this example, the Church is identified as a company running a business. In order to maximise its limited resources, it makes a deliberate plan to distribute and withdraw economic benefits. Its members are aware of the future isolation of the converts and use this isolation as a way to retain them without spending further economic resources.

The reformist villagers are well aware that Christians legitimise their assistance to non-Christians in the name of humanitarianism. They also admit that one of the purposes of religion is to rid human beings of sufferings irrespective of religious difference, so that, for instance, the donation of funds to those who suffer from disasters is not an inappropriate field for the Church's social activities. This admission, however, does not mean they approve of the Church's humanitarian activities. The reason is simple: if its assistance to followers of other religions is based solely on humanitarian grounds and no hidden intention is involved in it, there is no need for it to carry out these activities by itself or under its own name. In other words, the Church does not need to donate something directly to the *umat* Islam. What Christians should do instead is to collect funds and then donate them to the government or even to the *takmir masjid* in each region. Then, the government or the Islamic organisations will distribute them to those who suffer from disasters or from economic hardship. Seen from this perspective, the insistence of the Church that it should be the distributor of material assistance does have hidden implications. Pak Bibit put forward this view as follows, comparing it with world politics:

> Have you thought why America sent their army to Somalia or to the Gulf? Have you thought why America strongly supports South Korea rather than North Korea? Is it because she is so humane as to sacrifice herself to keep world peace? The answer is 'no'. There are underlying reasons America sacrifices her economic as well as human resources. ... The same logic applies to the activities of Christians in Indonesia. The donation of money by Christians to Muslims does not stem solely from humanitarianism. They have hidden intentions beyond the appearance.

As Pak Bibit mentioned, direct assistance from Christians to Muslims cannot be legitimised in any case. Therefore, the fact that these activities have been going on by the Church is proof that it does not give up its plan to Christianise the whole Muslim population in Indonesia. In this way, according to the reformist villagers, Christians have kept violating Decree No. 70 1978, which forbids proselytising activities toward those who already have a religion, and which prohibits the Church from giving out material benefits to Muslims.

Mixed marriage (*kawin campur*) is the second factor which is said to induce Muslims' conversion to Christianity. The experience of the reformist villagers easily supports this. In the Christian community of Kolojonggo, there are thirty-seven married couples. Of these thirty-seven marriages, five were between Christians, eighteen were between a Christian and a Muslim and fourteen were between Muslim couples, one or both of which later converted to Christianity. This relatively low ratio of marriages between Christians to the total marriages in the Christian community was partly due to the fact that no pressure had existed until quite recently for Christians to marry Christians or for Muslims to marry Muslims. When mixed marriages did occur, it seems to have been Muslims who changed their religion to Christianity. Of the eighteen mixed marriages discussed above, Muslims converted to Christianity in seventeen cases while in one case, husband and wife have retained their own religions so far.

The reformist Muslims understand this state of affairs well, so that mixed marriage is one of the frequently discussed topics in *pengajian*. In these discourses, Christians are depicted as immoral, being ready to use love, the most basic component of humanity, as a means to achieve their own ends. The typical marriage story goes as follows:

> A Christian girl approaches a Muslim experiencing hardship and lures him. After they fall in love and decide to marry, the Christian girl requests her future husband to convert to Christianity. As he is already blindly in love, he readily changes his belief.

As the conversion of one member of a Muslim family is a factor that may trigger the conversion of the whole family [9] and marriage is one of the easiest ways for Christianity to be imported into a particular family, the reformist villagers stress the issue of mixed marriage and how to tackle this. According to them, one of the best means of hindering mixed marriages is to prevent the formation of close relations between Muslims and Christians. As a villager put it, 'Muslim parents should work hard so that their children will love Muslims and not fall in love with non-Muslims.'

This emphasis put on marriage between Muslims seems to bring tensions to social life where mixed marriages have not been stigmatised until recently. In 1993-94, there was only one case of mixed marriage and, differing from the

---

[9] The conversion process of Pak Nadi's family to Christianity exemplifies how the presence of one Christian in a Muslim family may trigger the conversions of others. Pak Nadi's family was composed of three generations, his father-in-law, his wife, his brother-in-law and three children. In the 1980s, his wife was influenced by Christianity. Soon after this, she converted to Christianity. After her conversion, she tried to influence her children and succeeded in persuading two of them. The next target was her husband who converted in the early 1990s. As a result, her family was composed of four Christians and three Muslims. Her father and her son were also given several chances to become familiar with Christianity. Though they did not yet decide to convert to Christianity, they did not visit the *masjid*, appearing sometimes in the *kapel*.

previous mixed marriages, this aroused friction between the bride's and groom's family.

It was not certain how this couple, a Christian man, Pak Peno, and a Muslim woman, Bu Peno, had started their love affair. When the news of their affair reached me, it was when they had already decided to get married. Borrowing the perspective of the reformist villagers, this love affair was possible due to the weakness of Bu Peno's religiosity. Previously, she was not actively involved in Islamic activities and her visits to the *masjid* were confined to the first phase of the fasting month and special *pengajian*. In the case of Pak Peno, he was quite frequently present at the *kapel*, although he did not attend Sunday service every week. At the first stage when they decided to get married, religious difference did not seem to be a serious obstacle to their marriage. First of all, they themselves did not call their religious difference into question. The family of Pak Peno also did not object to the marriage since they believed Bu Peno would change her religion and the marriage would be celebrated in a Christian way. In accordance with their expectation, Bu Peno started to attend the Christian learning course. In a short while, however, the first obstacle to this marriage came from the side of Bu Peno. Her cousin who was an Islamic activist in Kolojonggo learnt that Bu Peno was going to change her religion. He made every effort to persuade his father to intervene in the marriage, an action effective enough to make Bu Peno reverse her previous decision. With the excuse that the learning course did not suit (*cocok*) her, she stopped attending the Christian learning course. However, at that moment, she did not seem to have decided not to change her religion to Christianity. Rather, it was likely that she reserved her decision, watching over the situations in both her family and Pak Peno's. The moment when she had to choose one of the two religions, however, came suddenly when her cousin who strongly opposed to her marriage ran over a passer-by with his motorbike. Later, this accident was interpreted to be caused by the fact that he had thought too deeply about Bu Peno's marriage and subsequent conversion until he had lost his control in the road. Whatever the actual cause of the accident might be, it worked as a turning point in her marriage. After hearing that the accident was caused by her, Bu Peno made up her mind not to change her religion and made her intention known to Pak Peno. After a few weeks, Pak Peno at last gave up his efforts to persuade Bu Peno. Instead, he decided to change his religion to Islam. This was a hard blow to Pak Peno's family and his parents did not approve of his marriage as a Muslim. The way they displayed their dissatisfaction with their son was somewhat extreme in village life. They did not attend the wedding ceremony which was held in Bu Peno's house. This step was followed by most of his kinsmen, so that only his uncle came to the bride's house as a representative of the groom's family.

In view of the Javanese social norm not to show one's real feelings in public, the absence of Pak Peno's parents and their kinsmen from Pak Peno's wedding seems to have been too extreme and this sort of reaction may not happen again in Kolojonggo. In spite of its abnormality, however, it shows the importance of religious identity as a factor in choosing one's spouse and the degree of friction which existed between Muslims and Christians concerning the issue of mixed marriages.

Apart from economic benefits and mixed marriages, what the reformist villagers enumerate as factors in causing conversion to Christianity include education in the Christian school, contact with Christian friends, involvement in a Western-style art group and indulgence in Western popular culture.

Many counter-measures were discussed by the reformist villagers to offset the proselytising activities of Christians. Deepening religious piety of Muslims to make them strong enough not to be tempted by the Christian mission was considered to be the most urgent one. The need to know more about Christian tactics, to give religious education to one's children, to improve the economic standard of Muslims and to intensify the welfare system in the *umat* Islam were also put forward. However, these measures are little more than principles and can hardly be realised with ease. The better and more practical way seems to be to clarify the boundary of the *umat* Islam and to strengthen the sense of collectivity within the *umat*, which will function to exert collective pressure on a Muslim who wants to change his or her religion. The effectiveness of this approach was actually proven when a Muslim girl gave up her intention of entering Christianity.

> When the third section of the *takmir masjid* meeting came to discuss miscellaneous things, Mas Toro asked for time. With a voice full of excitement, he began his speech. 'Before I speak, I ask forgiveness of everyone, if there is something inappropriate in my speech. Here, I'd like to discuss a problem of Mbak Tinah.' Then, he summarised a rumour that she had participated several times in the meetings of the Bible study group. After this, he added: 'I tell this story in order for us, especially Muslim youth in our hamlet, to reflect upon ourselves. When I first heard this story, I felt ashamed. I wondered why the activities of Muslim youth had deviated so far from the right track. Why aren't our religious programs designed to embrace all Muslim youth before ? Once again, I ask Muslims in Kolojonggo in general and Muslim youth in particular to recollect our previous activities. In addition, I request Muslim parents to pay more attention to their children and Muslim youth to take more

interest in their friends.' Without talking further about the problem of Mbak Tinah, he ended his remarks.

As Mas Toro mentioned, Mbak Tinah had attended Christian youth meetings. However, her attendance at these meetings did not mean her automatic conversion to Christianity. The Church decrees that someone who wants to be baptised should take instruction in Christianity for six months and Mbak Tinah had gone to these meetings just a few times, which was not enough to qualify her for baptism. The reason why she participated in these meetings was not clear. It was plausible that, as Mas Toro said, frequent contact with her close Christian friends might have played the major role.

It was unfortunate for her that publicisation of her intention preceded her actual conversion. A few days after the meeting of the *takmir masjid*, Mas Toro and a few others visited her. As they did not talk in detail about this meeting, it is difficult to know what discussion took place at that time between them. It might have been no more than making a simple suggestion or questioning her on the truth of the rumour. What is clear is that their unexpected visit conveyed a certain message to her. In Javanese social life where not many villagers are brave enough to express their hidden or real intention to others and where villagers are quite cautious about speaking directly of what they have in mind to others, this kind of simple but unexpected visit can mean something important. This visit could imply that their previous indifference to her was changed to deep concern about her. This show of interest in her behaviour clearly represented indirect pressure on her, alerting her to the fact that Muslims were monitoring her behaviour. As the Muslim youth expected, Mbak Tinah's visits to the *masjid* increased dramatically after their visit to her at home. A position was even given to her in the meeting to prepare for the fasting month, symbolising that she was fully incorporated into the *umat* Islam.

This success of the Muslim youth is somewhat exceptional. Their action seems to have been made possible by the fact that all of those involved in this incident belonged to the younger generation and somewhat aberrant behaviour could be more easily accepted, at least amongst themselves. However, if the news of an adult villager's conversion is heard, it would be unlikely that similar kinds of visit by adult Muslims would take place. They would not be brave enough to violate the social norms prohibiting direct involvement in others' private affairs until one is invited to do so by those directly connected with it.

In spite of this aberration, this example implies that the domain which was previously considered to be private is changing into that of collectivity. Conversion is no longer viewed, at least by some villagers, as an individual responsibility but a collective one. Islamic development and subsequent clarification of the boundary of the *umat* Islam have been the momentum bringing this change. When the boundary of religious identity can no longer be blurred, the religiosity of others is gradually incorporated as a concern of those who belong to the same 'in-group'.

This situation in Kolojonggo parallels the development at the national level in which the interpretation of religious freedom has shifted from the idea of *laissez-faire* to something that should be regulated. One of the factors which triggered this shift was the success of Islamic groups in prompting the stipulation of Decree No. 70 1978. Following this legalisation, Muslims have emphasised the need to interfere in religious life for the purpose of achieving religious freedom, as was exemplified by the inter-religious meetings (*musyawarah antara agama*) in Yogyakarta in 1983 and 1984. The primary aim of these meetings was to let delegates from the five official religions reach an agreement on ethical codes for followers of different religions. In the 1983 Yogyakarta meeting, the delegates agreed upon five ethical codes related to (1) construction of places of worship, (2) spread of religion, (3) marriage between different religious followers, (4) burial and (5) commemoration of religious days (Departemen Agama, 1990:19-48). Some of them go as follows:

(1) When building a new place of worship, the number of the population who will use that place and its distance from the existing place of worship of another religion should be considered; an ordinary house should not be used as a place of worship. [10]

(2) Proselytism should not be directed to a person or a group of persons who already have another religion.

(3) The ideal marriage is one between a man and a woman who have the same religion. Thus, marriage between a man and a woman who have different religions should be avoided (*dihindari*) and prevented (*dicegah*) as much as possible. When a mixed marriage takes place, guidance has to be sought in order for the newly married to carry out their religious practices respectively. [11]

---

[10] Apart from the regulations related to the spread of religion, Muslims were also successful in enacting a decree to regulate the construction of a church. The decree issued in 1969 necessitated permission from the government and from the residents of a certain area as a prerequisite to construct religious buildings (Proyek Perencanaan Peraturan Perundangan Keagamaan, 1980/81:87) while the decree in 1975 prohibited an ordinary house from being used as a praying house for a group on a regular basis (ibid.:91). These decrees could effectively control the expansion of missionary activities since Christians were forced to receive agreement from the Muslim population in order to build a church. The 1975 regulation made it almost impossible, at least in legal terms, for Christians to initiate missionary activities in a new area where no mission had been carried out previously since, according to the law, their private house could not be used for religious purposes and no church could be constructed.

[11] According to the marriage law passed in 1974, a certain marriage can be valid only when it is performed in a way prescribed by each religion (Badan Penelitian dan Pengembangan Agama, 1987/88:2). However, the different rules in each religion to regulate mixed marriages have brought about a situation in which all mixed marriages can be viewed as valid within the framework of the Indonesian legal system. This is because, of the five religions in Indonesia, only Islam has strict regulations governing mixed marriages: a Muslim woman cannot marry a non-Muslim man while

(4) The burial place prepared by the government is open to everyone who lives in a certain area irrespective of religion.

(5) In principle, the commemoration of the Holy Days of a certain religion should be celebrated and attended by those who profess that religion. However, those who belong to a different religion can also participate on this occasion on the condition that this visit is made to maintain family ties, good neighbourhood relation and community spirit (*kegotong-royongan*).

The behavioural norms between different religious followers are not confined to these five codes but are also expected to embrace all other domains of social life. Therefore, people are expected to be aware that their behaviour and speech could offend followers of other religions in everyday interaction. The spread of this emphasis on adequate behavioural codes to every level of the population has resulted in a gradual change to grasp the relations between followers of different religions. These have begun to be viewed as something that should be taken care of (*dipelihara*), cultivated (*dibina*) and taught in the family, school and community. This is a shift from the Old Order period when *laissez-faire* was a dominant concept in discussing such relations. In this framework, an individual or a given religious community was considered to be an entity fully responsible for making harmonious relations with other religious followers. With the shift of perspective, however, full responsibility is no longer given to an individual or a religious community since, according to Muslims, harmonious relations between people and groups having different religions cannot be attained without due attention and regulations. One Muslim intellectual puts the reason for this as follows:

> The meaning of religious freedom ... is that the parents who have a certain religion have to maintain and take care of their own religion among their family members lest they should change religion. If conversion of a member happens, it will cause instability in a family. It is not totally impossible that the proselyte will leave the family. This will lead to a situation in which the basis of religious freedom and harmony supported by mutual respect will disappear in that family (Sahibi Naim,1983:38-39).

One of the results of this emphasis on adequate behavioural codes has been that it demands people should monitor the religious identity of others with whom they interact. This is because they cannot behave appropriately unless they

a Muslim man may marry a Christian or Jewish woman on the condition that there are clear reasons for marrying a non-Muslim woman (Majelis Ulama Indonesia DKI Jakarta,1986:30). By contrast with Islam, Hinduism, Buddhism and Protestantism do not have clear guidelines to regulate mixed marriages while Catholicism tacitly admits the validity of mixed marriages by way of dispensation (Badan Penelitian dan Pengembangan Agama, 1987/88:5-10). This makes it possible for a Muslim marrying a non-Muslim to legalise the marriage in the national legal system since, seen from the perspective of the non-Muslim, a mixed marriage is valid.

know the religious affiliation of others. For example, Christians may offer pork or alcohol to Muslims and Muslims may use Arabic greetings to Christians if their religious identity is not clearly recognised. The only way to avoid these mistakes, which will jeopardise harmonious relations between different religious followers, is to be conscious of each other's religion. In brief, the emphasis on appropriate behavioural norms has made people include religion as a factor in their everyday interactions, has highlighted the importance of religious identity in social life and has transformed religious life, at least in the conceptual domain, from personal responsibility to what should be taken care of and guided by others of the same religion.

8.3. Superiority of Islam

The reformist villagers' discussions of the Christian mission or the negative picture of Christians that they support are ultimately underpinned by one fundamental idea: the superiority of Islam to Christianity. Their belief in superiority is clearly expressed in the stories of conversion to Islam. It is one's pursuit of the truth which leads one to Islam rather than the factors outside of oneself. A typical conversion story, presented by a preacher from the city in a *pengajian*, went as follows:

> I was born in a Catholic family and was educated in a Catholic school where I learned about Christianity and how to invite non-Christians into Christianity. As my knowledge deepened, I frequently argued with the priests over several religious issues but they could not respond to my questions properly. They just emphasised belief, evading the key questions of mine. This setback led me to knock at the door of the Protestant Church. There, I also debated with the clergymen but they could not satisfy me, either. Then, I was attracted to *kebatinan*. The impression that I got in the *kebatinan* group was better than my previous experiences in the Church, so that I wanted to be a cadre of that group. However, it turned out that the founder of that group had got his inspiration while performing Islamic ritual prayers. This discovery made me hesitate once again and I at last decided to resume my search for the truth. At that time, I was lucky enough to get in touch with people who had similar experiences to me, that is, people who had converted to Islam as a result of a long and painstaking pursuit of the truth. One of those to whom I addressed my problem was a famous Islamic leader who had studied in Cairo but who had once been a priest. Conversations with him at last strengthened my confidence that Islam was the answer that I had sought after for such a long time. I recited *sahadat Islam* in the office of the Department of Religion and added an Arabic name to my original one.

This sort of conversion story is not found among villagers in Kolojonggo. However, similar stories are heard about two families in which parents and children have different religions. For unknown reasons, Pak Toyo and his wife were Christians while one of their children was a Muslim. According to the reformist villagers, Pak Toyo, as an active Christian, has worked hard to persuade his child to accept Christianity, often with direct pressure or coercion. According to Mbak Sumi, Pak Toyo did not give money to his Muslim son whenever he did so to his other children. She said, 'I know this because I played in that house quite often when I was a child. ... To children, that kind of money matters a lot. Moreover, it was the time of poverty. Even a candy could make one feel the richest among one's friends.' The same tone is also found in the story of Pak Harto's family where two of his four children were Muslims. The *anak masjid* described Pak Harto as a cruel man devoid of fatherly love. Rumour had it that he objected to paying school fees for his Muslim daughter because she went to the *masjid*. He was also said to have forbidden his wife to prepare breakfast for his Muslim children during the fasting month, so that the girl had to get up at two in the morning to prepare it by herself.

What the story of conversion to Islam and the stories of Muslim children's hardship under the Christian parents try to convey is the contrast of 'the inner' to 'the outer', 'accident' to 'necessity' and 'strength of will' to 'easy life'. If it is material desire, job or romantic attachment (marriage) which induces one to convert to Christianity and just a short period of time is needed, it is the painstaking pursuit of the truth for longer period of time and the hardship which make conversion to Islam or the maintenance of the Islamic faith possible. To Muslims, this contrast is a proof that Islam is superior to Christianity. It is superior since conversion to Islam is a result of a long quest for the truth rather than of momentary vicissitude of mind and situational compulsion.

The equation between a search for the truth and the superiority of a certain religion cannot be understood without referring to the concept of *akal* (reason).[12] To the reformist villagers, *akal* is one of the key concepts with which to approach religion and to determine the rightness or incorrectness of a particular religion. Therefore, using *akal* in the quest for the truth is the right attitude of someone who accepts or rejects a certain religion. Their religious allegiance to Islam is also explained in terms of *akal*. They believe in Islam not because it is the only religion that has been available to them but because it 'makes sense' (*masuk akal*) while others do not. With this conceptual shift, they are described

[12] *Akal* originates from an Arabic word, *al-'aql*, meaning 'restraint from desire', 'prudence as opposed to weak reasoning (*lemah pikiran*)' and 'heart' (Harun,1986:5-7). In Indonesian, '*akal*' is used to mean mind, intelligence or reason. The reformist villagers define one of its meanings as 'power to think' *(daya pikiran)*. The popular idiom of '*masuk akal*' (to make sense) is in many cases interchangeable with that of '*pakai otak*' (to use brain).

not as submitting themselves to Islam blindly but as choosing Islam among various other possibilities.

The concept of *akal* is used by the reformist villagers in examining Christian theology. If Christianity 'makes sense', they argue, they will convert to it. Due to this emphasis on *akal*, one of the most frequently used ways of criticising Christianity takes the form of polemic: they question a certain concept in Christianity and show that it does not 'make sense'. Below is a conversation between a Muslim boy and a Protestant girl in their late teens, showing how the concept of '*akal*' is used by Muslims to evaluate Christianity. [13]

> As soon as Mas Gino and Mbak Padmi arrived at my place, it started to rain cats and dogs, giving them a chance to stay together in my place. Our conversation began as usual. I asked about their recent activities and we exchanged the gossip about other youth in the hamlet. When I and Mbak Padmi were talking about the Bible Study Group, Mas Gino who had kept silent for a while entered into our conversation. To my surprise, he asked her a question about Christianity: 'What is the relationship among *Tuhan* (God), Allah and *Bapak* (Father)? I heard these three terms were frequently used in Christian prayers. Until now, however, I cannot understand what is the exact relationship among *Tuhan*, Allah and *Bapak*?' Seeing his face filled with a smile and hearing the tone of his voice, I could easily recognise that he asked this question to tease her. Mbak Padmi hesitated for a while and answered that these three terms designated the same entity. 'Why do you use *Tuhan*, Allah, *Bapak* at the same time rather than using each of them individually?' he asked. 'That is just for emphasis and there is no other hidden meanings', she replied. Although the tone of her reply was rather aggressive, Mas Gino continued his questioning. 'Who is Jesus? Is he *Tuhan* or is he the son of *Tuhan*?' Mbak Padmi answered reluctantly, 'Jesus is the son of *Tuhan* as well as *Tuhan*.' At this point, I thought he would stop questioning, but he did not. Instead, he incorporated Maria into their conversation:
>
> 'Who is Maria?'
>
> 'Maria is the mother of Jesus.'
>
> 'Who made Maria pregnant?'
>
> '*Tuhan*.'

[13] As I have pointed out earlier in this chapter, no Muslims or Christians were willing to speak about religion with one another. The conversation in the text was the only one that I heard during my stay in Kolojonggo and in this respect, it was an exceptional case. This conversation might not have happened if the Muslim youth had not had a close relation with the Christian girl. At the time of this conversation, they were in love, which made it easier for him to speak about a taboo topic to her. His original intention seemed to tease her rather than to criticise Christianity.

'Whom did Maria give birth to?

'Jesus.'

'Is not *Tuhan* and Jesus the same?'

'Yes.'

Hearing her reply, Mas Gino responded in a way which did not seem to be appropriate to his original intention of teasing her: 'Does it 'make sense' that father and son are the same? Does it 'make sense' that *Tuhan* begot Himself? Definitely not!' He took a brief look at her and continued his interrogation: 'If *Tuhan* and Jesus had been the same entity, where was *Tuhan* while he was in this world? Was *Tuhan*, as Christians say, still in Paradise when He was in this world?' Still, there was no reply from Mbak Padmi. Although her silence made the atmosphere tense, he did not stop questioning: 'I cannot understand, first of all, *Tuhan* and Jesus are the same, existing in two different places and taking two different forms. In the ordinary course of reasoning (*secara akal*), is it possible that one can stay in two places in two different forms? Moreover, one of them took the form of a human being. How can *Tuhan* and a human being have the same form? ' Mbak Padmi did not answer his question nor make any other comment. A long silence was broken down when Mas Gino changed his topic: 'What is the difference between Catholicism and Protestantism?' He seemed to think this question was easy for her to answer. However, his guess was wrong. Mbak Padmi did not seem to have any clear explanation in her mind. After a pause, she answered that the Catholics worshipped (*menyembah*) Maria and every Catholic Church had the statue of Maria, an object of prayer for the Catholics. After answering, however, it seemed that she realised her reply was somewhat inappropriate. She tried to add another explanation, but she could not. Instead, what she did was to end our conversation by saying that 'I don't know much about it' in a somewhat loud and angry voice.
[14]

In this conversation, the concept on which Mas Gino relied to question Christianity was *akal*. He asked about the identity of God in Christianity and received the answer that the Son of God (Jesus) and Father of God (*Tuhan*) are the same entity. As the Son of God and Father of God cannot be the same entity and one cannot beget oneself in the ordinary course of reasoning (*secara akal*),

[14] After hearing her comment, Mas Gino tried to ease the tense atmosphere between them. He finished their conversation by referring to *Pancasila*: 'When I was in high school, I was taught that discussions on other religions are recommended by *Pancasila*. These discussions are not to disparage but to deepen our understanding of other religions, which will eventually help to achieve harmonious relations between followers of different religions. The previous question of mine, therefore, should be understood in this context.'

the argument of Christians that Jesus and *Tuhan* are the same entity, according to Mas Gino, cannot 'make sense'.

This sort of criticism of Christianity cannot be maintained unless one premise is satisfied. Muslims should be able to show that all teachings in the Quran 'make sense'. Two slightly different positions are taken by the reformist villagers: first, everything in the Quran 'makes sense' but the development of *akal* until now is not high enough for all of it to be understood and this gap is compensated for by revelation (*wahyu*); and second, not all of its contents can be understood by *akal* due to its absolute limitation and this is compensated for by revelation. The difference between these two positions may not be a trifling one. However, this germ of potential controversy has not been clearly recognised by the reformist villagers. Instead, they select one of the two positions dependent on the context. For example, when they use the concept, *akal*, as a step in criticising Christianity, they resort to the first position whereas, when they talk with other Muslims who are sceptical about certain Islamic teachings, the second position may be adopted.[15]

Whatever positions are taken by the reformist villagers, the way the concept, *akal*, is used is somewhat different from the way the English term, reason, is used since its application is based more on analogy than on empirical verifiability or falsifiability. In order to judge whether certain facts or ideas in Islamic teachings 'make sense', for example whether the teaching that Prophet Muhammad journeyed at the speed of light in *Miraj* 'makes sense' or not, the reformist leaders do not need to show a direct proof that this actually happened in the 7th century or it can happen now. Instead, what they use is a parallel example; the modern technological development makes it possible for human beings to journey as fast as sound, which was not imaginable at the time of the Prophet. This is then used as an example to show that people will be able to fly at the speed of light in the future, implying that the journey of the Prophet at the speed of light does 'make sense'. As the way to explain *Miraj* shows, the analogy to which the reformist leaders resort is also heavily dependent on an historical approach. They take several examples which had remained puzzles but which could later be explained with the development of science and use these to show that Islamic teachings 'make sense'. One of the most frequently used examples is the prohibition from eating pork, as a villager put it:

> By the Prophet, pork was categorised as forbidden. At that time, human beings did not understand why pork should be prohibited. Only the development of modern science showed that pork, compared to other meats, contained certain parasites endangering our health. This is the

[15] In general, the reformist villagers warn of the danger of extreme use of *akal*. According to them, *akal* should be applied to confirm the genuineness of Islamic teachings while the limitless use of *akal* may divert one from the right path.

secret of Allah (*rahasia Allah*). ... This example teaches us that the commands of Allah which do not seem to 'make sense' in the present time is not because these cannot 'make sense'. With the development of human *akal*, the Islamic teachings which have been regarded as incomprehensible will 'make sense' in the future.

Seen from the positivist philosophy, the conclusions that the reformist leaders draw from the above examples might not be easily accepted since these cannot be negated. When a certain teaching can be shown to 'make sense', for example if modern science shows that pork is more dangerous than other meats, this is used as a basis from which to argue that this Islamic teaching 'makes sense'. Although a certain statement is not yet fully clarified, however, this cannot be taken as proof that this statement does not 'make sense', since it is thought to be due to the limited development of *akal*. In this respect, no Islamic teaching is falsifiable. On the other hand, the reformist leaders have the last means of rationalising all Islamic teachings which do not seem to 'make sense': the Omnipotence of Allah. As one villager put it, 'Allah created everything in this universe, so why cannot Allah, the creator of human *akal,* do or command something which does not seem to 'make sense' ?' Seen from this framework, any proposal that Islamic teachings do not 'make sense' can not be accepted. The statement that Allah can do anything gives a rationale that everything can 'make sense' while this statement itself cannot be negated in any case. In this respect, the specific way the term *akal* is used by the reformist villagers allows them to believe that all Islamic teachings 'make sense'.

According to the framework which the reformist villagers adopt to criticise Christianity, all ideas and phenomena in human society including religion can be divided into three classes: those which 'make sense' such as the prohibition on eating pork; those which cannot be explained by the present state of *akal* such as the process of Creation [16]; and those which do not 'make sense' such as many beliefs in Christian theology. The Christian concepts which are considered not to 'make sense' by the reformist villagers include: the concept of Trinity; Original Sin and its inheritance; the Redemption of sin by Jesus Christ; several

---

[16] An Islamic leader at the regional level, Pak Pamung, whose name was well known to other Islamic leaders in Yogyakarta and who had widespread popularity among Muslims in the rural areas, proposed in a *pengajian* that even the process of Creation could be proven with *akal*. Pak Pamung based this idea on the research which he had carried out: he collected 22 kinds of soil and 21 kinds of fluid, mixed them and boiled the mixture. The material that he obtained from this was white and smelled sperm (*nutfah*). He then related this result to the teaching in the Quran that human beings originated from clay and fluid (he did not quote the verses in the Quran; for the use of clay and fluid in the process of Creation, see such verses as vi:2,xv:26 and xvi:4 in the Quran). Some of the villagers who attended Pak Pamung's *pengajian* with me mentioned that they were convinced by Pak Pamung's idea that virtually all Islamic teachings could be proven with *akal*. When I told this story later to several reformist leaders in Sumber and asked their opinions, they generally gave credit to Pak Pamung's efforts to prove Islamic teachings, although some of them suggested that the process of Creation was not proved by Pak Pamung's research.

self-contradictory verses in the Bible on the nature of God; and other contradictory statements in the Bible. They attack these problems resorting to an analogy based on *akal*: as 1+1+1 should be 3 rather than 1, so God, the son of God and Holy Spirit cannot be one; as the child cannot be responsible for the crime of his or her father, so no sin can be inherited from Adam by later generations; if Jesus Christ is God, He cannot ask of Himself the Redemption of sin; many passages in the Old Testament ascribe to God the human qualities of anger, shame, regret and so on and these are contradictory to the attribute of God transcending humanity; and while one passage in the Bible teaches that it was handed down only for the Jews, in another, the Bible was said to be revealed for all human beings.

These examples are used by the reformist villagers as proofs that theological themes in Christianity and the contents of the Bible do not 'make sense'. This enables them to argue that the Bible is not revelation from God. If it is from God, there should be no contradictions or inconsistencies in its contents which can easily be discerned by human *akal*. This argument eventually leads to the thesis that Christianity is a man-made religion which has totally deviated from the teaching of God and that Islam is superior to Christianity.

8.4. Summary

Christians and Muslims have co-existed in Kolojonggo since the first conversion to Christianity in the early 20th century. Until recently, the significance of religious difference between Muslims and Christians did not go beyond the religious domain. Villagers of one religion gathered on religious occasions but this grouping did not extend into non-religious life. In some cases, Christians were even included in the religious activities of Muslims and vice versa, as the exchange of foods and visits in the fasting month and at Christmas showed. As Islamic reform has accelerated, this situation has gradually changed. A clear line has been drawn dividing the *umat* Islam from the *umat* Christian, and villagers' consciousness of each others' religious difference has grown. This consciousness has been paralleled by the formation of the idea of 'in-group' and 'out-group' and, the exclusiveness of this concept has begun to extend into non-religious domains. It is now an important matter whether Muslims should make friends with Christians, may marry Christians, should choose a Christian in a election and should help Christians or not.

The clear awareness of religious difference has created tensions and friction between Muslims and Christians. Until now, these strained relations have not led to open conflict. Even verbal discord is seldom heard in public places where Muslims and Christians gather together. The maintenance of harmony in public life has been possible due to the effectiveness of the government's policy of imposing the ideology of *Pancasila* on public life and the pervading social norm emphasising harmony (*rukun*) in public. This does not mean, however, that the same attitude prevails within the 'in-group'. On the contrary, the reformist Muslims have been quick to point out offensive and provocative behaviour by Christians which jeopardises harmony between followers of different religions and they have tried to attack Christianity.

One of the issues of most concern to the reformist Muslims is the conversion of Muslims to Christianity. As a way of challenging this, Muslims wage an ideological war against Christians. In this ideological war, the main weapons they employ are *Pancasila* and the concept of *akal*. The concept of *Pancasila*, which is interpreted as not permitting any missionary activities among those who already confess a religion, is employed to highlight the unfair tactics used by the Christian mission. The concept of *akal* is used to show the logical absurdity of Christian theology, the truthfulness of Islam and the ideological dominance of Islam over Christianity.

The purpose of this chapter has been to examine the changing nature of the relations between Muslims and Christians in Kolojonggo. Apart from giving a better understanding of this relationship, the discussion has also provided a chance to look at the impact of the presence of Christians on the on-going process of Islamic development in Kolojonggo. As was indicated in Chapter III, Islamic development has opened a door for Muslim villagers to have intense contact with the scriptural tradition of Islam. The increasing religious knowledge, on the one hand, and the numerical increase of Muslims who make every effort to observe religious prohibitions and commands, on the other hand, have brought a diversification of the meaning of 'Muslim-ness'. At least to a certain segment of Muslims, especially those referred to as reformist villagers, the simple act of reciting *sahadat Islam*, once thought to be a sufficient condition of 'Muslim-ness', can no longer be regarded as a criterion to make someone a Muslim. They see it as merely the starting point. The differentiation made through this concept of 'Muslim-ness' has been recognised by the reformist Muslims, so that the term, 'Islam KTP', is used, even if not openly, to designate those Muslims who do not carry out their religious duties and who do not participate in Islamic activities.

The trend of the reformist villagers to divide the Muslim population into two, however, has not been fully developed[17] and an inclusive attitude is still retained by them vis-à-vis villagers belonging to 'Islam KTP'. One of the most important factors in maintaining this inclusive attitude is the presence of Christians and their threats to the *umat* Muslim. This makes it urgent for the boundary of the *umat* Islam to be drawn to embrace all Muslims, impeding the process of

---

[17] The recent study of reformist Muslims in Central Java shows that the core members of the reformist Muslims develop a dichotomised view of their own group and others. They regard themselves as the main vehicle of religious and moral excellence in village society while considering other Muslims as belonging to an unenlightened or heedless community (Irwan Abdullah, 1994:98-9). This situation may show one possible way the differentiation of villagers in terms of their religious outlook can be developed in rural Java.

differentiation amongst Muslims in conceptual and in social forms. As a result, the *umat* Islam is still defined in its most inclusive form, namely, as including anyone who is not a Christian, irrespective of his or her religiosity.

Chapter 9: Concluding Remarks

For the last few decades, Western scholarship has noticed that Islamic countries have been undergoing a fundamental change. Scholars of Islam employ such terms as Islamic resurgence, Islamic revivalism, Islamic reassertion, Islamic renaissance, and the re-flowering of Islam to grasp this change (e.g. Dekmejian,1985; Esposito,1983; Hunter,1988; Keddie,1994; Muzaffar,1986; Nagata,1984). These terms, though various, convey a common message, namely, Muslims' assertion of the centrality of Islam in their everyday life. The ways in which this assertion is manifested depend on the socio-economic, political and historical background of each region. In areas where Muslims' life is threatened by war, oppression from autocratic regimes or non-Muslims and where these threats are interpreted in religious terms, 'Islamic resurgence' may take the form of radicalism. In regions where Muslims' life is challenged by modern secularism, 'Islamic resurgence' may be directed at reinterpreting Islamic teachings and at reinstating Islamic values to accommodate them better to modern socio-economic and political realities.

In some sense, 'Islamic resurgence' may not be a specific feature of modern Muslim societies but an innate character of the history of Islam (see Dekmejian,1985; Maududi,1981; Voll,1983). Since the revelation came to the Prophet Muhammad, Muslims have reinterpreted Islam and applied it to their lives under changing historical circumstances. Nevertheless, there are reasons why the concept of 'Islamic resurgence' has been adopted widely to describe Islamic development in the modern era. On the one hand, we may attribute this to the expansion of the Muslim population for whom the question of the centrality of Islam comes to the fore. While the locus of 'Islamic resurgence' in traditional Muslim societies was placed mainly on religious specialists recognised as masters of religious texts (Eickelman,1992:652), that in the modern era has expanded to include the masses. In the consciousness of large number of Muslims, Islam has become a subject of 'objectification', so that such explicit and objective questions are asked as: 'what is my religion? Why is it important to my life? and How do my beliefs guide my conduct?' (ibid.:1992:643). With this shift, the process of reinterpreting Islam and of reinstating Islamic values at the centre of believers' lives, which was once monopolised by the religious elites, has become a concern of a wider circle of Muslims. On the other hand, the popularity of such a concept as 'Islamic resurgence' may be ascribed to a recent shift in the way of conceptualising Islam, a shift which has been precipitated by the concept of 'Orientalism'. According to Said, Western scholarship, in its efforts to understand Islam, has long been overwhelmed by an 'Orientalist' paradigm, namely, a view that 'Islam does not develop and neither do Muslims; they merely are (1978:317)'. In this paradigm, therefore, Muslims' life is supposed to be defined by Islamic doctrines, and the study of immutable doctrines is thought to be the right way of understanding Islam and Muslims. Said's critical evaluation has helped scholars of Islam to shift their focus from a search for an a-historical essence to an examination of the multiplicity of Islamic expression, and this allows them to understand better Muslims' continuing efforts to negotiate Islam in the process of conceptualising their life and of giving meaning to their historical, socio-political and cultural experiences. In this respect, the popularity of the concept 'Islamic resurgence' may be regarded as a reaction on the part of Western scholarship which has rediscovered the dynamics in Muslim society.[1]

Recent Islamic development in Indonesia has also been marked by such concepts as resurgence, revitalisation, revivalism, renaissance and reIslamisation (Hefner,1987a; Horikoshi,1976; Nakamura,1993; Pranowo,1991; Tamara,1986). The examples used to illustrate 'Islamic resurgence' in Indonesia, however, are less spectacular than those in other Islamic countries. Unlike 'Islamic resurgence' in Iran, no remarkable movement to implement Islamic values in Muslims' politico-economic life is evident in Indonesia. Some of the signs of 'Islamic resurgence' in Indonesia such as increasing participation in the fast, daily prayers and *Jumatan*, are what had occurred more intensively in other Islamic countries even before 'Islamic resurgence' was noticed. The same is true in the case of recent Islamic developments in Kolojonggo, which I have attempted to examine in this thesis. Islamic leaders' understandings of the Islamic scriptures might be no deeper than ordinary Muslims in other parts of the Islamic world and their efforts to incorporate Islamic values in their life are seen more clearly in their private life than in the political or economic spheres. In spite of these considerations, recent Islamic development in Kolojonggo can also be labelled as 'Islamic resurgence'. A group of Muslims has been created, who assert the centrality of Islam in everyday life, who try to understand things surrounding them not in terms of the categories which their elders have passed on to them but in terms of what they perceive to be Islamic, who negotiate what they perceive to be Islamic with their historical and socio-cultural realities, and who continue to objectify and question their Islamic ideas and practices. In this sense, their perspective on Islam contrasts sharply with that of their predecessors for whom Islam was taken for granted. 'Islamic resurgence' among Muslim villagers and a few characteristics of this process in Kolojonggo will be summarised below.

---

[1] Various other factors are discussed by scholars of Islam to explain recent 'Islamic resurgence'. Some of these are: an identity crisis precipitated by a sense of utter impotence and loss of self-esteem (Ahmed,1992; Esposito,1983; Hunter,1988); the reaction to Western domination after the post-colonial era (Ahmad,1983); disillusionment with Westernised government (Ahmad,1983; Dekmejian,1988; Hunter,1988; Keddie,1994; Muzaffar,1986); the spread of secularisation and the progress of Westernisation in Islamic countries (Ahmad,1983); disillusionment with the West (Esposito,1983; Muzaffar,1986); and the new-found sense of pride and power which resulted from the success of oil embargo in 1973 and from the Islamic revolution in Iran (Esposito,1983; Muzaffar,1986).

In Kolojonggo, a new phase of Islamic development started with the introduction of reformist Islam in the late colonial period. Before this time, Islam was deeply embedded in villagers' life: they were circumcised; their marriages were held in Islamic ways; new-born babies were greeted and the deceased were mourned with Arabic prayers; some of the important occasions in the Islamic calendar were celebrated; and the recitation of Arabic prayers was taught to children. However, as Islam was an integral part of villagers' life and no alternative form of perceiving and practising Islam was known to them, Islam was not a subject of conscious questioning but was taken for granted. No villagers were bothered much about whether certain practices were 'Islamic' or whether these were commanded, recommended or prohibited in Islam. Therefore, the significance of the introduction of reformist Islam was that it provided Muslims with the opportunity to come in contact with an alternative form of Islam to the traditionally practised one. By doing so, it increased the opportunities for villagers' Islamic beliefs and practices to become a subject of objectification, namely, a process by which the distinctions between these two streams of Islam could be highlighted and the 'Islam-ness' of both could be questioned, criticised and legitimised.

Reformist Islam's grip over Muslim villagers has strengthened rapidly throughout the last two decades. During this time, a group of reformist activists was consolidated in Kolojonggo, who tried to harmonise their religious practices and ideas with what they perceived to be Islamic values and to invigorate Islamic activities among Muslim villagers. Various factors have influenced the crystallisation of this group, including: the 1965 affair and subsequent government's policy in prompting villagers to confess their religion thereby removing the freedom to remain an atheist and to oppose religion; easy flow of information has allowed villagers to know more about Islamic development at the national or international level, which has been characterised as 'Islamic resurgence'; compulsory religious education in government schools and a longer period of schooling have provided the younger generation with greater exposure to regular religious education; and improving economic conditions have made it possible for villagers to mobilise a larger amount of economic resources for religious activities. Another factor which has also played a pivotal role in creating this group is reformist Islam's different emphasis on the way of learning Islam.

Unlike traditional Islam which considered the memorisation of the scriptures as the way of learning Islam, reformist Islam's emphasis is put on the understanding of the scriptures. To reformist Muslims, the memorisation of the scriptures is a praiseworthy work, but not a prerequisite for Muslims to make an attempt to understand the scriptures. Even those who do not know written Arabic should try to understand the scriptures translated into vernacular language. With this shift, to learn Islam by way of materials written in Indonesian is installed as a legitimate way to approach Islam and, subsequently the nature of religious knowledge and the basis of religious leadership have changed. Religious knowledge is regarded more as material that can be consulted in books rather than as that which is mnemonically 'possessed', while the qualification of religious leaders shifts gradually from a long apprenticeship under an established man of learning to a commitment to read written materials about Islam and a claim to interpret what Islam 'really' is (Eickelman,1978:511-12). When these changes take place, religious education in secular schools can facilitate the expansion of a group of people who claim religious leadership and who are considered leaders by others, in that an attitude and capability of religious leadership is not very different from that required to be a 'good' student in secular education. Although not all of those who received an extended period of religious education became agents leading Islamic development, the shift in the way of learning Islam, the nature of religious knowledge and the basis of religious leadership has created a group of Islamic activists more easily and rapidly than is the case where religious leadership requires a long apprenticeship under the established scholars.

After a group of reformist activists was crystallised and as its members initiated various religious programs, villagers have received more opportunities to recognise different religious behaviour among themselves. They can easily notice that there are villagers who carry out daily prayers and the fast, pay religious alms, attend other religious activities and try to observe Islamic rules and regulations, and those who do not. This different religious behaviour is interpreted by villagers as a reflection of different degrees of commitment to Islam, and such terms as 'Islam KTP' and '*anak masjid*' are employed to designate the different groupings of Muslim villagers. The equation of the outer, visible side of religiosity with its inner side in reformist Islam allows variations in the manifestation of religious life to be perceived and used by Muslim villagers as a way to differentiate themselves (cf. Pranowo,1991). In this framework, one's outer self is thought to be the delegate of one's inner self and one's outward behaviour is supposed to be unable to cover what is in one's heart.

The differentiation of villagers on the basis of their religious outlook parallels the diversification of the notion of 'Muslim-ness'. While the recital of *sahadat* or circumcision was once considered to be a sufficient condition to make someone a Muslim, the same notion of 'Muslim-ness' can no longer be accepted, at least for the reformist villagers. To them, these are just the starting point of being a Muslim, while 'Muslim-ness' should include the fulfilment of Islamic duties. If one is to be considered a Muslim, or more precisely, a pious Muslim, they suggest, one should carry out daily *sholat* and the fast, should participate in other religious activities and should observe various rules commanded by Allah. In this sense, the status of a Muslim perceived by the reformist villagers is not what can be obtained once and for all by reciting *sahadat* or circumcision, but what must be maintained with continuous renewal by performing Islamic duties and by participating in Islamic activities.

Although different religious behaviour between the reformist villagers and other Muslim villagers is clearly perceived, is interpreted in Islamic terms and is employed to explain non-religious behaviour, the pattern of interactions between them has not experienced a radical change. No reformist villagers try to involve themselves in the religious life of those belonging to 'Islam KTP', are willing to instruct people who carry out religiously forbidden behaviour or to make explicit the controversial aspects of others' religious behaviour in public. This attitude of the reformist villagers helps to create a social environment where the norm of harmony (*rukun*) is maintained and where villagers' different commitments to Islam do not become a source of social conflict. The peculiar situation of the *umat* Islam in Kolojonggo, namely, the existence of a substantial number of Christians, has also helped the maintenance of this state. This is because Christians are believed to be the biggest threat to the *umat* Islam, so that to embrace all Muslims irrespective of their religious orientations under the rubric of the *umat* Islam is thought to be one of the most urgent tasks by the reformist villagers. In this respect, the notion of 'Muslim-ness' retained by the reformist villagers is dualistic. When the religious behaviour of Muslims is discussed amongst the reformist villagers and when they evaluate others' religious behaviour in private, different commitments to Islam and different religious outlooks come to the fore and the concept of the *umat* Islam employed in these occasions incorporates only a certain segment of the Muslim population, namely, those who are ready to carry out religious duties and to participate in religious activities. However, when the presence of Christians is taken into account, villagers' different commitments to Islam are overshadowed by emphasis on the sameness, and the boundary of the *umat* Islam is defined in its most inclusive manner, namely, all those who are not Christians.

The impact of Christians on the on-going process of Islamic development in Kolojonggo is not confined to the ways the *umat* Islam is conceptualised. The existence of Christians has also left a deep imprint on the ways religious responsibility is perceived by the reformist villagers. When discussing the fulfilment of one's religious duties and one's responsibility for other Muslims, the reformist villagers generally emphasise their private character. Islam does not allow Muslims to intervene in others' religious life and no one will be responsible for others' wrong doings. This emphasis on personal salvation, however, is not the only way religious life is perceived by them. In other social situations, they highlight the collective nature of religious life and the need to intervene in religious life. They justify this intervention with the idea that freedom to practise religion in a multi-religious community cannot be attained without due attention and regulation. As a result, when a Muslim girl wanted to convert to Christianity, the reformist villagers were willing to intervene in this matter, justifying their action with the idea that her decision was not based on her free will but on compulsion or deceit. In this sense, the Christian presence in Kolojonggo has added a new element in the ways the reformist villagers grasp the nature of religious life. Although the private nature of religious life is not denied, the reformist villagers argue for collective responsibility for the benefit of guarding the privacy of religious life and religious freedom.

The existence of Christians in Kolojonggo has prompted the reformist villagers to defend the *umat* Islam from the alleged threat of Christians. One of the ways employed by them is to expose the absurdity of Christian theological tenets, which will eventually show the superiority of Islam over Christianity and the truthfulness of Islam. For this purpose, they rely heavily on the concept of *akal* (reason). They argue that many Christian teachings do not make sense (*masuk akal*) and use this argument as a proof that Christianity originated not from God but from human beings.

The frequent use of the concept *akal* in attacking Christianity seems to be a factor in reinforcing the tendency of reformist Islam to find rationales behind Islamic practices and ideas[2] and in allowing the reformist villagers to adopt *akal* as a tool to interpret their own religious doctrines. In the public discourse of Muslim villagers, therefore, it is not difficult to find villagers who rationalise Islamic teachings in terms of *akal*. For example, the prohibition on drinking alcohol is evaluated in the framework of 'advantage-disadvantage', namely, that the advantages one gains from drinking alcohol are far less than the disadvantages from drinking alcohol. The *salat* is sometimes interpreted to have practical advantages, namely, that it facilitates the flow of blood in the body. This emphasis on the search for the rationale behind Islamic teachings does not imply that they neglect the importance of faith. The statement that 'Allah commanded human beings to observe certain rules, so that Muslims should follow these rules', is considered as an absolute and unchallengeable proposition which explains all Islamic teachings and practices. However, the reformist villagers are of the opinion that faith cannot be maintained by itself but should be strengthened by the exercise of *akal*, which will eventually confirm the truthfulness of Islam.

The emphasis placed on *akal*, together with lack of an authoritative religious figure in Kolojonggo and its vicinity, has encouraged the reformist villagers to use their own independent reasoning and to base their understandings of Islam not solely on others' interpretations of it but on their own interpretations of the scriptures. They are also encouraged, and many are ready, to express their understandings of Islam in their own words, although they usually add an additional phrase, 'according to my own interpretation of Islamic teachings'. This attitude of reformist villagers makes it possible for a non-dogmatic, pluralistic and flexible approach to be instated as a way of understanding Islam.

---

[2] The concept of *akal* has been used by reformist Islam from its inception for attacking blind submission to the established scholars and for instating *ijtihad* as a right way to approach Islam.

The reformist villagers' emphasis on the rationales behind Islamic ideas and practices embodies a remarkable change that reformist Islam has brought to Kolojonggo. Whereas Islam once was a taken-for-granted subject, it is now, at least to the reformist villagers, a subject of conscious questioning. They raise questions about Islam as if they were objective observers, and search for answers which can rationalise their commitment to Islamic ideas and practices. In this respect, the change that reformist Islam has brought to Kolojonggo resembles a process of 'internal conversion', whereby what used to rest on habits now rests on rationalised doctrines (Geertz,1973:170-189), or a process of 'religious rationalisation', whereby religious interpretation of the world is strongly exposed to the imperative of consistency (Weber,1958b:324). [3]

'Religious rationalisation' proposed by Weber designates two interrelated processes, a process of systematising beliefs to make them more internally coherent, and a process of modernising beliefs to rid them of magical content (Bowen, 1993:322). The latter aspect of 'religious rationalisation' is also called 'the disenchantment of the world', a process whereby the image of the world is rationalised as being a cosmos governed by impersonal rules, deprived of concrete magic (Weber,1958a:282) and the sense of sacredness is gathered up and is concentrated in a nucleate concept of the divine (Geertz,1973:173-74).

Islamic development in Kolojonggo shows that the second process of 'religious rationalisation' has also taken place. The reformist villagers try to challenge and reformulate the nature of supernatural beings envisaged as intervening actively in villagers' life and to bring tangible consequences in human affairs. They equate supernatural beings with the malevolent *jinn* and condemn villagers' contact with them as *syirik,* the negation of the Oneness of Allah. These efforts, however, have not succeeded in attaining one of its goals, namely, to deprive supernatural beings of supernatural power and concentrate it in a monotheistic God. Supernatural power is still believed to be diffused to various supernatural beings who can be called, with the help of traditional magical practitioners (*dhukun*), by human beings to attain certain goals.

Compared with the reformist villagers, the role of those who work in the same domain as the *dhukun* but who employ different paradigms to interpret supernatural phenomenon in 'the disenchantment of the world' seems to be more

---

[3] This does not mean that a process of systematising religious ideas is a new phenomenon in Kolojonggo, initiated by reformist Islam. Even before the introduction of reformist Islam, the syncretic religious tradition in Kolojonggo was liable to the drive toward systematisation and the ideologues of this syncretic tradition, namely *dhukun*, were not unreflective adherents of it but tried to make their ideational system internally consistent. However, at that time, the locus of religious rationalisation was placed more on the traditional aspects of religion, which is now viewed to be non-Islamic by the reformist villagers. In this sense, it can be suggested that Islam started to be strongly exposed to the imperative of consistency only after the introduction of reformist Islam. For Weber's assumption that traditional religions lack systematic thought and his attribution of comprehensive rationality to the world religions, and anthropologists' criticism of his ideas, see Bowen, 1993:321-22 and Hefner,1993a:14-16.

significant in Kolojonggo. This is because their basic tenet is to bypass supernatural beings for obtaining supernatural power and to attribute supernatural power to a monotheistic God. If villagers can obtain the same result from a monotheistic God as they do from supernatural beings, there is no clear reason why they should resort to the *dhukun* who are strongly criticised by reformist Islam.

This distinctive rationalisation process seems to be one reason, among others, that the concept of God who is 'apart', 'above' or 'outside' of the concrete details of ordinary life in a rationalised world religion as is suggested by Geertz (1973:171) is not the only nature that Allah has in Kolojonggo. In addition to this, Allah inherits part of the nature that supernatural beings had and remains a Being who involves himself 'in an independent, segmental and immediate manner with almost any sort of actual event' (ibid.,172). In this way, the rationalisation process and subsequent concentration of supernatural power in Allah, a process which is still going on in Kolojonggo, does not result in a widening distance between human beings and Allah. Allah is still thought to be a Being who is close to human beings and whom villagers may call up for the fulfilment of their wishes related to the odds and ends of everyday life.

My experiences of living with Muslim villagers and of examining their religious practices and ideas allow me to adopt the same view as that proposed by Benda (1958:14) and Drewes (1955:286) in the 1950s, and by Nakamura (1993:180-83) in the 1970s, namely, that the history of Islam in Indonesia is the history of the expanding Muslim civilisation and its widening impact on the religious, social and political life of Indonesians. As I have attempted to show in this thesis, reformist Islam's grip over Muslims villagers has strengthened and a group of villagers has been created, who assert the centrality of Islam in their everyday life and who try to interpret their everyday experiences in terms of, and modulate their behaviour to, what they perceive to be Islamic values. This does not mean that the reformist villagers in Kolojonggo have been successful in achieving their ultimate goal of Islamising everyday life. On the one hand, as the persistence of rituals which are viewed, at least by some, to be related to syncretic religious tradition and as the use of non-Islamic themes to convey Islamic teachings by the *anak masjid* imply, traditional and local religious influences, which are not agreed unanimously to be Islamic, have not disappeared from villagers' life. On the other hand, the reformist villagers' efforts to Islamise everyday life have not touched on every aspect of their lives. Many of the socio-political issues such as economic inequality, corruption, social justice and the establishment of an Islamic state are seldom discussed by the reformist villagers and have not played a significant role in forging their Muslim consciousness. These limitations, however, do not seem to overshadow what the reformist villagers have achieved in the last few decades. Rather, it is better to consider their efforts to Islamise everyday life as an on-going process whereby the Islamic nature of taken-for-granted ideas and practices is questioned and those which cannot be brought into harmony with Islam are abandoned, not at one stroke but gradually. Seen within this framework, it is certain that the reformist villagers' efforts to Islamise everyday life will include much larger domains of their private and social life and that the questions which have not come to be foregrounded in their Muslim consciousness will be taken into more serious account in the future. This is all the more so since Muslim villagers consider their efforts to Islamise their life to be a ceaseless, or in some sense endless, struggle toward an ideal state of Islam.

Appendix A: Socio-Economic Developments in Kolojonggo before 1965

A.1. Economic History of Yogyakarta in the 19th century

At the peak of its power, the territory of Mataram was divided into three: the core areas surrounding the capital called *nagaraagung*[1] , the neighbouring areas of *nagaraagung* stretching into the central and eastern parts of Java called *mancanagara* and the territories in the northern coastal areas called *pasisir* (Moertono,1974:101). In the 17th and 18th century, the *pasisir* was gradually incorporated into direct Dutch rule while, following the British interregnum and after the Java War, the *mancanagara* was annexed by the Dutch Colonial government (Selosoemardjan,1962:27). Therefore, after 1830, Mataram incorporated parts of its previous *nagaraagung*, the Yogyakarta and Surakarta regions, under its sovereignty. This state of affairs continued until the retreat of the Dutch from Java in 1942. Throughout this period, the shrunken *nagaraagung* remained enclaves ruled by two partitioned kingdoms of Mataram under the supervision of the Dutch Residents.

Land in the *nagaraagung*, which was also called *Vorstenlanden* in Dutch, was liable to appanage (*lungguh*). Appanage referred to 'an assigned region where one has the right to gain from the land and the inhabitants a profit ... but which gives no rights on the land itself.'[2] The right to grant appanage was reserved for the ruler who was thought to have the sole proprietary right to the produce of the soil (Raffles,1965:137). Those entitled to receive appanage were royal families, court officials and favourites of the ruler.[3]

The appanage holders (*patih* or *patuh*) living in the city employed intermediaries (*bekel*) to manage their appanage (*kebekelan*). The main roles of the *bekel* who was selected from among the residents in a certain *kebekelan* were to extract products and labour from villagers and to transfer these to the *patih*. Apart from these, the *bekel* was also in charge of 'guarding order and tranquillity' (*njaga tata tenterem*) in his *kebekelan*. In so far as he could fulfil these duties, the *bekel*

---

[1] Due to the policy of the ruler of keeping his officials close to himself by providing them with appanages within the core areas and as a result of increase in the number of officials to support court life, the size of *nagaraagung* was gradually enlarged until, towards the end of the 18th century, it included the Yogyakarta-Surakarta areas and the Bagelen-Kedu areas (Moertono,1974:102).

[2] Van Vollenhoven, *Javaansch Adatrecht* (Leiden,1923), cited in Moertono (1974:117).

[3] The size of appanage varied in accordance with administrative rank in the case of court officials and with the closeness to the ruler in the case of royal families (Suhartono,1991:35). The number of *cacah* (landholding family) living in the appanage was a criterion to differentiate one appanage holder from others. In Mataram, each holder was called in accordance with the number of *cacah* such as *panewu* (thousand), *panatus* (hundred), *peneket* (fifty) and *panalawe* (twenty five) (ibid.:36).

was given the freedom to manage his *kebekelan,* a privilege which allowed him to be called 'a small ruler' (*raja kecil*) (Suhartono,1991:55). [4] He could expel peasants from his *kebekelan* (Selosoemardjan,1962:218) and could allocate *sawah* from one villager to another (Raffles,1965:145). This position gave the *bekel* room to use his power for his own benefit rather than for the *patih*'s. Mobilising the manpower of his subordinates, the *bekel,* for example, could convert uninhabited areas into *sawah.* As the individually developed land was akin to private property and was not liable to tax, this provided the *bekel* with a chance to accumulate wealth without being noticed by the *patih* (Carey,1981:xxxviii-xxxix).

Living in the *kebekelan* under the control of the *bekel* were peasant villagers. In terms of their access to land, they were classified into four: those who were given a right to cultivate *sawah* and access to a yard (*pekarangan*) to erect a house (*kuli kenceng* or *kuli sikep*); those who were given a yard but were on the waiting list for the allotment of *sawah* (*kuli kendo* or *kuli setengah kenceng*); those who had a house in someone's *pekarangan* (*tumpang*); and those who were not entitled to *sawah* nor a house, and boarded with another family (*tumpang tlosor*) (Moertono,1974:138). This stratification system was not a closed one where change of one's status from one to the *kuli kenceng* was blocked, but an open one where those who were ready to bear duties imposed on the *kuli kenceng* could be promoted as the *kuli kenceng.* The degree of openness in this system might be dependent on the size of available land and the population in each area. However, given that population density in the first half of the 19th century was far lower than in the early 20th century [5] , the *kuli kenceng* had to satisfy various duties which were not imposed on villagers of the other categories [6] and the *bekel* could acquire more labour force as the number of the *kuli kenceng* increased, it is likely that the promotion to the *kuli kenceng* might have not been difficult, if someone was determined to bear the duties of the *kuli kenceng.* [7]

[4] The freedom given to the *bekel* to manage his own *kebekelan* was comparable with the principles for organising state apparatus in Mataram: self-sufficiency and non-interference. The ruler granted the *patih* the right to govern their appanages autonomously and self-sufficiently and did not interfere in the matters happening there as long as order and tranquillity were maintained (Moertono,1974:88-92).
[5] In the first half of the 19th century, the population in Yogyakarta was less than 350,000 (*Koloniale Verslagen,* cited in Houben,1994:319). Later in the early 20th century, the population rose to more than a million (*Statistisch Jaaroverzicht Voor Nederlandsch-Indie,*1922-23).
[6] The duties of the *kuli kenceng* were as follows: first, they should pay half of the product from *sawah* to the *patih*; second, they should make occasional tributes in the forms of chickens, oil, wood and so on when the *patih* held a private feast and when two important Islamic Days (celebration of the birth of the Prophet Muhammad and of the end of the fasting month) came; and third, they had to supply corvée labour. They cultivated *sawah* allocated to the *bekel,* usually one-fifth of the total area available in a certain *kebekelan,* without compensation, participated in community works such as improvement of roads, ditches and bridges and were mobilised for other private and public works initiated by the *bekel,* the *patih* and the ruler (Suhartono,1991:39-43). Suhartono estimated that the total amount of corvée labour of the *kuli kenceng* reached 74 days a year (ibid.:41-2).
[7] According to village elders in Kolojonggo, *tumpang* (villagers holding neither *sawah* nor *pekarangan*), in the early 20th century, designated mainly the newly married groom who moved into his wife's *kebekelan* and lived with her family, and temporary migrant workers rather than the landless as the term implies. As the marriage of the newly wedded couple became stable and when the migrant workers

Although the position of the *bekel* was not based on heredity but on a contract between the *patih* and the *bekel*[8] and everyone was in principle eligible for the *bekel*-ship, the chance for ordinary villagers to be installed as the *bekel* was not high. They could not easily obtain one of the keys to be promoted as the *bekel*, namely, wealth to make an advance payment (Moertono,1973:132). Unlike the *patih* who did not maintain a close watch over the *bekel*, the *bekel* was in a position to scrutinise every villager in his *kebekelan*. Unless someone had a special relation with the *bekel*, the latter would never allow the former to gain as much wealth as he had (Selosoemardjan,1962:221). The difficulty for ordinary villagers to be promoted to the *bekel* implies that the rural populace was differentiated into two groups in the first half of the 19th century: the ruling class of the *bekel,* and their subordinates; peasant villagers. Although not based on a hereditary principle, this system encouraged the formation of a rigid boundary between the *bekel* and other villagers by giving the former room to use his power for his own benefits.

The second half of the 19th century saw a gradual erosion of the *bekel*'s previous position as a '*raja kecil*' and his transformation into a simple functionary to extract labour and tax from villagers. This change was brought about by factors both within and outside the appanage system. One of the challenges that the *bekel* faced from within was the segmentation of the *kebekelan*. The *patih*, who wanted to obtain extra revenues, adopted a strategy of increasing the number of *bekel* by dividing the appanage. The new *bekel*-ships thus created were put up for auction and given to the highest bidders.[9] The numbers of the *kebekelan* increased to such an extent that in 1883, there were *bekel* who had five households under their jurisdiction in Yogyakarta, while it was reported in Surakarta that one *bekel* supervised only a single household (Mulherin,1970-71:24).[10] The decreasing number of households under his control and the severe competition for *bekel*-ship meant that the *bekel* had less room to accumulate wealth and used more to retain his position (Takashi,1990:14).

The second factor contributing to the changes in the position of the *bekel* and to the socio-economic structure of rural villages in general was the massive influx of foreigners into the Principalities, who acquired leases from the *patih*. The system of leasing the appanage to foreigners began in the18th century by the

decided to settle down, which was symbolised by their marriages with the local women, the *pekarangan* to built a house and a plot of *sawah* were allocated to them. This comment implies that the number of the landless was, if any, only a few among the total villagers until the early 20th century.

[8] The contract between the *patih* and the *bekel* was recorded in a *piagam*, in which the duties of the *bekel* were minutely noted. For an example of a '*piagam*', see Moertono (1974:130-133).

[9] Van Kol, *Reisbrieven*, pp. 13-14. Cited in Takashi (1990:14-15).

[10] In 1910, there were 5750 *bekel* in Yogyakarta and the land under their control was 7200 *jung* (Takashi,1990:15). This indicates that the average size of the *kebekelan* was around 0.8 *jung* (3.2 *bau* or 2.24 hectares). In the case of Kolojonggo, the size of the *kebekelan* was much larger than the average. Around 17 hectares of *sawah* in Kolojonggo was under the control of three *bekel* before the 1920s, signifying that one *kebekelan* incorporated about 5.5 hectares of *sawah*.

patih who faced a shortage of money (Raffles,1965:273). When land and products at the disposal of foreign plantation owners expanded in the late 18th and in the early 19th century, the Dutch government, seeing its monopoly of coffee being threatened, restricted land leases in the government territories in 1808 and prohibited them in 1818 (Klaberen,1953:98). As the Principalities were excluded from this law, the Yogyakarta and Surakarta regions became the most attractive places for foreign planters, resulting in a dramatic increase in the areas of land leased to them. [11] In 1839, the area rented to foreign planters was 5210 *bau* (1 *bau* = 7096 m^2) (Houben,1994:267), while this increased to 45,616 *bau* in 1862 (ibid.) and 93,000 *bau* in 1890 (Takashi,1990:11).

When renting *sawah* from the *patih*, foreign planters did not have any intention of transforming the basic logic of the appanage system, namely, 'the land belonged to the ruler, the rights to the land belonged to the *patih*, the power over the land belonged to the *bekel* and the peasant simply belonged to the land' (O'Malley,1977:168). Instead, they adapted themselves to this system by positioning themselves between the *patih* and the *bekel*. They carried out the same duties as the *bekel* had borne for the *patih* and received the same rights that the *patih* had over the *bekel*, namely, the rights to use the land and to acquire free labour from the peasants. [12] As the area of the land they rented increased and their interest shifted gradually from indigo to sugar cultivation in the latter half of the 19th century, however, their presence became a major force in transforming the socio-economic structure of Yogyanese villages and the position of the *bekel*.

Under foreign sugarcane planters, the *sawah* was physically divided into two parts: one was called red (*abang*) and the other, blue (*biru*). This system, called *glebagan*, was instituted in accordance with the condition of land leases: the planter used half of the *sawah* for market crops while the peasants used the other half for food crops. The divided *sawah* was rotated each year, so that rice and sugarcane were alternately planted in a certain plot of the *sawah*. The *glebagan* system, however, could not be run as it was expected. First of all, it took more than a year for the sugarcane to be harvested, making it impossible for the planters to return the *sawah* to the peasants in a fixed time of the year. The result of this was that the actual period in which the peasants could cultivate the *sawah* for their own food crops was far less than a year, as Figure A 1 shows.

---

[11] Whether the prohibition of land lease to foreign planters ought to be applied to the Principalities or not had been a hot issue among the colonial administrators, and ceaseless changes in policy continued until 1883 when more freedom to do business in the Principalities was given to them (Houben,1989:189-93).

[12] In addition to paying land rent to the *patih*, foreign planters were asked to bring things such as glass, glasses, tools, clothes, lamps, rifles, furniture, horses and so on (Suhartono,1991:40-41). The role played by foreign planters made it possible for them to be called *bekel putih* (white *bekel*) or, in the case of the Chinese, *bekel cina* (Chinese *bekel*) (ibid.: 41).

Figure A-1: Use of *Sawah* under Foreign Planters

Month	Year 1												Year 2											
	J	F	M	A	M	J	J	A	S	O	N	D	J	F	M	A	M	J	J	A	S	O	N	D
Red section																								
Blue section																								

Land Use Under:
(A) Sugar Plantation Control   (b) Peasants' Control

■ Land Preparation   □ Rice

▨ Sugar-cane   ▨ Restoration of *Sawah*

▤ Sugar Harvest

Source: Modified from Anderson (1972:131).

Figure A-1 shows that the peasants could use the *sawah* only for half a year (see column for rice and restoration of *sawah*) within a period of two years. Excluding one and a half months to restore the *sawah* for rice cultivation, the actual period for cultivating food crops was around four and half months, which was shorter than the time needed to grow rice. For fear of being late and being punished by having their unripe crops removed by the planters, the peasants were frequently forced to resort to quick-ripening crops, which were of less value than rice or other principal food products (Selosoemardjan,1962:280).

The shortened period of using *sawah* was not the only hardship which the planters brought to the Yogyanese peasants. Different topological requirements and working processes in cultivating sugarcane escalated the amount of corvée labour that they should bear. It took around four to five months in a period of two years to convert the *sawah* which was used for sugarcane cultivation into the *sawah* for food crops and vice versa (see columns for land preparation and restoration of *sawah* in Figure A-1).[13] Harvest of sugarcane required more labour than that of food crops since each stalk of sugarcane had to be cut individually, tied and then delivered to the sugar factory. Selosoemardjan estimates that the peasants spent approximately 150 days on corvée labour and an additional five nights a week for night duties (1962:274-75), which was more than twice the amount of corvée labour estimated by Suhartono before the coming of the planters (1991:41-2)

The shortened period of using *sawah* and the increase in corvée labour shifted the value of holding the *sawah*. The *sawah* allocated to each peasant was called *sanggan,* literally 'a burden', a term unknown outside the Principalities (Selosoemardjan,1962:218). Some *kuli kenceng* opted to move into other areas where no sugar estates operated or even outside the Principalities

[13] For more about the process of converting the *sawah* for rice cultivation, see Anderson (1972)

(Soedjito,1957:11). Others chose to be daily labourers, discarding their status as *kuli kenceng* (van Mook,1958:315). However, not all of them could do so. The majority continued to hold their *sawah* because, except for working in the *sawah*, there were only a few ways of earning a living (Selosoemardjan,1962:218). Amongst the peasants who stayed in the village, a certain strategy had been developed to cope with the increasing labour demands: namely, to share the burden. This might be done in two ways. First, they could modify the traditional custom by requiring not only *kuli kenceng* but every villager liable for corvée labour. Second, they could allocate *sawah* to more villagers, which would increase the number of *kuli kenceng* eligible for corvée labour. The option which was chosen by the peasants in the Principalities was the second one, so an increase in the allocation of *sawah* to the landless was reported in the late 19th and in the early 20th century (Suhartono,1991:104).

The coming of the foreign planters weakened the position of the *bekel* in several ways. First, increasing labour demands from sugar plantation made it more difficult for the *bekel* to fulfil his duty as a supplier of corvée labour. When the *bekel* could not meet his duty, he had to face severe penalties. He was locked up in the jail (Selosoemadjan,1962:272-77) or was dismissed by the planters (Takashi,1990:17). On the other hand, increasing labour demands from the sugar plantation deprived him of opportunities to mobilise villagers for his own benefits, impairing his ability to accumulate wealth. Second, with the foreign planter came a new superior to the *bekel* called the *mandor*, an overseer of the supply of land and labour employed by the sugar plantation. In administrative terms, the *mandor* was not a superior of the *bekel*. However, his role and his easy access to the foreign planter gave him a power to treat the *bekel* arbitrarily. If a *bekel* had had the misfortune of displeasing his *mandor*, the latter could make a report to the foreign planter, which meant a severe penalty for him (Mulherin,1970-71:23-4). Third, in the process of being used as a medium to secure stable supply of labour and land for the foreign planter, the *bekel* could not use his traditional source of legitimacy: people's homage to the ruler. Instead, what he could use was physical force supported by the police. This allowed the relation of exploitation to be expressed more clearly, weakening the traditional authority of the *bekel*.

In brief, the changes in the second half of the 19th century made the position of the *bekel* less advantageous than before. His riches were siphoned off to renew his position as a *bekel*, his opportunities to accumulate wealth declined as the *kebekelan* were segmented and the peasants were mobilised for sugarcane cultivation, the traditional authority provided by his relation with the ruler was eroded and increasing labour demands from the sugar plantation made it difficult for him to fulfil his duty. With these changes, the independent power of the *bekel* was gradually impaired. He was no longer a *raja kecil* in his *kebekelan* but was identified more as a functionary employed by the planter. The deteriorating position of the *bekel*, however, did not mean an improvement of the peasants' position. They had to work longer for the foreign planter and could use their *sawah* for only a short period of time. In these circumstances, one of the ways adopted by the *bekel* and *kuli kenceng* to lessen their economic hardship was to share the burden by apportioning *sawah* to more villagers, thus increasing the number of people eligible for corvée labour.

A.2. Reorganisation in the Principalities

The economic system of the Principalities in the late 19th century was different from that in other parts of Java under direct Dutch rule. This system permitted free extraction of corvée labour, did not recognise individual right to the land and was based on the patron-client relation between the *patih* and the *bekel*, all of which had been gradually abolished outside the Principalities. As Dutch merchant capitalism was replaced by an industrial one based in the drive toward standardisation, centralisation, rationalisation and expansion in the late 19th century (Takashi,1990:18), a series of proposals were made to change the out-of-date system in the Principalities. The shift of colonial policy from the liberal *laissez-faire* to an 'ethical' one, combined with mass protests from peasants which had had no precedents in Yogyakarta, intensified the pressure for reform (van Mook,1958:310; Suhartono,1991:94-95). Finally in the 1910s, the reorganisation of the Principalities began.

In the matter of land, the reorganisation reaffirmed the principle that the land in the Principalities belonged to the ruler. However, it changed the way this principle was applied. While previously, the court officials and nobles had been given the right to use the land as compensation for their services, the reorganisation concentrated this right on the ruler (Suhartono,1991:95). As a replacement of the appanage, the ruler awarded an indemnity equivalent to the computed net income that the *patih* received from their appanage (van Mook,1958:321), while he levied taxes in the form of money to meet the cost to operate the administrative apparatus.

Second, the reorganisation abolished the system of *kebekelan* and instituted *desa* as the lowest administrative unit. Several former *kebekelan* were amalgamated into a *desa* [14] which was designed to accommodate functionally differentiated officials (ibid.:324). Each *desa* was supposed to be financially self-sufficient, so that parts of *desa* land were allocated as salary lands (*bengkok*) for the officials.

Third, the reorganisation redistributed the land to villagers and granted them rights to use, dispose and inherit the land. In principle, all adult male villagers who were capable of performing obligations to the village community and to

---

[14] The *desa* created after the reorganisation did not have the same population. The population in each *desa* reached 1500 to 2000 on the average, but it was not rare to see a *desa* with 3000 residents (van Mook,1958:323).

the state were eligible for an equal amount of *sawah* (Suhartono,1991:100; Takashi,1990:20). [15] The size of the land for distribution was not fixed but left to the situation in each *desa*. In the case of Kolojonggo, it was about 4000 m² of *sawah* divided into two, one located in the *biru* (blue) and the other in the *abang* (red) section, and about 2000 m² of *pekarangan*. [16] It is not certain whether the distribution of *sawah* instituted an equalisation of landholdings among villagers or not. As the distribution was implemented in already unequal power relations, however, it is plausible to assume that the former *bekel* had room to use his power to obtain more land than others. One of the ways employed by them to receive more land than the average was to register their children as recipients of the land (Suhartono,1991:102). In this respect, the reorganisation was unlikely to mean an equalisation of landholdings, although it surely helped for the land to be distributed evenly to villagers. The other benefit that the reorganisation gave villagers was the right to use their labour for their own benefits. Most corvée labour that they had borne for the *bekel*, the sugar planter and the *patih* was abolished [17] and the capitalistic labour relation was installed as a way to mobilise labour.

The last package of the reorganisation was to institute a tax system. Land tax was imposed on each landholder, the amount of which was dependent on the quality of land, and a fixed sum as household tax (*pajeg somah*) was levied (O'Malley,1977:179). In some areas of the Principalities, a fixed sum as water tax was also collected (Soemardjo,1959:18). The direct purpose of levying tax was to collect the revenue to pay the bureaucrats deprived of the appanage, but the tax system also played an important role for the survival of the foreign planters to whom the reorganisation gave the right to rent *sawah* [18] but no means to mobilise villagers' labour. As villagers had no way of earning money for paying taxes other than working in sugar plantations, the imposition of taxes worked as a mechanism to safeguard a stable supply of labour from the peasants without any compulsory measures.

With the installation of the reorganisation, the nature of land was transformed from non-commodity into commodity. Before the reorganisation, villagers could

[15] Those who qualified for land distribution were stipulated to be 'male villagers who were adult and strong' (*tiang jaler ingkang dewasa lan kiyat*) (Suhartono,1991:100).
[16] Takashi reports that around 3500m² (half a *bau*) was distributed to each villager (1990:21), while van Mook estimated each villager obtained approximately a fourth of a *bau* (about 1750 m²) (1958:327). The estimation of Selosoemardjan is much larger than that of Takashi and van Mook. He suggests that it was around 3/4 hectare of *sawah* in the lowlands while around 3 hectares of *tegal* (dry land) in the rugged areas (1962:223).
[17] The exception was the duty to work for the maintenance of dams and irrigation canals once a week (Selosoemardjan,1962:276).
[18] The reorganisation gave the foreign planters the right to rent *sawah* for fifty years without consent from the peasants (Selosoemardjan,1962:276). This indicates that the abolition of non-economic compulsion, one of the major purposes of the reorganisation, could not be fully accomplished from the beginning due to the vested interests of the foreign planters.

use land in so far as they met their duties as landholders, and when they could not fulfil these duties, it was transferred to others who were ready to do so. The same was true of the *bekel* who could secure his access to land as long as he held the position as a *bekel*. If he happened to lose this position or could not leave it to his heir, the *bekel* had to give up his right over land. In this sense, land was a source of riches but was not wealth itself and the investment of one's wealth in the form of land was inconceivable. After the reorganisation, the situation changed. An inheritable right was granted to landholders, limited transactions of land were permitted [19], and land could be converted into other forms of wealth. This implies that the barriers which prevented the investment of wealth in land were lifted and anyone who had riches large enough to buy land could do so in so far as they paid land tax. The transformation of the value of land, then, solidified the ground on which villagers could be polarised in terms of their landholdings. Whether this potential was actualised in the period after the reorganisation or not might be dependent on two factors: whether the amount of *sawah* distributed to each peasant was large enough to secure their economic reproduction and whether economic opportunities were distributed unevenly among villagers, so that one could accumulate riches much faster than others or not.

In Kolojonggo, each household was given about 4000 m² of *sawah*. As the *glebagan* system was at work, the size of *sawah* that landholders could use each year was just half of what they owned, while they could not get any income from the other half. Differing from the period before the reorganisation, the sugar plantation was stipulated to provide recompense for the late return of *sawah* at the rate of f 1 per month per 2000 m² (Soemarjo,1959:16) or f 6 for a half year. [20] Apart from the compensation, the sugar plantation bore the cost of restoring *sawah* for rice cultivation. For this work, the peasants holding 2000 m² of *sawah* could earn about f 1.9 every year. [21] After *sawah* was cleared up, the peasants planted rice. If the production was 29.8 *pikul* (1 *pikul* = 61.8 kg.) of unhusked dry rice per hectare (Scheltema,1986:181) [22] and the production cost reached 38

---

[19] In principle, the reorganisation prohibited landholders from selling *sawah* (to people living in a different village), renting out *sawah* for a share, selling products for a down payment and exchanging *sawah* (Suhartono,1991:110). For this purpose, a village council was formed to monitor transactions and the inheritance of land (Selosoemardjan,1962:220). In actuality, however, land was transacted freely between landholders living in the same village since the village council was controlled by those who were in a position to purchase *sawah* (Suhartono,1991:110).

[20] Selosoemardjan reports that the compensation for the late return of *sawah* was f 15 per hectare per month, a figure three times higher than that cited in Soemarjo. Given that land rent for one *bau* (0.7 hectare) of the second class *sawah* ranged between f 22.5 and f 7 per annum (Suhartono,1991:205), his estimate seems to be too high. Therefore the figure cited in Soemarjo is used in the text.

[21] According to my calculation from the sugarcane plantation in Kolojonggo in 1993, about 250 ditches were dug up in 2000 m² of *sawah*. As the sugar plantation paid 3/4 cent per ditch (Selosoemardjan,1962:279), the total payment for 2000 m² was estimated to be f 1.9.

[22] 29.8 *pikul* was the average production of rice between 1922-27 in the District of Bantul (Scheltema,1986:181).

percent of the yields (Gelpke,1986:61)[23] , they could obtain 3.7 *pikul* of unhusked rice per 2000m². In sum, a household holding 4000 m² of *sawah* could earn f 7.9 and 3.7 *pikul* of unhusked rice per annum. After land tax for *sawah* f 2.4, that for *pekarangan* f 1.3 [24] , household tax f 2, and water tax f 1 were subtracted, what was left to this household was f 1.2 (approximately 6 kg. of husked rice) [25] and 3.7 *pikul* of unhusked rice or 2 *pikul* (about 120 kg.) of husked rice. [26] This implies that 4000 m² of *sawah* could provide its holders with less than 0.5 kg. of rice per day. The second source of income was to work for the sugar plantation or as agricultural labour. By selling their labour, the peasants could earn about 1 kg. of rice per day (Soemarjo,1959:14-22; Selosoemardjan,1962: 277). Whether the income from the *sawah* and wage labour could meet the daily consuming needs of a household or not might be dependent on such factors as the population composition of each household and the availability of work opportunities. However, the income that they could earn was far less than what Yogyanese villagers regarded as sufficient (*cukupan*), namely, an income of 1200 kg. of milled rice equivalent for five family members (Penny and Singarimbum,1973:3-4).

In examining the economic viability of peasant households, the amount of income was not the sole factor to be considered. The stability of income also played a pivotal role in determining economic viability. By decreasing the level of consumption, peasant households could balance their budget to a certain degree without relying on more radical measures of selling their land or migration, as Soedjito describes: 'for one month after the harvest, small landholders ate rice three times a day, which was reduced to twice after that period and which finally became once when the paddy was ripening' (1957:131). Seen from this framework, economic conditions after the reorganisation were unfavourable for the Yogyanese peasants. First, the income that they could earn was not stable but fluctuated seasonally. Within the year, money was abundant from May to November. Rice

[23] 38 percent of production cost consisted of 20 percent for harvest, 6.3 percent for seeds and agricultural tools and 11.4 percent for *slametan* (ritual). Labour cost is supposed to have been met by family labour (Gelpke,1986:61).
[24] Below is the amount of land tax per hectare, cited in Soemarjo (1959:17):

	Class					
	I	II	III	IV	V	VI
Sawah	14.30	11.80	9.30	6.30	5.10	3.00
Pekarangan	11.60	7.70	5.10	3.40	1.70	0.80

As most *sawah* in Kolojonggo were classified as second class and most *pekarangan* as third class, the figures in the text were the land tax applied to second class *sawah* and third class *pekarangan*.
[25] From 1922 to 1930, the price of one *pikul* of husked rice in Javanese markets oscillated between f 11 and f 12.7 (*Statistisch Jaavoverzicht van Nederlandsch-Indie*, 1930).
[26] The conversion rate from unhusked rice to husked rice used in the text is 1:0.56, based on Iso (1986:288).

was harvested in April. From May, the sugar plantations paid compensation for the late return of *sawah*. From May to October or November, there were many opportunities to work as ditch diggers and harvesters of sugarcane. This bright phase ended after peasant households planted rice in December. The sugar plantation no longer needed a large amount of labour to manage sugarcane growth and work opportunities in the agricultural sector also decreased, whereas the rice, having been harvested in April, was already used up. At the worst point of their situation, therefore, peasant households had to survive with no money and little food while their rice was growing in the field (Selosoemardjan,1962:280). Second, the economic stability of peasant households was hampered by the lump sum of tax that they had to pay. Throughout the 1920s when the flow of money from the sugar plantations was smooth, the payment of tax could be met by them. However, when the Depression came in the 1930s and the sugar plantations curtailed the land reserved for sugar cultivation and lowered the wage cost (O'Malley,1977:187-190), land tax could not be easily met by the peasants.[27] They could borrow money or pawn valuables but these actions could not be taken endlessly. The last resort left to them was to sell land. By selling land, they could maintain their livelihood and be freed from the burden of land tax, an option which might not be totally a bad choice for them.

To summarise, the periodical fluctuation of money supply and land tax worked to hamper the capability of peasant households to overcome economic hardship by adopting the strategy of minimising consumption. In these circumstances, even a subtle change from within the household economy such as crop failure or sickness of a family member and from outside such as sudden shrinkage of work opportunities in the sugar plantation could easily disrupt any economic equilibrium that they maintained. Once disrupted, the equilibrium could not be restored with ease unless other economic opportunities were newly available.[28]

The villagers who could get real benefits from the establishment of private ownership of land were those working outside the peasant economy such as

---

[27] In the first half of the 1930s when the world depression hit the sugar industry in Yogyakarta, the foreign planters returned the land to the peasants, giving them a chance to cultivate *sawah* all year round. However, this change did not improve the economic condition of peasant households. They had to pay, in addition to the taxes they had paid before, the land tax that the sugar plantation had borne before the depression, while the price of rice dropped remarkably. The rice prices in 1933-40 were less than half of those in 1926-29 (*Indisch Verslag*,1941). The dramatic decrease in monetary income and the burden of paying tax after the depression seem to have been the origin of an expression that a few village elders in Kolojonggo still use: 'to buy money' (*tuku duit*). Similar expressions are used when they differentiate the period before and after the depression. They call the period before it *jaman murah duit* (the period when money was cheap) and, after it, *jaman larang duit* (the period when money was expensive).
[28] The *glebagan* system was another factor exacerbating the economic conditions of the landholders who sold their *sawah* since it was almost impossible for them to sell their *sawah* in both sections equally. When a peasant sold all *sawah* in one section, he had no *sawah* to cultivate once in two years, although he still owned half of his previous holdings.

village officials, large traders and regular employers in sugar factories, schools and offices run by the Dutch. The income that they could obtain varied in accordance with the kind of jobs and ranks [29] but their income made it easier for them to deal with the fluctuation of money supply and the need to pay a lump sum of tax. The economic condition of village officials is a good example of how advantageous their positions were. After the reorganisation, village officials received more than one hectare of the most fertile *sawah* as their salary land which was exempt from land tax (Takashi,1990:20). [30] As the land tax for first class *sawah* was f.14.30 per hectare (Soemarjo,1957:17) or more than one *pikul* of husked rice, tax exemption was a great benefit to them, apart from the products that they obtained from it. With this income, village officials and some of those who worked in non-agricultural sectors were in a position to take advantage of the opportunity that the reorganisation had provided, namely, to purchase land.

According to village elders in Kolojonggo, the pattern of land transactions after the reorganisation was not the same as it is now. It took place in a relatively longer period of time and the price of land was not fixed but dependent on the merits of each case. The first stage of a transaction usually started when a villager had nothing left to eat and had to borrow food from his or her wealthy neighbours. This borrowed food was supposed to be returned after the harvest with interest which was, according to some villagers, twenty percent of what the debtor had originally borrowed. When the debtor could not pay his or her debt back and if this went on for a while, he or she sold *sawah* to the creditor. At first, the selling was done only for one season (*tuku musiman*). The debtor transferred the right to use land for one season to the creditor while he or she cultivated it either as a sharecropper or as a wage labourer. If the debtor was fortunate enough to pay the debt back, land was returned after one season. If not, the period of selling land changed from one season to one year or a few years (*tuku tahunan*) until the ownership of land was shifted to the creditor. One of the factors which made it almost impossible for the debtor to pay the debt back was that, while land was sold by one season or by a year, the duty to pay land tax was not transferred from the debtor to the creditor. This debt bond made between villagers opened a way for land transactions to take place gradually and easily. The well-to-do villagers did not need to prepare a lump sum of money to purchase land but just kept lending small amounts of rice or money, which later could turn into land.

---

[29] According to two village elders who worked respectively as a primary school teacher and as a clerk in the office run by the Dutch, their monthly income in the 1930s was more than one quintal of rice.
[30] The salary land was apportioned to each official with the ratio of 4 (village head), 2 (deputy chief), 1.5 (secretary) and 1 (other officials) (van Mook,1958:324). In Sumber, the *lurah* received about 3.5 hectares of *sawah*.

A few features discussed above show a high possibility of land transactions in the post-reorganisation period, but the lack of written data makes it difficult to confirm this. The first data available for this purpose are the land registration records documented in 1943 under the Japanese colonial government. Although this register was not written in the late Dutch colonial period and does not contain any data concerning temporary transfers of *sawah*, the absence of other written materials necessitates its use as a base line to understand the structure of land tenure and the intensity of land transactions in the late colonial period. A modified version[31] of the land registration record in 1943 is presented in table A-1:

Table A-1: Landholdings in Kolojonggo in 1943

Size (ha)	No. of households	*Sawah* owned (percent)	Ratio of Blue/Red (Red = 100)[a]
0	16	0	-
< 0.3	11	10.5	31.7
< 0.5	13	31.5	73.4
< 0.7	4	14.2	59.8
< 1	3	15.1	54.6
> 1	2	28.7	52.3
Total	49	100	-

Source: Records kept in the *kelurahan* office
[a] Ratio of Blue/Red refers to the ratio of the size of *sawah* that a land owner had in the blue section to that in the red section (Red section = 100). For example, if a villager had 500 m² of *sawah* in the blue section and 1000 m² in the red section, the ratio becomes 50. For the convenience of discussion, the bigger part of *sawah* that a villager owned, whether it was actually in the red or in the blue section, is supposed to have been in the red section, while the smaller part, in the blue section.

The forty-nine households in table A-1 can be classified into three groups: those who owned less than 0.3 hectare of *sawah*, those who owned between 0.3 and 0.5 hectare; and those who owned more than 0.5 hectare. The first group was the greater in number but controlled only 10.5 percent of the total 17 hectares of *sawah* in Kolojonggo. Thirteen households in the second group held 31.5 percent. The average holding of this group was 4103 m², almost the same size of *sawah* said to have been distributed at the time of the reorganisation. However, it was not this group but nine households in the third group which controlled the majority of *sawah* in Kolojonggo. The third group owned 9.3 hectares or 58 percent of the total *sawah*. Of the nine households in this group, three were the heirs of the former *bekel*, and one, who owned 3.5 hectares of *sawah*, was the *mandor* (overseer) in the sugar plantation. Two of the remaining five were related

[31] Compared with the original data extracted from the village land registration, Table A-1 has two differences. First, it excludes the cases of inheritance which took place after the reorganisation, so that the land which was registered under the names of different heirs but which had been controlled by one household before the inheritance is considered to be undivided. This revision is made in order to differentiate the original households which had received the land at the time of the reorganisation from the households which inherited the land from their parents who were the original recipients of the land. By differentiating these two categories, it is expected to obtain more accurate data on land transactions. Second, table A-1 does not include the salary and pension land granted to those who had positions in the *desa* administration. The original data is presented in table A-2.

to the largest landowner as his son-in-law and his brother while the other three were ordinary peasants.

The extremely polarised landholding in table A-1 can not be explained except by referring to the accumulation of *sawah* by a few villagers through land transactions in the 1920s and 1930s. Although no written materials are available to show these transactions, the opinion of village elders supported this view. They remembered that a few landholders had been actively involved in buying land, while some of the land sellers of that time could still remember the land that they had sold to large landholders. Given the polarised land tenure in 1943 and the memory of village elders, it can be assumed, though oversimplified, that the first group in table A-1 consisted mainly of the households which had sold part of their holdings after the reorganisation, the second, which had retained their holdings, and the third, which had purchased *sawah*.

One of the features showing that landholders of less than 0.3 hectare of *sawah* constituted the main group that sold land is the ratio of the smaller part of *sawah* that they owned to the bigger one (see column for Ratio of Blue/Red in Table A-1). The *sawah* distributed at the time of the reorganisation was divided into two parts, one in the blue section and the other in the red section, and the size of each part was, although not the same, supposed to be balanced. Therefore, the more one was involved in land transactions, the ratio of the smaller part of *sawah* (which is supposed to have been located in the blue section in table A-1) to the bigger one (which is supposed to have been located in the red section) should be lower. [32] Table A-1 shows that the ratio is the lowest in the group of less than 0.3 hectare of *sawah*. Moreover, six of the eleven landholding households in this group had *sawah* only in one section, either blue or red. In the case of the second group, the ratio was 73.4. Of the thirteen households in this group, seven had a ratio higher than 80, three of which were higher than 90, and no household owned less than 1000 m^2 in either section of the *sawah*. The third group has a lower ratio than the second group, while no households in the third group had less than 2000 m^2 of *sawah* in either section of the *sawah*.

Another feature showing that the first group constituted the main group selling the *sawah* is the similarity in the size of *pekarangan* (yard) that nineteen households in the first group [33] and thirteen households in the second group owned. The average size of *pekarangan* owned by the nineteen households in the first group was 2430 m^2 while that owned by the second group was 2873 m^2.

[32] This proposition is based on an assumption that a villager could not sell (or buy) *sawah* in the blue and red section equally. For example, when a villager owning 2000 m^2 of *sawah*, half of which was located in the red section and the other half in the blue section, wanted to sell 500 m^2, it is unlikely, though not impossible, that he or she sold 250 m^2 from the red section and 250 m^2 from the blue section. In this respect, the more one was involved in land transactions either as buyers or sellers, the ratio of the smaller part to the bigger one (the bigger part = 100) would be lower.
[33] Of the twenty-seven households in the first group, eight households did not own *pekarangan*.

As *pekarangan* was distributed at the time of the reorganisation and the principle used in distribution might be the same as that for *sawah*, the similarity in the size of *pekarangan* can be regarded as an indication that the size of *sawah* received by the nineteen households in the first group and the thirteen households in the second group at the initial stage of the reorganisation might not have been as different as in 1943.

To summarise, table A-1 points out that a rapid process of polarisation in terms of landholdings took place in Kolojonggo over two decades after the reorganisation. [34] At one pole were a few villagers who had accumulated a large amount of *sawah* while at the other, a substantial number of villagers who sold their *sawah*, owning less than 0.3 hectare of *sawah* or changing their position from landholders to the landless. [35] The unfavourable economic circumstances in the 1920s and 1930s, amongst which were the seasonal fluctuation of income, heavy monetary taxes, and short period to use *sawah*, provided conditions in which peasant households could not fully use their adaptability and those who lost their economic equilibrium sold *sawah* for survival. In this respect, one of the aims of the reorganisation - namely to establish a strong tie between land and the peasants by giving the latter an inheritable right to the former (Selosoemardjan,1962:221) - could not be achieved in the long run. Instead, what the reorganisation installed was a capitalistic development in landownership which accelerated the alienation of the peasants from their land.

As long as the economic system which produced the polarised structure of landholdings continued, the gap between large and small landholders continued to widen. Large landholders could accumulate more *sawah* with the profit that they gained from the newly purchased land whereas small landholders or the landless had fewer resources to regain their land. These favourable conditions

[34] Comparable data showing the polarisation of landholdings are available in a village called Tumut placed around 10 kilometres westwards from Kolojonggo. Below is the structure of land tenure in Tumut in 1943 as is cited in Sato (1994:99). The figures in the table below show the size of land controlled by villagers and includes the salary land of village officials:

	Size Group						
	0	< 0.2	< 0.4	< 0.6	< 1.2	< 6.2	Total
Households	131	72	69	38	19	16	345
Area (%)	0	10.8	20.4	20.6	16.5	31.7	100

The above table shows that the polarisation of landholdings was also a prominent feature in Tumut, although exact comparison of the data between Kolojonggo and Tumut is impossible due to the lack of data on the land ownership in Tumut.

[35] Not all villagers who were classified as landless in table A-1 might be those who sold their whole *sawah*. Some of them were the migrants who entered Kolojonggo after the reorganisation and had had no chance to receive a portion of *sawah* nor *pekarangan*. In this respect, it is probable that those who owned neither *sawah* nor *pekarangan* (8 of 16 *sawah*-less households) might be the migrants, while those who owned more than 0.1 hectare of *pekarangan* but did not have any *sawah* (8 of 16 *sawah*-less households) might be the initial recipients of *sawah* who later lost it.

for the further differentiation of the peasants in terms of their landholdings changed in 1942 when the Japanese came to Java as a new colonial power. As the peasants were mobilised by the Japanese and later by the provisional Indonesian government for their war efforts, the pre-existing economic system could not work, slowing down the process of differentiation. When the rural countryside once again regained its peace, the economic system which had dominated the late Dutch colonial period was replaced by a new one.

A.3. Rural Economy in the Old Order Period

One of the first acts of the newly installed regional government of Yogyakarta was to abolish the economic system which had been at the heart of the peasants' hardship. Household tax was abolished in 1946, followed by land tax in 1951. Instead of land tax, the regional government instated income tax to which villagers who had paid more than Rp 6.00 of land tax (equivalent to approximately 0.4 hectare of the second class *sawah*) were liable (Selosoemardjan,1962:225). The *glebagan* system was annulled in 1948 (Soemarjo,1959:21). These measures helped to remove the negative value on land. Land was no longer a burden but the most reliable source of income and precious capital (Soedjito,1957:146).

In the 1950s, 0.2 hectare of *sawah* could produce about 500 kg. of unhusked dry rice per cropping. [36] When a household cultivated this amount of *sawah* with its own family labour, the production cost would amount 70-80 kg. of unhusked rice [37], leaving 420-430 kg. as net yield. If unhusked rice was converted to husked one at the rate of 1:0.65 (Fox,1991:80) and pounding was done by family labour, the household could secure about 275 kg. of rice. As double cropping was possible, this amount of rice could be harvested once every six months. This shows that 2000 m^2 of *sawah* could give its holders about 1.5 kg. of rice per day, an amount which was large enough to meet daily rice consumption of a family of five members [38], although not enough for other needs.

The benefits of this new economic system in the 1950s were distributed evenly to all landholders. Decreasing land tax and a longer period to use *sawah* provided large landholders with a chance to become wealthier, middle landowners with a better opportunity to secure their livelihood solely from the cultivation of *sawah* and small landholders with a better opportunity to survive without selling

[36] The yields (unhusked dry rice) per hectare in the 1950s ranged between 27.6 and 22.4 quintals (1 quintal=100 kg.), the average of which was 25.05 quintals (KSY,1957 and 1963).
[37] This consisted of 5 kg. of unhusked rice for seeds and 14 percent of the total yields for harvest (Soedjito,1957:135). Other labour processes such as ploughing, planting, weeding and fertilising are supposed to have been satisfied by family and *gotong-royong* labour, while the cost to celebrate ritual is not included, due to lack of data on it.
[38] According to Pandam, the daily consumption of rice in wealthy and middle-level families reached around 200 grams per person while that in poor families, 100 to 150 grams (1958:42).

their land. The affluence which middle landowners could enjoy in the 1950s was reflected in the influx of bicycles into rural villages, which had once been possessed only by government officials, the well-to-do village officials and a few merchants in the colonial period (Selosoemardjan,1962:256). About half of the total households in a Yogyanese rural hamlet is reported to have owned one or more bicycles, which cost 100 kg. of rice in the mid-1950s (Soedjito,1957:157). This changed the prestige symbol of wealthy villagers from bicycles to motorbikes (Soemarjo,1959:24), a situation which also applied in Kolojonggo.

Rising profitability of *sawah* cultivation in the 1950s brought a negative impact on the differentiation of peasants in terms of their landholdings. The abolition of land tax and of the *glebagan* system strengthened the economic position of small landholders while the changing value of land from that of burden to the most precious resource encouraged them to retain land, whatever size it might be. In the case of large landholders, a few constraints emerged which had a potential to block their economic capability to further the process of accumulating land. Before these will be discussed, the structure of land tenure in 1960 will be described:

Table A-2: Landholdings in Kolojonggo in 1960

Size (ha)	No. of Households			*Sawah* owned (percent)	
	1943[a]	1960[b]		1943	1960
0	16	21		0	0
< 0.1	6	12		2.7	4.5
< 0.2	6	14		5.0	10.7
< 0.3	10	15		13.6	19.7
< 0.4	6	5		12.1	9.2
< 0.5	6	3		15.4	7.2
< 0.6	2	2		6.7	6.2
< 0.7	2	3		7.0	10.3
< 0.8	0	0		0	0
< 0.9	2	0		10.0	0
< 1	0	0		0	0
> 1	2	3		27.5	32.2
Total	58	78		100	100

Source: Records kept in the *kelurahan* office
[a] The statistics for 1943 include the cases of inheritance and salary land, so that it is different from the data presented in table A-1.
[b] As was the case in 1943, temporary transactions of *sawah* by way of *tuku tahunan* and *tuku musiman* were not included in the statistics for 1960. Accordingly, the actual size of *sawah* that each household cultivated at that time may not coincide with the size of *sawah* presented in this table.

One of the most remarkable features in table A-2 is the increase in the number of households owning less than 0.3 hectare of *sawah*. Nineteen households were newly added to this group in 1960 and the size of *sawah* owned by this group rose from 21.3 percent to 34.9 percent. The increase in the number of small holders had also been a process characterising the colonial period. Compared with this, however, the process in the 1950s was different in that the increase in small landholders was not accompanied by the concentration of *sawah* among large landholders. On the contrary, the total area of *sawah* that landholders of more than 0.5 hectare owned declined from 51.2 percent in 1943 to 48.7 percent in 1960. The most important factor behind this change was inheritance. According to the Javanese custom, all children have the right to their parents' estates and valuables while no rules are systemised to give preferential right to the eldest child or the male (Koentjaraningrat, 1960:105-6). When applied to the inheritance of the *sawah*, this rule implies that, upon parents' death or even before it, the parents' *sawah* is inherited by each child rather than being kept by one of them. As a result, the inheritance of land in the family of large landholders meant the creation of several smaller landholders. In the 1940s and 1950s, thirteen cases of inheritance, of which nine involved the division of the *sawah*[39], were reported in Kolojonggo and 7.5 hectares of *sawah* previously owned by nine villagers were distributed to 26 villagers, 19 living in Kolojonggo and 7 living in neighbouring hamlets.

The second factor which changed the structure of landholdings was the commercial sale of *sawah*. However, the size of *sawah* which was transacted in the 1950s was far less than that in the colonial time. Two villagers sold 2190 m² of *sawah* while four bought 5535 m².[40] With these transactions, the ownership of 4.6 percent of *sawah* was shifted from one to the other. To understand better the impact of land transactions on the structure of land tenure, the same data were collected in five other hamlets in Sumber, which cover 70.1155 hectares of *sawah* and 41.9750 hectares of *pekarangan*. The result is as follows:

Table A-3: Land transactions in five hamlets in Sumber (1950-1964)

Year	Cases			Size	
	Sawah	*Pekarangan*	S + P	*Sawah*	*Pekarangan*
1950-54	4	3	0	0.2530	0.2040
1955-59	21	14	0	1.5670	0.5250
1960-64	12	8	2	0.8310	0.4710
Unknown	1	0	0	0.0915	0
Total	38	25	2	2.7425	1.2000

Source: Records kept in the *kelurahan* office.

Table A-3 indicates that 42 cases of land sales in the 1950s covered about 1.8 hectares of *sawah* and around 0.7 hectare of *pekarangan* or 2.6 percent of the total *sawah* and 1.7 percent of the total *pekarangan* in the five hamlets. These figures imply that accumulation of *sawah* by large landholders by way of land purchase did not take place on a mass scale. The size of landholdings of land

[39] The other four cases consisted of one case in which the family did not have *sawah* and of three cases in which the size of *sawah* was too small to be divided (less than 1000 m²). In the latter cases, the *sawah* was inherited by one heir while the *pekarangan* was divided among all heirs.
[40] The data related to land transactions were obtained from the records on land transactions kept in the *kelurahan* office. As these data only cover the cases of land transaction in which the title to land was legally transferred, these do not show a complete picture of land transactions in that period.

purchasers, as is shown in table A-4 below, also suggests that large landholders were not the major group to buy land. Of the 58 known cases of transaction, only two cases were carried out by landholders with more than 0.5 hectare. In this respect, the polarisation of landholdings by way of land sales which had dominated the colonial period was largely halted in the 1950s.

Table A-4: Size of *Sawah* owned by Land Buyers Before They Bought Land between 1950 and 1964

	Size of *Sawah* owned by Land Buyers				
	0	< 0.3	< 0.5	> 0.5	Unknown
Sawah buyers	10	19	3	1	5
Pekarangan buyers	15	4	4	1	1
Sawah & *Pekarangan* buyers	1	0	0	0	1
Total Cases	26	23	7	2	7

Source: Records kept in the *kelurahan* office.

The change in the structure of land tenure raises the question as to why the process of concentration of land in the late colonial period was largely stopped in the 1950s, although the economic condition of large landholders had not worsened. The first constraint to hinder the process of concentration of *sawah* was inheritance. In many cases, those who accumulated a large amount of land were middle aged in the colonial period, and the process of inheritance in their households started in the 1940s and 1950s. When large landholders had many children, inheritance meant a creation of several middle or, in some cases, small landholders. Although each heir was fortunate enough to receive more than one hectare of *sawah*, which was large enough to yield profits to purchase more land, however, inheritance worked in a negative way. On the one hand, the inexperience of the heirs in managing *sawah* might make it difficult for them to be directly involved in the expansion of their landholdings after inheritance. On the other hand, the higher education that many large landholders' children had received helped them to find jobs in non-agricultural sectors which were valued higher than those in the agricultural sector (Soedjito,1957:138). Irrespective of whether they stayed in the village or not, employment in non-agricultural sectors decreased their interest in agriculture and land accumulation.

The second factor was the improving economic condition of small and middle landholders. The abolition of land tax removed the expensive cost of holding land in the colonial period while the abolition of the *glebagan* system provided them with the right to cultivate *sawah* all year round, resulting in a rapid increase in the yields from the same size of *sawah*. These measures, then, made the holdings of *sawah* more advantageous than before and helped small landholders to maintain a certain degree of economic equilibrium in managing their household economy without resorting to selling their land.

In brief, the segmentation of land in large landholders' families, increase in the size of *sawah* that landholders could utilise, and the removal of outside pressure on landholders were some of the factors which hindered the process of polarisation of peasants in the 1950s. As a result, the previously differentiated structure of land tenure was largely maintained throughout this period or, considering inheritance in the families of large landholders, the gap between large landholders and smaller ones was narrowed.

The politico-economic developments in the first half of the 1960s had no major impact on the structure of land tenure. The high inflation rate in this period, although deprived the peasants of the sense of economic stability, played a role in reinforcing the importance of holding *sawah* as a safeguard against price fluctuation. On the other hand, the acceleration of the communist activities in the countryside worked to discourage large landholders' involvement in land purchase.

In Kolojonggo, the major change that the communist activists tried to achieve in the first half of the 1960s was to improve the economic condition of small landholders and tenants. Their campaigns aimed to reduce the interest rates on debt, to abolish the *ijon* system [41] , to change the sharecropping ratio from 5:5 to 4:6 (owner:sharecropper), to return the *sawah* which were sold for a fixed term (*tuku tahunan*) to its original owners, to collectivise agricultural working practices and to establish a cooperative. These programs, although backed by mass support from villagers, did not bring any tangible results to change the economic conditions of their supporters. Substantial concessions such as the replacement of sharecropping ratio and nullification of *tuku tahunan* could not be achieved due to severe opposition from large landholders, while the most fundamental issue of land reform was not located at the center of the communist program in Kolojonggo. This was because the size of *sawah* held by large landholders in Kolojonggo was, seen from the national standard, too small to be subject to redistribution. In Kolojonggo as well as in Sumber, no one had more than 5 hectares of *sawah*, the maximum size of landholding promulgated by the land reform act (Huizer,1972:33). On the contrary, the size that the largest landholder in Kolojonggo owned was just above 2 hectares, the official guideline used in the land reform as an appropriate landholding for a family (ibid.). [42]

[41] *Ijo* means 'green'. *Ijon* refers to a system in which the peasants sold paddy before harvest. As the peasants who used this system were in need of immediate cash, their bargaining power vis-à-vis rice traders could not be strong and the price agreed between them favoured the traders. Due to the campaign of the communist activists against the *ijon* system, rice traders did not dare to make transactions within the *ijon* system publicly.

[42] This does not imply that no action was taken by communist activists against large landowners. It is said that there were cases in which the sharecroppers delivered less than half of the products and this brought about confrontations between the group of communist activists and that of large landholders. However, these actions were not developed as a well-organised program in Kolojonggo. For more about direct actions taken by communist activists in the 1960s, see Lyon (1970:50-59).

Although the land reform was not a central issue in the communist programs in Kolojonggo, the stipulation of the national land reform law worked as a factor to discourage the involvement of large landowners in land transactions. They could not be certain whether another agrarian law would be introduced in the future to lower the limit on maximum landholding and whether the radical slogan of the communist activists, 'to return land to the peasants', would be realised forcibly to redistribute land to the tenants or not. In these circumstances, it was probably more advantageous for them to maintain the *status quo* than to purchase more *sawah*, agitating the heightened consciousness of the communist activists. Their reluctance to purchase land was reflected in the size and frequency of land transactions in 1960-64 (see table A-3). Compared with 1955-59, the size and frequency of land transactions in this period decreased.

Appendix B: The War of Words: Voices of the Christians

For quite a long time after I had started my research in Kolojonggo, I had an impression that Christian villagers, though a minority, were not in a weak or defensive position vis-à-vis Muslim villagers. Several factors helped me to gain this impression: first, the three Christian *kadus* of the total nineteen *kadus* in Sumber happened to live in Kolojonggo and in its two neighbouring hamlets. The *lurah* in Sumber and two of the eight officials in the *kelurahan* office were also Christians. [1] This composition allowed me to think that Christians represented themselves well, and in some sense, better than Muslims, in the village government. [2] Secondly, religious activities of Christians were no less prominent than those of Muslims. They gathered once a week to study the Bible, while the youth had their own independent weekly meetings. As the Protestant and Catholic villagers ran their religious meetings separately, I was sometimes invited to Christian gatherings up to six times a week (including two Sunday Services in the Protestant *kapel* (chapel) and in the Catholic Church). Thirdly, Christians showed much stronger solidarity than Muslims. When a *kendhuri* or other ritual was held in a Christian family, not only the Christians from Kolojonggo but those from neighbouring hamlets came to help the host. Four, Christians participated in public events more actively than Muslims. Their presence was more clearly visible in *gotong-royong* and in funerals, two of the most frequently held public events. I considered the solidarity of Christians and their active involvement in public affairs as manifestations of their confidence in village life. Fifthly, unlike the public discourse of Muslims, that in the *umat Kristen* seldom dealt with problems related to Islam and Muslims. As I assumed that frequent discussions about Christianity and Christianisation among Muslims were based on their feeling of crisis, namely, that the *umat* Islam was in danger from Christians' attack, I attributed the lack of the public discourse about Islam in the *umat Kristen* to their confidence in religious life. I supposed that it should be those in a weaker position who were more aggressive and were more conscious of the situation in which they were located than those in a stronger position.

As I directed my research more at the relations between Christians and Muslims in Kolojonggo, and especially after I met several priests and clergymen, my view changed gradually. I came to learn of their pessimistic evaluation of their situation in relation to Muslims, namely, that Muslims interfered in the internal affairs of the *umat Kristen* to the extent that the Church could not carry out its own

---

[1] One of the two RW heads and three of the five RT heads in Kolojonggo were also Christians.

[2] Around one fourth of the total population in Kolojonggo were Christians in 1993. According to the official statistics, about 10 percent of the total population in the *kelurahan* Sumber were Christians in 1990.

religious activities, these pressures from Muslims had become stronger, and, in spite of these, Christians had no power to defend themselves.

As my view of Christians' position shifted, I began to interpret my previous experiences from a different angle. Christians' active involvements in religious and social activities were considered more and more as an adaptive strategy to protect their community from the threats of Muslims. I started to interpret a long session announcing miscellaneous news about the Protestant villagers in Sunday services and Christians' frequent visits to other Christians in other hamlets as their deliberate efforts to build and to maintain solidarity among themselves. I began to consider Christians' inclusive attitude toward other Christians and their reluctance to vilify Christians, to evaluate other Christians' religiosity, and to criticise wrong doings of Christians as their attempts to embrace all Christians under the rubric of the *umat Kristen*, not discriminating one from the others. [3] Sometimes, this attitude seemed to go to an extreme, giving an impression that these efforts were desperate, as the following case shows:

> About ten minutes after the study session of the Bible study group for youth had started, Mas Gin and Mas Gun appeared. They did not sit with others who seated themselves in a circle. Instead, they found their seats outside the circle, leaning against the wall. It happened that they sat just behind me, giving me a chance to exchange brief greetings with them and to chat for a while. The study session went as usual. One girl who had been appointed as a chair person the previous week gave her exegeses of several passages in the Bible. After this, others made comments on her exegeses, adding their own interpretations. When the session finished and all participants lowered their heads to carry out a collective prayer, I suddenly felt a kick on my back. I looked back and found Mas Gin smiling at me. With his finger, he signalled me to come to him. As I approached him, he, still smiling, asked a question. It seemed that he tried hard to keep his voice down, but, his voice was much louder than the prayer that the girl was leading. 'Can you smell something from my mouth?' I tried to smell it, but I could not. I said, 'No'. Hearing this, he gave me a smile filled with pride and said, 'I had just finished half a bottle of whisky and came here.' His voice was still loud, so that other youth busy sending their messages to Father in Heaven (*Bapak di Syurga*) were certainly able to hear what he was saying. Mas Gin and Mas Gun

[3] In Indonesia, Protestantism and Catholicism are treated as if they are different religions. Many Muslims considered them two different religions, and a few Christians shared this view. In spite of this, the attitude of the Protestant villagers towards the followers of Catholicism or vice versa was inclusive and both of them emphasised the commonality that they shared rather than distinctiveness. This inclusive attitude was expressed more clearly in the domains which may not be considered as religious *per se*. For example, the Protestant *kaum* in Kolojonggo officiated at *kendhuri* in Catholic families and, when the Protestant *kaum* celebrated a *kendhuri*, a Catholic villager led the prayer, although the prayers of the Protestant and Catholic villagers were somewhat different.

had apparently been drinking alcohol together. Hearing our conversation, Mas Gun also gave me a big smile. When Mas Gin finished talking, the prayer that the girl was leading was clearly heard: 'Father (*Bapak*), please give us a strong faith, so that we may not go astray and follow the ways that Father taught to us. ... Father in Heaven, we have already listened to Your Words (*FirmanNya*). Please help us with Your Holy Spirit (*Roh Engkau yang Kudus*), so that the Language of Your Spirit (*Bahasa Roh Engkau*) may fill our life.' Now that I did not give him any praise, which he might have expected from me, nor showed any further interest, Mas Gin made another move. At this time, he pointed out a calendar on which a Western girl posed in her bikini. Noticing that I also looked at the picture, he positioned his thumb between index and middle fingers, a sign signifying sexual intercourse, and said that she was good to 'eat'. Mas Gun, who kept watching us, also took the same position and commented to Mas Gin, 'Please, 'eat'!' Then, they looked at each other and giggled for a while. The prayer finished and the next session began in which an organiser of the Bible study group gave a brief comment on the whole process of the meeting. Even in this session, Mas Gun and Mas Gin did not stop talking. As their previous interest was in sex, they started to talk about girls. Mas Gin said that he had recently got a magical operation to insert *susuk* (a small piece of gold or diamond) in his face to attract girls. Mas Gun did not want to lose. He began to talk about *ilmu* enabling him to attract girls, arguing that the group from which he had learned this *ilmu* was the most powerful one in Yogyakarta. When his story touched on how to obtain the *ilmu*, a topic which was interesting enough to draw my attention, they had to stop talking. The meeting ended and snacks and drinks started to be delivered.

In spite of this somewhat 'deviant' behaviour of Mas Gun and Mas Gin, they were never ostracised by other Christian youth. Although they usually participated in the study session as onlookers and their presence was visible only when the time to sing hymns came, they were never discouraged from attending the Bible study group. On the contrary, the organisers of the group showed interest in their participation. When they did not come to the meeting, the organisers did not forget to tell their sisters, who usually came to the meeting, to bring them the next week. The same attitude prevailed when some Christian adults evaluated the behaviour of Mas Gun, Mas Gin or any other Christian 'naughty youth' (*anak nakal*), whose names represented the epitome of 'naughty youth' to most Muslim villagers. [4] When I talked about juvenile delinquency

---

[4] According to villagers, the 'naughty youth' referred to those who did not study, drank alcohol habitually, took hallucinatory pills, flirted with girls, wandered around hamlet late at night, were unemployed without trying to find jobs, sang songs loudly and loved to get into arguments, and who, in spite of carrying out these behaviours, did not feel ashamed.

with the Christian *kadus* and asked him to enumerate the youth who might belong to the 'naughty youth', he did not include any Christian names in his answer. [5]

If the Christians' inclusive attitude toward other Christians can be considered as part of their conscious efforts to draw all Christians into the *umat Kristen*, a certain religious significance may be found in interpreting the following case.

> Around nine one evening, the Bible study meeting finished. When snacks and drinks ran out, Mas Hari, one of the organisers of this group, asked for the attention of the participants. First, he announced the venue and the time for the next meeting. Then, he proposed a plan which I could not understand properly. 'For the last few months, especially throughout the Christmas period, the money we collected reaches a reasonable amount. I think the time has come for us to carry out [something].' In spite of the ambiguity in his speech, no one asked any question about the 'something'. Seeing that there was no objection, Mas Hari added, 'I will go to Pak X's house on Sunday morning to see to [it]. If the condition is all right, I will get 'it'. According to my estimation, 'it' may cost about Rp 30,000 or so.' As he did not clarify what 'it' meant, his comments made me more confused, although everyone seemed to understand what 'it' meant. As Mas Hari changed the topic soon, I had to talk to him after most of the youth had gone home. "It' is a dog', Mas Hari said, 'We will buy a dog and eat together'. He talked to me for a while about the taste of dog meat and about diverse ways to kill dogs. He did not forget to say that he would deliver a portion to me, a proposal to which I responded with a smile. Irrespective of whether I said yes or no, it was clear to me that I would have a chance to eat it for dinner with my Christian landlord on Sunday evening. According to Mas Hari, this activity was a long tradition of the Christian youth in Kolojonggo. They collected contributions from the youth, usually between Rp 100 and 200, at the end of the Bible study meeting, waited until these reached a certain

[5] For almost seven months of my stay in his house, the Christian *kadus* did not intervene in my research nor in my private life except on one occasion. One night when we finished dinner together, he gave me a somewhat surprising advice: he did not care much about who visited my room late at night, but he worried about me a lot if the visitors were 'the naughty youth' who could have a negative influence on me. I tried hard to figure out why he talked about this matter at that particular moment, since many villagers visited me late at night after I had moved into his house and, consequently, he was quite accustomed to this. At last, I could find a clue. Before this conversation took place, Mas Noyo, a Muslim youth, visited my place several times. At first, I could not understand why Mas Noyo's visits triggered the *kadus* to give me such an advice in that, according to my own evaluation, Mas Noyo did not belong to 'the naughty youth'. Soon, I realised why the *kadus* categorised Mas Noyo as 'the naughty youth'. Mas Noyo had been unemployed for a few weeks and he was willing to make friends with 'the naughty youth', although he himself, for example, did not drink or gamble. After I understood why the *kadus* was so sensitive about Mas Noyo's visit, I asked the *kadus* to give me a few names of the youth who belonged to 'the naughty youth'. In his answer, he did not mention the names of any Christian youth, although some of the Christians were typical examples of 'the naughty youth' in Kolojonggo.

amount, bought dog meat and cooked it, sold it to Christian families, and re-contributed the profit to the Church. Mas Hari's plan was carried out without any problem. On the next Sunday afternoon, a few Christian youths gathered and cooked *dongseng* (a kind of stew) with dog meat. From about five in the afternoon, some made door to door visits to most Protestant households in Kolojonggo and to some in neighbouring hamlets, and sold the *dongseng*. As was expected, my landlord bought two portions, which were served at the dinner.

This case may be interpreted in diverse ways. However, it seems, at least to me, that it is difficult to understand this case without considering the minority position of Christians. We may interpret the practice of eating dog meat as a strategy of Christians to assert their religious identity. As a minority, Christian villagers have felt pressures to conform to the demands from Muslims. For example, the reformist Muslims prompted them, during the fasting month, not to eat, drink and smoke in front of Muslims, and even not to marry, not to make noise and not to sing hymns. [6] One of the ways to face these pressures may be to strengthen their solidarity by asserting their distinctiveness and by emphasising that they share this distinctiveness together. Dog meat seems to be a good medium to attain this purpose. Unlike other religious symbols, dog meat can convey a much clearer message of their distinctiveness from Muslims, primarily because it is a forbidden food for Muslims and because this prohibition is well known to villagers.

It is not certain whether the practice of sharing dog meat originated from Christians' deliberate effort to consolidate their group solidarity or not. If this was the case, we may regard this practice as an act of symbolic resistance. By selling dog meat to other Christians, they 'contaminated' Christians intentionally with what is forbidden to Muslims, and, by donating profits to the Church, they, at least symbolically, let all Christians share the money obtained in a forbidden way to Muslims but in a permitted way to Christians. If they did not do this intentionally, on the other hand, the practice of sharing dog meat may be considered as a coincidence: the Christian youth wanted to raise funds for the Church activities; some of them happened to choose dog meat for this purpose;[7] and, as they could not sell dog meat to Muslims, they sold it to

---

[6] Although Muslim villagers did not express these demands directly to Christian villagers, Christians seem to have been aware of these demands. In general, the Christians in Kolojonggo did not take Muslims' demands seriously, so that, for example, they did not stop smoking during the fasting month in public. A few Christians, whom I questioned about the Muslims' complaints, showed their anger to me, as a villager put it: if we cannot sing hymns during the fasting month or if we have to change the venues to sing hymns (some Muslims argued that if Christians wanted to sing hymns, they should do it only in places located far from the *masjid*), is Indonesia a nation of *Pancasila* or of Islam?'

[7] Although the economic situation improved dramatically since the 1970s, many villagers still could not afford to eat meat every day. As dog meat is relatively cheaper than beef, its taste is, according to some, better than chicken, and is thought to have medical efficacy by some, the selection of dog meat for fund-raising may be considered to be based on the personal preferences of some Christian youth.

Christians. [8] Irrespective of whether Christians deliberately chose dog meat or not, it seems to be obvious that the act of eating dog meat plays a role in clarifying Christian identity and consolidating the group solidarity. By eating dog meat, Christians feel that they are different from Muslims and they belong to the same in-group which can do what Muslims cannot do.

In Chapter VIII, I have examined the reformist Muslims' view of Christians, Christianity and Christianisation. Concerning almost all examples that the Muslims use to show the vicious intention of Christians and the absurdity of Christianity, Christians have things to say. The voices of Christians about these allegations from the reformist Muslims will be dealt with below. For the convenience of discussion, I will follow the sequence of my discussion in Chapter VIII.

It has been shown that the reformist Muslims attributed all sources of inter-religious conflicts to Christians and that this became the basis for them to construct a negative image of Christians. The argument that Christians ignored Muslims' religious activities, especially in the fasting month, was interpreted differently by Christian villagers. For example, when asked why he (a Christian) provided meals to the Muslim participants in a *gotong-royong* mobilised to improve his house, Pak Mulyo had a legitimate answer:

> If they (Muslims) vilify me [since I served meals to Muslims in the fasting month], this is intended to cover their negligence of the *umat* Islam. They do not know exactly what they are talking about and do not feel ashamed of what they have done to the *umat* Islam. Let's see. If all Muslims in Kolojonggo carry out the fast, why on earth do I have to serve meals? ... If I don't serve meals to the Muslim participants, they will go home and then start to vilify me since I did not serve them meals. If the situation is like this, which way do I have to choose?

If the reformist Muslims had heard Pak Mulyo's comment, they would have argued that what was wrong with him was to mobilise the *gotong-royong* during the fasting month. Although the context was somewhat different, another Christian villager had something to say about this argument:

> Is it possible that we [Christians] choose not to die in the fasting month? Is it possible for us to die at a specific time, so that *kendhuri* [after death] will not be celebrated in the fasting month? [If Muslims criticise the serving of meals at the funeral [9] or the mobilisation of Muslims to prepare

---

[8] Some Christian youth preferred this interpretation when they were asked why they selected dog meat rather than beef or chicken. They emphasised that choosing dog meat for fund-raising was incidental but distributing it only to Christian households was inevitable.

[9] It is a local custom that the host in the funeral provides food and drinks to those who come to the funeral. Until a few years ago, the host prepared meals for the guests, while in 1993-94, it was generally a slice of bread and a glass of tea. When a Christian died in the fasting month, the family

for a *kendhuri* after death in the fasting month] Please ask them to pray [to their God] not to take the souls of Christians in the fasting month!

The negative image of Muslims that Christians had was as strong as Muslims' negative image of Christians. Unlike the case of Muslims, however, the public discourse in the *umat Kristen*, such as sermons in Sunday services and at the end of weekly meetings, did not deal with any issue connected to Muslims and Islam. As a result, one of the important sources for Christians to construct a negative image of Muslims was their own experiences or the stories that they heard from others. Pak Mangku remembered his experience in West Java as follows:

> When I was a peddler, I wandered around almost every part of Java. One day when I was travelling in rural areas of West Java, I had to ask a hamlet head for a night's stay. He examined my identification card and allowed me to stay in his house for a night. While I was talking with him in the living room, his wife brought dishes of food for me, but strangely, she placed these in the room where I was supposed to sleep. I thought his family had already finished their dinner. However, this was not the case. Later, I could see them eating at the other part of the house. At first, I thought this was due to their local custom to let the guests eat separately. Just after I finished my meal, however, it turned out that my guess was wrong. I found that his wife washed the dishes and the glass that I had used seven times with soil. ... Can you imagine how I felt at that time? They might have been more fanatic than other Muslims. However, this experience shows how Muslims, a majority, think about Christians, a minority.

In the Christian discourse about Muslims, the terms *minoritas* (minority) and *mayoritas* (majority) were frequently used. They argued that (Indonesian) Muslims, though a majority, have a minority mentality, so that, unlike the tolerance and the generosity that the majority generally shows toward the minority [10], they oppress, discriminate against, vilify, and find fault with the minority. Two decrees issued in 1978, the stipulation of various rules to regulate religious life, especially, those of constructing church buildings, and mass-media were frequently mentioned examples to illustrate the minority mentality of Muslims. A Christian villager, for example, informed me that the studios to produce religious programs for TVRI (government broadcasting company) were different: the programs for Muslims were produced in Yogyakarta, while those

provided a slice of bread and a glass of tea. As hundreds of guests from dozens of hamlets came, all the guests were asked whether they wanted to eat and drink or not.

[10] It is not certain why Christians had an idea that the majority generally is tolerant to the minority. This is probably due to their assumption that, if they were in a position of the majority, they would treat the minority with love and affection.

for Christians, in Jakarta. 'Do you know why?' he continued, 'this is because they [the Muslims in the TVRI station in Yogyakarta] do not want to have the pulpit which Christian preachers use in their studio.'

Among ordinary Christians, one of the most frequently discussed issues was the discrimination in job-searching. They firmly believed that they were treated unfairly in applying for jobs in the government and private sectors due to their religious status. 'Once, my friend told me this story,' a Christian villager said. 'They wanted a new person in his office and several candidates applied for the job. The boss in his office examined their curriculum vitae one by one, but, in a few cases, it took just a few seconds for him to read them. Then he put them aside.' The explanation was simple. These were from Christians, and the boss, once he knew that these were from Christians, did not want to read them. Some Christians argued that they were forced to change their religion in order to obtain jobs, and that some of them did so. To those who had to change their religion from Christianity to Islam to obtain jobs, however, Christians generally gave no severe criticism. Jesus will understand the difficulty of such Christians and will give His love to them, they argued. They also believed that, if someone was forced to accept Islam, one's conversion was just nominal and one would be saved in the Hereafter.

Compared with the minority mentality of Muslims, Christians were thought to have a majority mentality. They were tolerant, did not discriminate against Muslims, and tried to love Muslims as the same creatures of God. 'All teachers in the Christian schools and universities are not Christians', a villager said. 'This is not confined to schools. Go to the Christian hospitals! There, we can find Muslim doctors, and probably they outnumber Christian doctors'. Another Christian added his comment, 'is it possible for Christians to work in an hospital run by Muhammadiyah? Impossible! They think Christians contaminate the hospital. Christians are dirty (*najis*), aren't they?'

Conversion was a critical issue among the reformist Muslims. They believed that Christians used vicious tactics to lure Muslims to Christianity, such as material benefits, marriages (one Muslim called this tactic *hamilisasi* or to make Muslim girls pregnant), education, art groups and so on. When asked to comment on Muslims' conversion to Christianity, all Christian priests and clergymen[11] stressed its voluntary nature, noting that there is no compulsion in Christianity. One of the proofs (*bukti*) that they used to show this point was the obligation of people who want to be baptised to study Christianity for an extended period of time. The Protestant Church obliges them to attend Christian learning courses held

---

[11] As ordinary Christian villagers did not want to talk about conversion, the passages below are based on the data gathered from my interviews with the Catholic priests and Protestant clergymen. I met two priests whose parishes were in Yogyakarta city, seven priests whose parishes were in rural Yogyakarta and two clergymen whose churches were in rural Yogyakarta.

either in the church or in each *pepanthan* (a Christian community which combines with an existing church temporarily until they can form their own church) for at least six months. In the case of the Catholic church, the period is a year. If the Church wants to increase its followers, they questioned, 'why do they make such a regulation which would hinder the expansion of the Christian population?' Many also pointed out that conversion has been the most sensitive issue between Muslims and Christians and that Muslims have tried hard to find fault with it. In these circumstances, even a small mistake by the Church will be severely criticised by Muslims and will bring a disastrous impact not only on a specific Church but on the *umat Kristen* in general. Accordingly, there is no reason why the Church would incite Muslims by doing something silly, which will jeopardise the basis of the existing *umat Kristen*.

I experienced this cautious attitude of the Church when I attended the course run by the Catholic Church for those who wanted to convert to Christianity.

> My proposal to attend the learning course for those who wanted to convert to Catholicism was readily accepted by a priest. He introduced me to a sister in charge of running the course, who informed me of the time and the place of the course. When I arrived at the convent (*Susteran*) a few days later, it seemed that I was a bit earlier than others. No participants in the course were there, except for the sister. After giving me a warm welcome, she started to talk first, asking me unexpected questions, 'Why were you (*saudara*) attracted by Christianity and why are you here to attend the course preparing for Baptism?' 'Was I attracted by Christianity?', I repeated her question in my mind. Her question confused me very much, in that, when I had met her before, I had explained clearly why I wanted to attend the course. Moreover, as I had visited the Church several times, I believed, my identity as a foreign researcher who studied Christianity was well known to the priest and sisters. By asking such questions, I thought, the sister treated me as if I was attracted by Christianity for personal reasons. I explained my research topics once again, emphasising that I attended the course as a researcher. Only when I finished talking and when she gave me her next remarks, I could understand partially why she asked these questions to me. 'From your remarks, it is clearly evident that there was no compulsion either from the Church or from Christians which forced you to come to this course. I understand your visit is based solely on your free will and on your independent decision. ... If one's intention to change one's religion is based on free will and on sound reasoning, our nation also permits it.'

It is not certain why the sister, who had already been informed about the reasons for my participation in the course, asked questions about what she might have known before. This might be to confirm what she had already known, or, as some of my Muslim friends with whom I discussed this experience suggested, this might stem from her deliberate strategy to impress a foreign researcher with the cautious attitude of the Church. What is certain, however, is that she asked the same questions of all new-comers in her course and received the same answer; that their participation was based not on compulsion but on their free will. Some Muslims who listened to this case argued that this procedure could not change their perception of the Church's vicious actions toward Muslims: if Muslims had already been lured by unfair tactics of Christians before they came to the learning course, whether their visits to it were based on their own free will could not change anything.

Two Catholic priests whose parishes were in the city and who, accordingly, managed a larger amount of material resources than those in rural areas, admitted that they assisted people irrespective of their religious affiliation. The priests and clergymen in rural areas mentioned that their Churches were not in a position to give economic assistance even to Christians. On the contrary, they sought donations and contributions from poor Christians to run their Churches. In these circumstances, they argued, it was impossible for them to give material assistance to non-Christians, an activity which all of them considered as the duty of the Church and which, if the situation permitted, they were willing to do. This was because the Church is obliged to help people, no matter what their religion may be. [12] All of them, including two Catholic priests in the city, denied the allegation

[12] When I visited a Catholic Church in the city, I had to wait for a while outside the priest's office since he was receiving a guest. Sitting in front of the office, I could see a man approaching me. It seemed that he also wanted to meet the priest. When I asked a question as to how long he had been baptised, he gave me a surprising answer, 'No, I am a Muslim.' He said he came from a rural village in Central Java to find a job in Yogyakarta. For several weeks, he had tried to find a job, but in vain until he had no money left and no places to go. He then remembered the story that the Church gave food and jobs for Muslims, and came to the Church to ask assistance. When the guest came out of the priest's office, I asked the Muslim man to meet the priest first. It did not take long for him to come out of the office. He gave me a brief comment, 'it does not work', and then quickened his pace to the street. When I met the priest, our conversation naturally lead to the Muslim man. 'Almost every day, a few Muslims come to the Church to ask assistance, although we have never given them jobs or any other material benefits.' The priest strongly denied the allegation that the Church assists Muslims to convert them to Christianity. 'When we assist non-Christians, these activities are carried out officially and directed not at individuals but at an organisation', he continued. Hearing my question as to why Muslims kept coming to the Church if the Church had never helped them individually, he attributed this to the vicious propaganda of Muslims. 'This is because Muslims propagate an idea that every Muslim, if they want to accept Christianity, will obtain assistance from the Church. Look at the man who came here earlier. He just believed the lie that Muslims spread intentionally and came here to get a job and food.' As I witnessed that the Muslim man's demands were rejected by the priest, I had nothing more to say about him with the priest. When I discussed this experience with some of the *anak masjid* in the following evening, however, they gave me a different interpretation. 'Do you think Christians are so stupid as to give assistance to Muslims in front of others? Moreover, you are a foreigner who will talk about your experience later in foreign countries. Are they stupid enough to reveal their secret to you ?', one of them commented. Another youth who had listened to my story expressed the same idea differently. 'What a pity he (the Muslim whom I met in the church) was! His fortune was really bad today ! ... If he arrived at the Church just a few minutes earlier than you, he would now have a job, a place to sleep

that the activities or the readiness of the Church to help non-Christians were aimed at luring Muslims and eventually at converting them to Christianity. To explain their position concerning this issue, some of them used an example of Romo Mangun, a Catholic priest who was famous for his social activities for the deprived. According to their version of the story, Romo Mangun prohibited the Muslims, who were moved by his self-sacrificing spirit and thus wanted to embrace Christianity, from becoming Christians. The message Romo Mangun delivered to these Muslims was, according to a priest, that 'you don't necessarily need to be a Christian when you want to be a good human being'.

Concerning mixed marriages, which were alleged to be used by Christians to lure Muslims, the priests and clergymen stressed its voluntary character. No Christians forced their future spouse or future in-laws to change religion from non-Christianity to Christianity. Some priests even said that they recommended strongly to the Muslim who would marry a Christian to fulfil his or her Islamic duties after the marriage. The same attitude pervaded their view of education: no Christians forced Muslim parents to send their children to the schools founded by the Christian organisations. As there were many schools founded by Muhammadiyah, they argued, the reason Muslim parents sent their children to Christian schools was simple: these schools gave a better education than Islamic ones. They also pointed out that Muslim students were encouraged to follow their own religion and that most, though not all, of them maintained their faith until they graduated from Christian schools. If this had not been the case, they argued, the Christian population in Yogyakarta would be far larger than now, since, for almost half a century, Christian schools had produced more graduates than Islamic schools. One of the priests had an opinion that education in Christian schools gave Muslim students better chances to be 'good Muslims'. This was because, unlike religious education in Islamic schools which put emphasis only on the formalistic and ritualistic aspect of religiosity, that in Christian schools stressed the inner dimension of religiosity. Accordingly, Muslim students who learned how Christians practised their religion would understand the importance of spirituality in their religious life and would put this into their practice of Islam.

In sum, the priests and clergymen had strong bases to reject Muslims' arguments that Christians employed unfair methods to lure Muslims. No material benefits were given to Muslims to convert them to Christianity and Muslims' marriages to Christians and Muslims' enrolment in Christian schools took place voluntarily. In some cases, Muslims' criticisms of Christians were used by the latter to show the 'minority mentality' which Muslims were supposed to have. 'Do you know the way Muslims criticise mixed marriages?' a priest asked to me. 'They argue

and food to eat. Therefore, it is your fault that he could not get a job. You have to find him and give him a job and food!'

that a mixed marriage takes place due to the priests who are unwilling to prohibit their followers from falling in love with non-Muslims.' Some of the priests believed that there were hidden intentions for Muslims to make these allegations: by attributing everything bad in the *umat* Islam to Christians, Muslims attempt to cover their failure in carrying out their religious programs toward other Muslims and try to avoid the blame that they deserve. They argued, it was not Christians but Muslims who should take care of and give guidance to their fellow Muslims and who eventually were responsible for them.

When asked about several theological issues raised by the reformist Muslims, Christian villagers generally had no idea how to defend Christianity against criticisms (see the dialogues between a Muslim boy and a Christian girl in Chapter VIII). Parts of the answer might be that public discourse in the *umat Kristen* did not deal with theological issues intensively but was directed more at learning the stories related to Jesus Christ and exegeses on these stories, on the one hand, and that many Christians did not consider themselves to be in a position to comment on these theological themes, on the other hand. They recommended me to go to the priests or to the clergymen when I asked troublesome questions. The priests and the clergymen agreed that ordinary Christians' understandings of theological themes in Christianity were not deep, although they evaluated this differently. Some attributed this to their lack of zeal to learn Christianity, while others, to the Church's emphasis on the inner aspects of religious life and on the realisation of God's love rather than on theological knowledge for the sake of knowledge.

This evaluation of the priests and the clergymen is closely related to one of their central frameworks for comparing Christianity with Islam. They considered Christianity to be a religion of faith (*iman*) but Islam to be a religion of rules and regulations. A priest quoted a passage from the Bible to show this difference: 'in Christianity, 'The Word became our flesh and lived in our body'[13] whereas in Islam, 'The Word became the written word and lived in the Book' (*Sabda telah menjadi tulisan dan tinggal di dalam buku*)'. As Islamic teachings are confined to the Book, according to some priests, Muslims are inflexible in understanding religion and are bound to be formalistic and legalistic, and observance of rules and regulations overshadows their faith. Their ideas are well expressed in the following example which was given by a priest:

> Let's say there is a Muslim astronaut revolving round the earth. When he or she wants to carry out *salat*, how can he or she decide the right direction and time for *salat*? This question will become a critical issue

[13] This is a literal translation of an Indonesian phrase, *Sabta telah menjadi daging kita dan tinggal di dalam tubuh kita*, which the priest mentioned without consulting the Bible. This phrase Yohanes,1:14) goes '*Firman itu telah menjadi manusia, dan diam di antara kita* (Yohanes,1:14)' in Indonesian or 'The Word became flesh and dwelt (lived) among us (John,1:14)' in English.

among Muslims. If some say that deciding the right time and direction is not an important matter, others would argue against it until death. If some propose a certain *fatwa*, others would fight against it to the extent that hundreds of Muslims will slaughter hundreds of other Muslims who do not agree with them. How about Christianity? Let's suppose Christians are commanded to pray at a fixed time. However, Christians will not fight each other to find an answer. To Christians, it is irrelevant to raise such a question. Why? Because we put emphasis on the inner side of religiosity. If the astronaut had an intention to carry out *salat* but he or she could not do it due to his or her uncertainty about rules, this would be received as *salat* by God.

Hearing this speech, the reformist Muslims probably say that the priest's understandings of Islam are totally wrong. [14] Irrespective of whether these understandings are right or wrong, however, the dichotomy of the inner and the outer and of faith and rules provide Christians with repertoires to defend Christianity from Muslims' theological attack, on the one other, and to argue for the superiority of Christianity over Islam, on the other hand.

According to the priests and clergymen, to observe rules and regulations is important in religion, but what is more important is to have faith, to understand religious teachings based on this faith [15] and to apply these in one's life. When the emphasis is placed on rules and regulations, this will naturally install a scriptural, legalistic and formalistic attitude as the most correct way to approach religion and will result in a neglect of faith. The religious life of the believers then will be overwhelmed by unproductive arguments concerning the right interpretation of the Scriptures, whereas the efforts of the believers to reappraise and to realise in their life what God truly intends to convey, a process which should be ceaselessly carried out, will lose ground in religion. The obsession with the literal interpretation of the Scriptures, which is supposed to characterise the *umat* Islam, was explained by a priest as follows: 'Before helping people suffering from AIDS, Muslims may argue first whether this act is written in the Quran as a recommended behaviour. It is not at all impossible for some to argue Muslims should not help those infected with AIDS since no passage in the Quran teaches that they have to do so.'

---

[14] See Chapter IV for more about the reformist villagers' emphasis on the inner side of religious life.

[15] A priest told me that there was no way for him to refute the argument that Jesus Christ was a clever impostor (*penipu besar*). According to him, the only way for someone to prove (the priest used the term, *membuktikan,* but I think the better term might be *yakin,* or to be certain) whether Jesus had been an impostor or God, is his or her faith and personal experiences. He then continued, 'in my case, my experiences and feeling (*rasa*) allowed me to believe (*percaya*) that Jesus was not an imposter but God.' Although somewhat extreme, the attitude of the priest showed the stress that Christian leaders put on faith.

The priests and the clergymen were of the opinion that Muslims' criticisms of a few theological themes in Christianity are based on their understanding that religious ideas should be interpreted literally. In this framework, therefore, it is possible to say: as Christians use three different names to call their God, there must be three Gods in Christianity; since Jesus was God and Jesus ate and drank, God in Christianity must do what human beings do; and since Original Sin is said to be inherited by human beings, people of these days must be responsible for Adam and Eve's sin. If they used the same framework as Muslims did, some of the priests suggested, they also agreed that Christianity has a few theological themes which seem to be illogical and irrational. However, according to them, this is not the right way to understand and interpret religious teachings. On the contrary, the right way is to look beyond the literal interpretation of religious teachings and to see their deeper meanings and, in some cases, to think about why God revealed these teachings to human beings. Seen from this perspective, the inheritance of Original Sin, for example, does not mean that we are responsible for the sin committed by Adam and Eve. Instead, it warns us that we as offspring of Adam and Eve are liable to commit sins. The same is true in the case of the three names of God. This does not mean that Christians worship three different Gods but that these names illuminate God's attributes in a way human beings can understand them. Several priests used the following comparison to convince me that the Trinity does not signify three different beings: people have diverse roles in a society and are called differently according to these. For example, one can be called father by his son, chief of an organisation by its members and teacher by his students at the same time.

In sum, the priests' and clergymen's framework for understanding religion makes it possible for them to defend Christianity from the criticisms of Muslims and to assert the truthfulness of Christianity. First is their emphasis on faith rather than on reason (or logical explanation). They argued that human beings cannot comprehend all religious teachings with their reason, nor did God recommend this attitude as the right way to approach religion. Second is their flexible attitude to the Scriptures. Although the equation of the Bible with the God's Word is not denied by them, they admitted that its contents were delivered in a language that human beings could understand, the Bible was recorded by human beings having their own subjectivity, it was transcribed from one to others, and accordingly, it may contain the bias of those who recorded and transcribed it.

The priests' and clergymen's emphasis on faith and on the spiritual side of religiosity shows that they share much in common with the reformist Muslims. This similarity, however, seems to be difficult for both Christians and Muslims to appreciate due to their somewhat 'prejudiced' preconceptions about the other religion. To Christians, Islam is the religion of rules and regulations devoid of faith and love, while to the reformist Muslims, the faith and belief that Christians have is useless since their faith and belief is directed to a false, man-made religion.

A lack of venues where Christians and the reformist Muslims talk about one another's religion seems to have played a pivotal role in producing and reproducing their mutual suspicion and their reluctance to understand each other. Somewhat ironically, the lack of common grounds has also been a factor in creating harmonious social life where no villagers disrespect the other religion, at least in the presence of the followers of that religion. So far, this atmosphere has dominated social life and no open conflicts have taken place between Christians and Muslims in Kolojonggo or in Sumber. It is my impression, however, that this does not seem to guarantee that the same situation will prevail in the interactions between Christians and Muslims. If reformist Islam gains a stronger grip over a much wider circle of Muslim villagers, if the expansion of Christianity continues at the same pace as it has done in the last few decades, and in so far as Muslims' concern about Christianisation is not expressed in a space which is shared by followers of both religions, it is not unlikely that the degree of friction will escalate and open confrontation will be considered an inevitable option.

Bibliography

Books

Abdul-Samad M.A.

1991 'Modernism in Islam in Indonesia with Special Reference to Muhammadiyah.' In M.C. Ricklefs, ed., *Islam in the Indonesian Social Context*, pp. 57-68. Victoria: Monash University.

Adnan, Zifirdaus

1990 'Islamic Religion: Yes, Islamic Ideology: No! Islam and the State in Indonesia.' In Arief Budiman, ed., *State and Civil Society in Indonesia*, pp. 441-477. Victoria: Monash University.

Ahmad. K.

1983 'The Nature of the Islamic Resurgence.' In J. Esposito, ed., pp. 218-229.

Ahmed, A.

1992 *Postmodernism and Islam: Predicament and Promise*. London and New York: Routledge.

van Akkeren P.

1970 *Sri and Christ: A Study of the Indigenous Church in East Java*. London: Lutterworth Press.

Alexander, J. & Alexander P.

1978 'Sugar, Rice and Irrigation in Colonial Java.' *Ethnohistory* 25:207-23.

1979 'Labour Demands and the 'Involution' of Javanese Agriculture.' *Social Analysis* 1(3):22-44.

Alfian

1989 *Muhammadiyah: The Political Behavior of Muslim Modernist Organization Under Dutch Colonialism*. Yogyakarta: Gadjah Mada University Press.

Ali Chasan Umar, M.

1980 *Makhluk-Makhluk Halus: Digali dari Al-Quran*. Singapore: Alharamain.

Amaluddin

1987 *Kemiskinan dan Polarisasi Sosial: Studi Kasus di Desa Belugede, Kabupaten Kendal, Jawa Tengah*. Jakarta: Penerbit Universitas Indonesia.

Anderson, B.

1965 *Mythology and the Tolerance of the Javanese*. Ithaca: Cornell University.

1983 *Imagined Communities: Reflections on the Origin and Spread of Nationalism*. London: Verso.

Anderson, G.

1972 'Plantation and Petani: Problems of the Javanese Sugar Industry.' *Pacific Viewpoint* 13:127-154.

Bachtiar

1985 'The Religion of Java: A Commentary.' In Ahmad Ibrahim (compiled), *Readings on Islam in Southeast Asia,* pp. 278-285. Singapore: Institute of Southeast Asian Studies.

Badan Penelitian dan Pengembangan Agama

1983/84 *Penerapan Wawasan Nusantara dalam Pembinaan Kehidupan Beragama: Pokok-Pokok Pikiran.* Jakarta: Departemen Agama.

1987/88 *Perkawinan Antar Agama.* Jakarta: Departemen Agama.

Benda, H.

1958 *The Crescent and the Rising Sun: Indonesian Islam under the Japanese Occupation, 1942-1945.* The Hague & Bandung: W. van Hoeve.

1972 'Christian Snouck Hurgronje and the Foundations of Dutch Islamic Policy in Indonesia.' In *Continuity and Change in Southeast Asia: Collected Journal Articles of Harry J. Benda,* pp. 83-92. New Haven: Yale University Press.

Berg, C.C.

1932 'Indonesia.' In H.A.R. Gibb, ed., *Whither Islam? A Survey of Modern Movements in the Moslem World,* pp. 239-311. London: Victor Gollancz Ltd.

Billah, M.M., et al.

1984 'Segi Penguasaan Tanah dan Dinamika Sosial Di Pedesaan Jawa (Tengah).' In S. Tjondronegoro and G. Wiradi, eds., *Dua Abad Penguasaan Tanah: Pola Penguasaan Tanah Pertanian di Jawa dari Masa ke Masa,* pp. 250-285. Jakarta: Yayasan Obor Indonesia.

Bjorkman, W.

1953 'Shirk.' In H.A.R. Gibb and J.H. Kramers, eds., *Shorter Encyclopedia of Islam,* pp. 542-44. Leiden: E.J.Brill.

Boland, B.J.

1982 *The Struggle of Islam in Modern Indonesia.* The Hague: M.Nijhoff.

Boon, J.

1979 'Balinese Temple Politics and the Religious Revitalization of Caste Ideals.' In A.L. Becker and A.A. Yengoyan, eds., *The Imagination of Reality: Essays in Southeast Asian Coherence Systems,* pp. 271-91. Palo Alto: Ablex.

Bourdieu, P.

1990 *The Logic of Practice*. Cambridge: Polity Press.

Bowen, J.

1993 *Muslims Through Discourse: Religion and Ritual in Gayo Society*. New Jersey: Princeton University Press.

BPS (Biro Pusat Statistik Indonesia)

Various issues *Statistik Indonesia*. Jakarta.

Bråton, E.

1989 'Safe is Ambiguous. Identity Management and Conditions of Islamization in a Central Javanese Village.' In M. Gravers et al., eds., *Southeast Asia between Autocracy and Democracy: Identity and Political Processes,* pp. 57-95. Aarhus University.

Carey, B.R.

1981 'Introduction.' In *Babad Dipanagara: An Account of the Outbreak of the Java War (1825-30)*. Kuala Lumpur: Art Printing Works.

Collier, W.

1979 *Declining Labor Absorption (1878 to 1980) in Javanese Rice Production*. Bogor: Agro-Economic Survey.

1981 'Agricultural Evolution in Java.' In Hansen, ed., pp. 147-173.

Collier, W., et. al. 1974 'Sistim *Tebasan*, Bibit Unggul dan Pembaharuan Desa di Jawa.' *Prisma* 6:13- 30.

1982 'Acceleration of Rural Development in Java.' *Bulletin of Indonesian Economic Studies* 18:84-101.

Cooley, F.

1968 *Indonesia: Church and Society*. New York: Friendship Press.

Cribb, R.

1990 'Introduction: Problems in the Historiography of the Killings in Indonesia.' In R.Cribb, ed., *The Indonesian Killings of 1965-1966: Studies from Java and Bali*, pp. 1-43. Victoria: Centre of Southeast Asian Studies, Monash University.

Dekmejian, H.

1985 *Islam in Revolution: Fundamentalism in the Arab World*. Syracuse: Syracuse University Press.

1988 'Islamic Revival: Catalysts, Categories, and Consequences.' In S. Hunter, ed., *The Politics of Islamic Revivalism: Diversity and Unity*, pp. 3-19. Bloomington and Indianapolis: Indiana University Press.

Departemen Agama, Yogyakarta

1990 *Munakahat Membina Keluarga Sakinah dan Keputusan Forum Dialog Pemuka-Pemuka Agama Prop. Daerah Istimewa Yogyakarta*. Yogyakarta: Kantor Departemen Agama.

Dhofier, Z.

1978 'Santri-Abangan dalam Kehidupan Orang Jawa: Teropong dari Pesantren.' *Prisma* 5:64-72.

Djajadiningrat, H.P.A.

1958 'Islam in Indonesia.' In K. Morgan, ed., *Islam-The Straight Path: Islam Interpreted by Muslims,* pp. 375-402. New York: The Ronald Press Company.

Drewes, G.W.J.

1955 'Indonesia: Mysticism and Activism.' In G.E.von Grunebaum, ed., *Unity and Variety in Muslim Civilization,* pp. 284-307. Chicago: The University of Chicago Press.

Echols, J. & Shadily, H.

1990 *Kamus Indonesia-Inggris: An Indonesian-English Dictionary*. 3rd edition. Jakarta: Penerbit Pt Gramedia.

Edmundson, W.

1994 'Do the Rich Get Richer, Do the Poor Get Poorer? East Java, Two Decades, Three Villages, 46 People.' *Bulletin of Indonesian Economic Studies* 30:133-48.

Eickelman, D.

1978 'The Art of Memory: Islamic Education and its Social Reproduction.' *Combibliomixedtive Studies in Society and History* 20:485-516.

1982 'The Study of Islam in Local Contexts.' *Contributions to Asian Studies* 17:1-16.

1992 'Mass Higher Education and the Religious Imagination in Contemporary Arab Societies.' *American Ethnologist* 19(4): 643-655.

Ellen, R.

1983 'Social Theory, Ethnography and The Understanding of Practical Islam in South- East Asia.' In M.B. Hooker, ed., *Islam in South-East Asia*, pp. 50-91. Leiden: E.J.Brill.

Esposito, J.

1983 'Introduction: Islam and Muslim Politics.' In J. Esposito, ed., pp. 3-15.

Esposito, J. (ed.)

1983 *Voices of Resurgent Islam*. New York & Oxford: Oxford University Press.

1987 *Islam in Asia: Religion, Politics and Society*. New York & Oxford: Oxford University Press.

Federspiel, H.

1970 *Persatuan Islam: Islamic Reform in Twentieth Century Indonesia*. Ithaca: Cornell University.

Fox, J. J.

1991a 'Managing the Ecology of Rice Production in Indonesia.' In Hardjono et al., ed., *Indonesia: Resources, Ecology, and Environment,* pp. 61-84. Singapore: Oxford University Press.

1991b 'Ziarah Visits to the Tombs of the Wali, The Founders of Islam on Java.' In M.C. Ricklefs, ed., *Islam in the Indonesian Social Context,* pp. 19-38. Victoria: Monash University.

1993 'The rice Basket of East Java: The Ecology and Social Context of Sawah Production.' In H. Dick, eds., *Balanced Development: East Java in the New Order,* pp. 120-157. Singapore: Oxford University Press.

Franke, R.

1973 *The Green Revolution in a Javanese Village*. Unpublished Ph.D. Thesis, Harvard University.

Geertz, C.

1963 *Agricultural Involution: The Process of Ecological Change in Indonesia*. Berkeley et al.: University of California Press.

1973 *The Interpretation of Cultures*. New York: Basic Books.

1975 *Islam Observed: Religious Development in Morocco and Indonesia*. Chicago & London: The University of Chicago press.

1976 *The Religion of Java*. Chicago & London: The University of Chicago Press.

1990 'Popular Art and the Javanese Tradition.' *Indonesia* 50: 77-94.

Geertz, H.

1961 *The Javanese Family: A Study of Kinship and Socialization*. Glencoe: The Free Press.

Gelpke, J.H.F.S.

1986 'Budidaya Padi di Jawa: Sumbangan pada Ilmu-ilmu Bahasa, Daerah dan Penduduk Hindia Belanda.' In Sajogyo et al., eds., pp. 1-98.

Gibb, H.A.R.

1953 *Mohammedianism: An Historical Survey*. London, et al.: Oxford University Press.

Guillot, C.

1985 *Kiai Sadrach: Riwayat Kristenisasi di Jawa*. Jakarta: Penerbit PT Grafiti Pers. Translated by Asvi Warman.

Guinness, P.

1986 *Harmony and Hierarchy in a Javanese Kampung*. Singapore: Oxford University Press.

Hadiwijono, Harun

1967 *Man in the Present Javanese Mysticism*. Baarn: Bosch en Keuning.

Hanson, G. (ed.)

1981 *Agricultural and Rural Development in Indonesia*. Colorado: Westview.

Hardjamardjaja, A.

1962 *Javanese Popular Belief in the Coming of Ratu-Adil A Righteous Prince*. Roma.

Hart, G., et al. (eds.)

1989 *Agrarian transformations: Local Processes and the State in Southeast Asia*. University of California Press.

Harun Nasution.

1986 *Akal dan Wahyu Dalam Islam*. Jakarta: UI Press.

Hayami, Y. and Hafid, A.

1979 'Rice Harvesting and Welfare in Rural Java.' *Bulletin of Indonesian Economic Studies* 15:94-112.

Hefner R.

1985 *Hindu Javanese: Tengger Tradition and Islam*. New Jersey: Princeton University Press.

1987a 'Islamizing Java. Religion and Politics in Rural East Java.' *The Journal of Asian Studies* 46(3):553-554.

1987b The Political Economy of Islamic Conversion in Modern East Java.' In W. Roff, ed., *Islam and the Political Economy of Meaning: Combibliomixedtive studies of Muslim Discourse*, pp. 53-78. London & Sydney: Croom Helm.

1990 *The Political Economy of Mountain Java: An Interpretive History*. Berkeley, et al.: University of California Press.

1993a 'Introduction: World Building and the Rationality of Conversion.' In R. Hefner, ed., *Conversion to Christianity: Historical and Anthropological Perspectives on a Great Transformation*. pp. 3-44. Berkeley & Los Angeles: University of California Press.

1993b 'Of Faith and Commitment: Christian Conversion in Muslim Java.' In R. Hefner, ed., *Conversion to Christianity: Historical and Anthropological Perspectives on a Great Transformation*. pp. 99-125. Berkeley & Los Angelous: University of California Press.

Hill, H. and Mubyarto

1978 'Economic Change in Yogyakarta 1970-76.' *Bulletin of Indonesian Economic Studies* 14:29-44.

Hinkson J.

1975 'Rural Development and Class Contradictions on Java.' *Journal of Contemporary Asia* 5:327-336.

Hobsbawm, E.J. & Ranger, T.O. (eds.)

1983 *The Invention of Tradition*. New York: Cambridge University Press.

Hodgson, M.

1974 *The Venture of Islam*. Chicago: University of Chicago Press.

Horikoshi, H.

1976 *A Traditional Leader in a Time of Change: The kijaji and Ulama in West Java*. Unpublished Ph.D. Thesis, University of Illinois.

Horvatich, P.

1994 'Ways of Knowing Islam.' *American Ethnologist* 21(4): 811-826.

Houben, J.V.

1989 'Economic Policy in the Principalities of Central Java in the Nineteenth Century.' In A. Maddison and G. Prince, eds., *Economic Growth in Indonesia 1820-1940*, pp.185-202. Leiden: Koninklijk Instituut voor Taal-, land- en Volkenkunde.

Houben, J.V.

1994 *Kraton and Kumpeni: Surakarta and Yogyakarta*, 1830-1870. Leiden: KITLV Press.

Hugo, G.

1985 'Structural Change and Labor Mobility in Rural Java.' In G. Standing, ed., *Labor Circulation and the Labor Process*, pp. 46-88. London et al.: Croom Helm.

Huizer, G.

1972 *Peasant Mobilisation and Land Reform in Indonesia.* The Hague: Institute of Social Studies.

Hunter, S.

1988 'Conclusion'. In S. Hunter, ed., *The Politics of Islamic Revivalism: Diversity and Unity,* pp. 281-86. Bloomington and Indianapolis: Indiana University Press.

Hüsken, F.

1979 'Landlords, Sharecroppers and Agricultural Laborers: Changing Labor Relations in Rural Java.' *Journal of Contemporary Asia* 9:140-151.

Hüsken F. and White B.

1989 'Java: Social Differentiation, Food production, and Agrarian Control.' In G. Hart, et al., eds., pp. 235-265.

Irwan Abdullah

1994 *The Muslim Businessmen of Jatinom: Religious Reform and Economic Modernization in a Central Javanese Town.* Universiteit van Amsterdam.

Iso Reksohadiprodjo and Soedarsono Hadisapoetro

1986 'Perubahan Kepadatan Penduduk dan Penghasilan Bahan Makanan (padi) di Jawa dan Madura.' In Sajogyo et al., eds., pp. 287-336.

Jay, R.

1963 *Religion and Politics in Rural Central Java.* New Haven: Yale University.

1969 *Javanese Villagers: Social Relations in Rural Modjokuto.* Cambridge, Massachusetts: The MIT Press.

Johns, A.H.

1987 'Indonesia: Islam and Cultural Pluralism.' In J. Esposito, ed., pp. 202-229.

Jones, Russell (compile)

1978 *Arabic Loan-Words in Indonesian.* London: the School of Oriental and African Studies, University of London.

Jordaan, R.

1985 *Folk Medicine in Madura (Indonesia).* Unpublished Ph.D. Thesis, Leiden University.

Kano, H.

1990 *Pagelaran: Anatomi Sosial ekonomi Pelapisan Masyarakat Tani di Sebuah Desa Jawa Timur.* Yogyakarta: Gadjah Mada University press.

Kantor Statistik Propinsi Daerah Istimewa Yogyakarta (KSY)

1957 & 1963 *Statistik Pemerintah Daerah Istimewa Jogjakarta*. Yogyakarta. Various issues *Daerah Istimewa Yogyakarta Dalam Angka*. Yogyakarta.

1990 *Struktur Ongkos Usaha Tani Padi Dan Palawija*. Yogyakarta.

1991 *Statistik Sosial dan Budaya*. Yogyakarta.

Kantor Waligereja Indonesia

1974 *Sejarah Gereja Katolik Indonesia*. Flores: Percetakan Arnoldus.

Keddie, N.

1994 The Revolt of Islam, 1700 to 1993: Combibliomixedtive Considerations and Relations to Imperialism. *Combibliomixedtive Study of Society and History* 36:463-487.

Keeler, W.

1987 *Javanese Shadow Plays, Javanese Selves*. New Jersey: Princeton University Press.

Khush, G.

1985 'Improved Rice Varieties in Retrospect and Prospect.' In *Women in Rice Farming*, pp. 455-465. Manila: International Rice Research Institute.

van Klaberen, J.J.

1953 *The Dutch Colonial System in the East Indies*. The Hague: Drukkerij Benedictus.

Koentjaraningrat

1960 'The Javanese of South Central Java.' In G. P. Murdock, ed., *Social Structure in Southeast Asia*, pp. 88-115. Chicago: Quadrangle Books.

1963 'Review of *The Religion of Java* by Clifford Geertz.' *Madjalah Ilmu-Ilmu Sastra Indonesia* 1:188-191.

1967 'Tjelapar: A Village in South Central Java.' In Koentjaraningrat, ed., *Villages in Indonesia*, pp. 244-280. Ithaca: Cornell University Press.

1985a *Javanese Culture*. Singapore: Oxford University Press.

1985b 'Javanese Terms for God and Supernatural Beings and the Idea of Power.' In Ahmad Ibrahim (compiled), *Readings on Islam in Southeast Asia*, pp. 286-292. Singapore: Institute of Southeast Asian Studies.

Lembaga Penelitian Dan Pembangunan Sosial

1968 *Ichtisar Statistik Tentang Geredja Katolik di Indonesia:1949-67*.

Lewis, B. et.al. (eds)

1965 *Encyclopedia of Islam: New Edition*. Leiden: E.J. Brill.

Lloyd, M.

1959 *The Protestant Church in Indonesia*. Unpublished M.A. Thesis, The American University.

Lyon, M.

1970 *Bases of Conflict in Rural Java*. California: University of California.

Majelis Ulama Indonesia, DKI Jakarta.

1986 'Tentang Perkawinan Antar Agama.' In Badan Penelitian dan Pengembangan Agama, 1987/88, pp. 25-32.

Manggistan

1986 'Produksi Padi di Jawa yang Tidak Mencukupi.' In Sajogyo et al., eds., pp. 99- 142.

Manning, C.

1987 'Rural Economic Change and Labor Mobility: A Case Study From West Java.' *Bulletin of Indonesian Economic Studies* 23:52-79.

1988 'Rural Employment Creation in Java: Lessons from the Green Revolution and Oil Boom.' *Population and Development Review* 14:47-80

Mansurnoor

1990 *Islam in an Indonesian World: Ulama of Madura*. Yogyakarta: Gadjah Mada University Press.

Maududi, S. Abul A'la

1981 *A Short History of the Revivalist Movement in Islam*. Translated by Al-Ash'ari. Lahore (Pakistan): Islamic Publications Ltd.

Maurer, J-L.

1984 'Agricultural Modernization and Social Change; The Case of Java Over the Last Fifteen Years.' *Masyarakat Indonesia* 11:109-119.

1991 'Beyond the *Sawah*: Economic Diversification in Four Bantul Villages, 1971- 1987.' In P. Alexander, et al., eds., *In the Shadow of Agriculture: Non-Farm Activities in the Javanese Economy, Past and Present*, pp. 92-112. Amsterdam: KIT Press.

McVey, R.

1965 *The Rise of Indonesian Communism*. Ithaca. Cornell University.

1983 'Faith as the Outsider: Islam in Indonesian Politics.' In J. Piscatori, ed., *Islam in the Political Process*, pp. 199-225. Cambridge: Cambridge University Press.

Mears, L.

1981 *The New Rice Economy of Indonesia*. Yogyakarta: Gadjah Mada University Press.

Moertono, S.

1974 *State and Statecraft in Old Java: A Study of the Later Mataram Period, 16th to 19th Century*. Ithaca: Cornell University Southeast Asia Program, Modern Indonesia Project, Monograph No.43.

Mohammad Zihid

1979/1980 'Hubungan Pemuluk Agama Katolik Dan Islam di Desa Ngawen, Muntilan'. In Moeslim Abdurrahman, ed., *Agama, Budaya dan Masyarakat: Ikhtisar Laporan Hasil-hasil Penelitian*, pp. 173-78. Departemen Agama RI: Proyek Penelitian Keagamaan.

Montgomery, R.

1974 *The Link Between Trade and Labor Absorption in Rural Java: An Input-Output Study of Jogyakarta*. Unpublished Ph.D. Thesis, Cornell University.

van Mook, H.J.

1958 'Kuta Gede.' In Institute voor de Tropen, ed., *The Indonesian Town: Studies in Urban Sociology*, pp. 277-347. The Hague: W. van Hoeve.

Mubyarto

1982 *Rural Development In Indonesia: Past Experiences and Future Policies*. Gadjah Mada University and United National Centre for Regional Development.

Muhammadiyah (Pimpinan Pusat)

1954 *Tafsir Anggaran Dasar Muhammadijah: Lengkap dengan Muqaddimah*. Jogjakarta: Pusat Pimpinan Muhammadijah.

1963 'Penjelasan Kepribadian Muhammadiyah.' In Umar Hasyim,1990, pp. 422-441.

1967 'Pedoman Pelaksanaan Muhammadiyah sebagai Gerakan Dakwah Islam and Amar Makruf Nahi Munkar.' In Umar Hasyim, 1990, pp. 181-186.

1968 'Rumusan Pokok-Pokok Persoalan Tentang Khittah Perjuangan Muhammadiyah', In Umar Hasyim, 1990, pp. 199-204.

1969 'Matan Keyakinan dan Cita-Cita Hidup Muhammadiyah: Keputusan Sidang Tanwir 1969 di Ponorogo.' In Umar Hasyim,1990, pp. 216-223.

1971 'Keputusan Muktamar Ke-38 Tentang Program Muhammadiyah Periode 1971- 1974.' In Umar Hasyim, 1990, pp. 234-238.

1978 'Keputusan Muktamar Ke-40 di Surabaya Bidang Program.' In Umar Hasyim, 1990, pp. 312-338.

1985 'Program Persyarikatan Muhammadiyah Periode 1985-1990: Hasil Keputusan Muktamar Muhammadiyah ke-41 di Surakarta, tgl. 7 s.d.11 Desember 1985.' In Umar Hasyim, 1990, pp. 370-421.

1991a 'Keputusan Muktamar Ke-42.' *Berita Resmi Muhammadiyah* 1991(1):7-20.

1991b 'Dakwah Dalam Era Teknologi dan Informasi.' *Berita Resmi Muhammadiyah* 1991(1):101-108.

Mulder, N.

1978 *Mysticism and Everyday Life in Contemporary Java: Cultural Persistence and Change*. Singapore: Singapore University Press.

1983 'Abangan Javanese Religious Thought and Practices.' *BKI* 139:260-267.

Mulherin, B.

1970-71 'The Bekel in Javanese History.' *Review of Indonesian and Malayan Affairs* 4/5:1-29.

Muzaffar, C.

1986 'Islamic Resurgence: A Global View.' In T. Abdullah et al., eds., *Islam and Society in Southeast Asia*, pp. 5-39. Singapore: Institute of Southeast Asian Studies.

Nagata, J.

1984 *The Reflowering of Malaysian Islam: Modern Religious Radicals and Their Roots*. Van Couver: University of British Columbia Press.

Nakamura, M.

1984 'The Cultural and Religious Identity of Javanese Muslims: Problems of Conceptualization and Approach.' *Prisma* 31:67-75.

1993 *The Crescent Arises over the Banyan Tree: A Study of the Muhammadiyah Movement in a Central Javanese Town*. Yogyakarta: Gadjah Mada University Press.

Nash, J.

1979 *We Eat the Mines and the Mines Eat Us: Dependency and Exploitation in Bolivian Tin Mines*. New York: Columbia University Press.

Naylor, R.

1991 'The Rural Labor Market in Indonesia.' In Pearson, et al., eds., pp. 58-98.

Netton, I. R.

1992 *A Popular Dictionary of Islam*. London: Curzon Press.

Noer, Delier

1973 *The Modernist Muslim Movement in Indonesia 1900-1942*. Singapore, etc.: Oxford University Press.

1978 *The Administration of Islam in Indonesia*. Ithaca: Cornell Modern Indonesian Project.

1983 'Contemporary Political Dimensions of Islam.' In M.B. Hooker, ed., *Islam in South-East Asia*, pp. 183-215. Leiden: E.J.Brill.

O'Malley, W.J.

1977 *Indonesia in the Great Depression: A Study of East Sumatra and Jogjakarta in the 1930's*. Unpublished Ph.D. Thesis: Cornell University.

Ong, A.

1988 'The Production of Possession: Spirits and the Multinational Corporation in Malaysia.' *American Ethnologist* 15:28-42.

Palmer, I.

1977 *The New Rice in Indonesia*. Geneva: UNRISD.

Pandam Guritno

1958 *Masyarakat Marangan: Sebuah Laporan Sosiografi ketjamatan Prambanan Daerah Istimewa Jogyakarta*. Jogyakarta: Universitas Gadjah Mada.

Papanek. G.

1985 'Agricultural Income Distribution and Employment in the 1970s.' *Bulletin of Indonesian Economic Studies* 21:24-50.

Peacock, J.

1978a *Muslim Puritans: Reformist Psychology in Southeast Asian Islam*. Berkeley and Los Angeles: University of California Press.

1978b *Purifying the Faith: The Muhammadijah Movement in Indonesian Islam*. California: The Benjamin/Cummings Publishing Company.

1986 'The Creativity of Tradition in Indonesian Religion.' *History of Religion* 25: 341- 351.

Pearson, S., et al. (eds.)

1991 *Rice Policy in Indonesia*. Ithaca and London: Cornell University.

Pearson, S., et al.

1991 'Recent Policy Influences on Rice Production.' In Pearson, et al., eds., pp. 8-21.

Peletz, M.

1988 'Poisoning, Sorcery, and Healing Rituals in Negeri Sembilan.' *BKI* 144(1): 132- 64.

1993 'Sacred Texts and Dangerous Words: The Politics of Law and Cultural Rationalization in Malaysia.' *Combibliomixedtive Study of Society and History* 35:66- 109.

Penny, D., and Singarimbun M.

1973 *Population and Poverty in Rural Java: Some Economic Arithmetic from Sriharjo*. Cornell University, International Development Monograph No.41.

Pickthall, M.

1930 (1989) *The Koran*. London: A Star Book.

Poerwadarminta

1939 *Baoesastra Djawa*. Batavia: J.B. Wolters' Uitgevers Maatschappij.

Pranowo Bambang

1991 *Creating Islamic Tradition in Rural Java*. Unpublished Ph.D. Thesis, Monash University.

Prawiroatmodjo, S.

1992 *Bausastra Jawa-Indonesia*. Jakarta: CV Haji Masagung.

Proyek Perencanaan Peraturan Perundangan Keagamaan

1980/81 *Peraturan Perundangan Yang Menyangkut Tata Kehidupan Beragama dan Pendirian Rumah Ibadah*. Departemen Agama.

Raffles, T.S.

1965(1817) *The History of Java*. Kuala Lumpur: Oxford University Press.

Rahman, F.

1980 *Major Themes of the Quran*. Minneapolis: Bibliotheca Islamica.

Rauws, J. et al.

1935 *The Netherlands Indies*. London & New York: World Dominion Press.

Ricklefs, M.

1979 'Six Centuries of Islamization in Java.' In N. Levtzion, ed., *Conversion to Islam*, pp. 100-127. New York and London: Holmes and Meier.

1981 *A History of Indonesia*. Bloomington: Indiana University Press.

1991 'An Unhelpful Contribution to the Study of Javanese Islam.' *Asian Studies Review* 14(3): 184-190.

Rodwell, J. M. (trans.)

1963 *The Koran*. London: Everyman's Library.

Roff, W.

1985 'Islam Obscured? Some Reflections on Studies of Islam and Society in Southeast Asia.' In M. Bonneff, et al. eds., *L'Islam en Indonesie* 1:7-34. Paris: Association Archipel.

Roosmalawati

1973 *Kehidupan Masyarakat Desa Triharjo Kecamatan Wates Kabupaten Kulon Progo, Dalam Tinjauan Sosial Ekonomi.* Unpublished B.A. Thesis, Gadjah Mada University.

Sahibi Nahim

1983 *Kerukunan Antar Umat Beragama.* Jakarta: Gunung Agung.

Said, E.

1978 *Orientalism.* London & Henley: Routledge and Kegam Paul.

Sajogyo and Collier, W.L. (eds.)

1986 *Budidaya Padi di Jawa.* Jakarta: Yayasan Obor Indonesia.

Sato, S.

1994 *War, Nationalism and Peasants: Java under the Japanese Occupation 1942-1945.* Asian Studies Association of Australia in Association with Allen & Unwin.

Scheltema, A.M.P.A.

1986 'Produksi Beras di Jawa dan Madura.' In Sajogyo, et al., eds., pp. 171-184.

Schweizer, T

1987 'Agrarian Transformation? Rice Production in a Javanese Village.' *Bulletin of Indonesian Economic Studies* 23:38-70.

Scott, J.

1976 *The Moral Economy of the Peasant: Rebellion and Subsistence in Southeast Asia.* New Haven: Yale University Press.

Sekretariat Umum Dewan Gereja-Gereja di Indonesia & Sekretariat Majelis Agung Waligereja Indonesia.

1978 *Tinjauan mengenai Keputusan Menteri Agama No. 70 dan No. 77 Tahun 1978 dalam Rangka Penyelenggaraan Kebebasan Beragama dan Pemeliharaan Kerukunan Nasional.* mimeo.

Selosoemardjan

1962 *Social Changes in Jogjakarta.* Ithaca: Cornell University Press.

Siegel, J. T.

1969 *The Rope of God.* Berkeley and Los Angeles: University of California Press.

1986 *Solo in the New Order: Language and Hierarchy in an Indonesian City.* New Jersey: Princeton University Press.

Singodimejo, Kasman

1969 *Renungan dari Tahanan.* Jakarta: Tintoamas.

Slamet, M.

1977 'Priyayi Value Conflict.' In *Religion and Social Ethos in Indonesia,* pp. 33-47. Victoria: Monash University, Centre of Southeast Asian Studies.

Soebardi, S.

1976 'The Place of Islam.' In E. McKay, ed., *Studies in Indonesian History*, pp. 39- 63. Victoria: Pitman Publishing Pty.

Soedarisman Poerwokorsoemo

1984 *Daerah Istimewa Yogyakarta.* Yogyakarta: Gadjah Mada University Press.

Soedjito Sostrodihardjo

1957 *Kedudukan Pemimpin di dalam Masyarakat Desa beserta Monografi.* Jogyakarta: Universitas Gadjah Mada.

Soemarjo

1959 *Desa Tjandi, Kalurahan Purwobinangun: Sebuah Laporan Sosiografi Ketjamatan Pakem, Daerah Istimewa Jogyakarta.* Jogyakarta: Universitas Gadjah Mada.

Stange, P.

1980 *The Sumarah Movement in Javanese Mysticism.* Unpublished Ph.D. Thesis, University of Wisconsin.

1984 'The Logic of *Rasa* in Java.' *Indonesia* 38:113-134.

1990 'Javanism as Text or Praxis.' Paper presented for the Asian Studies Association of Australia conference in Brisbane.

Sudjabat, W.B.

1960 *Religious Tolerance and the Christian Faith: A Study Concerning the Concept of Divine Omnipotence in the Indonesian Constitution in the Light of Islam and Christianity.* Unpublished Th.D. Thesis, Princeton Theological Seminary.

Suhartono

1991 *Apanage dan Bekel: Perubahan Sosial di Pedesaan Surakarta 1830-1920.* Yogyakarta: Pt. Tiara Wacana Yogya.

Supatmo

1943 *Animistic Belief & Religious Practices of the Javanese.* New York: East Indies Institute of America, mimeo.

Supomo, S.

n. d. 'From *Sakti* to *Shahada*: the Quest for New Meanings in a Changing World Order'. mimeo.

Syafri Sairin

1978 *Problems of Harvest Laborers in rural Yogyakarta.* Yogyakarta: Gadjah Mada University.

Takashi, S.

1990 *An Age in Motion: Popular Radicalism in Java, 1912-1926.* Ithaca and London: Corenell University Press.

Tamara Nasir

1986 *Indonesia in the Wake of Islam: 1965-1985.* Kuala Lumpur: Institute of Strategic and International Studies.

Tamney, J.B.

1987 'Islam's Popularity: The Case of Indonesia.' *Southeast Asian Journal of Social Science* 15:53-65.

Taussig, M.

1980 *The Devil and Commodity Fetishism in South America.* Chapel Hill: University of North Carolina Press.

Timmer, P.

1981 'The Formation of Indonesian Rice Policy: A Historical Perspective.' In Hansen, ed., pp. 33-43.

Umar Hasyim

1980 *Syetan Sebagai Tertuduh: Dalam Masalah Sihir, Pendudukan, Tahayul Dan Azimat.* Pena Mas Malaysia.

1990 *Muhammadiyah Jalan Lurus Dalam Tajdid, Dakwah, Kaderisasi dan Pendidikan: Kritik dan Terapinya.* Surabaya: Pt. Bina Ilmu.

1991 *Toleransi dan Kemerdekaan Beragama Dalam Islam: Sebagai Dasar Menuju Dialog dan Kerukunan Antar Agama.* Surabaya: Pt. Bina Ilmu.

Utrecht, E.

1973 'Land Reform and Bimas in Indonesia.' *Journal of Contemporary Asia* 3:149-164.

Voll, J.

1983 'Renewal and Reform in Islamic History: *Tajdid* and *Islah*.' In J. Esposito, ed., pp. 32-47.

Vredenbregt, J.

1962 'The Hadji: Some of its Features and Functions in Indonesia.' *BKI* 118:91-154.

Weber, M.

1958a 'The Social Psychology of the World Religion.' In H. H. Gerth and C.W. Mills, eds., *From Max Weber: Essays in Sociology*, pp. 267-301. New York: Oxford University Press.

1958b 'Religious Rejections of the World and Their Directions.' In H. H. Gerth and C.W. Mills, eds., *From Max Weber: Essays in Sociology*, pp. 323-359. New York: Oxford University Press.

1963 *The Sociology of Religion*. London: Methuen & Co Ltd.

Weiss, J.

1977 *Folk Psychology of the Javanese of Ponorogo*. Unpublished Ph.D. Thesis, Yale University.

Wertheim, W.F.

1956 *Indonesian Society in transition: A Study of Social Change*. The Hague & Bandung: W. van Hoeve Ltd.

1980 *Moslems in Indonesia: Majority with Minority Mentality*. Queensland: James Cook University.

White, B.

1976 'Population, Involution and Employment in Rural Java.' *Development and Change* 7:267-290.

1977 *Production and Reproduction in a Javanese Village*. Unpublished Ph.D. Thesis, Columbia University.

1983 'Agricultural Involution and Its Critics: Twenty Years After.' *Bulletin of Concerned Asian Scholars* 15:18-31.

1989 'Java's Green Revolution in Long-term Perspective.' *Prisma* 48:66-81.

Willis, A.

1977 *Indonesian Revival. Why Two Million Came to Christ*. California: William Barey Library.

Woodward, M.

1988 'The Slametan: Textual Knowledge and Ritual Performance in Central Javanese Islam.' *History of Religions* 28(1): 54-89.

1989 *Islam in Java: Normative Piety and Mysticism in the Sultanate of Yogyakarta.* Tucson: The University of Arizona Press.

el-Zein, A.H.

1988 'Beyond Ideology and Theology: The Search for an Anthropology of Islam.' *Annual Revie of Anthropology* 6:227-54.

Zoetmulder, P.J.

1967 *The Cultural Background of Indonesian Politics.* Columbia: Institute of International Studies, University of South Carolina.

www.ingramcontent.com/pod-product-compliance
Lightning Source LLC
Chambersburg PA
CBHW061243270326

41928CB00041B/3381